DERRIDA AND LAW

This book brings together an interdisciplinary range of scholars from across the spectrum of disciplines, generations, and geopolitical divides to revisit Jacques Derrida's account of law, violence, and justice.

Deconstruction is variously a philosophy of aporia, a method of patience, a practice of paradoxes, an ontography of uncertainty, a hermeneutics of escalation that sought not only to challenge metaphysical complacencies but also to transgress boundaries, test limits, and above all to provoke, invoke, and convoke thought. As a reworking of the philosophical tradition, its impact on law and legal theory became unavoidable in 1989 when Derrida, persuaded by the late Drucilla Cornell, came to address a law school audience on the mystical foundations of law. In a lecture – 'Force of Law' – that had global intellectual resonance, he startled the jurists by declaring that deconstruction 'is' justice. For some lawyers, it was a landmark thesis, a liberation. For others, it was deemed to be nihilist, a denial of all possibility of meaning, and so denounced as the equivalent of tearing up the constitution, or burning the flag. Some twenty years after his death, in this book, renowned Derridean scholars revisit this legacy. *Derrida and Law* offers a series of re-readings of 'Force of Law', and a conspectus of new reflections on Derrida's account of the violence of legality and the possibility of justice.

This book will appeal to philosophers, legal theorists, and others with an interest in deconstruction and Continental theory.

Peter Goodrich is Professor of Law at Cardozo School of Law, New York, and Visiting Professor in Social Science at New York University Abu Dhabi.

Anselm Haverkamp, Emeritus Professor of English at NYU, is Professor of Philosophy at LMU Munich.

Avital Ronell is University Professor of the Humanities and Professor of German and Comparative Literature at New York University.

Part of the
DISCOURSES OF LAW
Series

Series Editors

The publisher gratefully acknowledges the support of the Jacob Burns Institute for Advanced Legal Studies of the Benjamin N. Cardozo School of Law to the series *Discourses of Law*.

for information about the series and details of previous and forthcoming titles, see https://www.routledge.com/Discourses-of-Law/book-series/SE1036

A GlassHouse Book

DERRIDA AND LAW

Justice and the Violence of Legality

Edited by Peter Goodrich, Anselm Haverkamp, and Avital Ronell

Routledge
Taylor & Francis Group
a GlassHouse Book

Designed cover image: Portrait de Jacques Derrida à Berlin
Copyright: Photographe non mentionné / Archives Jacques Derrida / IMEC
Légende: portrait de Jacques Derrida numéroté, non signé

First published 2027
by Routledge
4 Park Square, Milton Park, Abingdon, Oxon OX14 4RN

and by Routledge
605 Third Avenue, New York, NY 10158

Routledge is an imprint of the Taylor & Francis Group, an informa business

A GlassHouse Book

British Library Cataloguing-in-Publication Data
A catalogue record for this book is available from the British Library

ISBN: 978-1-032-96431-7 (hbk)
ISBN: 978-1-032-96429-4 (pbk)
ISBN: 978-1-003-58941-9 (ebk)

DOI: 10.4324/9781003589419

Typeset in Sabon
by Apex CoVantage, LLC

CONTENTS

PART II
Force 157

ACKNOWLEDGMENTS

Twenty years in the making, reflecting a renewed sense of urgency around law and justice, coincident with the appearance of a new French edition of *Force de loi*, *voyous*, *fichus*, from Seuil, this May, the enigmatic novelty of an incalculable justice, of patience and rage emerges on the social stage. An outcrop of numerous events, occasions, chance conversations, temulence and tisane, this collect and collection aims, hopes and assays to invigorate further the force of Derrida's law. Travel, illness, interruptions, and abruptions give a certain floating valence to the expansions, digressions, savings and corrections that inevitably emerge when law and philosophy stage encounters. Our thanks, single and several, to the patience and enthusiasm of the contributors, and to the participants at colloquia in memoriam at Cardozo Law School and at New York University Maison Française, Derrida's old haunts. Our gratitude as well to those who contributed ideas orally, through gesture, in mad packets of letters, dance and electronic epistles, but who did not intervene with a chapter. All errancies, single and several, felicitous and egregious, veritable and divagatory, are our own.

CONTRIBUTORS

Isabelle Alfandary is a professor of American literature and critical theory at Sorbonne-Nouvelle University, philosopher, and psychoanalyst. She was president of Collège international de philosophie from 2016 to 2019. Her work focuses on the relationships between literature, philosophy, and psychoanalysis. She has published several monographs including *Derrida – Lacan: L'écriture entre psychanalyse et déconstruction* (Editions Hermann, 2016); *Science et fiction chez Freud. Quelle épistémologie pour la psychanalyse?* (Ithaque, 2021); *Le scandale de la séduction. D'Œdipe à #Metoo* (Puf, 2024).

Peter Goodrich is Professor of Law and Director of the Programme in Law and Humanities at Cardozo School of Law. An ardent advocate of the argute yet habile silent p, as in psithurism, ptomaine, cupboard, and rhubarb, he writes on forensic rhetoric, visual advocacy, law and literature, and juristic semiotics.

Anselm Haverkamp is Emeritus Professor of English at New York University, and Professor of Philosophy at LMU Munich. As Director of the New York University Poetics and Theory Program, he for years organized and taught 'Literature and Philosophy' seminars with Jacques Derrida and Stanley Cavell.

Juntao Lin is a PhD candidate in Comparative Literature at New York University. His works span political theory, translation, and modern Chinese literature and culture, with special interests in questions of revolution and history.

Phillip Mitsis is A. S. Onassis Professor of Hellenic Culture and Civilization at New York University and Academic Director of the American Institute for Verdi Studies. His research spans ancient philosophy, law and literature, and contemporary logic, with particular attention paid to judgment, affect, and the rhetorical life of norms. He is currently working on iterability without difference and modal collapse in S5 logic, and on a philosophical study of the history of the morality of hatred.

Chris Power is a doctoral candidate in French and German literature(s) at Rutgers University. He completed an MA in French Literature in Morningside Heights and another in German Literature in Middlebury, Vermont. He lives in Brooklyn with his kitten (Pixote).

Avital Ronell is University Professor of the Humanities and Professor of German and Comparative Literature at New York University, where she taught an annual seminar for ten years with Jacques Derrida. She has published many works inflected by deconstruction and hermeneutics. She was recently featured in the documentary film, 'Surviving Derrida: Avital Ronell's Politics of Friendship' (dir. by Jesús Mario Lozano, 2026).

Mangalika de Silva teaches cultural criticism, revolutionary theory, and film history and form at New York University. Her research interests are post-foundationalist political philosophy, critical race theory, insurgent politics, decolonial ecological thought, state formation, violence, and populist Buddhism. Her essays have appeared in peer-reviewed journals: *Social Text*, *Cultural Studies*, *Religion*, *Journal of Visual Culture*, *South Atlantic Quarterly*, *Canadian Women's Studies*, *Domains*, *Indian Book Review*, *Asian Women's Studies*.

Hent de Vries joined NYU in 2017 when he was appointed as the Paulette Goddard Professor of the Humanities. He is Professor of Religious Studies and serves as Chair of the Department. In addition, he is Professor of German, Comparative Literature, and Affiliated Professor of Philosophy. In 2025, de Vries was appointed IWLC International Chair Professor at Tsinghua University's Institute for World Literatures and Cultures, Beijing, China. In 2026, he was elected to the European Academy of Sciences and Arts. In 2023, a Festschrift with critical responses to his work by scholars in philosophy, religion, history, politics, and literary studies, was published under the title *Religion in Reason: Metaphysics, Ethics, and Politics in Hent de Vries*.

Erica Weitzman is Associate Professor of German and Affiliate Professor of Comparative Literary Studies at Northwestern University. Her publications include the monographs *Irony's Antics: Walser, Kafka, Roth, and the German Comic Tradition* (Northwestern UP, 2015) and *At the Limit of the*

Obscene: German Realism and the Disgrace of Matter (Northwestern UP, 2021), the co-edited volume *Suspensionen. Über das Untote* (Fink, 2015), and numerous journal and book articles on nineteenth- and twentieth-century German and European literature and thought. She is currently a fellow at the Berlin Institute for Advanced Studies/Wissenschaftskolleg zu Berlin, working on a project on 'bluster' as a rhetorical mode in mid- to late nineteenth-century German expository prose.

Robert J.C. Young is Julius Silver Professor of English and Comparative Literature at New York University, and Honorary Fellow of Wadham College, Oxford University. Among other works, he is the editor, with Jean Khalfa, of a collection of unpublished or uncollected work by Frantz Fanon, *Alienation and Freedom* (original French edition 2015, English translation 2018). He is currently completing a historical study of Fanon, *Fanon Questions*, together with an edition of Fanon's lost African writings, *Fanon en Afrique*. Young is Editor of *Interventions: International Journal of Postcolonial Studies*.

Dominik Zechner is Assistant Professor of German and Comparative Literature at Rutgers, The State University of New Jersey. He works on: modern prose and poetry; philology, linguistics, and the philosophy of language; psychoanalysis and critical theory. Zechner has published four books, including the recent monographs *The Violence of Reading: Literature and Philosophy at the Threshold of Pain* (Palgrave Macmillan, 2024) and *Kafka und das Problem der Endlichkeit* (Sonderzahl, 2024).

INTRODUCTION

Force and Law

Peter Goodrich

The focus of the present volume, collection, and set of librocubicularist exchanges is upon a curious and short-lived yet recurrent encounter between deconstruction and law. It plays a minor part in the larger history and context of the anglophone reception of French Theory. It is also a harbinger and one incident of what Haverkamp coined as 'deconstruction is or in' the American legal academy. It is a tale of peculiar companions or unlikely friends and is now lodged in the past, in significant part beyond memory or in the immemorial, as lawyers term absent sources or reference ghosts. It is half a century since *Of Grammatology* first appeared in a U.S. translation from Johns Hopkins University Press and haunted in advance – seldom read but much mentioned – a brief yet real reception in U.S. law schools, so much so that those associated with the nomenclature and style of deconstruction, accurately or more usually inaccurately, were deemed a real threat and were subject to a species of jurisprudential anathematization.[1] Yet, as Nietzsche opined, beware of killing your enemy, because you thereby immortalize him. Such, we argue, is the case with deconstruction. Derrida returns, grammatology lives on, dangerous supplements multiply, and deconstruction becomes a revenant. A brief recall of that history,

1 Translated by Gayatri Chakravorty Spivak, not without critics, as *Of Grammatology* (Baltimore: Johns Hopkins University Press, 1976), with a second edition, for the fortieth anniversary, and slightly revised translation in 2016. On anathematization, see Peter Goodrich, 'Deconstruction', in *Elgar Concise Encyclopedia of Legal Theory and Philosophy* (Aldershot: Elgar, 202); and also Pierre Schlag, 'A Brief Survey of Deconstruction' (2005) 27 *Cardozo Law Review* 741. For an intriguing instance of *damnatio memoriæ*, or erasure of a name, see Pierre Legrand, 'Jacques in the Book (on Apophasis)' (2011) 23 *Law and Literature* 282.

DOI: 10.4324/9781003589419-1

incursion, and, especially in the legal academy, that lost past can act by way of introduction and anticipation.

The advenient moments, arrival from France, came in two phases. There was first the seismic event for the humanities of Derrida's lecture at a conference at Johns Hopkins in 1966. A little-known figure from France, seemingly dwarfed by the presence of Jacques Lacan, Roland Barthes, Jean Hyppolite, Paul de Man, the irreverent and radical character of his intervention, 'Structure, Sign and Play in the Human Sciences', was as unexpected as it was novel. The argument, pitched against structuralist thought, against the fathers, was that "even today the notion of a structure lacking any center represents the unthinkable itself".[2] This decentering introduced the play of opposites that was to unsettle metaphysics with the history of signs, presence with absence, being with loss, certainty with undecidability. Addressing the relation of language to the social sciences, his immediate topic, "it is a question of systematically and explicitly posing the problem of the status of a discourse which borrows from a heritage the resources necessary for the deconstruction of that heritage itself. A problem of *economy* and *strategy*."[3] It was also a jurisprudential question of decentering and disrupting the normative and disciplinary inheritance, interrogating the order of discourse, the complacencies and certainties of discursive formations, and the presupposed meanings of dogma, maxim, and words of law. In the case of law as a discipline and professional practice, the play of meanings, the absence of certitude, the very idea of deconstruction were alien to juristic conventions of literalism, determinacy of meaning and specifically the rules of construction of textual meaning as a technical, black letter practice, and in the words of one legal historian, an algebra untouched by common use.

The second intervention was equally a surprise. It came in the form of a gathering point for the post sixties generation, and it was an unusual embrace of interdisciplinarity for Derrida to be invited in 1989 to give the keynote speech at a conference at a law school, on the barely conceivable topic of 'Deconstruction and the Possibility of Justice'. Cardozo School of Law was a new venture seeking to distinguish itself, and its faculty were different in that many had doctorates both in law and in another discipline. The keynote lecture, delivered and subsequently published in *Cardozo Law Review* to an international though muted jurisprudential reception, was titled '*Force de Loi*/Force of Law', and was printed simultaneously in French and English, on facing pages. It is this text that is the initial focus, the trigger of the present volume, the first self-conscious and nominate intervention of deconstruction

2 Jacques Derrida, 'Structure, Sign and Play in the Human Sciences', in *Writing and Difference* (New York: Routledge & Kegan Paul, 1978), 279.
3 Ibid., 282.

into legal institutions.[4] The address and exchanges that followed were to form the basis of a continuing relationship between Derrida and the Law School, as well as with New York University, and with Jay Bernstein and the philosophy department at the New School for Social Research.[5] The longer-term connection took the form of an annual visit and series of seminars, as well as subsequent conferences both at New York University, where Jacques was hosted by Avital Ronell and Anselm Haverkamp, and at Cardozo hosted by Drucilla Cornell and then Michel Rosenfeld, and latterly Peter Goodrich. These led most notably to a second Cardozo conference under the rubric 'On the Necessity of Violence for any Possibility of Justice' published in 1991, again in the *Law Review*,[6] and then in 1995 a conference and volume *Deconstruction is/in America*, curated by Anselm Haverkamp, then a professor of English at NYU and also a participant in both the prior law school conferences.[7] *Law and the Postmodern Mind*, to which Derrida again contributed a keynote address, 'For the Love of Lacan', was convened in 1994 and published in the *Law Review* in 1995, and the book of the conference in 1998.[8] Finally, just to close the stage, there was a farewell conference, postmortem, at the Law School, under the aegis of Haverkamp, Goodrich, Rosenfeld, and Ronell, in 2005.[9] Now, again, twenty years on, two decades adrift, a retrospective set of events focused on the lasting impact, the living on, the not yet and yet to come of Derrida's work and specifically the continuing force of 'Force of Law'.

The valence and interrogation of law addressed from the inside in the first part of the titular lecture is the inaugural theme of this collection, each chapter taking its point of departure from some aspect of the unstable binary of force and law. In brief and anticipation, force poses something of a paradox for lawyers in that it is generally the contrary of law, or to borrow from Sir Edward Coke's *Institutes*, "Force, *vis*, in the Common Law is most commonly taken in ill part, and taken for unlawful violence."[10] The conundrum

4 Jacques Derrida, 'Force de Loi: Le "Fondement Mystique de l'autorité"/Force of Law: On the Mystical Foundations of Authority' (1990) 11 *Cardozo Law Review* 920. The English version was later published in Drucilla Cornell, Michel Rosenfeld, and David Carlson (eds), *Deconstruction and the Possibility of Justice* (New York: Routledge, 1992).

5 My thanks to Michel Rosenfeld for alerting me to this.

6 The second law school conference was published as a special issue as 'On the Necessity of Violence for any Possibility of Justice' (1991) 13:4 *Cardozo Law Review*.

7 Anselm Haverkamp (ed.), *Deconstruction is/in America* (New York: New York University Press, 1995).

8 'Law and the Postmodern Mind' (1996) 16 *Cardozo Law Review*, and then in book form, Peter Goodrich and David Carlson (eds.), *Law and the Postmodern Mind* (Ann Arbor: University of Michigan Press, 1998).

9 'Derrida/America: The Present State of America's Europe' (2005) 27:2 *Cardozo Law Review*.

10 Sir Edward Coke, *The First Part of the Institutes of the Lawes of England. Or, A Commentarie on Littleton, Not the Name of a Man Only But of the Lawe Itself* (London: Society of Stationers, 1618), cap. 12, section 240, column 1.

of force of law is thus, as Derrida put it at length, that of the law-breaking character of lawful acts, and the violence of their enforcement. Starting with the question of force and weakness, it is evident that force is not law, but is what makes law possible, and determines what it is, in its application and enforcement. Force is difference and differential, playing into myriad rhetorical and conceptual instabilities of law, fissures and uncertainties that exasperate the exegete, frustrate the jurist, and make the critic smile. There is always work to do, and for Derrida force in its very difference and undecideability allowed precisely for the apprehension of plurality in rhetoric, signification, philosophy, and law. They need to be thought again, further, and in perpetual motion. There is a reason, therefore, that the early essay on force and signification ends with Nietzsche and the invective against sedentary thinking: "only those thoughts that come to you while walking have any value", any apprehensible force.[11] It is the dancing pen, the joyful wisdom or gay science of the terpsichore, of feet, ideas, words reeling, that drives creative cerebration and inscription. Force makes law what it is, but it is also, as Sir Edward Coke and the Anglican legal tradition more generally maintain, exterior to legality, the other of rule-bound reason and declarative theories of rule application. The irrational or violent quality of decision has to be confined by rules, tamed by normative expression, and indeed masked by the technicalities and argot of juridical reasoning.

It is at that point in the 'Force of Law', on the boundary, transgression, and imbrication of one with the other, after the dance of difference, that Derrida introduces the aphorism or epigram that "deconstruction is justice", that what is always in play in legal decision is the oscillation of the just and the unjust, the *fort/da*, to use Freud's expression, of justice in law and law in justice.[12] The preposition, in, is here a verb, but it equally bespeaks both an in-law, a relative by marriage, by contract and consent, as also inadequacy, where the prefix, in, signals a negative, as also does injustice, which is but a space away from doing what is just. Each contributor thus picks up the force of law, brings their own force, to speak critically and philosophically to lawyers. The endeavor attempts both to do justice to deconstruction, and to treat deconstruction as doing justice to law. It is a theoretical exegesis in the precise sense of addressing the degree to which ways of seeing law have changed, and jurisprudence – in its European sense of legal philosophy – has been influenced, affected, and impacted by a complex and quietly incendiary essay, which is even on occasion referenced in judicial decisions, and juridical deconstructions of terms, figures, images have been assayed, principally and respectively in contract law, copyright law, and patents, as well as in costs

11 Derrida, 'Force and Signification', 29.
12 Cornell et al., *Deconstruction*, 19.

hearings and insurance cases where 'forensic deconstruction' is applied to actuarial calculations and on occasion to the circumstances producing a crime.

If justice gives force to law, a theme intrinsic to all of the chapters, it also acknowledges that law is both necessarily and unjustly violent. Here the authors transition to the second part of the titular essay and the ways in which deconstruction breaks the law, the sense in which it changes the rules and proffers the force of rendering justice, of giving time and listening – Haverkamp's radical patience – to what is both outside and inside legality, the collision, extrapolated by Hent de Vries, of violence and the norm. Force is etymologically, conceptually, and legally tied to violence, and as much for this reason as for his constant and scrupulous attention to the Western philosophical inheritance, to the detail and desiderata of its texts, Derrida turns to Walter Benjamin's critique of violence and the crisis in the concept of law. Here Benjamin's Derrida meets Derrida's Benjamin, each giving new life to the other in tracing the mystical foundation of legality in acts of violence or states of exception that inaugurate a system and provide a basis for a new legal form. The ten commandments are broken and then inscribed again. First violence and then law. Cause and effect one might surmise or indeed hope as a dialectical mode of justice as resolution or combinatorial of different forces. Taking up Pascal's concept of the aporia of law's founding, Benjamin writes in the disturbingly contemporary context of a haunted and haunting text, an enigmatic and uneasy inscription in the spatiotemporal environs of "radical destruction, extermination, total annihilation, of the law and of right, if not of justice, and among those rights, human rights, at least such as these are interpreted within a tradition of natural law".[13] Antisemitism, impending holocaust, the portents of exile, expulsion, and war surrounded and continue to provide the atmosphere and context of any reading of Benjamin's critique as itself a haunting to the present day, with Derrida as the medium and as the deconstructionist at some symbolic species or sensibility of the Ouija board.

The reference is to a multiplicity of hauntings, of ghosts, revenants, specters, which themes are taken up in the form of domestic strikes, intimate blows, as also in international interventions and more often failures of decision and of action with respect to global standoffs, conflicts, wars. Avital Ronell, in an elaborate Afterword, takes up these violent themes and how they haunt by way of providing an account of the destinerrance of both Benjamin and Derrida, Walter and Jacques, in our contemporary context. The question of appropriating, reappropriating, expropriating Derrida in his relation to Benjamin takes track and traction through the history and theory of the passage from Derrida to Benjamin and back again. Two ghosts, specters of thought who address the aporetics of law and state in the context of their

13 This is from the asterisk footnote to Part Two of 'Force of Law', *Cardozo Law Review* 973.

violence, their injustices, as well as the force of their legitimations, foundations, and forms of authority. Here Derrida is most clear, and certainly more so than was Benjamin, that there is a necessary violence to law; force that has a ground, a foundation in justice, can be legitimate, authorized, philosophically reconciled. If there is no divine and bloodless violence, there is only exsanguination, mutilation, and death. It is that concrete sense of the force of law as a normative constraint upon violent anomie, death imposed in pursuit of a phantasm, a final solution, death without trace that is here subject to historical scrutiny and legal critique. Its value is captured well in Erica Weitzman's peroration in this volume, and can be repeated here, as a postcard, a letter, an envoi: "In this moment in which, yet again, nothing seems more fragile than the rights (and lives) of some, Derrida's call to ask who is sacrificed in the name of the law, including the law to come, bears rereading."

PART I
Law

1

DOING JUSTICE TO DECONSTRUCTION

Isabelle Alfandary

Today, deconstruction is bearing the brunt of the violent attacks unleashed against it in the public arena. On some political scenes, notably in France and the United States, it has become synonymous with the systematic and deliberate destruction of thought, culture, values and institutions. Despite the rhetorical precautions Derrida attempted to surround the term with, as if to contain its effects in advance, it has in some contexts become a hate word.[1]

Nothing could be more inaccurate than to identify "deconstruction" with any ideological movement, partisan or militant position whatsoever. Actually, this is precisely the criticism levelled at it by its opponents at the other end of the spectrum: that "deconstruction" lacks political courage, shuns commitment and is insufficiently clear in its conclusions. Neither nihilistic nor apolitical, deconstruction is not what it is made out to be. Not only because its meaning is not fixed or even stable, but because it is incessantly in the process of becoming in the multiplicity of sentences that are likely to be formulated on the basis of it,[2] but also because the opera-

1 In January 2022, a symposium was held at the Sorbonne in Paris, opened by the French Minister of Education at the time, entitled "Après la déconstruction, reconstruire les sciences et la culture" ("After deconstruction, rebuilding science and culture"). This conference openly attacked deconstruction and, beyond it, "French theory". In his introductory remarks, the Minister went so far as to denounce so-called "French thought" as a "virus" against which he hoped the conference would provide the "cure". This conference caused quite a stir in academia and the media, and led some of us to respond a year later, in January 2023, with another conference held at the Ecole Normale Supérieure, entitled *Qui a peur de la déconstruction?* (Paris: PUF, 2024).

2 Jacques Derrida, *Mémoires: For Paul de Man*, trans. by Cecile Lindsay, Jonathan Culler, Eduardo Cadava, and Peggy Kamuf (New York: Columbia University Press, 1989), 14–15.

DOI: 10.4324/9781003589419-3

tion, the motion it implies, while obviously not excluding judgment, grasps questions in a complexity that ethically obliges one to say and not to say, forcing us to a complexity inseparable from the idea of justice.

How can we explain the current fate of deconstruction? We might ask what it is about deconstruction that triggers such resistance, not only to its theses but even to its very name. We could begin by reexamining the term "deconstruction", which Derrida has chosen, for want of a better word.

It seems that we must return to this term again and again to clarify its meaning and justify its choice. Deconstruction is not – not only – the common name for Jacques Derrida's philosophical work, not even the name for the movement of thought that Derrida supposedly inaugurated. In fact, the philosopher used the word to moderate – if not downplay – it almost immediately: "Deconstruction takes place, it is an event that does not await the deliberation, consciousness, or organization of a subject, or even of modernity. It deconstructs itself. It can be deconstructed [*Ça se déconstruit.*]". The "it" [*ça*] is not here an impersonal thing that is opposed to some egological subjectivity. It is *in deconstruction* (the Littré says, "to deconstruct itself [*se déconstruire*] . . . to lose its construction").[3] There is no such thing as "deconstruction". Insofar as it suspends the attributions of the proper name, to speak of "deconstruction" implies running the risk of going astray at every turn: "there is no sense in speaking of *a* deconstruction or *simply* deconstruction as if there were only one, as if the word had a (single) meaning outside of the sentences which inscribe it and carry it within themselves."[4]

Consequently, there can be no sentence whose grammatical subject could theoretically be "deconstruction", nor any speaker who could ever claim to be its author. To paraphrase Derrida, deconstruction does not belong. It is the impersonality of a movement, of a motion, a drive, that the syntagm of "deconstruction" tries to grasp, no doubt clumsily and not without giving rise to some unfortunate equivocations and terrible misunderstandings.

Resistance to Deconstruction

Let's begin by noting that this term triggers defensive movements on both sides – on the part of its detractors as well as Derrida himself – which we cannot help but wonder about. The point here is not to psychologize, but simply to draw attention to the power of the conflicting motions that animate anyone who seizes upon the term "deconstruction" in a sentence, in

3 Jacques Derrida, 'Letter to a Japanese Friend', in David Wood and Robert Bernasconi, eds., *Derrida and Difference* (Warwick: Parousia Press, 1985), 5–6.

4 Derrida, *Mémoires*, 17.

the multiplicity of sentences that are likely to be formed from this word. The hypothesis I would put forward is as follows: the word "deconstruction" puts the speaker, whoever he or she may be, in a situation of having to defend themselves against it.

The so-called defense mechanisms uncovered by Freud relate to the ego as the unifying instance of the *psyche*. Defense is understood as a series of operations that Jean Laplanche and J.B. Pontalis describe as aiming to "reduce [. . .] to suppress any modification likely to endanger the integrity and constancy of the individual."[5] The aim of these operations is to protect against what the same authors call Freud's discovery of "this aggression from within that is the drive".[6] The defense mechanisms Freud discovers – the most common forms of which are repression, cleavage and denial – concern "internal excitations that we cannot escape".[7] As we can see, "defense" in Freud's sense of the term is not protection like any other: it is an (unconscious) measure taken in the face of a situation that threatens to become untenable, in the face of an internal conflict or unexpected source of displeasure that the subject cannot guard against, in the face of the risk of contact with a pathogenic knot that he or she is desperately trying to avoid.

If we continue along the path of this hypothesis of a defense intrinsically linked to deconstruction, what then could be the nature of the internal conflict or the origin of the displeasure that the subject would seek at all costs to avoid? Deconstruction touches on one or more knots, but also on an unravelable – what Derrida calls "indeconstructible" – justice. In *Specters of Marx*, he writes:

> This is where deconstruction would always begin to take shape as the thinking of the gift and of undeconstructible justice, the undeconstructible condition of any deconstruction, to be sure, but a condition that is itself *in deconstruction* and remains and must remain (that is the injunction) in the disjointure of the *Un-Fug*.[8]

This thesis from *Specters of Marx*, which anticipates the issues at the heart of 'Force of Law', makes justice escape from any system of legal-moral norms:

> Once one has recognized the force and the necessity of thinking justice on the basis of the gift (*without force, precisely* . . . without necessity, perhaps and without law) of thinking to the other as gift of that which one does

5 Jean Laplanche and Jean-Bertrand Pontalis, *Vocabulaire de la psychanalyse* (Paris: Presses Universitaires de France, 2009), 108; the translation is mine.
6 Ibid., 109.
7 Ibid.
8 Jacques Derrida, *Specters of Marx*, trans. by Peggy Kamuf (New York: Routledge, 2006), 33.

> not have and which thus, paradoxically, can only *come back* or belong to the other.[9]

What is the unavowable, the unbearable, the untenable conflict of deconstruction, and what are the positions that each party occupies in the face of this name?

The indeconstructible condition of all deconstruction exposes everyone to an inadmissible pressure. This conflict is to be understood in terms of space at least as much as time: it is that of the "out of joint" of justice beyond law and morality:

> Beyond right, and still more beyond juridicism, beyond morality, and still more beyond moralism, does not justice as relation to the other suppose on the contrary the irreducible excess of a disjointure or an anachrony, some *Un-Fuge*, some "out of joint" dislocation in Being and in time itself, a disjointure that, in always risking the evil, expropriation, and injustice (*adikia*) against which there is no calculable insurance, would alone be able to *do justice* or to *render justice* to the other as other? A *doing* that would not amount only to action and a *rendering* that would not come down just to restitution?[10]

In this respect, justice could be seen as the *omphalos* of deconstruction: despite what Derrida calls "[t]he hyperanalyticism with which I identify 'deconstruction'",[11] there would be a stopping point, a point beyond which it would not be possible to go, not strictly speaking an indeconstructible point but an unanalyzable point, a structurally blind spot. This is how Derrida defines the navel of the Freudian dream:

> There is often a passage [a place, *eine Stelle*] in even the most thoroughly interpreted dream which has to be [*man muss*] left obscure [*muss man oft eine Stelle im Dunkellassen*] this is because we become aware during the work of interpretation that at that point there is a tangle [*Knäuel,* like a ball of yarn] of dream-thoughts which cannot be unravelled [*der sich nicht entwirren will*] and which moreover adds nothing to our knowledge of the content of the dream. This is the dream's navel [*der Nabel des Traums*], the spot where it reaches down into the unknown. The dream-thoughts to which we are led by interpretation cannot, from the nature of things, have any definite endings [*mussen bleiben ohne Abschluss*]; they are bound to branch out in every direction into the intricate network [*in die netzartige*

9 Ibid., 32.
10 Ibid.
11 Jacques Derrida, *Resistances of Psychoanalysis*, trans. by Peggy Kamuf, Pascale-Anne Brault, and Michael Naas (Stanford, CA: Stanford University Press, 1998), 35.

> *verstrickung*] of our world of thought. It is at some point where this meshwork [*Geflecht*] is particularly close that the dream-wish grows up, like a mushroom out of its mycelium.[12]

This point beyond which there is no possible analysis, and which is inextricably linked to the figure of the unknown, could be related to the problematic of the encounter with pure singularity in the experience of justice. The metaphor of the *omphalos* coincides with the Freudian syntagm of "*Jenseits*" – which Derrida translates as "*not beyond*", playing on the equivocation of the syntagm in French "*pas au-delà*" – a syntagm that the English translators have rendered as "step (not) beyond".[13] It is this same German syntagm and its French translation that Derrida will make much of in his rereading of the death drive discovered by Freud in the 1975–1976 seminar 'Life Death'.[14] It is the complex knotting of justice and deconstruction that I would now like to consider.

Destructive Drive?

Let's start with a detour into psychoanalysis and its relationship to deconstruction. Psychoanalysis, as Derrida understands it, is a power of deconstruction, despite its complicity with metaphysics – a complicity the philosopher has been trying to protect psychoanalysis from since his inaugural text on Freud ('Freud and the Scene of Writing').[15] The thinking of the archive inaugurated by Freudian psychoanalysis throws metaphysical categories, such as the concept of time, which are supposedly stable and homogeneous, into disarray. But there's more. According to Derrida, psychoanalysis discovers the violence inherent in any archive, and the death drive it necessarily conceals. The archive, as Derrida understands it from Freud, is no longer simply synonymous with memory:

> It is what I called earlier, and in view of this internal contradiction, *archive fever.* There would indeed be no archive desire without the radical finitude,

12 Ibid., 14.

13 Jacques Derrida, *Life Death*, trans. by Pascale-Anne Brault and Michael Naas (Chicago: University of Chicago Press, 2020), 18.

14 "Let me announce by way of anticipation that it is toward a certain other thinking of the beyond, of beyond, of the *Jenseits* of Nietzsche and of Freud, and especially of the *step (not) beyond* [*pas au-delà*] of Blanchot, that I would like to lead this seminar" (Derrida, *Life Death*, 5).

15 "The necessity of an immense labor of deconstruction of the metaphysical concepts and phrases that are condensed and sedimented within Freud's precautions. The metaphysical complications of psychoanalysis and the so-called human (or social) sciences (the concepts of presence, perception, reality, etc.). Linguistic phonologism" (Jacques Derrida, *Writing and Difference* [London and New York: Routledge, 2005], 248).

> without the possibility of a forgetfulness which does not limit itself to repression. Above all, and this is the most serious, beyond or within this simple limit called finiteness or finitude, there is no archive fever without the threat of this death drive, this aggression and destruction drive. This threat is *infinite*, it sweeps away the logic of finitude and the simple factual limits, the transcendental aesthetics, one might say, the spatio-temporal conditions of conservation. Let us rather say that it abuses them. Such an abuse opens the ethico-political dimension of the problem. There is not one archive fever, one limit or one suffering of memory among others: enlisting the in-finite, archive fever verges on radical evil.[16]

Insofar as it implies an exteriority ("*a certain exteriority*"[17]) and what Derrida calls "*a technique of repetition*",[18] the archive is threatened by the logic of repetition, or even repetition compulsion,[19] the other Freudian name for the death drive. "The archive always works, and *a priori*, against itself",[20] writes Derrida, who argues in the same breath that "the death drive is above all *anarchivic*".[21] In its very structure, the archive is a failure to remember, a hypomnesis. Archive fever is the archive put to death by the archive itself. Yet deconstruction as practiced and taught by Derrida seeks to excavate the archive in an attempt to grasp its logic or contradiction, and as a result finds itself de facto affected – infected – by the fever it carries. Once again, we shouldn't be overly surprised by the virulence of the resistance generated by deconstruction, or by the misunderstandings about its so-called "destructiveness". Deconstruction has an intimate, inescapable and inextricable relationship with the death drive, and its "knowledge", coextensive with its undertaking to reread the texts of the metaphysical tradition, inevitably leads it to cross paths with the death drive.

The fever of the archive that Derrida elaborates throughout his 1993 conference is a fever that can be understood not only as the fever of the mortifying drive that eats away at the archive but also as the fever of the burning desire for origin:

> The *trouble de l'archive* stems from a *mal d'archive*. We are *en mal d'archive:* in need of archives. Listening to the French idiom, and in it the attribute *en mal de,* to be *en mal d'archive* can mean something else than to suffer from a sickness, from a trouble or from what the noun *mal* might name. It is to

16 Jacques Derrida, *Archive Fever: A Freudian Impression*, trans. by Eric Prenowitz (Chicago: University of Chicago Press, 1996), 19–20.
17 Ibid., 11.
18 Ibid.
19 Ibid., 12.
20 Ibid.
21 Ibid., 10.

> burn with a passion. It is never to rest, interminably, from searching for the archive right where it slips away. It is to run after the archive, even if there's too much of it, right where something in it anarchives itself. It is to have a compulsive, repetitive, and nostalgic desire for the archive, an irrepressible desire to return to the origin, a homesickness, a nostalgia for the return to the most archaic place of absolute commencement.[22]

Yet since 1967, Derrida has never ceased to question the concept of origin and that of the originary. From *Of Grammatology* to *Archive Fever*, in a way this has been all Derrida has done, and in doing so, his thought has resonated with the fever it brings to light – to the point of sometimes seeming to merge with it. The so-called nihilism that deconstruction is criticized for may be understood as an effect of its proximity, its familiarity with the archive and its exposure to the impulses beyond the pleasure principle that are at work in the questions and texts it addresses.

Derrida considers the question of the drive to be a philosophical issue of the utmost importance. Whereas the drive for mastery (*Bemächtigungstrieb*) was already present in Freud's work, the psychoanalyst regarded it as just another pregenital drive, while Derrida elevates it to the rank of drive of drives. He writes in *The Post Card*: this drive for mastery, for which "It is always a question of knowing who is the 'master', who 'dominates', who has 'authority'",[23] is the drive that organizes the entire drive system, and serves as the "transcendental predicate"[24] of the drives: "In other words, the motif of power is more originary and more general than the PP [Pleasure Principle], is independent of it, is its beyond."[25] In so doing, Derrida takes up and corrects the theory of drives that Freud reworked in 1919 in *Beyond the Pleasure Principle*. But the Derridean refoundation – rectification – of the theory of drives is not intended solely to complement the Freudian metapsychology: the drive for mastery, which Derrida holds to be different from the death drive or the repetition compulsion, and which "gives us with what to describe them",[26] is of interest far beyond the sole field of application of psychoanalysis: "You can see that this word (*Trieb*) is everywhere. It pushes up everywhere, it pushes up everywhere there is pushing. . . . This *Trieb* is indeed destined to cover the totality of what is, namely the world."[27]

22 Ibid., 91.
23 Jacques Derrida, *The Post Card: From Socrates to Freud and Beyond*, trans. by Alan Bass (Chicago: University of Chicago Press, 1987), 404.
24 Ibid., 405.
25 Ibid.
26 Ibid.
27 Jacques Derrida, *The Beast and the Sovereign*, vol. 2, trans. by Geoffrey Bennington (Chicago: University of Chicago Press, 2011), 158.

Defending and Illustrating Deconstruction

In 'Force of Law', Derrida defends himself tooth and nail against the attacks of nihilism to which deconstruction has been subjected:

> Under the hypothesis that I shall only touch lightly upon for the moment, what is currently called deconstruction would not correspond (though certain people have an interest spreading this confusion) to a quasi-nihilistic abdication before the ethical-political-juridical question of justice and before the opposition before just and unjust, but rather to a double movement.[28]

He defends himself and deconstruction, correcting misunderstandings and denouncing the malevolence it has generated. At the same time, he acknowledges the problematic identification of his own name with the name of deconstruction. Here is his response to those who accuse him of a guilty nihilism, all the more perverse for being the result of an act of judgment:

> The sense of responsibility without limits, and so necessarily excessive, incalculable, before memory; and so the task of recalling the history, the origin and subsequent direction, thus the limits of the concepts of justice, the law and right, of values, norms, prescriptions that have been imposed, and sedimented there, from then on remaining more or less readable or presupposed. And to the legacy we have received under the name of justice, and in more than one language, the task of a historical and interpretative memory is at the heart of deconstruction.[29]

Deconstruction thus sets itself the task (*Aufgabe*) of recalling history, origin and meaning. It is by no means a work of destruction, nor is it revisionism. Quite the opposite, in fact. However, Derrida – as the Kantian that he is – immediately reminds us that this task is inseparable from an exposure of the determinations – and therefore necessarily the limits – of these concepts. Deconstruction, insofar as it proceeds from a movement of reading, brings contradictory and disconcerting conditions to light.

Derrida takes care to explain what he calls the "two styles" of deconstruction: "One takes on the demonstrative and apparently ahistorical allure of logico-formal paradoxes. The other, more historical and more amnesic, seems to proceed through readings of texts, meticulous interpretations and genealogies."[30] Insofar

28 Jacques Derrida, 'Force of Law', in Drucilla Cornell, Michel Rosenfeld, and David Gray Carlson, eds., *Deconstruction and the Possibility of Justice* (New York: Routledge, 1992), 19.
29 Ibid.
30 Ibid., 21.

as deconstruction "suspends" in its analytical movement the concepts it intends to apprehend, it may appear to be caught up in a movement of indecision, inertia, even inclined to a renunciation of judgment. But this is not the case. However dizzying, it doesn't shirk its task. But it takes its time. It has no choice but to take time. Derrida defends the movement of deconstruction, its own temporality, its patience, the meticulous rigor it requires, which presupposes enduring a certain deferment, a *différance*, that is in no way a shirking of the responsibility that commits it. Quite the contrary, insofar as deconstruction primarily questions responsibility – understood as the capacity to respond. But the questions it poses must remain open for a time, and the movement of spacing that constitutes its very gesture presupposes a suspension of judgment that has nothing to do with a refusal to judge:

> This responsibility toward memory is a responsibility before the very concept of responsibility that regulates the justice and appropriateness (*justesse*) of our behavior, of our theoretical, practical, ethico-political decisions. The concept of responsibility is inseparable from a whole network of connected concepts (property, intentionality, will, freedom, conscience, consciousness, subject, self, person, community, decision, and so forth) and any deconstruction of this network of concepts in their given and dominant state may seem like a move toward irresponsibility at the very moment that, on the contrary, deconstruction calls for an increase in responsibility. But in the moment that an axiom's credibility (*crédit*) is suspended by deconstruction, one can always believe that there is no more room for justice, nor for justice itself, nor for theoretical interest directed toward the problems of justice.[31]

Derrida argues that responsibility requires us not only to suspend judgment but also to support the gap that the deconstructivist method introduces into the concepts themselves: this form of "épochè"[32] is a moment "without which, in fact, deconstruction is not possible".[33] The immensity of the task set by the philosopher, who is well aware of the solidarity that exists between concepts that are as canonical as they are delicate to handle, is clear to see. The task is nothing less than to unravel the entire skein of metaphysics. And although Derrida is not inclined to indulge in the slightest psychologism, he acknowledges that this structurally necessary moment is not without a certain "*anxiety*",[34] which distantly echoes *Angst*, the an-

31 Ibid., 20.
32 Ibid.
33 Ibid.
34 Ibid.

guish before the indeterminate that Heidegger speaks of in *Being and Time*, and which is distinct from *Furcht* – fear – which relates to a definite object. Deconstruction understood as practice is not without effects on concepts as well as those who handle them: "This moment of suspense, the period of *épochè*, without which, in fact, deconstruction is not possible, is always full of anxiety, but who will claim to be just by economizing on anxiety?"[35]

Derrida denounces the bad faith that consists in pretending not to understand the movement of deconstruction, its necessity of difference, its structure of suspension, but he recognizes how much this method, if it is one, triggers anguish and sometimes vertigo – bordering on the unbearable more than on the undecidable. This structural unbearability lodges in the question of justice, of its indeconstructibility, preventing us from judging too quickly, from ever judging, if not without remorse, then at least without haunting. Derrida maintains the structural necessity of the dissatisfaction – which can become unbearable – that deconstruction generates: "For in the end, where will deconstruction find its force, its movement or its motivation if not in this always unsatisfied appeal, beyond the given determinations of what we call, in determined contexts, justice, the possibility of justice?"[36] In this respect, justice would not only be the *omphalos* of deconstruction, the "step (not) beyond" of the analyzable; it would take the place of an appeal, a driving force for deconstruction itself.

"I Know Nothing More Just Than What I Today Call Deconstruction"

Derrida does more than defend himself and deconstruction in this passage from 'Force of Law'. Not only does he maintain that justice is the question par excellence of deconstruction ("such a deconstructive line of questioning is through and through a problematization of law and justice"),[37] but he goes so far as to say that he knows "nothing more just than what I today call deconstruction (nothing more just, I'm not saying anything more legal or more legitimate)."[38] What Derrida "today call[s] deconstruction", and whose attributes he has set out, is deconstruction per se. Insofar as it is defined by "its force, its movement and its motivation", deconstruction seems to name a *dynamis* (a potential, an inactual force), but also an *energeia* (an actual force) that Derrida seeks to support and espouse not in the name of truth but in the name of justice.

35 Ibid.
36 Ibid., 20–21.
37 Ibid., 8.
38 Ibid., 21.

Is deconstruction wrongly associated with undecidability? It all depends on what one means by this. Derrida reminds us that a decision that doesn't "go through the ordeal of the undecidable would not be a free decision",[39] but moreover, he argues that the undecidable with which deconstruction is concerned, the undecidable that looks at it, and suspends and delays its hasty judgment, stems from "the experience of that which, though heterogeneous, foreign to the order of the calculable and the rule . . . is still obliged . . . to give itself up to the impossible decision while taking account of laws and rules."[40] The undecidable belongs to the order of the incalculable, of what is to come, of that which comes and cannot be anticipated.

Derrida's deconstruction, however, cannot be reduced to a mere observation of the undecidable, of an abstract justice wounded by the impossibility of the incalculable to which it is supposedly and tragically reconciled. The call of justice, however imperfect, cannot remain unanswered: "And so uncalculable justice *requires* us to calculate".[41] Only the demand for justice obliges, "requires", to say and re-elaborate tirelessly, without the answer ever being fully satisfying, nor fully tranquilizing. At the end of the chapter 'The "Mystical Foundation of Authority"', Derrida states: "Nothing seems to me less outdated than the classical emancipatory ideal."[42] And he adds a paragraph in which it becomes clear how deconstruction both obliges and exposes us:

> But beyond the identified territories of juridico-politicization on the grand geopolitical scale, beyond all self-serving interpretations, beyond all determined and particular reappropriations of international law, other areas must constantly open up that at first can seem like secondary or marginal areas. This marginality also signifies that a violence, indeed a terrorism and other forms of hostage taking are at work.[43]

There's nothing simple or reassuring about posing the question of justice, or exposing oneself to the constant threat of its reappropriation by law – even international law. We need only look at current contemporary conflicts. Deconstructive thought is restless, constantly on the lookout for motives for reappropriation that it must flush out, perverse motives that it must denounce – even at the risk of making oneself unpopular. In analyzing the chain of "autoimmune pervertibility of democracy",[44] Derrida takes

39 Ibid., 24.
40 Ibid.
41 Ibid., 28.
42 Ibid.
43 Ibid.
44 Jacques Derrida, *Rogues: Two Essays on Reason*, trans. by Pascale-Anne Brault and Michael Naas (Stanford, CA: Stanford University Press, 2005), 34.

the example of colonization and decolonization in Algeria, which "were both autoimmune experiences wherein the violent imposition of a culture and political language that were supposed to be in line with the Greco-European ideal".[45] While not pitting settlers against the colonized, Derrida draws attention to a mirrored "auto-immune process": "To immunize itself, to protect itself against the aggressor (whether from within or without), democracy thus secreted its enemies on both sides of the front so that its only apparent options remained murder and suicide."[46] The young Algerian regime, having fought a war of independence that "in the name of the political ideals extolled by the colonial power",[47] had to put an end to the electoral process "in order to save a democracy threatened by the sworn enemies of democracy."[48] The least we can say is that the political price to be paid for such analyses, which are dictated by the demand for justice, is undoubtedly not small – even if, once again, Derrida does not equate colonial power with the colonized people.

Does deconstruction end up being an unbinding force, by dint of exposure to the drive for mastery and the death drive, whose circuits it tirelessly tries to dismantle? In 'Force of Law', Derrida insists on the proximity between justice and what he calls "the worst": "Left to itself, the incalculable and giving (*donatrice*) idea of justice is always very close to the bad, even to the worst for it can always be reappropriated by the most perverse calculation."[49] Deconstruction has an intimate knowledge of the drive for mastery, and as such is constantly threatened by it with perverse appropriation. Deconstruction's close ties with the drive for mastery bring us to the shores of aporetic madness or the violence of given death. Derrida refuses to mince his words, and confesses his distrust of the word "force", whose equivocity leaves no one in peace, and is always likely to be turned into *Gewalt* (violence), if it is not always imbued with it: "What remains is that I've always been uncomfortable with the word force, which I've often judged to be indispensable."[50] To read this remark, which is anything but incidental, is to understand the extent to which "force of law" strictly echoes "the right to justice" – justice being at the confluence of motions as inextricable as they are irreducible.

45 Ibid.
46 Ibid., 35.
47 Ibid.
48 Ibid.
49 Derrida, 'Force of Law', 28.
50 Ibid., 7.

2

IN THE WAITING ROOM OF INJUSTICE

Pascal, Kafka, Derrida

Robert J.C. Young

> "Nous avons attendu la justice et elle ne vient point."
>
> Blaise Pascal, *Prophéties* VI

Abandoning the precision of the Pascaline for theories of probability around 1654, with this remark Pascal sketched out the course of the everlasting fissure between the law and the possibility of justice, the justice for which we continue to wait. In the twenty-first century, after the eras of Franz Kafka and Samuel Beckett who did nothing but rewrite Pascal for their own times, the wait for the event which manages not to happen continues amidst uncertainty, anxiety and the evanescence of the law itself. We have always been waiting for justice to become aligned with the law, but that unrealized possibility slips further and further from us.

What can Jacques Derrida add to Pascal? He has been put in an impossible situation. Asked to speak about 'Deconstruction and the Possibility of Justice', the topic already begs the question.[1] If justice has to be consigned merely to the realm of possibility in the very title of the colloquium, it must necessarily also exist close to the jurisdiction of the impossible and the unjust, forcing justice to resort to the imaginary, the deceiving but only genuine host of its possibility. But then who better to confront the alluring temptations of mere possibility than Derrida, celebrated philosopher of delay,

1 Jacques Derrida, 'Force de loi: le "fondement mystique de l'autorité"'/'The Force of Law: The Mystical Foundation of Authority' (1990) 11:5/6 *Cardozo Law Review* 920–1045; a version of the English translation reproduced in *Deconstruction and the Possibility of Justice*, ed. by Drucilla Cornell et al. (Routledge, 1992), 3–67.

DOI: 10.4324/9781003589419-4

deferral, *décalage*? How might "deconstruction" transform a situation that Pascal in the seventeenth century was already characterizing thus: "We call justice whatever might can enforce" ("et ainsi on appelle justice ce qu'il est force d'observer").[2]

As he freely admits, Derrida can chart the slippages between law and justice, but he cannot arrest them. No more than the transmutations that occur as he pushes justice, power and law across languages in his pursuit of justice's posited possibilities. He soon finds himself brought up before Walter Benjamin's essay 'Kritik der Gewalt', which as Benjamin himself puts it, expounds the relation of "gewalt" "to law and justice". The "Gewalt" in the title is usually to some extent mistranslated as "Critique of Violence" even though the primary meanings of *Gewalt* – power, strength, force, judicial power, authority – do not necessarily carry a negative connotation.[3] Violence as such enters only when power is exercised with a damaging intention or context, as in the phrase "gewalt antun" (commit violence). In reading Benjamin, Derrida duly worries about the issue of the potential or realized act of enforcement of the law as it moves from the relaxed abstractions of the general to the particularities of a case. That pushes him to effect further transversals by moving the law into French, producing a random translational bounce in a different direction that rehearses Benjamin's own metaphor of translation as the chance trajectory of colliding billiard balls. It is impossible for Derrida to analyze Benjamin's essay without reaching for the two adversarial words for law in French, "loi" and "droit", colliding "the law" with right(s), prescription and entitlement. Justice, meanwhile, continues to lurk in the aporetic realm of the impassable impossible, that is, in the realm of injustice. Until there is justice, there will always be only the relentless equivocations of injustice, injury, impairment, indignity, inequity, iniquity.

II

Sliding along the alphabet from i- to l-, from injustice to law, between injustice, justice and law there is always the silent barrier of the k. The letter "K" plunges itself into ambivalence, as in today's K-shaped economy. After the firm downstroke with which it begins, the pen breaks into two sideways strokes that point incompatibly in different directions up and down, northeast and southeast at the same time. Those such as Kierkegaard and Kafka who bear the heavy burden of carrying the letter capitalized at the forefront

2 Blaise Pascal, *Pensées and Other Writings*, trans. by Honor Levi (Oxford: Oxford University Press, 1995), 30; *Pensées de Blaise Pascal*, 2 vols. (Paris: P. Didot L'aîné, 1817), I: 193.

3 Walter Benjamin, *Selected Writings, Volume I, 1913–1926*, ed. by Marcus Bullock and Michael W. Jennings (Cambridge: Harvard University Press, 1996), 237.

of their names are condemned to a permanent state of ironic incongruity, can never escape the either-or with which K taunts them, consigning them to a vacillation all too discernible in their writings. In order to try to escape his nominal fate, Kierkegaard resorted to one pseudonym after another, producing over a dozen in the course of his life. The titles of his books bristle with equivocal dyads, dualities and dichotomies: after his first book on irony as such, in his next, *Either/Or,* Kierkegaard went further in reformulating the ambivalence of the second strokes of the letter "K" by producing two pseudonymous authors for the text. The opening capital letters of their names, V and A (Victor de Eremita and A) not only mimic horizontally the form of the second strokes of K but mirror and invert each other.

When transmuted into Johannes de Silentio, the author of *Fear and Trembling,* Kierkegaard enacts the dynamics of his own name's opening capital letter by introducing inexorable doubt into the story of Abraham and Isaac from Genesis that despite its sudden resolution continues to haunt us with its possibility of injustice, of the theologically and morally unacceptable, so much so that Kierkegaard rewrites it into multiple clinamina. Each version takes the form of a narrative swerving repetition that attempts to assuage the unjust monstrosity, the "motiveless malignity" as S.T. Coleridge describes Iago, of God's selfish command that Abraham should kill his own son as a sacrifice to God himself, arbitrarily and unjustly requiring the hundred-year-old Abraham to foreshadow God's own decision to sacrifice his only son. God's motive for doing so is clear in the case of Jesus, whose birth, though miraculous, was scarcely less so than Isaac's – for Sarah is so "old and well stricken in age", so well into the hundred and twenty-seven years of her life, that when she overhears God telling Abraham that she will bear him a son she breaks out laughing, a moment to be commemorated in his name.[4] God has a reason for sacrificing his son, but when after Isaac is born so miraculously late in life God commands Abraham to kill him, it is, we are told, simply to tempt him, an arbitrary tease to see if he will disobey him. Just kidding. As Kierkegaard relates in one of his revisionary versions of the story:

> It was a quiet evening when Abraham rode out alone, and he rode to Mount Moriah; he threw himself down on his face, he prayed God to forgive him his sin, that he had been willing to sacrifice Isaac, that the father had forgotten his duty to his son. He often rode his lonesome road, but he found no peace. He could not comprehend that it was a sin that he had been willing to sacrifice to God the best that he had, the possession for which he himself would have gladly died many times; and if it was a sin,

4 Genesis 18:12–13 KJV.

> if he had not loved Isaac in this manner, he could not understand that it could be forgiven, for what more terrible sin was there?[5]

For Kierkegaard, this prompts the question of the possibility of the teleological suspension of the ethical and of the law: for Abraham to have followed God's command would have been nothing less than a sin in itself. The father is required to forget his most important duty as a father to protect his own son, in the face of God's command to kill him – which in itself would involve his committing the sin of disobeying the very first of the Ten Commandments. Except that, when God commands Abraham to do this in Genesis 22 he has not yet prescribed the Ten Commandments, which do not make their appearance until Exodus 20. The story of Abraham and Isaac thus occurs, quite literally in a temporal sense, before the law. At this point, the relationship between God and Abraham is based only on a legal agreement, a "covenant", which means that at this point, God's command to Abraham to kill his own son is not yet definable as a sin, any more than it would have been for Abraham who had in fact himself just cruelly cast out Hagar the Egyptian and the son that she had borne him into the wilderness of Beersheba. If disobeying God's command amounts to a sin, it is only to the degree that it breaks the agreement that Abraham will follow God's orders. Everything in Genesis and the first nineteen chapters of Exodus occurs before the arrival of "the law"; before that the law exists only as God's performative command, as it was for Adam and Eve. Until Exodus 22 there is no "the law" in the sense of a set of general articulated prescriptions that must be obeyed if not always understood. At this stage, if the law is, as it were, out there, it is almost impossible to know whether or not one has broken it, because it is inaccessible other than in the form of performance, that is, God's command, which is as entirely unpredictable as a President's, a mode that suffuses the Old Testament throughout even in its form of writing. As Erich Auerbach describes it, that involves:

> the externalization of only so much of the phenomena as is necessary for the purpose of the narrative, all else left in obscurity; the decisive points of the narrative alone are emphasized, what lies between is nonexistent; time and place are undefined and call for interpretation; thoughts and feelings remain unexpressed, are only suggested by the silence and the fragmentary speeches.[6]

5 Søren Kierkegaard, *Kierkegaard's Writings VI: Fear and Trembling/Repetition*, ed. by Howard V. Hong and Edna H. Hong (Princeton: Princeton University Press, 1983), 13.
6 Erich Auerbach, *Mimesis: The Representation of Reality in Western Literature*, trans. by Willard R. Trask, with an Intro. by Edward W. Said, 50th anniversary ed. (Princeton: Princeton University Press, 2013), 11.

Like God himself, the law as law is inaccessible, the very situation, in fact, of the other bearer by name of the mark of the split K, K. in Franz Kafka's novel *Der Prozess*. There the law's inaccessibility is articulated explicitly in the fable which appears in the last chapter before K.'s unjust death, 'Vor dem Gesetz', usually translated as 'Before the Law' or, in French, 'Devant la loi', also the title of Jacques Derrida's essay on Kafka's story.[7]

In the Biblical version of the story of Abraham and Isaac, Abraham simply accepts God's command and never seeks to question or understand it, thus demonstrating his "faith" but more obviously his unwavering obedience even if the command confuses his faith. God's unknowability occurs literally "before the law" because, as has been said, at this point in the Bible the law has not yet been laid down. The unknowability, unpredictability and inaccessibility of God is at its extreme because the law has not yet arrived. This is also exactly the situation in Kafka's story, in which the "vor" of its title could equally well indicate a temporal relation to the law. The law is still in process, in the process of formation, as it always is. In the story of the man from the country who has to wait before the gate of the law that he is never allowed to enter, the prohibition is applied because the law is itself not yet present; it may be anticipated but it does not yet exist. The countryman arrives too early. He waits at the gate expectantly, but there is nothing there, only a series of doorkeepers, each one of which, the doorkeeper claims, is more terrible than the last. The law is nothing but the power that is enforced upon the luckless countryman who arrives because he imagines the law as being directly accessible. As Pascal put it, "[t]he good of mankind requires them to be deceived".[8] Law is force, and justice is whatever power can enforce.

III

In obeying God's commands, God states that Abraham will thereby "keep the way of the Lord, to do justice and judgment".[9] God's way is "to do justice and judgement", which suggests that God's way is identified with the law, even if as yet the law is nothing more than a series of performative commands. But the strange concept, "to do justice", as Derrida observes, is soon undercut four chapters later when God's cruel and perverse command in the story of Abraham and Isaac raises the questionable relation of God's law to justice that will never disappear. The matter is articulated most forcibly in the book of Job, whose patience exceeds even that of Kafka's countryman.

7 Franz Kafka, *The Trial*, trans. by Mike Mitchell (Oxford: Oxford University Press, 2009); Jacques Derrida, 'Before the Law', in Derek Attridge, ed., Christine Roulston, trans., *Acts of Literature* (London: Routledge, 2017), 181–220.

8 Pascal, *Pensées*, 25.

9 Genesis 18:19, KJV.

The Book in some sense takes the form of prolonged extended questioning of the Genesis story, of what is involved when God exercises his power "to do justice and judgment". As Job's friend Bildad the Shuhite asks: "Doth God pervert judgment? or doth the Almighty pervert justice?"[10] And if so, what becomes of justice, which exists, after all, only for humans?

God's "way" may be to do justice and judgment, but does that apply to his law, or to the law in general as it appears in Kafka's story? Law offers plenty of judgments, but does it offer more than the possibility of justice, whose contradictions and instabilities perhaps, as Derrida claims, can be located and unravelled by deconstruction? Unravelled in its irredeemability. If law is distinct from justice, as Derrida argues, then its justice must be unmediated, its judgments must be just. Justice ought to be a word that grammatically can take no adjective other than just. For once it is qualified – as in Sir Thomas More's complaint of England's "extreme justice" for example – then it will no longer be justly just, can no longer be the entity that it claims to be, namely justice, just as for Abraham to keep the way of the Lord is also to become guilty of a sin. When we ask for justice, should we rather ask for a just justice? Or should we recognize that nothing is intrinsically just, that like everything else it moves with the times, that justice is nothing but strength and power, and that, like law, as Pascal puts it, justice too "has its periods", subject to the vagaries of time, fashion and force.[11] There may be law, but not "the law" that embodies a universal principle of justice.

Law nevertheless identifies itself with justice as if they were the same – judges of the highest courts are called "Justices", even "the Hon Mr Justice". But since justice can always be qualified, can always be unjust, partial, law must leave unmediated its theological origins, its identification with the vengeful justice of the Lord for whom the law means obedience to his will whether or not it is just or lawful. So the defendant today when brought "before the law" and asked if he or she pleads "guilty or not guilty", guilty or guiltless as the Bible puts it, finds themselves back in the Garden of Eden. For to have to plead at all already implies the desperation of guilt. And no one can plead "innocent", because to be truly innocent you cannot have a concept of guilt. Before the law, we are all always already guilty, even if only negatively so.

But does it even make sense to suggest that "the law" exists in a philosophical sense, as Derrida implies, suspended as it is between the particular and the universal? Can it exist or be discussed as if independent and distinct from the lived experience of its incarnations in historical, geographical, and linguistic realms? Kafka himself lived in and travelled between imperial environments – Prague, Berlin – in which two very different forms of law were operative, the

10 Job 8:3, KJV.
11 Pascal, *Pensées*, 23, 25.

Austrian and German legal codes respectively.[12] The countryman assumes, however, that there is simply the law in general. This is because, as an alternative English translation of the title of the story puts it, he too remains always "outside the law". Finding himself outside the law, in the course of his wait the countryman discovers that the law is literally nothing. There is no inside. There are laws: when we say "it's the law" we use the term the law to indicate the existence of a specific law. But there is no substantive entity that we can ever encounter or experience as "the law". And of course, as the class dynamics of the story also suggests (contrast the subservient behavior of the doorkeeper in the story of the visit of Josef K. to the merchant's house),[13] the subaltern non-elite countryman will always be outside the law in the sense that the law will always be made for others, certainly not for him. It is also a matter of class, and it is this that the doorkeeper understands.

IV

Before and after it was published as a free-standing story in 1915, Kafka's parable 'Before the Law' was recited by a priest in a cathedral, inserting the question of law into its originary theological framework. Indeed, as with the story of the merchant who "consults a man versed in the law", when Kafka writes of "the law", it often turns out to be indistinguishably legal, moral, and theological, and thus irresolvable in any conventional form:[14]

> "How do you imagine it will end?" asked the Priest. "I used to think it would turn out all right," said K., "now I sometimes even doubt that myself. I don't know how it will end. Do you know?" "No," said the Priest, "but I fear it will end badly. They think you are guilty. The trial will probably not get any further than one of the lower courts. At least for the moment they think your guilt is proven." "But I'm not guilty," said K., "it's a mistake. How can a person be guilty anyway? We're all human, every single one of us." "That is correct," said the priest, "but that's the way guilty people talk."[15]

K., it seems, has committed as much a sin as a crime, like Meursault in Camus' *L'Étranger*.[16] And indeed, K.'s arrest seems to have been put into operation proleptically, since it is almost immediately followed by his sexual

12 Kafka, *The Trial*, xx.

13 Franz Kafka, *Diaries*, trans. Ross Benjamin (New York: Schocken Books, 2024), 357–358.

14 Derrida, 'Before the Law', 183.

15 Kafka, *The Trial*, 151–152.

16 In Camus' *L'Étranger*, Meursault is convicted as much (if not more) because he did not appear to grieve his mother's death as for the murder of the Arab.

assault on Fräulein Bürstner, in which he commits at once a sin and a crime in an act of narrative retrocausality. Like God, the all-seeing law operates in a continuous present, outside human perceptions of temporality. His arrest anticipates the crime that he will commit shortly afterwards. Even if K. does not see it himself, his guilt is apparent to the reader from this act that occurs the very same evening as the arrest. By placing his parable 'Before the Law' in a cathedral in a story about a trial, Kafka broadens the idea of the law to include the moral aspects of the assault, staging the inextricable implications of law with theology, on which the authority of law must be based for all the reasons spelt out by Benjamin in 'Critique of Violence.' The law is founded on theological as well as state violence. Within the novel, the unending Talmudic interpretations of the story make up a narrative of analytic reversals that end in an interpretation in which the positions of the doorkeeper and countryman reverse, like Hegel's master and slave, leading to the ultimate triumph of the latter. But the closing inference that it is the doorman, not the countryman, who is deceived is not left at that, for what appears as a final conclusion is then expressly stated not to be final: " 'It means that the world is founded on untruth.' K. said this as a final comment, but it was not his final verdict." As judge and priest, the two men stage for the reader the novel's own infinite interpretability and ultimate, in the literal sense of the word, incomprehensibility. There's no use, we're told, in trying to discern "the meaning" of *The Trial* any more than that of 'Before the Law.' Neither has a "meaning" as such – but then how many things that human beings experience in life have "*a* meaning"? Writing often involves an attempt to give stories, experiences, meanings, but language is not a code; if interpretations are required or possible, then there will never be "a" meaning. The story leaves something absent inside us for which we search, like the *objet a*.

V

Nevertheless, it is all the more curious that once the discussions between K. and the priest about the story have shown us that we shouldn't expect to produce a definitive interpretation of *The Trial,* we read Kafka in his diaries recounting a striking episode in 1915 in which he recites some of his work aloud to Felice during a rare moment of doubtless still stilted intimacy.

> F. said: "How good we are being here together." I was silent as if during this exclamation I'd lost my hearing. For two hours we were alone in the room. Around me nothing but boredom and hopelessness. We have not yet had a single good moment with each other during which I would have breathed freely. With F. I never had, except in letters, the sweetness of the relationship to a beloved woman as in Zuckmantel and Riva, only boundless admiration, subservience, sympathy, despair and self-contempt.

> I also read to her, the sentences became disgustingly jumbled, no connection with the listener lying with her eyes closed on the sofa and silently taking it in. A lukewarm request to be permitted to take a manuscript with her and copy it. During the doorkeeper story ["Before the Law"] greater attention and good observation. The meaning of the story dawned on me for the first time, she too grasped it correctly, then, to be sure, we plunged into it with coarse remarks, I started it.[17]

It was thus only *after* he had written it, and in the erotic context of a performative act of reading it aloud to a woman whom he desired lying on the sofa before him, that the meaning of his own story finally became apparent to Kafka, as it did simultaneously to his lover. The dawning of the meaning of the story turns out to be a highly erotic experience, prompting them to "plunge into it with coarse remarks", followed by the odd additional phrase "I started it". In any Kafka novel, this grasping and plunging between them in a disgusting jumble always indicates some sort of physical, sexual encounter. Unlike the infinite interpretations exchanged between K. and the priest, between Franz Kafka and Felice Bauer, interpretation on this occasion is notably not at issue. The meaning, intriguingly, seems to be sexual and erotic, or perhaps it is rather that the mutual discovery of the meaning provides an irresistible catalyst for psychosomatic attraction and love-making. Kafka of course never discloses what this meaning of the story that they both discovered actually was: like God's law, it only exists in the performative moment. Nevertheless, intriguingly, the anecdote suggests that the uninterpretable story does in fact have a meaning after all, that readers could finally access its meaning if not the law, that the parable works like the other side of 'An Imperial Message', in which there is a written message but the letter simply never arrives at the destination of its waiting recipient. However, no sooner do we take that satisfaction than we read Kafka's later text 'On Parables' in which he writes that "all these parables really set out to say merely that the incomprehensible is incomprehensible".

Here though Kafka does *not* say that the parables are incomprehensible, i.e. that we cannot know their meaning. Rather he offers what is not quite a tautology: the parables are saying that "the incomprehensible is incomprehensible", in other words, that God himself is beyond our human understanding, our own finitude. As Coleridge puts it in 'The Eolian Harp' (1795):

> For never guiltless may I speak of him,
> The Incomprehensible! save when with awe

17 Kafka, *Diaries*, 386.

I praise him, and with Faith that inly feels;
Who with his saving mercies healed me,
A sinful and most miserable man,
Wildered and dark.[18]

"In the darkness [the man from the country] can now perceive a radiance that streams immortally from the door of the Law". The impossible condition of finite human understanding before God, the incomprehensible, returns us not just to Abraham receiving God's command that he kill his own son, but to the inference in 'Before the Law' that law and justice must always remain incompatible, an incompatibility brutally staged in the final chapter of *The Trial*, in which far from facing the court for his trial and receiving the law's promised justice for which he holds out to the end, K., already deemed guilty, is taken out by state assassins and, watched by an unknown onlooker from the top-story window of a nearby house, is viciously murdered "like a dog" – a vengeful, ignominious killing whose public brutality adds the further punishment of shame, a common practice and pleasure for state torturers and assassins – think of the death of Patrice Lumumba, for example, who was forced to eat his own words, to eat the paper on which they were printed while being filmed – before being killed.

So too, like Abraham's planned sacrifice of his son Isaac while being watched from on high by the angel of the lord, K.'s public death, propped on a boulder in the quarry, takes place in the dark aporia of humiliation that lies between the law and justice. *Summum jus, summa injuria.*

18 S.T. Coleridge, 'The Eolian Harp', ll. 58–63, in J.C.C. Mays, ed., *Poetical Works, The Collected Works of Samuel Taylor Coleridge*, Bollingen Series (Princeton: Princeton University Press, 2001), I: 234–235.

3

IS DECONSTRUCTION JUSTICE?

Peter Goodrich

There is a celebrated moment in 'Force of Law', where Derrida announces that "Deconstruction is justice".[1] Deconstruction cannot itself be deconstructed because it is not, variously, an analysis, a critique, or a method, but rather an attack from within, an internal dismantling, a process, happening and event. In the present excursus I will take the three-word conjunction in its positive material connotation and ask to what extent justice as an institution, and the judgements and decisions of common-law courts of justice in anglophone jurisdictions, have embraced and been impacted by deconstruction. Is there, after Derrida, a minor jurisprudence of deconstruction, meaning an operative play of attention to juristic excesses of meaning, the undecidability of legal texts? Has there been a relay or transmission of at least aspects of the theory and practice of textual construction, of the literary qualities of legal utterances? In the alternative, does the fear of exposure of indeterminacy, of the enigma of plurality of meanings, force judgments to bend towards fictions of certainty in judicial dispositions? The injustice at the heart of justice, the before and outside the law that necessarily intersects in decisions, has tended to threaten jurisprudence and do violence to the quietude of the norm. It is a question initially of hauntology. A matter of the passage of signs, attributions, communal thought and thought processes into the institution and practice of case law. To what extent, if any, and if so in what forms has

1 Jacques Derrida, 'Force of Law: The "Mystical Foundation of Authority"' (1989) 11 *Cardozo Law Review* 919, 945, and in the original French "La déconstruction est la justice." One should note also that in *Memoires for Paul de Man* (New York: Columbia University Press, 1986), 18 Derrida had claimed "America is deconstruction", the place being appropriated as the name of deconstruction in progress, a move that also led to Anselm Haverkamp (ed.), *Deconstruction Is/In America* (New York: NYU Press, 1995).

DOI: 10.4324/9781003589419-5

our subject, Emeritus Derrida, entered law and specifically legal judgment in the modality of judicial decisions and so also case outcomes? The inquiry, in sum, mortar and balance, is into the question of the effects of deconstruction being thought as internal to justice.

It is in the first instance itself a deconstructive question, in which what is at issue is an untranslatable homonymy in which the Derridean philosophy of the exorbitance of the text gives pause to law and not least through its challenges to core jurisprudential concepts of structure, center and determinacy of meaning. The play of sense and sense making has a certain irreverence and initiates spectres that I pose here in relation to common-law cases and the casuistry of their elaborate written determinations. The goal is a close analysis of the internal structure of the textual elaborations of the reasons for judgments in a set of anglophone cases that have recourse to the term and on occasion to the concept of deconstruction. The preliminary question, and initial reception, is that of a certain negative reaction to the intimidating prefix, 'de', of deconstruction, or *dé de déconstruction* and its impact as an undoing, which is to say the phantasm of haunting, influence or at one point the (momentary) perceived threat of an internal hæmorrhage, of a hermeneutic derailing of the community of precedential thought. Deconstruction, whose performance sees the structure of law, its medium, fall apart, at least in nominal appearance seems to pose an existential threat to the legal establishment. It was ever likely to face resistance. Time, however, now close to half a century of usage in multiple contexts, has softened the reactions and opened the possibilities of interpretation. Tracking the movement of legal thought, can it be said that the late Derrida is summoned before the law with any force or frequency? A question that he would want to ask and which thus has to start with being late, a spirit, a looming figure, *en retard*, dead and so necessarily before the law as it is enunciated now, and also outside the law of the living, but then also and necessarily, to a degree, also in the view, presence and conusance of decision.[2] The haunting is that of a name, Derrida, that has passed, no more one, more than one, contributing to the force of the not yet. It is also that of the process, deconstruction, associated with the nomination that has joined the vast host of figures of thought that make up the spectral community or micro-ontology, in our instance, of anglophone jurisprudence, common-law cerebration and determination.

The initial point to make is that continental theory is cited less often than the already infrequent references to classical philosophers, to Aristotle, Plato or,

2 I use the term conusance in its old legal sense of cognition – cognizance – that takes account of other jurisdictions and by extension knowledges. It suggests a version or reference to the old maxim that philosophical, medical and poetic authorities ought to be cited: *auctoritates philosophorum, medicorum et poetarum sunt in causis allegendæ et tenendæ.*

for the more Anglican inclined judiciary, Lewis Carroll, or Charles Lutwidge Dodson, proffering *Alice in Wonderland* and Humpty Dumpty.[3] I am not concerned with legal academic receptions, minimal and discarded as they generally were in anglophone law schools, or in any direct sense with the literature of critical legal studies that for a brief moment flaunted deconstruction as a talisman, a totem that rapidly became taboo.[4] In the US legal academy, which, as is remarked in 'Force of Law', has an institutional presence in legal and judicial practice, deconstruction was anathematized early on, and by the mid-1990s deconstruction was no longer a presence or force. In other common-law jurisdictions with undergraduate law programs, discussion of Derrida and deconstruction continued, but in the nebula or nephophile dominions of academic closed-circuit circulation. That is a story for another occasion, a narrative of which is incidental to judicial uses of deconstruction save in the singular sense that the culture wars of the 1980s and 90s, now returned with vivid vim and vicious vigor, gave the prefix, the word de-construction, a negative connotation, and confined it within scare quotes. Not being much engaged in theoretical debates, outside the youthful tripos curriculum, or lingering interest in literary criticism, the judiciary pay scant attention to such academic brouhaha, but one might nonetheless expect a certain aura of anathema, of negative sentiment to accompany whatever slight presence and use deconstruction may have in the *communis opinio* and written judgements of common lawyers. In what follows I will trace an initial, superficial and defensive judicial response to the word and event of deconstruction into a less obvious and more positive if inchoate

3 *Brayshaw v Partners of Apsley Surgery* [2018] EWHC 3286 (QB) Spencer J. (Plato); *People v Nesbitt* 199 N.Y.S.3d 850 (2023) Rebecca L. Town J. (Plato and Aristotle); *Investor's Compensation Scheme v West Bromwich Building Soc.* [1998] 1 BCLC 494, 527i per Leggatt L.J. (Alice in Wonderland); and in the House of Lords, Lord Hoffman discusses Humpty Dumpty [1998] 1 BCLC 494, 549c. One can also note Joseph Raz, a successor to Hart at Oxford, who notes that reconnecting to philosophy meant from Plato to Hegel, to the 'greats', Raz, 'Responsibility and the Negligence Standard' (2010) 30 *Oxford Journal of Legal Studies* 2.

4 There are exceptions, such as Michel Rosenfeld, *Just Interpretations* (Los Angeles and Berkeley: University of California Press, 1992) or the essays in the edited collection, Pierre Legrand (ed.), *Derrida and Law* (Abingdon: Routledge, 2009). The history of CLS is beyond my scope here, but the brief version of the story is set out in Steven M. Teles, *The Rise of the Conservative Legal Movement: The Battle for Control of Law* (Princeton: Princeton University Press, 2008), cataloguing how the Olin Foundation injected millions of dollars into conservative law and economics programs in US law schools. On UK CLS, which never had much if any direct professional purchase, there is Douzinas et al., *Postmodern Jurisprudence: The Law of Text in the Texts of Law* (Abingdon: Routledge, 1991); and Peter Goodrich, 'The Critic's Love of the Law: Intimate Observations on an Insular Jurisdiction' (2000) 10 *Law and Critique* 343; and then Costas Douzinas and Adam Gearey, *Critical Jurisprudence* (Oxford: Hart, 2005) and also Jacques de Ville, *Jacques Derrida: Law as Absolute Hospitality* (Abingdon: Routledge, 2011). For a general account of the anglophone confusion of legal theory, see J. Desautels-Stein and C. Tomlins (eds.), *Searching for Contemporary Legal Thought* (New York: Cambridge University Press, 2017).

incorporation in case law references or a minor jurisprudence emergent in common-law jurisdictions. Since the early 2000s, the structure, sign and play of deconstruction have had a limited but nonetheless surprising presence in judicial reasoning, and especially when the subject matter of the case requires close textual scrutiny. The reversal of binaries, the elaboration of alternate meanings and the politics of writing, of scribble, writing-power, as Derrida coined it, leads inevitably to a play upon the traditional certitude of 'black letter' legal rules, and an opening to view the contingency of the structural constraints of the social history of letters and their communal interpretations.

Negative Connotations

Excluding the relatively frequent appearance of construction companies with names such as Deconstruction Inc. or Ltd, the substantive use of the neologism, while superficial and thus somewhat incidental, is often cautionary.[5] It arrives as a term caught up with the aura of the culture wars and there are certainly moments of antagonism to the use of the concept. In the Canadian case of *Maughan v University of British Columbia*, a student sued the university under the Civil Rights Protection Act. The question before the court was the admissibility into evidence of web postings allegedly seeking support and funding for the lawsuit. The arguments made in the postings are therefore incorporated by reference, and specifically by quotation, into the decision. Here the citations introduce deconstruction into the decision four times, but as a label, in the mode of railing against the "anti-deconstruction, anti-gay, pro family values agenda" animating the two-decades-long antipathy to radical critique in the Humanities in American universities.[6] There is reference as well to the "moral panic" accompanying such antipathies and a lament that it diverts focus from civil rights violations to poststructuralist theory and expert testimony. In that spirit, or in resistance to the spirit of deconstruction, there are certain and continuing moments of judicial recalcitrance in the face of attempts to play with divergent meanings in precedent texts and judgments.

Deconstruction asks the impossible according to an Australian judge in a trademark decision in which a footnote references 'Force of Law' explicitly, citing pages 3 and 26–28; the reference is appended to the judgement, noting the Applicant's argument, that it needed more time to review the opponent's

5 As for instance, to take two examples, *Northeast Constr. Group, Inc. v Deconstruction Inc.*16 A.D.3d 207 [2005] where Deconstruction Inc. was successful in defending against a claim; *Werner Deconstruction LLC v Siteworks Serv., NY, Inc.* 2022 WL 4631078, action for summary judgment unsuccessful. For a UK example, see *Kelly v KPH Deconstruction Services Ltd* [2017] UK ET 23001111.

6 *Cynthia Maughan v University of British Columbia* [2007] B.C.J. No. 2876 para's 5, 8, 9.

evidence, but was irrelevant: "Aside from some critical legal theory that this line of argument might evoke", the Applicant had received all that was due. The text dismissively cited is probably the observation that "left to itself, the incalculable and giving (*donatrice*) idea of justice is always very close to the bad, even to the worst because it can always be reappropriated by the most perverse calculation".[7] The judge was reluctant to give time to the Applicant, because decisions have to be taken, and at the same time opening to the possibility that acting in justice is very close to injustice was not a deliberation that he wished to open up. In a similar vein, in a recent South African case concerned with deciding the appropriate forum for an action in delict against the Iranian government, the harm of deconstruction, the phantasmatic threat is deemed even greater. One of the issues raised was that of the highly contentious doctrine of 'act of state' that grants the sovereign immunity from civil actions. Here the plaintiff sought to extract multiple meanings from the precedent law and challenge the blanket immunity on the ground that breach of the terms of the competitive tender for provision of a national mobile phone network in Iran was a matter of private law and not of sovereign action. The judicial rebuttal of the attempt to argue that the term sovereign act, dispensation in older law, was being used indiscriminately, was that "[i]t is always possible to break down the cases into different factual categories, and deconstruct the law into a fissiparous bundle of distinct rules."[8] These are clearly viewed as negative attributes of the deconstructive process whose divisiveness in multiplying meanings troubles the calm of precedential rulings as binding authorities.

In English and US common law there are similar concerns as to the fissiparous, furcating and potentially frictive consequences of deconstruction.[9] Fears are expressed that arguments will splinter, decisions will become incoherent and general doctrinal propositions fall apart in the face of what is in essence philological choice coined as undecidability. The undecidable moment of decision became the indeterminacy thesis in the short-lived legal theory jargon of the day, and on occasion critique of the incoherence of the particulars, the play of binary oppositions engaged in their construction, was deemed to threaten veridiction based upon the 'as if' or *verum* of law, and

7 *Homelink Real Estate v Maxwell Investments* (2019) 147 IPR 140, footnote 3. Derrida is pointing to the legal requirement of decision: "justice, however unrepresentable it may be, doesn't wait. It is that which must not wait. To be direct, simple and brief . . . a just decision is always required immediately, 'right away'."

8 *East Asian Consortium BV v MTN Group Limited and other* [2023] 1 All SA 632 (GJ) para. 227. The same expression appears earlier in a UK Supreme Court decision, *Belhaj v Straw* [2014] EWCA Civ 1394 (per Lord Sumption).

9 See more recently, for example, in *The Serious Fraud Office v Hotel Portfolio* [2021] EWHC 1273.

in extension, the stability of the text of the constitution itself.[10] As one judge archly put it in a patent case: "What is obvious – and what is not obvious – is not a matter that can further be deconstructed or defined. The word 'obvious' means what it says".[11] In another instance, the Judge, in a domestic abuse case, views deconstruction as both irrelevant and as symptomatic of a lack of politesse, and divagation of tone:

> Dr X's letter continues to deconstruct my judgment line by line, suggesting that "perhaps the judge can provide a definition" for this or "clarification" of that "would be useful here". This tone serves no obvious purpose other than to demonstrate Dr X's disrespect for the court.[12]

There is also of course the question of qualification to deconstruct, the inherent dialogism of the text, the intersectionality of language, which on one occasion leads the English Court of Appeal to a vigorous reprimand in an insurance case: "No deconstruction of the policy should be undertaken by the costs judge", it being necessary to emphasise that "costs judges [do] not have the expertise to second guess the insurance market still less to deconstruct a policy into constituent parts."[13] A loose or vernacular and non-philosophical usage for the purposes of exclusion of the concept, but nonetheless a sense of an expansion of the process of interpretation, an admission of the argot, a glimpse of the spectre haunting law, of things out of joint. In another case from the first decade after Derrida's demise, again concerned with costs and dismantling the construction of an insurance premium, the judge reiterates that "[t]here is no basis whatsoever upon which the court could or should deconstruct the premium", as the calculation was based on exposure to risk whose calculation a court could neither adequately nor properly dismantle into constituent figures or structural composition.[14] Elsewhere, and in similar vein, there is derogatory dismissal of deconstruction as indulging in

10 Indeterminacy was the critical legal bowdlerization of Derrida's concept of undecidability: "I do not believe I have ever spoken of "indeterminacy," whether in regard to "meaning" or anything else. Undecidability is something else again . . . un-decidability is always a determinate oscillation between possibilities (for example, of meaning, but also of acts)", Jacques Derrida, *Limited Inc.* (Northwestern University Press, 1998), 148.

11 *Nicoventures Trading Ltd v Philip Morris* [2021] EWHC 5, para. 60. The Judge then, of course, goes on to provide a highly selective view of the obvious: "In light of the common general knowledge of a person skilled in the art, and the pleaded prior art, having construed the inventive concept of the claim in question".

12 *M v F* [2023] EWFC 53 (B) para. 34.

13 *Peterborough and Stamford Hospitals NHS Trust v McMenemy, Reynolds v Nottingham University Hospitals NHS Foundation Trust* [2017] 6 Costs LR 973; [2017] EWCA Civ 1941.

14 *Motto and Others v Trafigura Ltd* [2011] EWHC 90207 (Costs).

"nitpicking point by point" negative analysis of a Refugee Appeals Tribunal decision, which is deemed "impermissible . . . parsing and picking apart of the [Tribunal] findings".[15] In greater detail, one court opines "[a] micro-deconstruction of an administrative decision is not appropriate" because "a micro-specific critique of isolated sentences in a lengthy decision, combined with a failure to situate that critique within the context of the decision as a whole is not appropriate".[16]

The first point can thus be summarized in terms of a certain negativity, and consequent caution, a quotidian and vernacular, translated wariness as to the destructive potential of deconstruction, conceived as a culturally loaded, often rather vague exposure of the internal structures that in hierarchically constituted form undo the apparent logic of a judgement through destabilization and multiplication of meanings. The concern expressed is that it can unsettle certainty, lift the veil of doctrine or look too closely beneath the surface of the text, here the numbers that are subject to judgement. While one can argue that the complacency of legal reason is threatened by close scrutiny, that is only part of the issue in that it is degrees of focus, assumptions of meaning and the expertise of the party doing the deconstruction that causes the principal and legitimate concern. In that it is numbers, not text, that are the subject of these judgments, they also involve an expansion of object although it is the assumptions and purposes of the calculations, the linguistic justifications, that are subject to the internal process and multiplication. The surprising view that judges are on occasion unqualified to disassemble certain texts, judgements of the European Court of Justice,[17] the calculation of insurance premiums, the quantification of costs, elements of a patent or trademark, goes against the view of judicial omniscience[18] and suggests a certain spectral haunting of a figure associated with deconstruction, though as Derrida opined, one in the main unconnected to any reading of the texts that announced the concept. It is a derivative, somewhat nebulous, mildly disapproved term for a species of critical, teasing and unsympathetic, close reading.

There is then an umbratical, negative living on, an inheritance from the culture wars and perhaps also from the critical legal disquisitions academical

15 *PO v MJELR* [2010] IEHC 513.

16 *Krupecki & J.A.M. v Minister for Justice and Equality* [2018] IEHC 505 para. 14.

17 *British Horseracing Board v William Hill* [2005] EWCA 863 (Civ), [2006] IP & T 210, per Lloyd LJ, on the attempt by BHB to link the investment in building a database to the official list of runners that the defendant betting firm was using: "This involves a process of deconstruction of the ultimate database which was rejected by the ECJ".

18 I refer here to David Campbell, 'The Proof of Judicial Omniscience Act (UK)', in Goodrich and Zartaloudis, eds, *The Cabinet of Imaginary Laws* (London: Routledge, 2021), 146: "Since the passage of the Human Rights Act 1998, the demand for judicial omniscience has, however, grown astronomically."

around indeterminacy, nihilism and fear of the legal text breaking up and losing meaning.[19] What is significant is that this particular ghost, the persistence in spectral modality, in the circulation, albeit in the scarcely defined nominal form of Derrida's neologistic catchword, is rarely seen. The anxiety is seldom manifested and, if so, generally in superficial and brief form. The threat is more an irritant than an attack. As Brooke LJ in the English Court of Appeal put it, as early as 2003, in a case concerned with dismantling how an insurance premium was calculated, whether it was for allocation of risk or in part for provision of services related to handling claims, a "central issue . . . is whether the master was entitled to lift the veil and to be influenced by what was actually being provided in return for the premium allocation".[20] The judge responded that this was in the circumstances necessary and inevitable and thus dismissed the negative connotations asserted vividly by the complainants that 'deconstruction' of a premium would allow "endless arguments as to the appropriateness of different elements of a premium . . . and make assessment a nightmare".[21] In the face of dismissal by the complainant's counsel, the Court hints at an emergent jurisprudence and defends deconstruction as a dismantling that can be used legitimately to weigh the structuring elements of the pricing of the insurance. The detailed question concerns the meaning of a provision in The Access to Justice Act 1999 under which premiums paid could be recovered in costs under the policy where a claim was successful.[22] The premium could not be taken at face value as the cost of the coverage provided but rather had to be broken down into risks covered by the policy and purchase of "entitlement to other benefits" additional to the coverage purchased – such as costs of adjustment and assessment, claims' vetting, claims' handling. To track the structuring of the premium cost as between premium properly so called and further services being charged for, or expenses incurred by the insured as conditions of the policy, required a "deconstruction schedule". Derrida haunts the judgment, at least in the sense that the word, used four times in the reasoning of the decision, is directly concerned to undo the assertion of certainty as to the meaning of premium and to reorient the hierarchical opposition between coverage and expenses so as to give a greater weight to additional expenditures that

19 The aspersion of nihilism, of tearing up the constitution, has been mainly an academic scare discourse in early reactions to critical legal studies, and soon forgotten. See Owen Fiss, 'The Death of Law' (1989) 72 *Cornell Law Review* 245; Paul Carrington, 'Of Law and the River' (1986) 34 *Journal of Legal Education* 222.

20 *Re Claims Direct Test Cases* [2003] 4 All ER 508, 528.

21 Ibid., 524.

22 Access to Justice Act 1999 s. 29, which for the sake of completeness provides: "Where in any proceedings a costs order is made in favour of any party who has taken out an insurance policy against the risk of incurring liability in these proceedings, the costs payable to him may . . . include costs in respect of the premium of the policy."

do not form part of what is generally, and here in Parliamentary language, meant by the costing of an insurance premium.

A Minor Jurisprudence

As the interpretation of the different contexts and meanings of 'premium' indicate, and by a circuitous route of indirection, a trajectory of lexical expansion of law's theoretical vocabulary can be faintly discerned. The concept of deconstruction hovers, unattributed but recognizable, haunting as a foreign presence the positivistic determinacy and reasoning, the *ratio decidendi*, meaning here the major language, the dominant mode of juristic elaboration of decision. The ghost is a necessarily minor presence, a spectral and umbratical, or in another language penumbral influence upon judicial reasoning. It is *obiter dictum*, a digression or *secessus* that in thoroughly Derridean fashion can slowly come to invert the apparent order of dominance and meaning. The minor, to borrow from Deleuze and Guattari's famous essay on Kafka, is always potentially a subversive use, an alien imagination and revision of the major language and here of the dominant mode and method of legal discursive elaboration.[23] As an emergent minor jurisprudence, a foreign tendency within the legal corpus, it manifests initially as a willingness in appropriate circumstances to 'lift the veil' and deconstruct the binary oppositions that produce, as the occasion may require, the premium number, or the textual proposition, the doctrinal rule or code provision, the clause of a statutory rule, in light of its context and composition, language used and conceptual hierarchies assumed in elaboration.

If deconstruction has taken the form of a minor topic and term in adversarial and judgmental elaborations, it has also by virtue of this very fact gained a certain recognition and as adumbrated, even when utilized negatively, has claimed a presence and performed a role. The greater and increasingly positive reception of the concept has still and necessarily been low key, covertly positive, camisado. It has been seen nominally and substantively in the use of a technical neologism 'forensic deconstruction'[24] in relation to disputes involving accounting procedures. The term as a positive operation of

23 Gilles Deleuze and Félix Guattari, *Kafka: For a Minor Literature* (Minneapolis: University of Minnesota Press, 1976).

24 *R (L) v Serious Fraud Office* [2018] EWHC 856 (Admin) para. 111: "Ms Callaghan QC, for the third Interested Party, undertook a forensic deconstruction of the specific reasons advanced in the letter of 19th September 2017 by ABC LLP (see paragraph [41] above). There is much force in her submissions." The earliest use of the term is in *Jelson Ltd v Secretary of State for Local Government* [2016] EWHC 2979 referencing a "forensic deconstruction of the point, which to my mind is wholly convincing". The point at issue was the "rapid and deliberate" submerging of certain figures that required being taken into account.

interpretation acts as a general synonym for careful and painstaking dismantling of arguments, seeking the flaws in the assumptions, the hierarchies and oppositions, that generate the conclusions claimed to be derived from them. The reasons of reason or laws of law, to put it more grandiosely, are appropriate subjects of casuistic inquiry, for methodological excurses and moments of epistemic reflexivity. In that spectre and spirit, another court announces the need for a little "light deconstruction" prior to disaggregating a set of figures, while other courts reference "critical deconstruction", and on another occasion it is "creative deconstruction" that is required to make sense of a judgment.[25] Hardly the opening of the floodgates but nonetheless a moment and mobilization of legal significance and an instance of intrication that must in turn be given its context and legal history.

There is a certain obvious correlation and sympathy between casuistry and deconstruction, between the legal close scrutiny of texts, the exegetical labor of lawyers for whom, as Sir Edward Coke put it, "each syllable is known and significant in law"[26] and the unsettling event, the philosophical opening of juridical textuality to the play of meaning and the divergent possibilities of sense. Law and deconstructive theory are both heavily rhetorical endeavors, both in their way operate to take apart and reconstruct; both are hermeneutical exercises intended to have effects. The judge in deciding and the philosopher in having an impact on the institution. If deconstruction is justice, it is a question of giving time and analysis to the manner and meaning of composition of judgments. It is also, for Derrida, the aspiration that rather than deconstruction being only speculative, theoretical, academic, that it also "lead to something more consequential, to *change* . . . to intervene in an efficient and responsible though always, of course, very mediated way, not only in the profession but in what one calls the *cité*". More than ever, he continues, the academy is "less than ever a monadic or monastic ivory tower that in any case it never was. And this is particularly true of law schools."[27] That deconstruction is justice is here to be understood as a political challenge, a desire for institutional impact, for a species of *effectus*, and for justice as giving time, listening, attending to the sources and composition of the arguments triggering institutional action. It is, to borrow from Anselm Haverkamp's

25 Respectively *Dukes Bailiffs v Breckland Council* [2023] EWHC 1569 (TCC); *Sharp v Blank* [2019] EWHC 3096 (Ch); and *R (Oss Group) v Environment Agency* [2007] EWCA Civ 611.

26 *James Osborne's Case*, in 10 *The Reports of Sir Edward Coke* 130: elaborating on "words significant and known to the sages of the law, but not allowed by the Grammarians, nor having countenance of Latin".

27 'Force of Law', 933. In the earlier work *The Truth in Painting* [1978] (Chicago: University of Chicago Press, 1987), 19: the materiality of practice is posed in terms of "the historical forms of pedagogy, the social, economic or political structures of this pedagogical institution. It is because deconstruction interferes with solid structures, 'material' institutions, that it is always distinct from an analysis or a 'critique'."

phrasing, a matter of radical patience as the ground of just interpretations.[28] So, moving from the negative, the defensive warding off, the inclusive exclusion of deconstruction from legal determinations, the arbitrium of the cut, so as to maintain a degree of appearance of control, we can turn to the positive institutional effects in the incalculable moment of legal decision.

Start with the process of deconstruction, the happening or event of meaning generation, the hermeneutic force of the rhetorical play. A decision from 2004 takes on the question of the meaning of deconstruction directly in determining whether the removal of a beneficiary from a trust had been valid. Prior case law being split on the point of whether the beneficiary needed to also sign the revocation, the court addressed a question of method, as to how to interpret conflicting precedents. The salient paragraph proposes that

> As part of our present task, we are also called upon to construe decisions from other courts of appeal interpreting section 2280. Those decisions are not binding on us. Further, the language of an opinion must be construed with reference to the facts of the case, and the positive authority of a decision goes no further than those facts. A decision is not authority merely for what it says, but for the points actually involved and actually decided. Applying this rule, we are free to deconstruct the language of decisions from other courts of appeal and reassemble their true meaning and effect.[29]

The issue, for the sake of comprehending this deconstructive exercise, was whether a Trust, in this case that of one George Marx, that stipulated that any changes to the Trust were to be made in writing and signed by both Marx and the Trustee, precluded enforcing a revocation that removed the plaintiff from the trust but was not signed by the Trustee. Under the relevant Code section 2280: "Unless expressly made irrevocable by the instrument creating the trust, every voluntary trust shall be revocable by the trustor by writing filed with the trustee." Arguing at length that the previous case law had "obscured the true meaning of section 2280" the California Court of Appeal concluded that as the Trust did not expressly declare itself irrevocable, and did not stipulate that the method of amendment in the Trust itself was the exclusive mode of modification, it was sufficient that the revocation was in a writing signed by the Trustor but not by the Trustee. The relevant deconstruction was of the relation in the precedents between express, explicit and implicit exclusivity. If a method of modification specified in the trust was highly specific, did that imply that it was expressly exclusive? That,

28 Anselm Haverkamp, 'Radical Patience: Deconstruction's Fall into History' (2005) 27 *Cardozo Law Review* 547.

29 *Huscher v Wells Fargo* 18 Cal.Rptr.3d 27 (2004) at 31.

according to the Court, depended upon the degree of specificity. Where, as with the Marx Trust, it "is not explicitly exclusive and is not sufficiently detailed to be implicitly exclusive", an alternative method can be used.

The *Huscher* decision exhibits the dance of deconstruction, the "play of absence and presence",[30] in judicial hands and a logic internal to the case law that allows for a reversal of the binary hierarchy of explicit and implicit, at least insofar as the deconstruction of the gradations of the implicit limits the scope of exclusivity and restrains the precedence of the explicit. A later California Court of Appeal decision offers the most direct definition of the juridical use of deconstruction, resorting to Merriam-Webster's online dictionary to proffer that "[t]he term 'deconstruct' is used in this opinion to mean 'to take apart or examine in order to reveal the basis or composition of, often with the intention of exposing . . . flaws."[31] It is, to use the first citation used in the Oxford English Dictionary, there for reform. The case involved an action in negligence by the father of an alcoholic beverage consumer, who had been shot by police, against the defendant brewing company. His son, a student at Pacific Fresno University, had drunk two cans of the defendant's product and his behavior had become erratic, disoriented and paranoid. He took a shotgun into the backyard and started firing at random. The police were called and when he appeared with the shotgun over his shoulder, he was shot. The issue to be construed was whether the multi-ingredient drink was unreasonably dangerous to the consumer or whether it was a common consumer product whose dangers would be known. In the instant case the defendant, who expressly adopted a "deconstructionist approach", failed to prove that the dangers were common knowledge, because the drink was adulterated with ingredients that they failed to list. It contained alcohol and caffeine, a known stimulant and a known depressant, but it also contained other additives, specifically guarana, taurine and wormwood, whose attributes were not common knowledge. The interactive effects of the ingredients took it outside of the immunity given to common consumer products and the court's corrective deconstruction allowed the case to go forward to trial.

The general sense of deconstruction as a mode of intervention, as a dismantling of structures that can then be reformulated, gains greater focus and precision in specific substantive domains of law and distinct transaction types. Where the word deconstruction is used in a colloquial vernacular sense to signal decomposition, demolition, break up into parts, it plays a relatively marginal, or a less distinctive role in judgement, and while it is clearly a transplant, an insertion of a deterritorialized philosophical concept, it is not

30 Jacques Derrida, 'Structure, Sign and Play in the Human Sciences', in Jacques Derrida, eds., *Writing and Difference* (Abingdon: Routledge, 2001), 369.

31 *Fiorini v City Brewing* 231 Cal.App.4th 306 (2014).

used in its properly philosophical sense. It is a sleeper, a nascent and inchoate seed term awaiting its moment of growth and recognition. That, of course, is the fate and fortune of the minor. It exists as potential, ambivalently adopted, an inclusive exclusion that can be instanced in an English defamation case where a "skillful and detailed deconstruction" seeking to support the meaning for which the litigant contended was deemed a "somewhat artificial and strained exercise"[32] but nonetheless helpful for the judge's interpretation of the meaning of the language subject to complaint.

The claimant, Jusan Technologies, a corporation sole, holding funds for Nursultan Nazarbayev, the former president of Kazakhstan, argued that it was distinct from and defamed by the accusation that it, a passive holder of the funds, was "a corrupt vehicle" through which the President maintained control over illegally obtained monies. As the President "and his cronies" ran the fund, the claimant's case failed. The deconstruction endeavoring to show the person and the corporation to be distinct was unsuccessful, and the articles were held to be factual. The patient reading, the derailing and refabrication of the language used to determine "the single natural and ordinary meaning of the words", added depth and legitimacy to the judgement, an inkling of institutional reform or of Derrida's neologism making a difference. As the case in question was in effect brought by the "former dictator of Khazakhstan" in relation to media reports of his having hidden a £6 billion empire in the UK, the decision, expressly influenced by the attempted deconstruction of the texts, resulted in protection of the press and media outlets by affirming the truth of their reporting. Interestingly, what was in play was a battle of deconstructions, alternative processes and dismantlings by the respective litigants, and then the adjudicative reformulation of the judge whose hierarchical superiority in the process allows for the leap from the incalculable to the determinate, from justice to law.

The textualist bent and free play of deconstruction in litigation and decision has its most obvious remit or jurisdiction in cases that turn on hermeneutic questions, including defamation, but more often interpretation of prior law, statute or precedent, where it is applied to literary texts or semiotic representations relating to patent, trademark or copyright. The binaries involved in patent and trademark cases raise frequent oppositions of prior and post, extant mark and application for distinctive registrations, similarity and *différance*. These oppositions are frequently visual, infringement being of the visual design of fabric patterns, of touchpads or of patented insulin pumps as in *Insulet Corporation v Roche Diabetes Care Ltd*, where it is the deconstruction of the design drawings patented that forms the basis of comparison and

32 *Jusan Technologies v Bureau of Investigative Journalism* [2023] EWHC 2581 (KB).

decision.[33] In infringement of trademark cases, where the issue is whether, for instance, the Spanish mark K Kerasol is infringed by the English mark Kerashot being used for a similar hair product, required extensive linguistic scission of syllables to determine if kera and sol were sufficiently different from Kera and shot to allow for registration. It was held that anyone reasonably fluent in English and Spanish would perceive a difference but that the general public would not discern any adequate distinctiveness to the Kerashot mark and so the registration was refused because deconstruction of the terms failed to disclose any significant originality.[34] In similar vein, where a case was brought to register the sign RELY-ABLE as a distinctive trademark, the visual distinctiveness did not overcome the phonetic similarity to everyday usage and in the absence of any conceptual ambiguity, together with the visual obviousness of the ruse of misspelling the word, allowed the court to conclude that

> The deconstruction of an adjective into its verbal root and its adjectival suffix is not unusual in a language such as English, and even less so for the relevant public, which is made up of highly attentive specialists, as the applicant recognises in its pleadings. It follows that the sign RELY-ABLE will, despite the misspelling, be immediately perceived and understood by the relevant public – even specialised – as meaning ‘reliable’, without the need for any interpretation.[35]

The *différance* of relyable, the being imprinted of the imprint, the visual trace lacks legal difference for the purposes of trademark and would be viewed as a deliberate misspelling.[36] Here the court dismisses the *différance* as a registerable trademark, where deconstruction would attribute a greater significance to it, as a unique word, a simulation affirmed in dance and laughter,[37] but the issue is canvassed judicially. Able to rely plays on reliable, but a Y for an I is a typographic revision that does not introduce any novelty beyond the standard meaning of trustworthy, a synonym although visually different with the phonetically indiscernible penultimate letter of the alphabet substituted for the ninth. Where the issue is semantic rather than lexical, as in the mark,

33 *Insulet Corporation v Roche Diabetes Care* [2021] EWHC 1933 (PAT).

34 *CareAbout GmbH v Office of Harmonisation for the Internal* Market [2015] All E.R. (D) 187 (Dec).

35 *Boehringer Ingelheim International GmbH v Office for Harmonisation* [2013] Official Transcript at para 21.

36 Jacques Derrida, *Margins of Philosophy* (Chicago: Chicago University Press, 1982), 3, discussing *différance* as “a writing within writing whose different trajectories thereby find themselves, at certain very determined points, intersecting with a kind of gross spelling mistake, a lapse in the discipline and law which regulate writing and keep it seemly”.

37 Ibid., 27.

the scope for deconstruction and indeed its quiet reception has been more expansive, and the material institutional effect that much greater.

Literary Excursions

In *Haraguchi v Superior Court*, a case from 2006, the prosecutor, Attorney Joyce Dudley, had published a novel, *Intoxicating Agent*, featuring a protagonist markedly similar to herself, who vigorously prosecutes a rape case involving an intoxicated victim.[38] The novel was published and was being actively promoted by the author shortly before she was due to prosecute the petitioner for the alleged rape of an intoxicated victim on facts strikingly similar to those of the fictional case. Seeking recusal of Dudley, the petitioner claimed that there was an improper intermingling of the facts of his case with the facts portrayed in the novel. The defendant is portrayed as having a

> "bloated" face, a "protruding belly," and "filthy hands." "Talk about felony ugly, [Danner] thought, he looks just like the pig he is!" "Felony ugly," the author notes, is "[a]n in-house expression used by some prosecutors to describe a defendant who fits the stereotype of a perpetrator of the crime for which he is charged." Danner was "saddened . . . especially because Cantera turned out to be so despicable." 'This dirt bag really did a number on her [Diana].' Danner said to herself, " 'I'll get you, you heartless bastard . . . for Diana's sake.' "[39]

The alleged victim, in contrast, is described in glowing terms, devoted to family, community, job and friends, involved in charitable endeavors with children and the elderly. The recusal action makes the argument that the facts in the novel and in the trial are too similar, leading to the fear that fact and fiction were conflated by the publication of the book. Elements of the case files had been used in the fiction, and the prosecutor's investment in promoting the book made it probable that her impartiality and ability to exercise prosecutorial discretion were compromised. There was, in sum, a conflict of interest, an intrusion into prosecutorial offices of financial interests and emotional predispositions.[40]

Here the binary hierarchies multiply exponentially and one can witness a variation on the deconstructive dictum *il n'y a pas de hors texte* in the

38 Joyce Dudley, *Intoxicating Agent* [2004] (Infinity Publishing: N.P., 2006).

39 *Haraguchi v Superior Court* 143 Cal. App. 4th 846 [2006] 848.

40 The California Supreme Court reversed the decision on the recusal petition in *Haraguchi v Superior Court* 43 Cal.4th 706 (2008), determining that the "Court of Appeal deconstructed the author's acknowledgements" but failed to evidence that the conflict was sufficiently extreme to require recusal.

mode of there being no outside of the prosecutorial office. The opposition between victim and perpetrator is contextually weighted heavily against the defendant, as also the gradient of the gender opposition between female and male, innocence and guilt. Lifting of the veil indicated promotion of dual causes, a stark binary of office and authorship, deconstruction here signalling "*plus d'une langue*, more than a language, and no more of *a* language".[41] Which latter point, requiring a reading, construction of meaning to the sentence, appreciation of the sententiousness in sense, forces circumspection and an attention to the affect of *inventio*, the alien interior to thought. Perhaps the most extreme example of this *plus d'une langue* operational in a legal decision reverts again to a literary case, this time involving copyright infringement and the insertion of a cryptogram in the body of the judgment handed down.

In *Baigent and Leigh v Random House,*[42] the issue was whether there had been copyright infringement of the earlier work, *Holy Blood, Holy Grail* in the later blockbuster *The Da Vinci Code* authored by Dan Brown.[43] The relevant legal questions are, first, whether *Holy Blood, Holy Grail* was an original work meriting copyright protection, and second, if it was sufficiently novel, had its copyright been infringed by substantial copying? The trial judge, who remarks at one point that "I am no literary person",[44] engages in an expansive deconstruction of the original work, and breaks the Central Theme of the earlier book into 15 constituent points or elements that were sufficient to constitute an original copyrightable work. These elements are then counterposed to the structure of the later work and a majority of the 15 themes are found to be present in the *The Da Vinci Code*. The requirement of substantial copying, however, was not met. Partly because the earlier work had a nebulous and indiscernible structure and so could not be substantially copied, and partly because there was only an insignificant amount of language copying. The expression was thus Dan Brown's, and it is primarily the expression that is protected. The asserted structure, which

41 Jacques Derrida, *Memoires for Paul de Man*, trans. by Cecile Lindsay, Jonathan Culler, Eduardo Cadava, and Peggy Kamuf (New York: Columbia University Press, 1989), 15: "If I had to risk a definition of deconstruction, one as brief, elliptical, and economical as a password, I would say simply and without overstatement: *plus d'une langue* – both more than a language and no more of *a* language."

42 [2006] EWHC 719 (Ch). Affirmed in *Baigent and Leigh v Random House* [2007] EWCA Civ 247. For discussion of this decision, see Thom Giddens, 'The *Imago Decidendi* of *Baigent v Random House*', in Thom Giddens, *The Typography of Law* (Edinburgh: Edinburgh University Press, 2026); and Peter Goodrich, 'Legal Enigmas: Antonio de Nebrija, *The Da Vinci Code* and the Emendation of Law' (2010) 30:1 *Oxford Journal of Legal Studies* 71.

43 Michael Baigent, Richard Leigh, and Henry Lincoln, *Holy Blood, Holy Grail* (London: Jonathan Cape, 1982); and Dan Brown, *The Da Vinci Code* (New York: Doubleday, 2003).

44 *Baigent* [2006] 474.

the judge defines as "an architectural edifice of ideas",[45] of *Holy Blood* fell away when examined.

The Court of Appeal affirmed the trial court judgment and explicitly referenced the "deconstruction and reconstruction"[46] but misses what is the most striking feature of the judgment handed down by Peter Smith J. sitting in the High Court of Chancery. This is the fact that the Judge inserted a series of bold and italicized single letters throughout the decision. There is brief mention of a coded message in the High Court judgment, "but nothing turns on it".[47] A loss of nerve and a looking away on the part of the appellate judges, because no letter or syllable is unknown or insignificant in law, and because a great deal, the motivation of judgement and the judicial image of invention are coded in the statement. The letters formed an encryption,

S m i t h y c o d e J a e i
e x t o s t g p s a c g r e
a m q w f k a d p m q z v

which when disencrypted using the sequence of the Fibonacci code utilized in Brown's novel, reads "Smithy Code who are you Jackie Fisher Dreadnought". The detail of argument has been made elsewhere and so for present purposes the deconstruction of the textual comparata did no more than evidence the vanishing character of the claimed structure of *Holy Blood, Holy Grail*, and so a lack of substantial copying. It also generated an enigma, a coded statement encapsulating in necessarily opaque, umbratical and indirect form that justice is deconstruction, that the incalculable moment of decision takes the form of an image which is always, as Ovid remarks, more than it seems. The specific image, the Delphic statement provided here as a literary riddle, is an enigma replete with forgotten references and plural possible meanings. An irresolvable moment of initiation that equally deserves its own deconstruction as a figure of decision, the image that triggers.[48] The juggernaut of the successful novel *The Da Vinci Code* gains expression in the figure of Dreadnought which, as its name suggests, was the ship with the largest and greatest number of guns on the seas at the time of its launching. The image is of an unstoppable force and signals, amongst other indications, Peter Smith J's apperception that the mega selling novel was by virtue of its success

45 *Baigent* [2006] 470.
46 *Baigent* [2007] para. 104 (Rix L.J.).
47 *Baigent* [2007] para. 3 (Lloyd L.J.).
48 I term this, for those with legal training, the *imago decidendi* or image of decision. See Peter Goodrich, '*Imago Decidendi*: On the Common Law of Images' (2017) 1:1 *Art and Law* 1; and at greater length, Peter Goodrich, *Judicial Uses of Images: Vision in Decision* (Oxford: Oxford University Press, 2023).

and its numbers quite independent in real terms from the rather lame and disorganized bumboat *Holy Blood, Holy Grail*.

What is most interesting and vital in the use of the encryption – the typographogram – is the excess, the internal reordering of letters, the productive flaw in the judgement that deconstructs and reformulates. It is a dramatic instance of *plus d'une langue*, of a happening, an event, at the heart of the decision. The Appellate Court dictum that nothing turns on it is in surface terms legally correct but shortsighted and hermeneutically inapposite. The exact words were that the Judge

> was prompted by the extensive use in DVC of codes, and no doubt by his own interest in such things, to incorporate a coded message in his judgment, on which nothing turns. The judgment is not easy to read or to understand. It might have been preferable for him to have allowed himself more time for the preparation, checking and revision of the judgment.[49]

The reprimand, which ended any hope of further elevation on the bench, is peculiar for immediately pointing out that two extremely significant things turn on the encryption. These were clarity of composition and lack of proofreading of the judgment, rendering the precedent opaque and obstructive to reading. Being law, these would seem to have a degree of gravity, which the Court avoids addressing. Worse, the trial judge's engagement with the literary facts, his enthusiasm for the deconstruction and reconstruction of the two novels is reprimanded rather than commended. The decision would appear to expose too much in that the deconstruction produces a new language and mirrors in that aspect, in cryptographic form, the behemothic novelty of *The Da Vinci Code*. It performs what it decides and in doing so judges its judgement through a manifestation of the figure of invention. It is there that the conjunction of deconstruction and justice is most evident, in the specific enigma of the decision that materially changes language, produces novel meanings and potentially signals institutional reform. It is in that spirit that the condition of forensis is changed by the event. It can act as the opportunity of engaging with one final instance of reception, one further reverberation of impact. A case that Jacques would have found intriguing.

The cryptogram or coded message is also of course an instance of *différance*, a homonymy that is not apprehensible phonically but only visually. Changes in typography here signal another level of meaning and play a poetic interpretative role, even and especially where Justice Smith is seeking on the surface of the text to indicate that the "judgment is not a work of fiction

49 *Baigent and Leigh v Random House* [2007] para. 3.

(I hope)".[50] Even more archly or, better, with greater oratorical denial, the Supreme Court of Ireland deems it necessary to preface its conclusive decision in an exhaustive case of insurance litigation with the opination that

> [l]egal agreements are not poetry intended to have nuances and layers of meaning which reveal themselves only on repeated and perhaps contestable readings. . . . It is important to remind ourselves . . . that the process is not the deconstruction of the text, but rather the interpretation of an agreement.[51]

The negative incorporation of fiction, poetry and other apparent markers of deconstruction as somehow opposed to interpretation or as too much hermeneutics gains a further and highly poetic deployment and inventive use in a case involving an unfair dismissal suit. Nadine Quashie was a third-year university student in accounting and finance, who worked intermittently for 18 months as a lap dancer for the respondent club, Stringfellows.[52] There was a standard form contract drawn up by the club that listed her duties and appended the club rules for dancers, but this contract was never shown to Quashie, nor signed by her. The house rules are detailed and in some regards peculiar. She was required to work a certain number of nights and on certain specified days. She was to report at the beginning of the evenings she worked to the 'house mother' and pay her a fee which was not returnable. Her own pay was provided by customers in the form of 'heavenly vouchers' which were subsequently converted into cash by the club and after commissions and fines had been deducted the remainder, if anything, was paid to her. In private law terms, she was in a relation with the club and subject to a number of mandatory rules. The legal question raised by her claim of unfair dismissal was whether, under the Employment Rights Act 1996, she was an employee, or self-employed and so outwith the protections of the legislation. A question of contract law and of whether there was an agreement, express or implied, of employment.

Quashie, as a student, worked on a part-time basis at the club for 80 weeks prior to being dismissed on the assertion that she had been dealing drugs. The Employment Tribunal dismissed her claim on the basis that although there was an expectation of continued employment on both sides, there was no contract because of a lack of mutuality of obligation in the periods she was not working, and because the club had never paid her. Her earnings were

50 Ibid., para. 358.
51 *The Law Society of Ireland v The Motor Insurer's Bureau* [2017] IESC 31, para. 12–13 (O'Donnell J.).
52 *Quashie v Stingfellows Restaurants* [2012] IRLR 536.

provided by customers. On appeal the successful argument was "Mr Hendy's deconstruction of the four points that led the judge to conclude that there was no mutuality."[53] In sum, there was an obligation to pay the dancer; she had to pay the 'house mother' and also pay the club commissions; she was obliged to work as directed; she was subject to fines if she did not abide by the rule book, and so took the risk of not earning enough to cover her costs. The crux of the matter, addressed by the deconstruction of the relationship, is that when she worked she was apparently in a spot (discrete) contract with the club, but even 80 weeks of spot contracts do not create mutuality of obligation if both parties can walk away at any point. Quashie was, in the eyes of the Tribunal, both naked as a dancer and without legal clothes. The apposite term for such lack of commitment is *nudum pactum* as distinct from *pacta vestita*. The deconstruction, however, not only lifted the veil covering the Tribunal's reasoning but also led the Employment Appeal Tribunal to provide her with a carapace, the integument and cloth of a global, overarching umbrella contract.

Where parties are in a relation of mutual recognition over time an overarching umbrella contract is generated to give effect to the legitimate expectations of the parties and in some views, in this case, to a good faith obligation of employment. Understood in relational terms the umbrella is an implied commitment inferred from the overarching relationship, the patterns of performance and the expectations for flexibility and adjustment that accompany the behavior of the parties over time:

> the test is not whether it is necessary to imply an umbrella contract, or whether business efficacy leads to that conclusion. It is simply whether there is a sufficient factual substratum to support a finding that such a legal obligation has arisen. It is a question of fact, not law.[54]

In the case of *Quashie*, there was a contract of employment each night that she showed up for work and the question is whether in between work nights, whose rota bound her, she was under cover of an employment relationship. For the Employment Appeal Tribunal the regular character of the work, the fact that she was obliged to show up as the rota assigned, needed permission to take time off, mitigated to the conclusion that her regular performance of work, the expectation of work and the obligations that accompanied her work "enured into an employment relationship under one umbrella contract".[55] This decision was in turn reversed by the Court of Appeal on

53 *Quashie* [2012] 53.
54 *Hafal Ltd v Miss K. Lane-Angell* [2018] UKEAT/0107/17/JOJ.
55 *Quashie* [2012] 62.

the grounds of lack of mutuality of obligation during the intervals between working.[56] The cover of the umbrella was removed and it is accurate to say that claims for such umbrella obligations have generally been hard to prove successfully in employment contexts as well as commercial transactions of service or supply.[57]

The immediate conclusion from *Quashie* being quashed, and Mr Hendry's deconstruction being reversed, is that global or umbrella contracts still have to push against the repression barrier or convention carrier of legal formalism and its conception of discrete, isolated, solipsistic agreements. Deconstruction suggested a different reading, a dismantling of the structure of relationship, the hierarchy of antinomies, to generate a novel concept and protection of the apotropaic legal armature of the umbrella. A question of style to be sure, and Derrida does remark that "it passes itself off for what it passes itself off for".[58] In the context of lap dancing, the plaintiff bares herself to perform and entertain on a weekly basis for a club that strictly regulates both the time and manner of her performing and her compensation. It seems reasonable to take that context into account and to play on the maxim *il n'y a pas de hors texte*, signifying that there is always deferral of meaning and play of interpretation, that the implication from the facts should expand to include the circumstances and vulnerabilities of the student lap dancing for a year and a half, as well as the stringency of Stringfellows' rules of employment. Deconstruction, in sum, was the avenue to opening that possibility, to expanding the contextual meaning of 'mutuality of obligation' to take account of the broader hierarchies in the relevant matrix of fact.

Conclusion

This short conspectus of judicial uses of deconstruction over the last three decades offers few conclusions or any graph of impact zones. It is clear that

56 *Stringfellows Restaurants v Quashie* [2012] EWCA Civ 1735, para. 13: "Without some mutuality, amounting to what is sometimes called the 'irreducible minimum of obligation', no contract exists." To give a sense of the difficulty of meeting the criteria for implication of an umbrella contract, see, for examples, *Uber v Aslam* [2021] ICR 657; *Johnson v Transopco* [2022] EAT 6; *Mackie Motors v RCI Finance* [2022] EWHC 1942 (Ch); in all of which cases the plea failed, the umbrella remained furled.

57 *Baird Textiles Holdings Ltd v Marks and Spencer plc* [2002] 1 All ER (Comm) 737 dismissing the claim of an umbrella contract from 30 years of extremely close commercial relationship and myriad spot contracts. The Court teetered on the edge of acknowledging an umbrella, and looked to context and conduct, the non-textual relationship but stepped away from finding the overarching protection. For commentary advocating for umbrella contracts in this context, see Linda Mulcahy and Cathy Andrews, 'Baird Textiles Holdings v Marks and Spencer plc', in Rosemary Hunter et al., eds., *Feminist Judgments: From Theory to Practice* (Oxford: Hart Publishing, 2010), 189.

58 Jacques Derrida, *Spurs: Nietzsche's Styles* (Chicago: Chicago University Press, 1979), 127.

the term has made its way into the legal dictionary and is used in a general sense to mean demolition and dismantling of words, signs and structures. Thus, K Kerasol could be protected, RELY-ABLE, despite its *différance*, was not. In a very lengthy copyright case involving an official database, to take up another instance, the British Horseracing Board sued the betting firm William Hill for infringing their database by using the data in their online betting business. The case went through the English courts to the European Court of Justice [ECJ] and returned on the question of whether BHB had created, verified, obtained or gathered the information in the database such as to bring it within the sui generis right provided by art 7 of Directive 96/9.[59] Resisting the process of deconstruction of the assemblage of the database as being contrary to the conclusions of the ECJ, it was determined that the finished database was distinct from the list of qualified runners published and used by William Hill, and thus did not involve investment in the "obtaining and verification" of the contents of the database, but rather simply "gathered" the information from which the published list that the defendants were using was composed.[60] Distinguishing creating from obtaining and verifying, as distinct again from gathering the information, it is clear that deconstruction has work to do and is used and eventually rejected in this instance as going beyond the surface implied by the EU Directive. The minor jurisprudence is thus best described as nascent yet burgeoning. Advocates and judges on lower benches, often engaged most directly with factual discovery, deconstruct to make sense of numbers, figures, images, defamatory articles, purloined expressions in books. Their excursions presently are frequently overruled but when the judges involved climb to higher courts, the narrative and decision outcomes may well change. Presently it is simply worth observing that reversal is nonetheless an acknowledgment, a negative incorporation, a suppressed concept that will ceaselessly press against the repression barrier and convention carrier of legal formalism. That is the deconstruction to come, the not yet of an emergent language.

Insofar as Derrida was concerned with change not in semiotic or not only in semiotic systems but also in material institutions, the process and event of internal dismantling and reformulation of legal categories do also allow for the conclusion from this brief conspectus that a limited assertion that deconstruction is justice is permissible and apposite. The impact or effect is one of opening legal meaning to a wider range of connotations, a degree of play on the possibility of other senses and sensibilities, a giving of time so as to do justice to the judicial text. There is a minor jurisprudence, an emergent body of thought and practices that incorporate a deconstructive patience and

59 *British Horseracing Board v William Hill*, op.cit. n.9, 212.
60 *BHB v William Hill*, 218.

suspension of belief, that are willing to challenge the process through which structures and in our case legal institutions are produced and reproduced. What that means in common law is a reversal of prior assumptions, a radical patience that allows time for the exploration of context and possibility, such that juxtapositions can be delineated, comparisons made and differences noted in the combinatorial that comprises the structure in question: "following the consistency of its logic, [deconstruction] attacks not only the internal edifice, both semantic and formal, of philosophemes, but also what one would be wrong to assign to it as its external housing, its extrinsic conditions of practice".[61] The hermeneutic presuppositions of legal textual and interpretative practice incorporate both negatively and increasingly positively the process, happening and a fleetingly recognized event of deconstruction as an aspect of judicial practice. In juristic terms it perhaps makes most sense to talk of deconstruction as an ever present potential, a spectral resource for legal thought, an opening to extraneous, which is to say contextual and relational, opportunities. In review of the final cases, where deconstruction was carried out in detail, the result was to generate novel juxtapositions and conjunctions, new forms of expression and encoding of judgment. In the last case the contextual undressing produced an appositely apotropaic umbrella to protect a vulnerable student who had been forced by circumstances to remove her clothes.

61 Derrida, *Truth in Painting*, 19.

4

NASORUM VIS

Hate Inside and Outside the Law

Phillip Mitsis

Anecdote I: *Odium Narium*: A Descent Into Hate and an Assent

I went down yesterday to catch a train in the West Fourth Street station near my apartment. For those who have not braved the Gehenna of the NYC subway system of late, the overpowering graveolent, sulphurous, and fetid airs emitted from various ancient and freshly deposited effluvia, effluxions, extravasations, exsanguinations, sting the eyes, assault the proprioception, and not only penetrate to the soul but also evade the snuggest of N95 masks. As is my wont, I began searching for my accustomed spot to cling to in order to avoid being pushed onto the subway tracks, when through the Stygian gloom my eyes dimly alighted on a poster of the Metropolitan Transportation Authority. It had been newly plastered on the column where I was planning to employ what rock climbers call a 'side-pull' grip. "Hate Has No Place in Our Transportation System", it brusquely declared. "Hmmn, really?" I muttered under my breath. "I certainly hate the smell of this godforsaken subway." And I also wondered whether posting such a high and mighty declaration, which struck me as a passive-aggressive prohibition masquerading as public information, was really all that lambent an idea in the first place, since it seemed destined to backfire and at personal cost to me. To whit, in the yeasty old days when there were heated controversies over the laws that enforced fines and jail time for public expectoration, the number of incidents of spitting on subway posters promulgating anti-spitting ordinances dramatically burgeoned to several thousand sprayings per week. Encountering such shrines of *lex scripta infecta* would hardly be very high on my bucket list, but, more to the immediate point, would my underground safe space by displaying this advertisement against hate similarly begin to incite misarchist

DOI: 10.4324/9781003589419-6

defiance of the Authority's threatening ordinances and fines? And who would be the collateral damage?[1]

By the same token, it was argued by pundits at the time that expectoration laws cruelly curtailed a healthy god-given natural impulse, targeted individual freedoms ad hock, and ceded to the government far too much power over cuspidorial choice. Ontotheological divines, of course, appealed to divine soterologies and Jesus's promise of eternal salvation. And, as usual, even in those days of rampant TB, the medical establishment could not manage to agree about the potential health risks or benefits of public spitting. After all, wasn't it good, all things considered, to get the poisonous stuff out? A few do-gooder organizations tried to act as peacemakers by handing out free sputum flasks in an attempt to appease both sides and avoid insurrection, but that compromise too found legal and moral opponents amid all the partisan strife. As a consequence, a series of fascinatingly complex legal conundrums arose in the face of this flood of looganic liquidity that proved both divisive and destructive, if not at times borderline deleuzional. But what I find truly remarkable is how closely the welcoming and rejecting of spit by pro and anti spitters – hostispittlety, as it were – mirrors arguments about the benefits and harms of hate throughout the long polar arc of the western philosophical tradition, even if nowadays arguments in its favor have become rather muted. The same obmutescence holds true, I'm afraid, for spitting, at least since the days of Punk gobbing, notwithstanding Carla Lonzi's brave manifesto in favor of philosophical sialoquence.[2]

In any case, it's not to be denied that sputum and spittoons have now been widely nosed out by hate as the numero uno subway menace thought to be facing the general public. Accordingly, let us return to the postered column where I was standing, but where hate itself enjoyed no legal standing. Having come to the conclusion that AI-designed hate flasks were still somewhere off in our collective future, I looked up again at the words "has no place," and found myself attempting to meditate slightly more sequaciously about whether by means of my own powers alone, I could ever hope to adhere to this mandate to abrogate all hate and thereby not snub my strap-hanging obligations to the Authority. To whit, I asked myself flat out, even if I really tried to abrogate all hate so that I might stand tall and true in the presence of hate's absence, could I all by my lonesome,[3] even with the best of training and

1 Within six months of first writing these lines, at least two people have been pushed onto the tracks from my very spot, one fatally. MTA police, for obvious reasons, have refused to speculate on any causal connections with their new signage.

2 Carla Lonzi, *Sputiamo su Hegel, la donna clitoridea e la donna vaginale: e altri scritti* (Milan: Rivolta Femminile, 1974). Cf. John D. Thomas, *Great Expectorations: The Cultural History of Saliva from Jesus Christ to Iggy Pop* (New York: Strayhorn Press, 2012).

3 F. Nietzsche, *On the Genealogy of Morality*, trans. by M. Clark and A. J. Swensen (Indianapolis: Hackett Publishing, 1998), 25: "At this juncture I cannot suppress a sigh and one last

steely discipline, ever fail to hate and abhor such olid fumes, even if I learned to admire the marvelous workings of the olfactory compounds that produced them? Or might I ever be induced to offer a prevenient welcome to these foul-smelling excrescences just by studying their daedal genesis? Or even as an admittedly rather desperate last resort to *l'optimisme*, by channeling Marcus Aurelius might I be able to catch a sniff of these noxious mephitic vapors without retching if I came to understand their necessary beneficent and sanative role in Providence's universal Panglossian design?

Alas, I must confess that the more I resorted to such *nostra* and *doctrina philosophiae* even with these hard-nosed *Wissenschaften* as my aides-de-camp, the more freeing myself from the illaqueable snares of hate became impossible. All my efforts kept miserably failing and all my noes to hatred vanished, since my relentlessly misological and non-enthymemetic nostrils were positively rhinorrheatic with unchecked hate. Ratiocinate until the cows came home, still my nose's disgust and hatred persisted unmoved, unabated, and unrepentant. It seemed, therefore, that not only had hate found *seine heimat für sein Leben und Werk* where it was now cheekily thumbing its gorgonic nose at the enemy's own sign but that its enmitic underground laws were being aided and abetted by a vital *vis* of my very own nose and its gnosic canons – with, *hélas*, nary a peep of protest from all of those quondam therapeutic *Wissenschaften*. Indeed, when faced with the nose's *l'elisir d'odio*, these oligophrenic bashi-bazouks, these Dulcamaran knowledgeships and apostate mountebanks strummed their noses in an echopractic polyphonic flouting of the Metropolital Transportation Authority's authority to deny hate hostipitality. Poltroonish louts that they were, they servilely offered hate not just a place *conspirate*, but a warm and welcoming scentuary *sine die*. Faced with these Mephistophelean betrayals, I ask, how could I on my own hope do anything but begrudgingly give assent, even if only under my increasingly dyspneic breath, to the compulsions of *odium narium*? But enough of this shamefully derivative and breezy *La coscienza di Zenose*. In short, utterly spiflicated and beaten down, I admitted defeat and threw in the (s)ponge.

I. Hate Inside the Law: Force, Decision, and the Repressed Genealogy of Aversion

If this surrender reads as theatrical, that is because it is. It belongs to a theater of diagnoses where what is on display is not resolution but exposure. What

hope. What do I find absolutely intolerable? Something which I just cannot cope alone with and which suffocates me and makes me feel faint? Bad air! Bad air! That something failed comes near me, that I have to smell the bowels of a failed soul! . . . Apart from that, what cannot be borne in the way of need, deprivation, bad weather, disease, toil, solitude? Basically we can cope with everything else, born as we are to an underground and battling existence."

collapses along with nasal fortitude is the familiar fantasy that judgment arrives first with the body following obediently behind. Instead, the order reverses itself. The nose does not wait for permission or continuances; its aversion already registers disturbance before reason finds its words.[4] Of course, to continue lingering in this atmosphere of anecdote would merely indulge the symptom while ignoring the structure that renders such betrayals ordinary, even necessary. So what demands attention now is not the mere farce of bodily capitulation but the conceptual economy that receives without argument these prior refusals and expulsions, and then proceeds as if nothing had happened. How are such presentiments and prejudgments named, authorized, or disavowed once law and ethics step onto the platform? How is it that some injustices reek before they can be named? It is precisely at this juncture, where the body's comedy insists on being taken seriously, that Derrida's 'Force of Law' is unavoidable. By now it has become one of those texts that one does not so much encounter as inherit, cite, ritualize, or resist. It has been quietly presupposed across legal theory for a generation so that its central claims now risk appearing self-evident, even almost polite. Written at a moment when critical legal studies, deconstruction, and political theology found themselves in an awkward embrace, 'Force of Law' arrived less as a doctrine than as an irritation. "Law cannot be disentangled from force, and justice will not consent to being called law." The argument proceeded not by settled theses but by applying pressure, worrying and bending the distinctions through which jurisprudence ordinarily secures its authority. Law, Derrida exposed, comes into being through a decision that cannot be fully justified in advance, a moment in which reasons arrive late and authority begins without guarantee. He names this origin mystical not to perfume it with transcendence, but to mark the point at which justification gives out and law nonetheless takes hold. There is no law without force, no norm without imposition, no justice without exposure to undecidability, and to deny this is not merely naïve but to cling to a consoling fiction in which legality under its golden pince-nez sees itself innocent of its own effects. Yet it is precisely here, where force is acknowledged most uncompromisingly, that a hesitation appears – a hesitation before the sign of hatred and the refusal that precedes judgment. In 'Force of Law', force does not arrive as a momentary excess but settles in, stabilizes, repeats itself, and becomes livable,

4 I should point out from the outset that the proboscations I am excavating from the midden of the encyclomisopedia of western philosophy track Peter Goodrich's waggish profundities in 'Proboscations: Excavations in Comedy and Law' (2017) 43:2 *Critical Inquiry* 361–388: verum animo satis haec vestigia parva sagaci/sunt, per quae possis cognoscere cetera tute./ namque canes ut montivagae persaepe ferai/naribus inveniunt intectas fronde quietes,/cum semel institerunt vestigia certa viai,/sic alid ex alio per te tute ipse videre/talibus in rebus poteris caecasque latebras/insinuare omnis et verum protrahere inde. (Luc. *DRN* 1. 402–409).

a part of the everyday life of legality rather than its exception. It is rendered as structure, while hatred is politely ushered aside, treated as derivative, pathological, or simply not quite the law's concern. The founding cut is duly acknowledged, yet the forces of aversion released by that cut remain largely unthematized – the repulsion, the refusal, the sense that something must not be permitted to remain. This absence is not incidental. It reflects a deeper inheritance within Derrida's work that quietly shapes his accounts of justice, hospitality, forgiveness, and responsibility. Derrida is prepared, even insistent, to think of force without innocence, but he draws back from hatred that sits uneasily in the moral register in which law prefers to speak. The result is that 'Force of Law' risks repeating a familiar modern configuration in which law confesses its violence at the level of principle while disavowing the affective labor through which exclusion, punishment, and refusal are stabilized, repeated, and lived in practice. To first bring this configuration into sharper relief, I first turn to archaic Greek reflections on law, beginning with Homer and Hesiod – an archive Derrida himself intermittently invokes but never attempts to fully inhabit. In *Rogues* he briefly gestures toward Hesiod when discussing sovereignty and founding violence, but there the Greek material is refracted through an Abrahamic optic, read as a scene of sacrificial authority rather than as a cosmology of separation, measure, and generative aversion. I suggest that this sacrificial re-inscription and theological domestication obscures something crucial. In Hesiod, law does not arise from obedience to a transcendent demand, but from a violent cut within the family itself and a refusal of the suffocating proximity of the father that opens space for time, memory, and normativity. Hatred is not a moral failure but a world-making power. Accordingly, by tracing hatred from its aristocratic visibility in Homer, through its cosmic and juridical centrality in Hesiod, we can begin to recover a conception of aversion as internal to law rather than outside and opposed to it. This genealogy does not rehabilitate hatred indiscriminately, since it distinguishes between parasitic, obsessive, or resentful forms of hatred and those forms that function as boundary-drawing, discriminating, and preservative of civic order. The Greeks, I argue, understood something that modern legal theory has difficulty admitting, that law depends not only on force and reason but on trained capacities of refusing and expelling what must not be admitted, tolerated, or forgiven. Only against this background, moreover, does Derrida's later work on hospitality, immunity, forgiveness, and responsibility come fully into view. The rhetoric of unconditional welcome, the suspicion of exclusion, and the ethical valorization of openness are not departures from 'Force of Law', but extensions of its unresolved tension. When hatred is denied conceptual dignity at the foundation of law, it returns displaced as administration, humanitarian moralism, colonial governance, or as bodily reflex rather than acknowledged judgment. By the same token, what presents itself as ethical purity often conceals an unexamined economy of aversion. The point, then, is not to bypass Derrida's account of law, nor to diminish the enduring force of 'Force of Law' as it circulates within critical legal thought. Rather, it is to remain with one of its unresolved tensions, staying attentive to the aporias and textual pressures that Derrida himself so carefully stages, but finally leaves open. If justice is to remain more than a pious name for undecidability, however, it must reckon with the affective conditions that make decisions possible and durable. In this genealogy, law does not begin in Ricœurian solicitude. It begins with a cut.

To begin to see what is at stake in this displacement of hatred, it is worth returning to the archaic Greek world where hospitality and enmity were articulated together, not as moral opposites but as mutually implicating practices, for it is only there that the 'no' can be seen as constitutive rather than reactive. Derrida's sustained engagement with hospitality, from *Adieu à Levinas* to *Of Hospitality*, trembles between two incompatible imperatives: the injunction to welcome the other without condition and the structural necessity that any welcome must involve a gate, a door, a threshold, and therefore a decision to say no. The Greek lexicon already names this tension without embarrassment. *Xenia* is haunted by *xenos*, the stranger who may be guest, enemy, barbarian, god, or spy, and as David Konstan has shown, *xenos* in Homer does not yet mean "the Other" in a moralized sense, but simply "the stranger," the one whose intentions and affiliations are undecided.[5] Hospitality toward foreigners is thus never a standing obligation but a precarious, voluntary act, extended at risk and always shadowed by the possibility of refusal or violence. To open the door is exposure, to close it is denial; both are intelligible only because hatred and love are already in play as discriminating orientations rather than as pathologies. Derrida remains faithful to this aporia and chooses, characteristically, to dwell on its hinge, but what he does not do is grant aversion and hatred (*misos*) the same ontological dignity he accords to love and hospitality. Hatred appears instead as an effect of fear, hierarchy, or ignorance, a symptom of premature closure rather than a condition of ethical sense. What the ancient material suggests, however, is that hatred need not be understood only at the level of its excesses or corruptions. Attended to structurally rather than diagnostically, *misos* names the capacity to draw a line between what may be welcomed and what must not be, between what can be loved and what must be opposed. It is this capacity, rather than any moralized doctrine of hostility, that the Homeric poems will make hatred visible as a civic and perceptual competence, prior to its later ethical domestication. In this register, the 'no' is not merely the limit of hospitality

5 David Konstan, 'Making Friends with Foreigners: Xenoi in the Homeric Epics', in Eustathia Papadodima, ed., *Ancient Greek Literature and the Foreign* (Berlin: De Gruyter, 2021, Trends in Classics Supplementary Volume), 29–54.

but the transcendental condition of its intelligibility, and the ethics of welcome depends on the disciplined capacity to hate rightly.

II. The **Contest** *and the Problem of Aristocratic Hatred: Homer Between Honor and Law*

The *Certamen Homeri et Hesiodi* stages, in schematic form, a misrecognition that will reverberate throughout later reflections on law. In this work, which preoccupied Nietzsche, Hesiod is crowned victor over Homer in the contest for Greece's greatest poet because he is taken to sing of agriculture, peace, and civic usefulness, while Homer is dismissed as a poet of war. The judgment is meant to be ethical as much as aesthetic. Poetry that instructs the city in orderly life is preferred to poetry that dwells on slaughter. Yet this contrast mistakes surface for structure. What it fails to register is not only the distinctiveness of Homer's violence, but the different work hatred is doing in Homer and in Hesiod. Homer's poems do not merely depict violence, they anatomize the affective conditions under which violence becomes intelligible, bounded, and judged. We see a baseline phenomenology of hatred in its aristocratic form, which functions in relation to honor, truthfulness, recognition, and mortality, prior to its moralization, propaedeutics, or juridical refinement. It appears less a moral attitude than a perceptual capacity, a way of sorting friend from enemy, truth from deception, life from death, in a world where judgment is immediate and the stakes are absolute.

In the *Iliad*, hatred is inseparable from clarity. Achilles' famous declaration that he hates deception "as the gates of Hades" (Il. 9.307 ff.) binds *misos* (hatred) to mortality and truth at once. To hate what lies is not here a moral abstraction but an existential reflex. Deception threatens the integrity of honor and exposes one to death under false pretenses. Hatred is an alerting mechanism, a sharpened sensitivity to what endangers one's standing among equals. It is no accident that Achilles' language repeatedly couples hatred with visibility and concealment, with what is shown and what is hidden in the heart. Hatred names the refusal to tolerate duplicity in a world where one's life depends on reliable signs.

Odysseus complicates this picture without abolishing it. His celebrated cunning introduces a distance between inner intention and outward speech, but this distance does not dissolve hatred; it redistributes it. Odysseus, too, claims to hate deception "as the gates of Hades," even as he practices it (*Od.* 14.156–157). The point is not hypocrisy, but the strain placed on aristocratic judgment once survival requires indirection rather than face-to-face confrontation. Hatred here becomes reflexive, turned back upon itself, yet it remains bound to the same demand for intelligibility and survival. One hates deception even as one deploys it. The poems do not resolve this tension but make it visible. Hatred remains bound to truth, even as truth itself becomes stratified, situational, and perspectival. What persists is the sense that hatred tracks danger before law, before institution, before justification.

It is crucial to note what is not yet present in Homer's texts. There is no conception here of hatred as a moral vice in need of eradication, nor for that matter of love as a universal solvent. What we see instead is an aristocratic sensorium in which hatred functions as an immediate capacity of discrimination. One hates what threatens honor, kin, oaths, or survival. One hates what lies or what brings shame. Hatred is not yet generalized but keyed to persons, actions, and visible affronts. It belongs to a world of face-to-face recognition and mortal risk.

This is the point at which Nietzsche's nose[6] briefly reenters, not as authority, but as a diagnostic excess. Nietzsche's insistence that truth is first "smelled" before it is argued captures something essential about Homeric judgment. The nose names a bodily attunement to danger and falsity that precedes reflective justification. But by elevating his sensitivity into a sign of his own uncanny and sovereign olfactory privilege, Nietzsche risks converting what is in Homer a shared aristocratic capacity into the mark of a solitary oracle. Homer does not sanctify a privileged oracular nose, he distributes perception across a social world in which hatred is intelligible because its objects are publicly contestable and can be challenged, answered, and avenged. The *Certamen*'s preference for Hesiod thus occludes the specificity of Homeric hatred. By treating Homer as merely bellicose, it overlooks the way his poems articulate the affective groundwork upon which later notions of law will build. Aristocratic hatred is limited, visible, and answerable to honor. It does not yet found institutions, but it establishes the necessity of boundaries. It shows that not everything can be tolerated, not every claim can be accepted, not every stranger can be trusted. In this sense, Homer prepares the problem of law without yet resolving it. At the same time, Homer's world exposes the insufficiency of aristocratic hatred as a basis for order. Because hatred remains situational and personal, it cannot stabilize a cosmos or a city. The same capacity that sharpens judgment also fuels cycles of retaliation. The poems are acutely aware of this danger. They show how hatred clarifies and destroys, how it preserves honor and invites ruin. What they do not yet provide is a mechanism for transforming hatred from an episodic response into a structuring principle. In Homer, hatred operates within

6 "May I venture to indicate one last trait of my nature which creates for me no little difficulty in my relations with others? I possess a perfectly uncanny sensitivity of the instinct for cleanliness, so that I perceive physiologically – *smell* – the proximity or – what am I saying? – the innermost parts, the 'entrails', of every soul . . . I have in this sensitivity psychological antennae with which I touch and take hold of every secret: all the *concealed* dirt at the bottom of many a nature". F. Nietzsche, *Ecce Homo*, trans. by Walter Kaufmann (New York: Vintage Books, 1967), 8.

a world of warriors, calibrated by honor, lineage, and divine proximity, constantly exposed to the risk of death. It is enacted in visible confrontations whose stakes are immediately legible within that hierarchy. Hesiod shifts the register entirely. Hatred is no longer confined to agonistic encounters among warriors but is displaced to the origins of the world itself, where it functions as an act of separation and measure. What is at stake is not just a movement from war to peace, but a transformation in the role hatred plays. It ceases to be merely reactive but becomes generative, no longer answering to insult or loss, but producing the conditions under which order, memory, and law can come into being. Where Homer binds hatred to honor and mortality, Hesiod binds it to separation, measure, and time as we move from visible conflict to constitutive incision.

III. *Certamina Divini Hesiodi et Derridae: Hatred, Memory, and the Juridical Birth of Time*

If Homer gives us what later vocabularies will call hatred as an aristocratic capacity for perceptual discrimination, Hesiod effects a more radical transformation, one in which antagonism is no longer episodic or situational but inscribed into the very architecture of reality itself. What in Homer remains bound to persons, affronts, and moments of judgment is, in Hesiod, displaced into a cosmogonic register, so that the *Theogony* does not merely recount violence among gods but articulates the conditions under which order, temporality, and normativity become possible at all. At the center of this account stands the castration of Ouranos by Kronos, an act of refusal so elemental that it resists moralization in any familiar register, not because it is ethically opaque but because it precedes the very field in which ethical evaluation could arise. This act is not simply an episode of familial drama but the inaugural incision through which *nomos*, measure, and law first come into being. Conflict here does not stand opposed to order; it is the means by which order is first wrenched into existence.

In Hesiod's account, the violent severing of heaven from earth forces distance, interval, and space into a world previously collapsed into suffocating immediacy, so that what had appeared as unbroken presence is cut apart, and with that incision time itself begins, since presence can no longer remain uninterrupted, just as justice becomes thinkable only once separation makes judgment possible. The cut is thus at once cosmological and juridical, not because it regulates an already existing world, but because it brings a world into being through a founding act of division, so that Hesiod's cosmos is not born of reconciliation or harmony but of refusal, of the necessity that something be torn away if anything else is to appear at all. In this sense, what later moral vocabularies will name hatred functions here not as a moral attitude but as a negatively generative principle, the power to declare an intimacy intolerable and a proximity destructive, as when the father's endless embrace becomes unlivable and the son's act intervenes to impose distance. This is not yet ethics, but it is already an ontology shaped by normativity, since the incision inaugurates measure and proportion, and law, in its earliest form, appears not as command but as the imposition of separation itself.

The importance of this act becomes clearer when we attend to Hesiod's invocation of the Muses, for the poem begins by calling upon the daughters of Mnēmosynē (Memory), a gesture that is not ornamental but revelatory, since it shows that memory, discourse, and law are co-originary.[7] The Muses can speak only because the primal cut has already taken place, because remembrance presupposes separation, the ability to distinguish past from present and to hold what is no longer immediate at a distance sufficient for narration. Memory here is not passive retention but an active incision, dependent on the interruption of the father's endless presence and on the refusal of origin as total immediacy, so that without hatred's cut there would be no memory, no story, no law, but only undifferentiated continuity.

This point is crucial for understanding the juridical dimension of Hesiod's poetry, in which problems of text, trace, and inscription are already at work, since Hesiod's world is one in which normativity emerges together with inscription. The *Theogony* itself performs what it narrates, offering a regulated access to origin through a mediated account that replaces immediacy with sequence, and writing here already functions as a juridical apparatus, stabilizing memory, fixing distance, and allowing normativity to endure beyond the moment of

7 Plotinus already worries about the temporal instability of Hesiod's account when he asks how the Muses who are daughters of Zeus and Mnemosyne could claim first hand knowledge of the castration of Ouranos, an event that precedes their own creation (*Enn.* 3.7.11.15–20). The question complicates the authority and temporality of Hesiod's *logoi*, a difficulty Paul de Man long ago taught us not to resolve too quickly by appeal to narrative coherence or mythical distance. In *Rogues*, Derrida returns to this scene in the context of sovereignty and *nómos*, reading the castration of Ouranos (*Theog.* 155 ff.) as a foundational act of violent, sacrificial power that establishes authority by interrupting and mastering time, an act that is at once paternalistic, patriarchal, and ipsocentric (p. 17). As is well known, the word *nómos* does not occur in Homer (see Thanos Zartaloudis, *The Birth of Nomos*, vol. 1 [Edinburgh University Press, 2019]), and it is therefore natural to look to Hesiod for an inaugural moment of law where the term explicitly appears. But such a move is neither genealogically exhaustive nor textually or temporally stable. Derrida's Hesiodic emphasis tends to privilege those strands of *nómos* that resonate with Judaeo-Christian concerns about mystical authority, while eliding the role of hatred and aversion in the force of law, along with a rhetoric of atemporality that finds its most systematic articulation in Plato. A similar elision is at work in Heidegger's account of *Gewalt* and *Díkē* as emerging from *Eris* in Heraclitus (cf. 'Force of Law', 6), and for closely related reasons. In each case, the displacement of hatred allows law to acknowledge violence in principle while obscuring the affective operations through which authority is sustained.

force.[8] Refusal is built into this economy not as an affect to be purged, but as the enabling condition of distance and legibility. One cannot write law without cutting oneself off from origin, nor remember without refusing presence.

At this point the divergence from Derrida's preferred genealogy begins to come into view. When Derrida, particularly in *Rogues*, gestures toward Hesiod in his discussion of sovereignty and founding violence, the Greek material is tacitly reframed through an Abrahamic lens, so that the origin of law is imagined as a scene of sacrificial obedience in which the father stands before a transcendent demand, prepared to kill the son at the command of an invisible Other.[9] Authority is founded, on this model, through responsiveness to what exceeds genealogy, and violence is justified, if at all, by appeal to a stranger-God who interrupts familial bonds from without. Hesiod's myth does not conform to this structure. There is no transcendent guest who commands the cut, no external voice that authorizes violence in the name of obedience. The violence is immanent, genealogical, and directed inward, and law arises not through submission to the wholly other but through revolt against a suffocating sameness that threatens to collapse all difference.

The consequences of this divergence are far-reaching. In the Abrahamic scene, law and hospitality are knotted together through sacrifice, since the household is founded on an obedience that exceeds kinship and the possibility of welcoming the stranger becomes structurally central. In Hesiod's cosmos, by contrast, hospitality never fully detaches from the drama of procreation and succession. Gods devour their children, castrate their fathers, and displace their predecessors, and each act of exclusion is aimed not at the foreigner but at an intimacy that has become intolerable. Law emerges here

8 Cf. Pietro Pucci, *Hesiod and the Language of Poetry* (Baltimore: Johns Hopkins University Press, 1977) for a brilliant deconstruction of the doubleness of the *logos* that Hesiod receives from the Muses and that produces further paradoxes, contradictions, doubles, polysemies, and ambiguities throughout the rest of Hesiod's text.

9 So too in 'Force of Law', with a wonderfully apophatic gesture, Derrida traces this symbolic foundational (g)nomic moment in "carnivorous sacrifice" (*FL*, 18) that "is essential to the structure of subjectivity, which is also to say to the founding of the intentional subject and to the founding, if not of the law, at least of law {droit), the difference between the law and law {droit), justice and law {droit), justice and the law here remaining open over an abyss. I will leave these problems aside for the moment, along with the affinity between carnivorous sacrifice, at the basis of our culture and our law, and all the cannibalisms, symbolic or not, that structure intersubjectivity in nursing, love, mourning and, in truth, in all symbolic or linguistic appropriations." (*FL*, 19) Many of Derrida's chief interlocutors – Kierkegaard, Benjamin, Levinas, etc. – focus on law and justice through the theological prism of Abraham and Isaac (on which, Cf. Robert Young, this volume). I worry, however, that this tends to elide the deeply embedded and specific role of hate in the ancient Greek force of law and its structured intersubjectivities along with its corresponding rhetoric of atemporality that found its most influential expression in Plato and his successors – and which is ultimately rooted in Homer's depiction of the mutual deconstructive alluviations among truth, hate, and authority, and their sedimentations.

not from the welcome extended to the stranger, but from the violent regulation of kinship itself, so that aversion is oriented inward rather than outward, directed against what is too close, too encompassing, too immediate to allow a world to take shape at all. What this contrast clarifies are two different genealogies of law, one grounded in sacrifice to transcendence, the other in immanent division.

Hesiod thereby shows that the founding violence of law is not merely a performative act that cannot be justified in advance, but an affective refusal that creates the very conditions under which justification, memory, and normativity can later operate.[10] What Derrida names the "mystical foundation of authority" captures the structural opacity of this origin, but Hesiod allows us to see its affective content. The foundation is not only undecidable; it is marked by strife, blood, proximity, and revolt. To acknowledge this is not to glorify violence, but to recognize that law's emergence is inseparable from aversion. By embedding strife into the origin of cosmos, memory, and writing, Hesiod radicalizes the problem that Homer merely stages, since what later vocabularies will call hatred no longer appears simply as a response to affront but as the condition under which order itself becomes possible. Yet this does not license indiscriminate hostility. On the contrary, it opens the question that will dominate subsequent Greek thought, namely how this primordial capacity for refusal can be disciplined, educated, and rendered compatible with communal life. That question is taken up explicitly by Plato, for whom aversion is no longer primarily a cosmological operation but becomes a psychological and pedagogical problem, one that must be trained, redirected, and interiorized if it is to serve rather than corrode the city. The transition from Hesiod to Plato thus marks not a rejection of aversion, but its domestication within law through its translation into the life of the soul.

IV. Plato's Bi-Narium: Nomos, *Hatred, and the* Pharmakon *of Law*

Plato inherits from Hesiod a world already structured by incision, separation, and memory, but he refuses to leave aversion at the level of theogonic origin. His intervention is neither to abolish nor to celebrate it, but to submit it to rational education. What Hesiod presents as a cosmic necessity, Plato translates into a juridical and pedagogical problem. How can the capacity for refusal that founds order be trained so that it preserves rather than corrodes communal life? The answer, developed across the *Republic* and the *Laws*,

10 Here one might appeal to Benjamin's distinction between founding and conserving violence. W. Benjamin, *Toward the Critique of Violence* (Stanford, CA: Stanford University Press, 2021). For a subtle account of the relation to Derrida, cf. A. Haverkamp (ed.), *Gewalt und Gerechtigkeit: Derrida – Benjamin (*Frankfurt/M: Suhrkamp, 1994).

is unambiguous. Hatred is not an accident of moral failure, it becomes one of the primary affective instruments by which virtue is formed, maintained, and protected. The danger lies not in hating, but in hating the wrong things. Correspondingly, in Plato's *Lysis,* Socrates raises a question that puts an end to aristocratic Homeric hate and its subjective laws of authority and sovereignty. He dialectically coerces his interlocutors into agreeing that one is only a friend to those who are good and an enemy to those who are bad, thus saddling friendship and, indirectly, hospitality *(xenia)* with a new normative moral constraint (*Lys.* 213a ff). What makes someone either worthy of friendship or hate is no longer one's own particular whims or desires. Hate must be aimed at what is evil, which endows it with a new impersonal and objective moral focus that, as we shall see, Plato makes fundamental to his *nomoi*. And Plato being Plato, these laws must be epistemologically grounded in a metaphysics of *ousia* and *aletheia*. Plato's starting point is strikingly frank. Education does not begin, he insists, with reasoned argument, but with the gradual alignment of pleasure and pain, love and hatred, through which the soul is first oriented in the world. Long before it can grasp an account (*logos*), it is already being shaped by what it is trained to welcome and what it is trained to recoil from (*Laws* 653b1–c3). This formative work is not an unfortunate prelude to rationality to be overcome once reason arrives, but the very condition under which rational judgment becomes possible. To love the good is inseparable from hating the bad, and the virtuous soul is not one that has transcended hatred, but one that has learned to direct it rightly. Hatred here is neither blind aversion nor irrational excess, but a form of discriminating refusal, a capacity to set limits that reason by itself cannot enforce.[11]

The juridical significance of this claim becomes explicit when Plato turns from individual education to the ordering of the city. A polis that cannot hate injustice, he argues, cannot survive. (*Laws* 689a4–c2). Love of the good, in its full philosophical sense, is rare and demanding. Hatred of injustice is more widely available and more easily mobilized (*Laws* 862d-e).[12] For this reason, Plato repeatedly emphasizes that law must work with hatred rather than

11 In an echinate verse (Luke 14:26) that daily tests the ingenuity and Greek of evangelical bloggers, Christ says: "If anyone comes to me and does not hate (*misei*) his own father and mother and wife and children and brothers and sisters and even his own soul, he is not able to be my follower" (my translation). This verse was extremely important for traditions of monasticism, but also gives theological backing to Plato's point about the importance of hate in setting moral boundaries. To love Christ properly, one must hate everything outside of him.

12 Plato would therefore oppose Derrida's claim that the essence of law is affirmative and not prohibitive (*FL*, 6–7) because he thinks that while its essence includes both, it must be strongly prohibitive given his psychological pessimism, hence his emphasis on the moral importance of hatred in law, which helps prevent one from falling into moral evil. Moreover, unlike Derrida, he is not interested in the relation of law and affirmations of our

against it. Punishment, exclusion, and prohibition are not merely deterrents, they are pedagogical acts that cultivate shared aversions. Law, in this sense, is an institutionalized *pharmakon* that is both poison and cure, capable of corrupting when misapplied and of preserving when rightly administered.

This *pharmakon* is not an incidental metaphor but the very condition of Plato's legal thinking. Laws must be written, Plato insists, precisely because living reason cannot be present everywhere at once, cannot see, hear, or judge in all places and at all times. Writing fixes norms, stabilizes commands, and makes law portable, but in doing so it also introduces rigidity, repetition, and the ever-present risk that what was once measured judgment will harden into blind application. Plato is acutely aware of this danger and never forgets that writing both preserves and poisons. Yet his response is not to renounce law, nor to indulge the fantasy of a city without coercion or exclusion. Instead, he insists that law must be thickened from within. Written statutes require preambles, explanations, and above all a pedagogical surrounding that trains citizens to feel rightly about what the law welcomes and what it forbids. Hatred, in this register, is not expelled by writing but folded into it. The written law becomes the city's durable memory of refusal, the inscription of what must not be tolerated, repeated not because it is always perfectly just, but because the city cannot afford to forget what it has learned to reject. It is precisely this ambivalence that Derrida seizes upon in his analysis of the *pharmakon*, where writing appears as both remedy and poison, supplement and threat, preserving what it simultaneously risks deforming. Plato's anxiety about writing thus becomes, in Derrida's hands, a paradigm of undecidability itself. Yet when this analysis is brought back to Plato's account of law, something else comes into view. Plato does not merely fear writing's corruptive potential. He relies on it. Writing is not only the site where law risks rigidity and misapplication, it is also the means by which collective refusal is stabilized, transmitted, and made durable. The *pharmakon* here names the ambivalence of inscription itself. What preserves judgment also exposes it to repetition, drift, and misuse. Hatred understood not as blind animus but as the city's settled capacity to refuse does not function as the poison, but as what writing seeks to hold in place and render governable. To purge law of its coercive or aversive dimension in the name of ethical purity would be, for Plato, not a moral advance but a civic abdication, leaving the city without the resources to defend itself against what it has already learned it cannot tolerate. Plato's insistence on hatred's pedagogical role also clarifies the stakes of his metaphysics. When he claims that the philosopher must hate falsehood and love truth, he is not offering a psychological aside but articulating a

freedom, since the latter holds little value for him. Hence paternalism and prohibition go hand in hand.

normative demand (*Republic* VI 485b–c). Truth is not simply contemplated. It is guarded and the philosopher's hatred of falsity functions as a boundary-maintaining force, excluding what would dissolve the integrity of knowledge. Even the gods, Plato insists, must hate evil because benevolence without exclusion is incoherent. Love that does not know how to refuse becomes complicity.[13] What emerges, then, is a conception of law in which hatred is internal rather than antagonistic. Yet Plato is equally clear about the danger. Hatred that is not educated becomes destructive and can become directed at persons rather than actions. When fueled by desires uncontrolled by reason, it can degenerate into resentment and cruelty. The task of law is to prevent this degeneration by redirecting hatred toward what is genuinely destructive of communal life. Hatred, like writing, is a *pharmakon*, both indispensable and dangerous, necessary and unstable.

This Platonic configuration sharpens the problem that 'Force of Law' inherits but does not resolve it. Derrida is willing, indeed compelled, to consider law's force, its violence, and the undecidable moment of its institution, yet he hesitates before granting hatred the same conceptual standing. The result is a theory in which law can acknowledge its coercion while ethics continues to insist on openness. Plato would find this division unintelligible. For him, the very possibility of justice depends upon the education of aversion. Without trained hatred, law's force lapses into arbitrariness; without law's inscription of refusal, hatred itself becomes anarchic.

Plato thus marks a decisive moment in the genealogy traced here. Hatred has moved from aristocratic perception in Homer, through cosmic incision in Hesiod, into juridical pedagogy, and philosophical attainment. It is no longer merely reactive or generative, but normative. The question that now presses, and that Derrida will confront in a different key, is whether modern legal theory can acknowledge this dependence without reverting to moralism or authoritarianism.[14] It is to that question, and to the fate of hatred in the

13 Or mere association or presumably even tolerant openness: "Is it not probable or even inevitable that the result will be exactly the same as whenever someone, living among the wicked habits of bad men, does not hate (*misei*) but accepts and even delights in (*chairēi*) them, yet blames (*psegēi*) them merely in a spirit of play, as if being in a dream about one's own wickedness? Then, to be sure, inevitably the person so delighted becomes similar (*homoiousthai*) to whatever they delight in, even though ashamed to praise it. Yet what greater good or evil would we say befalls us so inevitably?" (*Laws* 656b ff). And we might add, what greater challenge for hospitality?

14 Utilitarians have restricted their analyses of hate to the particular liberal problem of a society's tolerance for hate speech. In some sense, Derrida follows in this tradition, while unmasking, however, the pitfalls of language, the power and political dynamics that make attempts at suppression always reinterpretable, provisional, and contestable. The complexities of "hate speech' within his general views of freedom of speech must be set aside here, see Jacques Derrida, 'The University Without Condition', in Peggy Kamuf, ed. and trans., *Without Alibi* (Stanford, CA: Stanford University Press, 2002), 202–237, esp. 205. But hate speech is nonetheless

wake of Kantian morality and Derridean undecidability, that the argument must now return.

Anecdote II. Derrida, the Telephone, and Hegel's Secret

For several of the years Derrida was teaching at NYU he sublet my apartment, which was well furnished with Greek and Latin texts, much music, and very little heat. In the living room hung Salvatore Puglia's *Abstracts of Anamnesis*, a work Derrida knew well and admired, in which images embedded in glass panes reflect and refract one another without stable anchoring in memory or historicity.[15] Derrida was, as I used to say, a perfect tenant. He paid a generous supplement, left no trace, and, more importantly, proved remarkably adept at deflecting the bill collectors who were then pursuing me with some vigor. At the time I was sleeping in my office to make ends meet. A friend of mine, a philosopher from Princeton with whom I was writing a paper, came to New York to work and tried repeatedly to reach me by phone. Instead he found Derrida on the other end of the line, wonderfully evasive about my whereabouts, perhaps even my existence. The exchange escalated linguistically, edging toward one of those stylized impasses familiar from the Searle–Derrida controversies, until my friend finally exclaimed, in exasperation, "My god – who is this? Who am I speaking with?" The answer came calmly: "Jacques Derrida." "Oh really," my friend replied. "Well then tell Mitsis that Hegel called and is trying to get in touch with him." The remark was met without protest. Hegel's name appears, but no Hegel is on the line. What is present instead is a missed connection, a summons that fails to land. A displaced authority is invoked as if it were still operative, still entitled to receive and resolve the calls of the past. What the anecdote records then is not mockery but recognition. Something had gone astray, not a disagreement, but a transmission. What is misrouted in this failed call is a secret, which offers an excuse, in a Derridean spirit, to pass on another larger secret: the secret of hatred, or more precisely, the place hatred occupies within

typically construed in these contexts as hating something not necessarily hateworthy. For Plato "hate speech" and "love speech" would merely be two sides of the same coin – what distinguishes them is the moral quality of the object of speech; for instance, hate speech against genocide or racism, would be good, while love speech in favor of evil is something bad. Hate and love are strictly evaluated by their objects; they have no particular independent moral value. To embrace "love" can be horrific, if that means, say, the love of torture. To say "hate has no place here" is as uninformative as "love has no place here". Both love and hate are merely floating signifiers whose value depends on their objects, however themselves aporetic, and a decision.

15 Jacques Derrida, 'Sauver les phénomènes (Pour Salvatore Puglia)', in *Contretemps* in 1995. Cf. Christopher Fynsk, 'Anonymous Figures', in *Abstracts (of Anamnesis)* (Onassis Foundation for Hellenic Studies, 1995).

contemporary moral and legal thought. Modern philosophy learned early to treat this secret as something best kept hidden, displaced, or purified away. Kant famously banished both love and hate from the moral law, leaving duty cleansed of affect. Hegel, for all his dialectical ambition, largely accepts this purification, transforming conflict into reconciliation at the level of Spirit. What appears to survive as negation is stripped of its affective insistence. Refusal becomes a task for *aufgehoben*, hatred an embarrassment to be outgrown. The secret is preserved only by being denied conceptual dignity.[16] What was not passed on, and what Kant withheld from Hegel, and Hegel from Heidegger, is the ancient recognition that modernity found increasingly difficult to tolerate. Aversion, hatred, and refusal are not accidental residues of judgment but among its enabling conditions. A rough contemporary of Kant, Edmund Burke,[17] the soul of conservatism, could still say without embarrassment that hatred of injustice was a providential endowment, and that gentleness purged of what he called "charitable rancour" produced not virtue but complicity. This was not an appeal to passion against reason, but a recognition that judgment requires the capacity to reject, to draw lines that reason alone cannot draw without remainder. The secret here is not that hatred exists, but that law depends upon trained forms of refusal while insisting on speaking as though it does not.

The aim of the anecdote, then, is not to revive Hegel, nor to stage yet another return to dialectical reconciliation. It is to let Hegel's name mark a structural absence, the trace of a line of thought modern philosophy did not take. The unanswered call signals not an error but a foreclosure, the interruption of a transmission in which aversion, refusal, and the affective labor of judgment were progressively displaced in favor of reconciliation, purification, and ethical abstraction. Recovering what was lost does not require reopening the drama of Geist or founding acts of sovereignty, but retrieving some of the apparently forgotten histories that preceded them. One such recovery leads not forward, but sideways to the Stoics. For if Hegel's philosophy of history rendered the ancient world a preparatory stage surpassed by modern reason, Stoic thought offers a counter-image.

16 For instance, in Kant hatred returns in pedagogy as *Verachtung*: "If the child, for example, lies, it must not be punished but rather met with contempt, and it must be told that in the future one will not believe it, and the like," 9.481. *Lectures on Pedagogy*. 9.481 (trans. Louden).

17 "A kind Providence has placed in our breasts a hatred of the unjust and cruel, in order that we may preserve ourselves from cruelty and injustice. They who bear cruelty, are accomplices in it. The pretended gentleness which excludes that charitable rancour, produces an indifference which is half an approbation. They never will love where they ought to love, who do not hate where they ought to hate" (Edmund Burke, *Letters on a Regicide Peace*, vol iv. To the Earl Fitzwilliam, 62).

V. Ratio certe Cogit: *Stoic Reason and the Force of Law*

Derrida writes that "it was normal, foreseeable, desirable that studies of deconstructive style should culminate in the problematic of law (*droit*), of law and justice," and that this interrogation must begin

> by destabilizing or complicating the opposition between nomos and physis, between thesis and physis – that is to say, the opposition between law, convention, the institution on the one hand, and nature on the other, with all the oppositions that they condition.
>
> (*FL, p. 8*)

Deconstruction has indeed pursued this task in multiple registers, often by returning to Greek materials. Yet it has not fully confronted a persistent silence concerning hatred – one that is not accidental, but historically mediated. This silence is traceable, I suggest, to the decisive influence of Hegel's history of philosophy, particularly his account of post-Aristotelian ethics. Hegel's narrative effectively occludes the role that hatred and aversion play in ancient moral and legal thought, above all by misconstruing the philosophical and institutional moment in which the Greek Stoics disengaged hatred from the force of law while redistributing it into the pedagogical and practical structures of assent, refusal, and avoidance. That redistribution continues to shape the afterlife of 'Force of Law' (see Section VII).

Hegel's understanding of ancient philosophy is governed by his conviction that, after the culmination represented by Plato and Aristotle, Greek thought entered a period of decline. The Hellenistic schools – Stoics, Epicureans, Skeptics – are treated as symptoms of this regression. The explanation is familiar: the Macedonian conquests destroyed the ethical substance (*Sittlichkeit*) of the polis, forcing philosophy to abandon its objective, political vocation in favor of an inward, apolitical subjectivity. The loss of civic life allegedly produced a corresponding collapse of philosophical ambition, replacing systematic reflection with therapeutic techniques of self-management.[18] Hegel's account of law during this period is fully continuous with this diagnosis. The Stoic turn inward appears, for him, as the triumph of abstract subjectivity over ethical life:

> Subjectivity, as abstract self-determination and pure certitude only of itself, dissolves within itself all definite realization of right and duty. It passes judgment within itself, determines solely out of itself what is good,

18 Cf. Katerina Ierodiakonou, 'Introduction: The Study of Stoicism: Its Decline and Revival', in Katerina Ierodiakonou, ed., *Topics in Stoic Philosophy* (Oxford: Oxford University Press, 1999), 1–22.

> and makes this self-produced good its content. It bestows reality upon a good which is at first only presented and intended. The self-consciousness, which has reached absolute return into itself, is conscious of itself as something over which nothing that exists or is given to it can or ought to have any power. This tendency to look within, and know and decide from oneself what is right and good, assumes a more general form in history, appearing at epochs such as that of Socrates, the Stoics, etc., when the accepted ethical principles could not satisfy the better will. When the visible world has become untrue to freedom, the will no longer finds itself in the established morality, and is forced to seek the harmony, which the actual world has lost, in the inner ideal life. Since the right, which self-consciousness acquires in this way, is formal, everything depends upon the nature of the content, which it gives itself.
>
> *(Philosophy of Right, trans. Dyde, p. 117)*

Hegel is wrong on two counts. Historically, the social and institutional mechanisms of Greek life did not collapse in the way his narrative requires; many remained strikingly continuous under Macedonian and Diadochic rule. More importantly, the Stoics did not "decide from themselves" what was right and good in anything like Hegel's sense. To see this, it is helpful to recall Henry Sidgwick's judgment that Stoicism marks the decisive transition "from the ancient to the modern manner of ethical thought."[19] By this Sidgwick means a conception of morality grounded in universally valid rules of law cognizable by reason and not dependent on positive legislation. In contrast to the Platonic-Aristotelian priority of the Good and of virtue, Stoic ethics is structured around the apprehension of a moral code. Kant's moral philosophy – minus Zeus – would be unthinkable without this Stoic inheritance.[20] Far from retreating into subjectivism, the Stoics articulated a rigorously jural conception of morality, one that profoundly shaped Roman jurisprudence. Hegel's diagnosis reverses the direction of dependence.

The transition is visible already in the opening lines of Chrysippus' *Peri Nomou*:

> The law is king over all things human and divine. Law must preside over what is honourable and base, as ruler and as guide, and thus be the standard of right and wrong, prescribing to animals whose nature is political what they should do, and prohibiting what they should not do.
>
> *(SVF III.314)*

19 Henry Sidgwick, *Outlines of the History of Ethics for English Readers*, 5th ed. (London: Macmillan and Co., 1906), 7.

20 Cf. Stephen Engstrom and Jennifer Whiting (eds.), *Aristotle, Kant, and the Stoics: Rethinking Happiness and Duty* (Cambridge: Cambridge University Press, 1996).

Whatever we make of the Stoic analogy between morality and law, or of their claim that universal moral laws are discoverable by reason, these theses emerged in response to specific historical and ethical pressures. Schematizing brutally, the Stoics transformed the traditional opposition between *nomos* and *phusis* into what appeared to their opponents as an oxymoron: *nomos phuseos*, the common (*koinos*) law identified with Zeus, with providential reason itself. Cicero's later translation of this doctrine as *lex naturalis* proved fateful, weakening the Stoic position by rendering nature merely adjectival and reintroducing the need for an external ground or enforcer. It is precisely this gap that Derrida addresses when he asks after the reason of reason or the law of law.

Yet the Stoic formulation resists this regress. Greek grammatical usage makes room for a familiar semantic elasticity in the genitive: the "of"-relation may mark either an objective relation, in which a norm takes its object (law *concerning* nature), or a constitutive or source-like relation, in which what follows the genitive is that from which the norm itself issues.[21] Read objectively, *nomos phuseōs* reinstates the familiar gap between norm and world, inviting the demand for an external ground or enforcing authority. Read constitutively, however, law belongs to nature as its own activity. The latter is the Stoic view. Here there is no separation between *nomos* and *phusis*, no external ground to be supplied, no sovereign moment of institution. Zeus is not a legislator standing over nature but the immanent rational ordering of nature itself. *Ratio certe cogit*: reason itself compels, without an impulse beyond itself.

This alternative conception of reason was explored with particular acuity by Carlo Diano in *Forma ed evento* (1952).[22] Diano emphasizes the Stoics' nominalism and their rejection of stable universals in favor of an ontology of

21 I thank Gayatri Spivak for bringing to my attention comparative Sanskrit data and Saussure's account in *De l'emploi du génitif absolu en Sanscrit: Thèse pour le doctorat présentée à la Faculté de Philosophie de l'Université de Leipzig* [= On the Use of the Genitive Absolute in Sanskrit: Doctoral thesis presented to the Philosophy Department of Leipzig University] (Geneva: Jules-Guillaume Fick, 1881). For the complexities of Derrida's rather indirect reception of Stoic linguistic theory through Saussure and Jakobson, see Russell Daylight, 'The Originality of Saussure', In Russell Daylight, ed., *What If Derrida Was Wrong About Saussure?* (Edinburgh: Edinburgh University Press, 2011), 33–49.

22 For this immanent conception of law and rationality, see Carlo Diano, *Forma ed evento* (Neri Pozza: Venice, 1952), esp. the chapters on *logos* as continuous articulation rather than static form; *Form and Event*, trans. by Tim Campbell (Fordham: New York, 2020). Diano's account draws explicitly on early Greek Stoicism, particularly the identification of law (*nomos*) with living rational order rather than enacted statute, and the conception of *logos* as an ongoing event rather than a fixed ground. For the Stoic background, see Diogenes Laertius, *Lives of the Eminent Philosophers*, ed. T. Dorandi (Cambridge: Cambridge University Press, 2013) 7.87–89 on law as "right reason in command," Cicero, *De legibus* 1.18–19 (with the usual caution about Latinization), and Epictetus, *Discourses* 1.28 on rational avoidance (*ekklisis*) and assent.

events governed by a continuously active *logos*. Stoic reason is not a contemplative mind that sees, but a rational movement that never ceases. It has no founding moment, no external authority, no messianic horizon. Temporality is not oriented toward redemption or culmination, and sovereignty has no inaugural act.

This Stoic detour matters for Derrida and the deconstruction of *nomos* and *phusis* not because it resolves the aporias he identifies, but because it reframes the field on which they arise, inviting us to ask whether the very appeal to a problem of grounding – so central to Derrida's analysis – already presupposes a conception of reason and normativity that Stoic immanence refuses. From a Stoic perspective, what would then require deconstruction is not only the opposition between law and nature, but the assumption that normativity must be thought in terms of founding moments, external grounds, or binary alternatives at all. At the same time, this reframing shows that the Platonic domestication of hatred within law does not exhaust the ancient resources for thinking normativity and force, since Stoic natural law, though not instituted through violence, does not thereby eliminate exclusion or aversion, but redistributes them into the structures of assent, refusal, and avoidance that govern rational practical agency. Hatred is not eradicated on this model; it is displaced, and the consequence is significant, for aversion appears not merely as the residue of a failed foundation or the symptom of an originary violence, but as an unavoidable condition of intelligible order, whether law is conceived as instituted or immanent. In this way, the Stoic model sharpens rather than weakens Derrida's emphasis on undecidability, since hatred returns not as an origin to be mourned or confessed, but as a practical necessity that theory cannot fully purify. This logic comes into particularly sharp focus in Hegel, for whom the marginalization of hatred is not incidental to his account of law and political life, but one of its explicit ambitions. The greatness of the modern state, Hegel writes, functions as a controlling element precisely insofar as it renders "revenge, hate, and the like passions . . . inoperative and powerless," so that in a large and well-ordered polity "family relations and other private ties" lose their ethical primacy and give way to "an habitual regard for universal interests and affairs".[23] Hatred thus appears not as a structural feature of normativity, but as a residual affect tied to private attachment and insufficiently mediated social forms, and its eclipse is presented as an ethical and political advance. One of the most striking consequences of this purification appears in Hegel's account of modern warfare, where "modern wars," he insists, "are carried on humanely," since "one person is not set in hate over against another," personal hostilities are no longer required, and in the army as an army "enmity is something undetermined, and

23 G. W. F. Hegel, *Elements of the Philosophy of Right*, ed. by Allen W. Wood, trans. by H. B. Nisbet (Cambridge: Cambridge University Press, 1991), 239.

gives place to the duty which each person owes to another."[24] Hatred here is not sublimated but neutralized, displaced by role, duty, and institutional abstraction, and what this abstraction conceals, as Avital Ronell has shown in her analyses of authority, is not the disappearance of hostility but its relocation into the tonalities of address – summons, repetition, insistence – through which power continues to bind without appearing to strike. What disappears from view is not violence itself, but the affective economy through which exclusion, refusal, and hostility continue to operate under the guise of impersonality, in short, the ethics of the drone.

VI. A Return to Law's Force

With this genealogy now murmuring in the background, we can return to 'Force of Law'. Derrida's central claim that law is constituted by a founding violence that cannot be fully justified by prior norms appears not so much as a scandalous paradox, but as a late, reflective articulation of a problem visible already in archaic Greek thought. The institution of law requires a decision that cannot be deduced from rules that do not yet exist. Justification follows, if at all, only after the act has taken place. Derrida's insistence on this point remains one of the essay's lasting contributions to legal theory and breaks decisively with positivist dreams of self-grounding legality and with moralist hopes that law might be purified of force. At the same time, however, what the genealogy of hatred brings into focus is not what Derrida says, but what his conceptual economy quietly brackets. In 'Force of Law', force is granted full ontological and rhetorical dignity. Decision, violence, performativity, and iterability are named, analyzed, and affirmed as unavoidable. Justice, by contrast, is positioned as an excess, an undeconstructible horizon that forever judges law without coinciding with it. The structure is elegant and powerful, yet also asymmetrical. For while force is theorized as constitutive, aversion and hatred are left hovering at the margins, treated as moral contaminants rather than as internal conditions of decision. This asymmetry is not accidental. Derrida's account of undecidability depends upon a careful ethical posture in which decision must be exposed to risk but not guaranteed by rules, while remaining ever open to the other. Thus, to decide responsibly is to pass through the ordeal of not knowing. What this posture resists, however, is any positive theorization of refusal as such. The 'no' that institutes law is presumed structurally, but its affective dimensions – repulsion, disgust, hatred – are treated as if they belonged to a different register, one that ethics must work to neutralize rather than to educate. Accordingly, what results is not the disappearance

24 Hegel, *Elements of the Philosophy of Right*, 339.

of refusal, but its displacement. Law can confess its violence at the level of principle, while the work of aversion is left to operate elsewhere, untheorized and largely unowned.

This displacement surfaces explicitly in Derrida's later reflections on hospitality, where the problem of force reappears not at the level of institution but at the level of the body. In his dialogue with Habermas, Derrida asks whether a hospitality "protected by an immune system against the wholly other" could still count as hospitality at all.[25] The question is telling. An immune system does not deliberate or justify but discriminates, rejects, expels. It sneezes. To invoke immunity is already to concede that openness without refusal is untenable. What appears then is not a retreat from ethics, but its biological underside: the admission that the capacity to welcome presupposes the capacity to refuse, and that refusal is never purely rational but affective, visceral, and bodily. Read in this light, Derrida's question about hospitality anticipates the difficulty 'Force of Law' leaves unresolved – how law is to act, decide, and exclude once refusal has been rendered ethically suspect but practically unavoidable.

VII. Decision Without Ground: Afterlives

From this bodily, and in a precise sense immunitary, scene the afterlife of 'Force of Law' opens not as a contest of interpretations or a lineage to be mastered, but as a shared condition in which Derrida's work continues to circulate, unsettle, and demand response. What is at stake in speaking of an "afterlife" here is not influence, reception, or doctrinal succession, but the persistence of a problem once Derrida's central insight has been absorbed. What has been inherited is not a doctrine, nor even a determinate method, but a predicament that many of Derrida's readers recognize as their own. Force can be thought without innocence, justification can no longer pretend to come first, and yet decisions must still be made, lines drawn, exclusions enacted, all without the comfort of secure grounding. Alongside this recognition, however, there persists a hesitation, a tactful reserve, even embarrassment around refusal itself, not because refusal has vanished, but because its affective dimension no longer enjoys an authorized place within ethical or juridical discourse. Aversion and hatred are treated as though they belonged to a register too crude, too bodily, or too politically volatile to receive conceptual dignity, as though they could be acknowledged only as dangers or residues, but not avowed as reasons. Ethics, in this configuration, leans toward openness, exposure, and infinite responsibility, while the affective labor

25 Jacques Derrida, *Philosophy in a Time of Terror: Dialogues with Jürgen Habermas and Jacques Derrida* (Chicago: University of Chicago Press, 2003), 129.

through which decisions become livable is displaced, translated, or rendered polite. What is missing is not language as such – Derridean discourse is rich in names for limits, aporias, and interruptions – but a vocabulary that can authorize refusal as a ground of judgment rather than merely registering it as a threat to ethical purity.

It is at this juncture that Derrida's thought often can take on a spectral hue. Risk is articulated as unbounded, hospitality as exposure without horizon, forgiveness as "pure,"[26] responsibility as a demand that cannot close upon itself or come to rest. These formulations do not mark an oversight or a lapse, but a deliberate ethical intensification meant to prevent law from mistaking its authority for justice and from taking comfort in its own decisions. This ethical openness has rightly been admired for refusing complacency and for keeping law exposed to what exceeds it, yet it also leaves a practical and philosophical question of how decisions are to be made, sustained, and inhabited once the capacity to refuse has been rendered ethically suspect while remaining practically unavoidable. The difficulty is not that refusal disappears, but that it can no longer speak in the first person as a justification. It may operate

26 On forgiveness Derrida's position is most sharply formulated in his insistence that "pure" forgiveness, if it is to be anything other than reconciliation, excuse, therapy, or political calculation, can only forgive the unforgivable; otherwise it collapses back into an economy of exchange in which pardon is granted because it is deserved, requested, compensated, or socially useful. See Jacques Derrida, 'On Forgiveness', in Mark Dooley and Michael Hughes, trans., *On Cosmopolitanism and Forgiveness* (London: Routledge, 2001), 25–60. Derrida's formulation is in explicit philosophical dialogue with Vladimir Jankélévitch's postwar insistence that certain crimes – above all those bound to what he calls the "imprescriptible" – cannot be absorbed by ordinary moral time, neither excused nor "closed" by forgetfulness, and that in some cases forgiveness is precisely what would be morally obscene. See Vladimir Jankélévitch, *Forgiveness*, trans. by Andrew Kelley (Chicago: University of Chicago Press, 2005); and Jankélévitch, *L'Imprescriptible* (Paris: Seuil, 1986). What changes when antiquity is placed beside this modern aporetic, however, is that the central puzzle is no longer whether forgiveness can be "pure," but whether the modern grammar of interpersonal forgiveness is even available as a moral category in the first place. David Konstan argues that the fully interpersonal notion of forgiveness, as a moral overcoming of blame that restores a damaged relationship as such, is not a concept articulated in Greek and Roman antiquity in the modern sense, and that the relevant ancient practices are more often concerned with reconciliation, forgetting, forbearance, or the restoration of civic order than with a distinct ethical act of forgiving. See David Konstan, *Before Forgiveness: The Origins of a Moral Idea* (Cambridge: Cambridge University Press, 2010; repr., 2012). Set against this backdrop, Derrida's "unconditional" forgiveness begins to look less like an intensification of an ancient economy than a distinctly post-Kantian pressure placed upon moral life, one that risks displacing the older, harsher, and perhaps more discriminating question of how one is to recognize and hate what is evil without thereby surrendering the possibility of restored relation. Looking back to antiquity in this way does not refute Derrida's aporia, but it deconstructs the apparent self-evidence of the modern ideal of openness, showing how much the contemporary valorization of forgiveness presupposes the repression, rather than the education, of aversion and hatred.

and address, but it cannot not avow itself. The afterlives of Derrida's work unfold not by correcting this difficulty or supplying what is missing, but by lingering where his thought strains against its own limits and by experimenting in different sites of pressure with ways of giving body, normativity, and practice to a responsibility that cannot remain purely aporetic.

The first sustained pressure on this configuration emerges unsurprisingly at the level of the body. The body appears here not as metaphor or foundation, but as the site where the deferral of refusal becomes untenable. Before refusal can be theorized, justified, or administered, it is endured somatically as recoil, fatigue, vulnerability, and risk. The body is where openness encounters its limit not as a concept but as a condition of survival. If Derrida's ethics pushes exposure toward an infinite horizon, several of his closest interlocutors have lingered precisely where that horizon meets its breaking point, insisting that openness is never encountered in the abstract but always borne by bodies that can be wounded, exhausted, or undone. The question that arises then is not whether openness is ethically admirable, but how it is lived without becoming destructive. Risk, on this view, is not an ethical posture one adopts at will but a lived condition, and correspondingly hospitality is not a metaphysical ideal but a trembling practice that may fail under its own generosity. The threshold ceases to function as a partition of thought alone, but becomes a site of sensation, where warmth, fear, vulnerability, recoil, and defense are negotiated moment by moment, and where the ability to say 'no' appears less as a moral failure than as a condition of endurance.

It is in this lived, precarious dimension that Anne Dufourmantelle's countersignature beside Derrida's name in *Of Hospitality* acquires its distinctive force. Her insistence that hospitality is first of all risk does not spiritualize exposure or translate it into moral heroism, but insists on its embodied cost. To welcome is to accept the possibility of being injured, altered, or undone, not as an abstract ethical demand but as a corporeal event with palpable consequences. Where Derrida renders hospitality as an aporia that must remain open, Dufourmantelle insists on its temporality and finitude. Risk is borne by finite bodies, at particular thresholds, under conditions that may not permit endless openness. The language she develops – of trembling, pulse, and exposure – does not negate Derrida's ethics but stresses what it tends to leave implicit: that openness without the capacity for refusal is not ethical excess but self-erasure. The immune system she invokes is not an alibi for exclusion purified of violence, but a living defense that knows how to reject without allowing aversion to congeal into cruelty.[27] Dufourmantelle's intervention is

27 Anne Dufourmantelle, 'Zero Risk?', in Steven Miller, trans., *In Praise of Risk* (New York: Fordham University Press, 2019), 33 ff.

not a metaphysical critique, but an existential conclusion: an ethics that cannot survive embodiment cannot guide action.

Something parallel, though articulated on a different plane, is at work in Emanuela Bianchi's return to *physis*. What she exposes is not merely a political or ethical blind spot, but a recurrent metaphysical tension. She explores the ways that form secures itself by marking off what it cannot fully assimilate. The remainder that results – often gendered, sexualized, and insistently embodied – returns not as an external interruption, but as a symptom of philosophy's own aspiration to purity.[28] Matter appears here as an unwanted guest, too proximate, too alive, too resistant to formal capture, and thus perpetually in need of management, exclusion, or neutralization. Aversion, on this account, is not an accidental passion that bursts in from without, but one of the structural operations by which form maintains its coherence and protects itself from collapse. Read alongside Hesiod's incision and the Stoic redistribution of aversion into practices of assent, refusal, and avoidance, Bianchi's argument can be heard not as a total genealogy of metaphysics – given Democritean, Cynic, Epicurean, Sceptic, etc., traditions – but as a critique of a Platonic strand within a much older conversation about how order, legibility, and endurance are purchased through acts of separation. What modern philosophy often treats as pathological affect reappears in her hands as a condition of intelligibility itself, a reminder that form, no less than law, lives by what it cannot wholly welcome.

Taken together, these bodily and ontological lines of thought make it difficult to sustain the idea that responsibility can remain purely spectral. Bodies do not live on infinite openness, they survive by learning where to stop. Exposure without limit is not ethical excess but self-erasure, and hospitality that cannot say 'no' risks becoming indistinguishable from violence. Without celebrating or even acknowledging hatred, this work nonetheless restores aversion as a condition of life, insisting that decision and action require a capacity to refuse what cannot be indefinitely deferred. What emerges here is not yet a theory of law, nor is it meant to be. What is forced into view instead is a limit that ethical openness cannot indefinitely postpone. Bodies must stop. Forms must exclude. Life must refuse in order to persist. The body thus becomes the first site where Derrida's ethics is tested and strained by the demands of survival. The question that now presses is how these limits are translated, stabilized, and contested once law itself must act. And it is this movement from lived exposure to institutional decision that propels the argument toward

28 Emanuela Bianchi, 'Necessity and Automaton: Aleatory Matter and the Feminine Symptom', In *The Feminine Symptom: Aleatory Matter in the Aristotelian Cosmos* (New York: Fordham University Press, 2014).

normativity, where refusal can no longer merely be endured but must be articulated, justified, and enforced.

Once law itself is asked to act under these conditions, a different pressure comes into view. Undecidability may describe the condition of judgment, but it cannot by itself sustain the demands placed on institutions that must decide here and now, allocate responsibility, and draw lines whose consequences are anything but abstract. The question that presses is no longer whether law can avoid violence, but how it can act without either masking its coercion or abandoning its claim to justice. At this point, the problem of aversion ceases to be merely ethical or phenomenological and becomes fully juridical. Refusal must no longer simply be endured or managed at the level of the body, but articulated, justified, and enforced within institutions that cannot indefinitely defer decision. It is in this space that Drucilla Cornell's engagement with Derrida becomes especially instructive, not because it supplies foundations where Derrida withholds them, but because it insists on thinking how undecidability is borne by institutions that must nevertheless legislate, adjudicate, and punish. Cornell does not seek to domesticate 'Force of Law' into moral rules, nor does she retreat from Derrida's exposure of law's groundlessness; rather, she asks how justice can remain oriented once justification no longer precedes action.[29] Her appeal to aspirational rights is neither moral consolation nor a metaphysical guarantee, but a juridical realization of a practice of orientation, a way of marking certain harms as intolerable while acknowledging that such markings are always provisional, contested, and enforced. In this respect, Cornell's project implicitly recovers a Platonic insight without adopting Plato's metaphysics. Law cannot educate, protect, or rehabilitate unless it is able to say, with authority, that some things must not continue. What Cornell brings into view, especially for law, is that orientation already implies refusal and aversion. To say that rights guide judgment is to say that certain injuries must stop, that certain exclusions will be upheld, and that the authority to say 'no' cannot be indefinitely deferred without emptying normativity of force. Her work thus occupies a difficult middle position between Derridean openness and the older juridical demand, already articulated by Plato, that law must cultivate not only love of the good but hatred of injustice if it is to function at all.

As Peter Goodrich has repeatedly emphasized, law does not merely apply norms but performs them through rhetoric, tone, repetition, and exclusion, so that every declaration of right also inscribes a refusal that is managed,

29 Drucilla Cornell, *The Philosophy of the Limit* (New York: Routledge, 1992), 31–58; *Beyond Accommodation: Ethical Feminism, Deconstruction, and the Law* (New York: Routledge, 1999), 59–92, 165–198.

masked, or redescribed as neutrality. What appears from this rhetorical perspective as procedural form or stylistic excess is in fact one of the primary sites where aversion is translated into institutional action without ever being named as such. Costas Douzinas presses this point further by refusing to let it remain at the level of ethical orientation or juridical style. Where Cornell asks how law can sustain commitments to justice without foundations, Douzinas asks how those commitments are forged, contested, and reworked in histories of struggle. For him, human rights and justice arise from antagonism, from conflicts in which something is refused and something else is wrested into visibility.[30] Here Douzinas comes closest to the ancient recognition, already present in Hesiod and sharpened by Plato, that law is born not only from disciplined agreement but from the containment of conflict. Hospitality, recognition, and inclusion are never innocent gestures but sedimented outcomes of legal and political conflict, stabilized through institutions that remember refusals even as they redescribe them as universal norms. What liberal jurisprudence often disavows as resentment or hostility is the affective register through which injustice becomes legible and contestable. Douzinas thus restores to Derrida's legacy what Derrida himself hesitated to name directly. Law's normative force is inseparable from the affective energies of resistance, and that refusal – sometimes experienced as anger, sometimes as hatred – is not a pathological remainder but one of the conditions under which juridical transformation becomes possible.

One does not need to look far for a scene in which law refuses without hatred. Derrida's own formation in colonial Algeria offers a quietly exemplary case. As a Jewish child under French rule, he was first included within the legal order, then excluded by Vichy decree, and later re-included, all without explanation, justification, or acknowledgment. No animus was required for the withdrawal of citizenship, and none was named when it was restored. Law acted through reclassification alone. Recognition was suspended and reinstated as a matter of administrative fact. What occurred was neither persecution nor reconciliation, but a form of exclusion that did not need to announce itself as exclusion. This juridical oscillation is instructive. It shows how refusal can operate most efficiently when it does not appear as refusal at all. Hospitality was not violated, it was never offered. Hatred did not erupt, it was unnecessary. Law withdrew recognition while maintaining its appearance of neutrality. The violence lay not in overt hostility but in the ease with which belonging could be revoked and returned without residue. Read against this background, 'Force of Law' appears less as an

30 Costas Douzinas, *The End of Human Rights* (Oxford: Hart Publishing, 2000); Costas Douzinas and Adam Gearey, *Critical Jurisprudence* (Oxford: Hart Publishing, 2005).

abstract meditation on founding violence than as a theoretical clarification of a lived legal grammar: exclusion without avowal, decision without affect, force without declared enmity. What disappears in such moments is not aversion itself, but the language by which aversion might be owned as judgment rather than absorbed into procedure. Placed here, Derrida's Algerian experience does not function merely as biography. It shows how exclusion can be enacted most powerfully when it is rendered impersonal, procedural, and affectively neutral. This is precisely the form of refusal that later afterlives of 'Force of Law' will confront on a global scale. Once aversion is displaced into administration, the problem is no longer how law justifies violence at its origin, but how it governs populations while insisting on its own ethical restraint. The question becomes how refusal operates when it is no longer avowed as judgment, but redistributed into policy, care, and responsibility.

It is at this point that postcolonial critique enters as a necessary clarification of the stakes. Gayatri Spivak's *Critique of Postcolonial Reason* tracks the consequences of a juridical and ethical language that expands responsibility while systematically foreclosing resistance. What appears as inclusion is often a reconfiguration of domination, and what presents itself as care is frequently a mode of management.[31] The subaltern is not excluded outright, but absorbed into a discourse of ethical solicitude that renders refusal unintelligible.[32] Opposition is converted into responsibility, resistance into testimony, anger into injury. Aversion does not disappear; it is redescribed in terms that deprive it of political force. Undecidability migrates into policy, where decisions are made continuously but without avowed antagonism. Robert Young sharpens this diagnosis by insisting on the colonial genealogy of such arrangements. Returning Derrida to the scene of Algeria, Young shows that colonial hospitality was never separable from appropriation. The offer of inclusion already presupposed possession, and recognition was inseparable from control. The settler's open hand concealed a chain of command, and refusal – when it occurred – could only appear as hostility or ingratitude. In this context, hatred is not a moral excess but a resource of survival.[33] To refuse is not to fail ethically, but to resist incorporation into a system that thrives on neutralizing conflict. What liberal jurisprudence

31 Gayatri Chakravorty Spivak, 'Righting Wrongs' (2004) 103:2–3 *South Atlantic Quarterly* 535–537, esp. the sequence where she distinguishes her sense of responsibility from "duty of the fitter self," then describes supervisory benevolence and the subaltern as "above/below," tokenization, and "written to dictation."

32 Gayatri Chakravorty Spivak, 'Responsibility' (Fall 1994) 21:3 *Boundary* 2: see esp. early pages on "being responsible to the question of responsibility," and the discussion of "setting-to-work" and institutional risk.

33 Robert J. C. Young, *Postcolonialism: An Historical Introduction* (Oxford: Blackwell, 2001), 'Derrida in Algeria', 411–426.

disavows as resentment or hostility thus reappears as the only available form of political clarity.

If the postcolonial turn shows how refusal is absorbed into governance, the final afterlife to be considered concerns how law continues to speak once its grounds have been exposed and its aversions displaced. Here the problem is no longer primarily one of foundation or normativity, but of address, and how authority persists, repeats itself, and demands response in the absence of any secure justification. Avital Ronell does not ask how law can be legitimated after undecidability, nor how justice might be grounded once foundations have been withdrawn. She asks instead how authority sounds when legitimacy can no longer be secured.[34] In her account, authority survives as a voice that continues to call, test, provoke, and insist precisely because it cannot bring itself to rest.[35] What Derrida names as founding violence returns here not as an origin to be confessed or mourned, but as the compulsion of address itself. Law does not strike but it wears down subjects who are summoned again and again, interpellated by demands that cannot fully justify themselves and yet cannot be ignored. Refusal, lacking an authorized place, reappears not as judgment but as fatigue, evasion, irritation, or breakdown. Hatred is neither theorized nor redeemed but displaced into symptom, where it continues to do work without acknowledgment.

Peter Goodrich brings this condition back into the legal scene with particular historical and contemporary sharpness. His jurisprudence treats law not as a system of rules, but as a dense rhetorical field in which images, gestures, tones, and figures do the work that doctrine prefers not to name.[36] Law, on this view, does not merely decide. It senses, sniffs, anticipates contamination, sanitizes, and deodorizes. Its exclusions are legible not only in statutes or judgments, but in obsessions with hygiene, security, efficiency, and risk. These are not metaphors but diagnostics that show how aversion continues to animate legal practice even where it has been officially disavowed as passion or prejudice. The law knows how to say 'no', but the difficulty lies in learning how to acknowledge that knowledge without disguising it as neutrality, professionalism, or role.[37] Ronell and Goodrich

34 Avital Ronell, 'Have I Been Destroyed? Answering to Authority and the Politics of the Father' (2010) 21:1 *Differences: A Journal of Feminist Cultural Studies* 48–62.

35 Avital Ronell, *The Telephone Book: Technology, Schizophrenia, Electric Speech* (Lincoln: University of Nebraska Press, 1989), 'Delay Call Forwarding', esp. 1–10; Avital Ronell, 'Authority', in Barbara Cassin et al., eds., *Political Concepts: A Critical Lexicon* (New York: Fordham University Press, 2011), s.v. "Authority."

36 Peter Goodrich, *Legal Discourse: Studies in Linguistics, Rhetoric, and Legal Analysis* (London: Palgrave Macmillan, 1990).

37 Peter Goodrich, *Oedipus Lex: Psychoanalysis, History, Law* (Berkeley: University of California Press, 1995).

stage the rhetorical and auditory consequences of refusal deferred and allow us to hear what law sounds like when it cannot avow the limits it enforces. What they reveal is not the absence of hatred, but its transformation into verbosity, repetition, and procedural excess. Law continues, but it continues by speaking and speaking, rather than by deciding. What is lost is not force, but the capacity to name force as judgment rather than as mere procedure.

VII. Conclusion. L'à-venir exige un nez

At this point it becomes difficult not to recall how unembarrassed philosophy before Kant was about naming the affective stakes of judgment. In Homer, hatred of deception is inseparable from love of truth and survival among equals. In Hesiod, strife and refusal are not pathologies but the very conditions under which the world, law, and memory can emerge. In Plato, hatred of injustice is not an unfortunate residue to be suppressed, but an educable capacity without which neither virtue nor law can endure. Even the Stoics, so often misread as eliminating affect, relocate hatred rather than erase it, redistributing it into rational practices of assent, refusal, and avoidance. None of these figures imagine that judgment could proceed without affect or that law could be sustained by openness alone. What they assume, without nostalgia or innocence, is that to love the good is already to hate what destroys it. What is lost in the modern displacement of hatred is not merely a vocabulary but a structure of moral orientation. The ethical idiom that emerges in the wake of Derrida often speaks as if love could be purified of hatred, as if openness could be sustained without aversion, and as if responsibility could remain elevated so long as it avoids naming the affects that make judgment possible. The question that now presses is not whether we can refuse injustice, but whether we can acknowledge – without nostalgia or brutality – that some things rightly provoke hatred, just as others rightly call forth love.

This chapter has offered some glimpses of what it means to live on with Derrida's questions of whether law's force can be thought without innocence, while aversion and hatred, left unowned, continue to govern elsewhere. Derrida becomes spectral here because those who follow him must supply what his ethics of openness could only gesture toward: body, risk, history, and the disciplined power to refuse. The task that emerges, however, is not to expunge or to disguise hatred, but to refine it. To love indiscriminately is to collapse into sentiment, while to hate discriminately is to think. *Nomos* was once a fence, not its absence. Hospitality without the painful power to say 'no' is not ethical purity but another, quieter form of domination. Law knows this already in practice. Its difficulty lies in learning how to say it without disavowal.

What has been traced here is not an account of Derrida's influence in general, nor a verdict on the trajectory of deconstruction in law, but a way of reading how one persistent difficulty has been taken up, displaced, and made livable across its afterlives. This persistence would hardly have surprised Derrida himself, who is reported to have said that one of the two things he hated more than anything was complacency.[38] Following the thread of refusal and aversion is not meant to elevate it as the key to engaging Derrida's work, of course, but to stay with a problem that 'Force of Law' exposes without resolving – a problem that returns whenever law must decide, exclude, and coerce while still laying claim to justice, when, in other words, olfaction must precede benefaction. As deconstruction continues to diagnose the aporias of the force of law, it should not forget to smell out the deodorization of force and law, and the efforts to render aversion anosmic by redescribing it as neutrality, role, or duty. My *nasorumque narium vis* alerted me to the possibility that I might hate, not without some justification, though perhaps without legal permission, the smells in the subway. Do genocide, racism, sexism, mindless indifference to suffering, injustice, or cruelty smell any better, and does the hatred of them have no place in a full deconstruction of justice? Should deconstruction no longer indulge itself in keeping a secret that should not be kept?[39]

38 The other being "vulgarity". Benoît Peeters, *Derrida: A Biography*, trans. by Andrew Brown (Cambridge: Polity, 2013), 418.

39 I would be remiss if I did not thank all the deconstructionists who through the years have indulgently welcomed this gerund grinding philologist into their fold, beginning foremost with my teacher, then colleague and friend, Pietro Pucci, who introduced deconstruction to the field of Classics after hearing Derrida's famous intervention at Johns Hopkins – and also the cohort at Cornell in the heady '70s, including Jonathan Culler, Neil Hertz, Cynthia Chase, David Grossvogel – and, of course, Derrida himself. Now some fifty years later, I am immensely grateful to the editors of this volume, Peter Goodrich and Avital Ronell, along with Robert Young who have endlessly iterated that earlier welcome. To Gayatri Spivak I owe a series of searching questions about Saussure and to Nick Pappas a veritable *potami* of ideas and references.

5
JUSTICE WITHOUT FORCE

Hent de Vries

In preparing my remarks for the Cardozo Law School conference in April 2024, commemorating Jacques Derrida's conception of law, as well as in finalizing the present chapter, I could not help but recall a personal story, which I will relate here in all brevity. A few years after the epochal Cardozo Law School symposium held in October 1989 under the heading *Deconstruction and the Possibility of Justice,* I had an unexpected phone conversation with Derrida related to the keynote address he had presented there. I had fond and profound memories of this first academic event I ever attended in the United States, as I had only just two months before arrived from overseas at Johns Hopkins University, Baltimore. I did not present at the conference in New York, where Derrida read the first half of his suggestive 'Force of Law: The Mystical Foundation of Authority,' but I listened and learned, and got a rough sense of the stakes of the technical debates as well as of the wider intellectual, moral, and political landscape in which his thoughts intervened at the time.

Ever since that formative moment, questions of religion and law, self-determination and violence, all of them centered around the early problematic of "the theologico-political" as well as around the emerging debates regarding "the secular" or "the postsecular" in contemporary modernity, have been firmly on my mind. Indeed, these at the time highly topical concerns (and one wonders what has changed in the meantime) also allowed me to revisit much earlier interests, which I had pursued during my studies in the Faculty of Law, devoted to public finance and social democracy. I had pursued these inquiries during a break from my more formal "theological" studies at my alma mater, Leiden University, in the Netherlands, where my main focus until then had been on the philosophy of religion and on

DOI: 10.4324/9781003589419-7

Hellenistic Judaism. Little did I know that these seemingly diverging topics overlapped in more than one way and, indeed, converged in the overarching question of the meaning and force of justice and law, of their very idea and also practice. In retrospect, these interrelated fields and their guiding questions have continued to guide me in my ongoing efforts to educate myself further in a recent series of advanced seminars on religion and law at NYU, in direct as well as indirect conversations with the substantial work done by some of my distinguished colleagues there.[1]

Unbeknownst to me, Derrida had been given my telephone number by Werner Hamacher, my inimitable and much-regretted host, responsible for bringing me to the German Department at Johns Hopkins as a postdoctoral affiliate, in 1989. In Baltimore, we had talked about an essay I had just completed and that would eventually be published in the German issue of Johns Hopkins's journal *Modern Language Notes*, in the Spring of 1992, entitled 'Anti-Babel: The "Mystical Postulate" in Benjamin, de Certeau, and Derrida.' In a greatly revised and expanded form, this essay would eventually become a central chapter of my *Religion and Violence: Philosophical Reflections from Kant to Derrida*, published ten years later.[2] Werner had, again without my knowledge and to no small consternation on my part when I finally learned this, passed on this early article to Derrida, who, having read it, promptly called me. With the infinite generosity so many of us, even if often undeservedly, have experienced over the years, Derrida kindly responded to the basic thrust of my reading and gave me all the necessary encouragement to further pursue my inquiries into his work, which I had begun in my dissertation and which were further inspired and informed by a 1989 seminar he offered in Paris, and several seminars he directed at Johns Hopkins, all of which left their traces in my own subsequent work.[3]

1 See notably my '*Invocatio Dei*, la discipline de la tolérance, et la vérité de la vérité. J.H.H. Weiler et la Constitution de l'Europe,' special issue on 'Les religions et la question de la vérité', Yves Charles Zarka and Philippe Capelle, ed., *Revue Cités* No. 62, 2015, 27–61.

2 See my 'Anti-Babel: The "Mystical Postulate' in Benjamin, de Certeau and Derrida' (1992) 107 *Modern Language Notes* 441–477, and *Religion and Violence: Philosophical Reflections from Kant to Derrida* (Baltimore and London: Johns Hopkins University Press, 2002, 2006), translated by Marlène Jouan, with a new preface as *Religion et violence: Perspectives philosophiques de Kant à Derrida* (Paris: Éditions du Cerf, 2013). The chapter also appeared in Hebrew translation as *Dat Ve'Alimout: Derrida Ve'ha Teologi Politi*, trans. Guri Arad and Michal Ben-Naftali (Tel Aviv: Resling Publishers, 2012).

3 See notably my *Minimal Theologies: Critiques of Secular Reason in Theodor W. Adorno and Emmanuel Levinas*, trans. by Geoffrey Hale (Baltimore and London: The Johns Hopkins University Press, 2005), the expanded and completely revised edition of my dissertation *Theologie im pianissimo. Zwischen Rationalität und Dekonstruktion* (Kampen: J. H. Kok; Leuven: Peeters Publishers, 1989), and *Philosophy and the Turn to Religion* (Baltimore and London: The Johns Hopkins University Press, 1999, 2000).

What I had claimed in the aforementioned essay, albeit not without hesitation and trepidation, as this was my first tentative effort to revisit 'Force of Law,' since having attended the original Cardozo symposium, was that Derrida's overall argument in his keynote lecture, delivered on that occasion, *obliquely* drew on very similar thoughts formulated many years earlier by Michel de Certeau in the first volume of his *La Fable mystique* (*The Mystic Fable*). This remarkable parallel, albeit lodged in an *indirect* reference, was one that, in all fairness, might have been only apparent to whoever had also read Derrida's moving written homage to de Certeau himself (as I happened to just have done for reasons completely unrelated to understanding 'Force of Law'). Derrida's homage took the form of an in memoriam, entitled '*Nombres de oui* [A Number of Yes],' and was republished in the volume (or, in its English translation, the first tome of) *Psyché*.[4]

Derrida did not disagree with my conjecture in his friendly phone call, which happened when I had returned to teaching in Europe, this time at the University of Amsterdam, but during the academic quarter when I was visiting at the Institute for the Advanced Study of Religion at Chicago's Divinity School in the late spring of 1993, where he reached me in my office. Indeed, de Certeau's work was, I realized even more so after that conversation, a crucially important – if not uniquely determining – inspirational source and discursive repository for the very motif of a presumed "mystical foundation of authority," itself central to the rigorous argument of 'Force of Law.' There was no doubt on my mind that the invocation of the mystical gave this text far greater depth and breadth than could be found in, say, Derrida's 1984 '*Déclarations d'indépendance* [Declarations of Independence].' And, as I rightly suspected at the time, the motif in question was indicative of a *deeply pragmatic* register in Derrida's oeuvre, of which so much was still to come in the years that followed. As it would turn out, these later writings, roundtables, and lectures would address the modern post-Hegelian constellation and reconfiguration of "faith and knowledge," as they presented themselves in ever newer forms of religion and technological media, all of which placed the traditions and legacies of so-called positive and negative or apophatic theologies in a dramatically, often spectacularly, novel light, anticipated by only a few (Henri Bergson being a case in point).[5]

4 Jacques Derrida, *Psyché. Inventions de l'autre* (Paris: Galilée, 1987), 639-650; *Psyche: Inventions of the Other*, Volume II, ed. by Peggy Kamuf and Elisabeth Rottenberg (Stanford: Stanford University Press, 2008), 231-240.

5 See my 'Les deux sources de la 'machine théologique: Une note sur Derrida et Bergson', in *Cahiers de l'Herne* (Paris, 2004), 255–260; 'The Two Sources of the "Theological Machine": Jacques Derrida and Henri Bergson on Religion, Technicity, War, and Terror', in Creston Davis, John Milbank, and Slavoj Žižek, eds., *Theology and the Political* (Durham: Duke University Press, 2005), 366–389.

Following J.L. Austin's *How to Do Things with Words* and drawing on examples from law and jurisprudence, de Certeau had characterized 16th and 17th century "mystic speech" in Western Europe, notably France and Flanders, in terms of what one might call an *absolute performative*. By this he meant a *modus loquendi* and *modus agendi*, which circumvented the stale alternative of *either* adopting *or* heretically criticizing theological theses or doctrines, dogmas and rituals. Instead, de Certeau argued, "mystics" inhabited and lived their presumed opposed theoretical theses and existential dispositions altogether differently, taking them *spiritually* or, as we might now say, counter-factually and virtually, as the *occasion* required. Avoiding the "constative fallacy" whose pitfalls Austin had sharply diagnosed, the mere hypothesis and postulation of epistemic premises and statements of any given discourse (whether religious, ecclesial, legal or other) – accompanied as they tended to be by their normative imposition or their potential and no less categorial negation and denial (i.e., *dénégation*) once they seemed firmly established – was shown by de Certeau to *first of all* require and *subsequently* rely on some form of *positing*. The latter's *Setzung* or *Satz*, followed by its all too often ill-fated *positivity*, based as this latter was on the logical and ontological predicament of all predication (discursive and other), was thus shown to inevitably end up in a *performative contradiction* of sorts. Among the most telling was, perhaps, Derrida's own early example that "*Dieu déjà se contredit* [God already contradicts Himself]."[6] But, of course, the insight that all theological statements have to circumnavigate the standing risks of conceptual idolatry or, more broadly, of heterodoxy and heresy or blasphemy, such that, strictly speaking, only God could have a theology of God (as the dialectical theologian Karl Barth once mused), dates back to the beginnings of Biblical theology and has haunted the so-called Abrahamic religions of the Book no less and no more than it did others.

In the longest footnote of his 1987 *De l'esprit: Heidegger et la question* (*Of Spirit: Heidegger and the Question*), Derrida had characterized the absolute performative in terms of an "originary affirmation." As he observed, the latter – as a "mystical postulate," we might say, in its own right – precedes, accompanies, and further eludes the traditional distinction between so-called kataphatic and apophatic, positive and negative statements of a purely descriptive-constative nature (each of them caught in the very "fallacy" Austin decried with regard to both their mention and use). In addition, Derrida intimated, this "originary affirmation" was one *without fixity or firmity* (*fermeté*) and, hence, must be rendered in "*perverformative*" terms. Independently, Werner Hamacher, in a

6 For a discussion, see my 'On Inexistence, Divine and Other', in Tarek R. Dika and Martin Shuster, eds., *Religion in Reason: Metaphysics, Ethics, and Politics in Hent de Vries* (London and New York: Routledge Publishers, 2022), 270–374.

1989 lecture and essay, entitled '*Afformative, Strike*,' likewise presented at the Cardozo Law School conference devoted to *Deconstruction and the Possibility of Justice*, would come to define a related motif in Walter Benjamin's essay '*Zur Kritik der Gewalt*' ('Toward the Critique of Violence') with a neologism, namely as an "afformative." Like 'Force of Law,' Hamacher's essay teased out the finesse of Benjamin's Marxian-cum-messianic thought. Benjamin, he noted, had seemingly deliberately harped on Georges Sorel's 1908 *Réflexions sur la violence* (*Reflections on Violence*), while remaining at a certain remove from this theorist's own concept and practice of a revolutionary syndicalism with its culminating moment of the "general strike" (as he would also steer clear from Sorel's eventual veering off into fascist registers, with their emphasis on the need for social myths and their dismissal of parliamentary democracy).

***

With the motif of the "originary affirmation" and "mystical postulate of authority" in hand, institutional and pragmatic arrangements of whatever nature are exposed by Derrida's aforementioned writings as hanging over an unavoidable and ultimately inescapable abyss, one that inaugurates, but also potentially questions and dismantles, their established histories, while remaining fundamentally unintelligible and, indeed, extralegal on these institutional legacies' contingent critical and juridical terms. Instead, a chasm, it seems, *opens up beneath* as well as *hovers over and beside them* as an at once *promising* and *threatening* suspension of causes and reasons or rules. And while these critical terms and their organizing concepts, at least in the history of Western thought, had long enabled the explanation, interpretation, and justification of ancient, modern, as well as contemporary phenomena of the greatest possible variety, awareness of the abysmal chasm revealing itself beneath, around, and beyond them does not, on Derrida's account, imply or require the no less fateful cessation of epistemic and normative forms of assessment and judgment per se. Its suspension of belief in the very world as we find it does not so much paralyze our thinking and acting but rather brackets the *naturalistic* rendition, justification, and interpretation of both. Derrida's finer point and overall argument, therefore, are *phenomenological* – and, in this sense, Husserlian, Heideggerian, and Levinasian – through and through.

Suggesting a near-Pascalian sense of *depth* and *expanse* of at once infinitely *small* and infinitely *vast* spaces that inhabit and surround us, thus making room for the *virtual* archives and repositories of limitless possibilities and impossibilities, the "mystical postulate" reigns supreme and, hence, has both the first and last word. That we can look at and engage things and situations from the angle of what, in terms of whatever "exists," must be considered as *inexistent*, strictly speaking, allows us to do so as if for the first and for the last time. But doing so also implies that we cannot thereby invest ultimate importance in what we say and do (or, alternatively, refrain from saying and doing).

But then again, to state as much should not delude us. The "mystical postulate's" logic or operation is not that of a quasi-theoretical proposition that could be deemed either true or false, at least not on the basis of criteria that have been established *post hoc*, after the fact, and that, hence, do not hold sway over it in any determined, much less decisive, way. This said, the alternatively – at times, simultaneously – emerging possibilities and impossibilities that resurge from the absolute, immemorial past are *coextensive* with, if often unobserved and unrealized in, the present we live in.[7] And to the extent that they do not announce and materialize themselves here and now, they remain a wild card in the principally unknowable future, all of whose further occasions for thought and for agency will, likewise, prove to be as many potential springboards for both the best and the worst (with much else in between).

Stepping-stones and potential stumbling blocks alike, these occasions – *quasi-miraculously*, without any necessary, sufficient or otherwise determining cause – make themselves nonetheless known. They manifest or, in the religious idiom, *reveal* themselves not only *for all eyes to see* but also allow and invite us to *set all things aright.* At the very minimum, they do so for all those who are willing and able to pay minute and sustained attention. And this means: for those who follow up and follow through, and only thereby *call these virtual opportunities into being*, more precisely, out of *inexistence* into some form of worthwhile, indeed, worthy existence as it were. This, and nothing else, is their *apocalyptic* modality, whose moment and momentum are what make histories tick and, at times, epochal. When and where this happens, it does so in the verificatory, authenticating or pragmatic process of truth-making, without which such occasions and their callings may well sink into oblivion forever. And this, unmistakable as their announcement might further have seemed to be to some (and was surely also "in fact," as a "fact of

7 One might say that any iteration of past possibilities inscribes change in the repetition, the "non-synonymous substitution" of which Derrida speaks, thus precluding the age-old and Nietzschean assumption of an "eternal recurrence" or "repetition of same." But then again, if with every occasion or possibility absolutely everything is possible in principle if not thereby in fact – according to the stringent "logic" of the *tout autre est tout autre* (here: every next, that is, other possibility is "every bit other"), then not even the possibility of the self-same repeating itself all over again, reminiscent of the early Christian doctrine of the *apokatastasis ton pantoon* or *restitutio in integrum* (cited by Benjamin) can be dismissed out of hand. This motif of redemption, of everyone and all things, ultimately rejected by the Church as it condemned Origen of Alexandria, must be regarded as revealing a standing – if, paradoxically, also perennially contestable – possibility, come to think of it. Cf. Michael Jennings, 'The Will to Apokatastasis: Media, Experience, and Eschatology in Walter Benjamin's Late Theological Politics', in Colby Dickinson and Stéphane Symons, eds., *Walter Benjamin and Theology* (New York: Fordham University Press, 2016), 93–109.

reason" or "total social fact," as Kant and Marcel Mauss respectively said), will always and everywhere remain a standing risk. The occasions in question are fleeting instants, nothing more. This said, where and whenever they are recognized for which they truly might be or yet become, they can be turned into instances of total transformation that are nothing short of revolutionary.

Derrida never failed to note that any such (quite literally) existential call or calling forth, from inexistence into existence – and, *a fortiori*, any further calling from mere existence into the verification and justification that its *perfectibility* requires in turn at ever deeper and wider levels – is worthy of its name *if and only if*, in retrospect, it *might* very well *not* have resounded, had remained *unheard* or *unseen* and *not* quite lived up to. By the same token, regarding the future, it also inheres in the very essence or structure of the eventual (or, in the Heideggerian jargon, evental) "to come [*à venir*]" that *nothing* or *nothing much* may ever arrive, there and then. The future event in question may well turn out to be that nothing happens in fact. The future may well reveal that there was no future at all. The future, then, is an absolute contingency, a *creatio ex nihilo*, a *creatio continua*. One might call it a *standing miracle*, thus acknowledging that its presumed fatefulness (or, as Derrida reminds us, *Ananke* [Ἀνάγκη]) remains a matter of chance (*la Chance*), just as historical determination must fundamentally and ultimately be considered a mere appearance (a *Schein*, as thinkers from Immanuel Kant, Karl Marx and Theodor W. Adorno would wisely insist throughout).

With this in mind, the parallels between de Certeau and Derrida regarding the putative necessity of assuming a "mystical postulate" and "originary affirmation," respectively, are striking. In my view, they continue to offer an important interpretive key to our contemporary understanding of the *theologico*-political – and, hence, not merely national-philosophical – foundations and infatuations with both State and legal authority. They do so in far more *systematic* and *revealing* ways than they have, thus far, been given credit for.[8] Well

8 A further point I had earlier taken away from Derrida's incisive reading in 'Force of Law' was his, in my eyes, justified worry about Benjamin's invocation of and apparent fascination with a presumably "bloodless" divine violence. For this expressed concern, Derrida would be taken to task by several Benjamin scholars. And, while the jury is still out on this matter, I continue to feel that Derrida was right to intimate (perhaps unwittingly echoing what Stanley Cavell had once remarked of the reception of Ludwig Wittgenstein's later work) that, surely, it was "possible that Benjamin was wrong about some things." Anyway, why Derrida's unease with this part of Benjamin's *Toward a Critique of Violence* was not only textually grounded but, moreover, fully consistent with his own wider views on religion and violence could, I felt at the time and to this day, certainly be demonstrated in all necessary detail. In fact, as I argued in *Religion and Violence*, the worry expressed regarding Benjamin extended to Levinas's and, as he would himself leave no doubt, Derrida's own writings as well. The underlying argument is as simple as it is daunting. If the conditions of possibility of the best and worst (and much else in between) are fundamentally "the same," then at no point we are free of – or morally and politically immune to – violence in both the historical or

beyond the invocation of a divinely ordained or natural law and sidelining the modern preoccupation with the murky waters of blood and soil as in juridical doctrines defining forms of national belonging rooted in *ius sanguinis* or *ius soli* – and even independent of our current tempered hopes that the rulings of international courts of law and human rights will carry the day at long last – the quasi-transcendental and seemingly theological motifs and moments, modalities, and at times moods that inform Derrida's preoccupations with "law" remain of "*relevance*." But, in what sense exactly?

While Derrida steers clear from an all too assertive "apocalyptic tone" in modern philosophy, in sync in this with Kant,[9] these (for lack of a better terminology) *theologico-political* considerations continue to shed light on the cluster of problems that organize his concept of constitutional, international humanitarian law, and of jurisprudence, where his references stretch from G.W.F. Hegel to Carl Schmitt to Nelson Mandela, and from the early twentieth-century preoccupation with non-state actors "in a time of terror" to the ever-expanding phenomenon of "rogue" and "failed" states, immigration and the laws of hospitality, cities of refuge, and rights to literature. With this preoccupation in mind, one can only imagine the level of dismay and despair Derrida would have overwhelmingly felt and, no doubt, lucidly voiced at the dismal state of our present world. And, as Victor Hugo quipped, Derrida recalled in a series of interviews, "what tomorrow will be, no one knows."[10]

* * *

Deconstruction and the Possibility of Justice was a surprising, ambiguous title as it intimated that there was a somewhat problematic, in any case, *non-necessary* or *less than self-evident* relationship between deconstruction, its ethics and politics or concept of justice, on the one hand, and the founding and constitution as well as preservation of law, whether in a nation, state, republic or federation, each of these requiring the interpretation and application in its jurisprudence or so-called rule of law, on the other. Put differently, so the conference's title implicitly asked, it seemed: did deconstruction truly hold its own in the legal considerations and deliberations so clearly at stake not only in a nation's court of law,

empirical, not to mention transcendental or metaphysical, senses of this worrisome concept and its incalculable practices. It is this intrinsic complicity, which Kierkegaard, speaking of *horror religious* in *Fear and Trembling*, expressed succinctly (see my *Religion and Violence*, 123–209), that should give us pause in our thoughts, acts and judgments, legal and other.

9 See my *Philosophy and the Turn to Religion*, 359 ff.

10 Jacques Derrida and Elisabeth Roudinesco, *De quoi demain . . . Dialogue* (Paris: Fayard, Galilée, 2001); *For What Tomorrow . . .: A Dialogue*, trans. by Jeff Fort (Stanford: Stanford University Press, 2004).

but also in matters of international law, where state and non-state actors tended to go either "rogue" or wallow in merely "vacuous" moralistic declarations?[11]

But this was not all. The Cardozo conference's title further seemed to allow for the contrary "possibility" that deconstruction was, perhaps, unique in that it was especially well-placed to spell out and justify at least the *quasi-* or *simili-*transcendental, if not thereby also the historical or empirical, conditions, not merely of distributive justice (seen in terms of, say, Rawlsian "fairness"), but of an infinite, if not thereby *de facto*, much less *de iure*, divine justice to boot. And to do so, it was suggested, required radically and resolutely breaking away not only from constitutional "originalism," but from legal "positivism," "realism," "pragmatism" or even any conception of the so-called "common good," which would ultimately be based on either natural law or theocratic premises.

This much, at least, seemed abundantly clear at the time. Deconstruction, as Derrida presented it, did not render justice downright impossible or unlikely; nor, for that matter, could deconstruction ever be conceived, practiced, let alone instituted, as *the only possible* or *justifiable* path towards the perfection or, rather, perfectibility associated with the principal "infinity," inscribed in its very concept – an assumption Derrida inherited from Levinas and which governs 'Force of Law's' crucial distinction between existing, established or adjudicated law [*le droit*] and aspirational, if unfounded, justice [*la justice*] from beginning to end. What good, then, might deconstruction contribute to our understanding and – as theory and praxis go hand in hand here – litigating and settling legal disputes, both old and new?

Derrida's numerous accounts of our being "before the law [*devant la loi*]" remind us in the clearest possible terms that there ought – and, in the long run, perhaps, could – be no force, in any case, no legitimate authority, without justice (emphatically, that is, not merely procedurally understood). A presumed *status naturalis* in which *homo homini lupus* or in which there is a principal war of all against all could not be sustained in the end (i.e., all by itself, even in terms of its own ends). For the same reason, a purported *status civilis* could not come into existence, much less be sustained, were it not for an *idea of justice* – and, hence, the *force of just law* – that founds and maintains its very legitimacy and order of things. While the first, feared, imagined or postulated state (i.e., of mere force without any justice) may well be the nightmare from which humanity has sought to gradually wake up since its earliest beginnings and, indeed, is its *de facto* default, alas, the second (i.e., of a

11 For an excellent discussion, see Alexandre Lefebvre, *The Image of Law: Deleuze, Bergson, Spinoza* (Stanford: Stanford University Press, 2008).

powerless idea of justice without real force) is the downright nihilistic, cynical, and hypocritical station we are presently at.

***

Ever since a US president, for the first time in history, was, just a few blocks from Cardozo Law School, put on trial – one of many still to come, one had every reason to believe and trust at the time, even though claims of presidential, executive immunity had already been summarily granted by a Supreme Court ruling mostly in his favor – it has been hard to suppress a mounting sense of bafflement and despair, followed by indignation and rage.[12] As a layperson, one could certainly be forgiven to wonder aloud why, if Donald J. Trump, indicted with an ever-growing mountain of actionable evidence (according to several grand juries, across the nation), was constantly let off the hook, anyone else in this country, often on the basis of lower types of misdemeanors and felonies, that is, far lesser crimes, could so easily end up in prison at all. And prisons, now often run and exploited by private, profit-based companies, are in the US nationwide full to the rafters, mostly filled with average, working-class people, people of color, and members of immigrant populations, who were often all too quickly and summarily convicted for what, on closer scrutiny, would readily reveal themselves to be, in fact, much smaller legal offenses.

Further, one could rightfully go on to ask why there were apparently so many ways to endlessly delay a former (or even current) president's day in court to face a potential conviction and eventual consequences that no one else could surely avoid when held to the very same legal standards (as the law, constitutional scholars and criminal lawyers agree, would surely require).

All in all, then, at least to the untrained eye, there was no other conclusion possible: ultimately, *might dictated right*, in this case, in this country at this point, and fear and cowardliness, if not the counterintuitive possibilities of appeal after appeal (for those who could afford it) did the rest. Clearly, "some animals" were "more equal than others," as George Orwell, an avid student of authoritarianism, well knew. A cult of personality that put even Stalinism

12 Lest we forget, these trials had been preceded, if not prepared, by congressional investigations, as documented in *The Mueller Report*, presented with related materials by *The Washington Post*, Introduction and Analysis by reporters Rosalind S. Helderman and Matt Zapotosky (New York and Toronto: Scribner, 2019); they were accompanied by a host of other criminal indictments, as summarized in *The Trump Indictments: The Historic Charging Documents with Commentary*, Introduced, annotated, and with supporting materials by Melissa Murray and Andrew Weissmann (New York: W.W. Norton & Company, 2024); and then there was the scathing final report by Special Prosecutor Jack Smith (https://www.justice.gov/storage/Report-of-Special-Counsel-Smith-Volume-1-January-2025.pdf, accessed March 30th, 2025).

to shame, it seems, ruled the day. To make matters worse, the present-day rule of law, at the very least in Trump's case – and in that of those whom he pardoned or whose ongoing investigations by the Justice Department he quickly shut down, on the sole basis of their demonstrated loyalty and political as well as financial interest to "the don" (as the conservative *Drudge Report* continues to call him) – effectively proved the existence and ruthless deliverance of *class justice* all over again. Justice lacked force – the force of the better argument, it seems, and that of enforcement – and, hence, was not "served."

It needs little additional proof that international law and its rule fared hardly better. Why even countries that signed the treaty establishing the International Criminal Court (ICC) – not the USA and not Israel, but, among others, most of the states that make up the European Union – would so much as even consider hesitating to fulfill their legal obligation and detain those against whom international arrest warrants for suspected war crimes and crimes against humanity had been issued,[13] is truly dumbfounding and explains that "something's rotten" (echoing Shakespeare's *Hamlet*, Act I, Scene 4) in the state of the world overall. And yet, it should have been clear all along that there's no justice but justice *done*; indeed, the latter primarily is "what makes law," this, nothing else, is its "normative force."[14]

***

With the benefit of hindsight and without the current predicament firmly in sight, Derrida's prevailing and remaining theorem, therefore, may well have been precisely this: the *apparent* strength and *false* legitimacy of force and violence, throughout most of human history, is just *what there is*. It is nothing short of a law of *blind nature* that the weak suffer, the less privileged vanquished, and the invisible remain unseen and unspoken for. This, all by itself, should render *naturalisms of all stripes* ethically and politically suspect *at a minimum*. Morally and legally speaking, no "is" yields an "ought," that is, no normative and justified "must" of whatever sort follows immediately, much less necessarily, from any historically or empirically given – hence, absolutely contingent, be it positive or negative – state of affairs. Nor are the affairs of state ever a legal, much less moral or political, justification by themselves.

13 Cf. https://www.politico.eu/article/israel-pm-benjamin-netanyahu-hungary-icc-arrest-warrant/ (accessed, March 30, 2025); https://www.reuters.com/world/dutch-see-options-netanyahu-visit-despite-icc-arrest-warrant-2024-11-29/ (accessed, March 30, 2025); https://www.euronews.com/my-europe/2024/12/03/fact-check-where-do-eu-countries-stand-on-iccs-arrest-warrant-for-netanyahu (accessed, March 30, 2025).

14 Liam Murphy, *What Makes Law: An Introduction to the Philosophy of Law* (New York: Cambridge University Press, 2014). See especially the chapters on 'The Normative Force of Law' and 'What Makes Law? Law beyond the State,' 109–182.

Conversely and paradoxically, justice *without* strength or some other force would be neither *equal for all* – that is, infinite through and through, up and down, left and right, addressing and redressing not only the present, but past and future alike – nor so much as even rooted in the procedural *fairness* of due process and diligence (protected by the proverbial "long arm of the law"). In Derrida's somewhat technical formulation of the problem: "Applicability, 'enforceability,' is not an exterior or secondary possibility that may or may not be added as supplement to law. It is the force essentially implied in the very concept of *justice as law* (*droit*)."[15]

As a consequence, if the prevailing force in "force of law" comes down to mere or brute force – meaning uninformed and no longer guided by critical normative considerations or even constraints – then a Republic, beginning with its Declaration of Independence, Constitution and Bill of Rights, is, not to put too fine a point on it, *simply no more*. Its written, spoken and even unwritten law will be a fig leaf at most. The language of law, even when and where invoked, will be a purely nominal affair, a *flatus vocis* with no *fundamentum in re*. The law thus served and will serve the hegemonic economic and ideological interests of the neo-feudal capitalist *nomenklatura* alone. And while this term originally referred to state-socialist bureaucratic elites in the former Soviet-dominated Eastern European bloc during the period of the Cold War, the oligarchic one percent of our time expects and behaves no differently.

To think of and administer justice, then, requires that one "enforce the law" by insisting on its rightful "applicability" in its very concept and practice. As Derrida reminds us, "Law is always an authorized force, a force that justifies itself or is justified in applying itself, even if this justification may be judged from elsewhere to be unjust or unjustifiable." As the latter will often or strictly speaking even always be the case, this basic and guiding principle confirms each and every law's essential *imperfection* and no less essential – that is, at once logically implied and normatively necessary – *perfectibility*. It belongs to the very concept, founding and maintaining of law that it is nowhere *set in stone*. There is, as Montesquieu knew, a *spirit of laws* (*esprit des lois*), which is precisely why the latter are not self-grounding, self-explanatory or self-executing, but require a quasi-, rather than merely extra-, para- and post-legal performative act – indeed, an enacting force and interpretive violence – each step of the way. It is this act, then, that, as it were, *makes up* the lawful process as it goes (and as far as it goes). Seen from the perspective of law and jurisprudence, this act itself comes *out of nowhere*, *from elsewhere*, as, phenomenologically speaking,

15 Jacques Derrida, 'Force de loi: Le "Fondement mystique de l'authorité"'/'Force of Law: The "Mystical Foundation of Authority"' (July/August 1990) 11:5–6 *Cardozo Law Review* 920–1045, 925.

echoing Jean-Luc Marion, any genuine "revelation" must do. To state as much, nothing else, *is* the "mystical postulate" of all genuine "authority" (legal and other). And this fundamental insight extends to all institutions, including to those that establish and guarantee the "right to philosophize [*droit à la philosophie*]," to allude to yet another important title of Derrida's that is relevant to his thoughts on law.

As a consequence, *legal perfectionism*, used here in analogy with *moral perfectionism*, using the term often identified with the school of thought called American Transcendentalism and adopted by Stanley Cavell in exemplary fashion for modern epistemological, axiological and aesthetic purposes in conversation with ordinary language philosophy, inspired by the later Wittgenstein and J.L. Austin, may well provide one of the more plausible ways of receiving and further developing Derrida's central intuitions in this matter. Speaking of *deep pragmatism*, as I have suggested elsewhere,[16] thus giving further philosophical backup to Derrida's own conception of "pragrammatology," may yet be another. Both designations – legal perfectionism and deep pragmatism – I would now claim, honor the overarching, if negative, metaphysical insights into the ineradicable nature (if one can still say so) of "skepticism" and as Cavell says, its "truth". Yet they also steer clear of entertaining "unnatural doubts,"[17] especially where normative questions – and those concerns involve regulative or policy-driven matters – are what need debating and pursuing. In such cases, "our word," uttered indirectly and inadvertently or explicitly and deliberately, will be "our bond."[18] Before and beyond any further moral or legal considerations, the unacknowledged or, ideally, acknowledged act in question will be the deed we need to make good upon.

There is, Derrida writes, "no such thing as law (*droit*) that doesn't imply *in itself, a priori, in the analytic structure of its concept*, the possibility of being 'enforced,' applied by force."[19] Indeed, he adds, it is of secondary relevance "whether this force be direct or indirect, physical or symbolic, exterior or interior, brutal or subtly discursive and hermeneutic, coercive or regulative, and so forth."[20] Just the same, the notion and conscious assumption of infinite – and, in this precise structural sense, perhaps, divine – justice (again, "the mystical postulate of authority," as Derrida, echoing

16 See my 'Introduction: Why Still "Religion"?', in Hent de Vries, ed., *Religion – Beyond A Concept* (New York: Fordham University Press, 2008), 1–98.

17 Cf. Michael Williams, *Unnatural Doubts: Epistemological Realism and the Basis of Scepticism* (Princeton: Princeton University Press, 1995).

18 See my 'Must We (NOT) Mean What We Say? Seriousness and Sincerity in the Work of J.L. Austin and Stanley Cavell', in Ernst van Alphen, Mieke Bal, and Carel Smits, eds., *The Rhetoric of Sincerity* (Stanford: Stanford University Press, 2009), 90–118.

19 Derrida, 'Force de loi/Force of Law', 925.

20 Ibid., 926.

Montaigne, Pascal and de Certeau, says in 'Force of Law') holds down-to-earth, at first founded, but then also established and legally upheld principles that together form the very forms and rule of law, *critically in check*. It does so, not by introducing a meta-critical, mega- or master-criterion – in Derrida's terms, a "transcendental signified" – that would put an end to the chain of signifiers, once and for all, but recalling the place and role of an "empty" (i.e., rigorously and resolutely, negative metaphysical or, indeed, dialectical) function instead. The latter instance, "always pending [*toujours en instance*]," as Derrida, with reference to Maurice Blanchot, wisely recalls, reveals that law in whatever capacity is never quite final, let alone just, even if fair. If we're all equal "before the law," the law, no matter its doctrinal, divine, natural or positive concept, cannot all by itself, by its own force, account, much less stand in, for that very fact. Faced with and compared to this "fact of reason" or "total social fact," to parody Kant and Marcel Mauss here in one breadth, the law comes *too late*, remains *too distant* and fulfills *too little*. If the law thus reveals itself to be absolutely contingent, if not created, then at least postulated on the basis of, well, nothing (i.e., nothing historically or empirically determinate, preconceived or preordained), then *its* power is nowhere absolute. If it is, at most, delegated (called for and calling out by no one in particular, by *Niemand*, as Heidegger says of "call of conscience"), then it stands to reason to insist on its *fallibility* and *perfectibility*, first and foremost. It would be a bloody mistake, then, to pretend that some "bloodless divine violence" or, for that matter, any "general strike," might *all by itself* be able to overcome the law's structural incompleteness and, thereby, its *systemic injustice*, its essential inability to just get things right, without further ado.

If that sounds and feels like adopting an all too nihilistic proposition (based indeed on a *nihil*, we found), then it is worth remembering that, as Adorno said, in awe of Samuel Beckett, every attempted overcoming of nihilism tends to be infinitely worse than the compromised state it seeks to put halt on or end to. The "good conscience," here and elsewhere, should be the "bad" one, while any form of self-righteousness, whether of complacency or complicity, should remain *anathema*.

***

With these and related insights and arguments, assuming I have interpreted them justly and fairly up to this point, Derrida has not only anticipated but given an enduringly unique and useful take on several among the most interesting and, indeed, wide-ranging motifs and observations introduced by leading scholars in constitutional law and the philosophy of law in recent years. I am thinking of the law's "invisible" aspect in its ability of "curving" the social space (in Laurence H. Tribe's work), of the "rule of law's" required "thoughtfulness" (to use Jeremy Waldron's phrase) as well as its "moral practice" (to add Scott Hershovitz's), and even of the legal orientation towards a differently conceived "common good" (to end this list with Adrian Vermeule, who, it must be added, takes this motif, originally introduced by Gaston Fessard and others, in very different political directions than Derrida ever would).[21] And, perhaps, this is what the concept and practice, the founding and administering of law have always stood for.

"Derrida's law," to return to our Spring 2024 Cardozo colloquium's title, treats these tropes and admitted common places with special – phenomenological or, perhaps, we should rather say quasi-transcendental – rigor. Moreover, this methodic stringency has distinctive Hegelian and Marxian, that is, speculative and dialectical, if not downright historical materialist, resonances. These latter are no less worthy of further inquiry in this legal context than are Derrida's excursions, here and there, into pragmatism, insofar as his conception of law manifests itself, as already indicated, in a "pragrammatological" register. In so doing, his analysis echoes Aristotelian and later Gadamerian efforts at articulating the meaning and force of *phronesis* qua practical wisdom. These similarities are unmistakable, even though the nuanced differences among all these authorities should not be ignored. This will have to be for another occasion, however.

Instead, in the remainder of this chapter, I will argue, somewhat counterintuitively, that "Derrida's law," as discussed in 'Force of Law' and related texts, finds its first and, perhaps, most important expression in his treatment of Hegelian *Sittlichkeit*, often translated as "ethical life," a notion which, in turn, relies on – or eventually ties in with – that of Absolute Knowing (*das absolute Wissen*). Put differently, Derrida's concept of and appeal to an equally infinite and absolute justice is not coincidentally *sittlich* in a strikingly Hegelian no less than Marxian orientation toward this overarching motif. "Derrida's law," on this reading, takes on the unmistakable formal features and material qualities of a Hegelian Marxism – or, if one prefers, post-Marxian Hegelianism – and does so in ways that have not yet been fully explored, much less exhausted, and that remain of philosophical, moral, and political relevance to us, "today."

Sittlichkeit, broached by Derrida as a central topic in Hegel in his massive 1974 *Glas* (*Clang*) first and foremost, *prefigures* his later, no less suggestive and far-reaching remarks on "messianicity," the "New International" and "democracy-to-come," in *Spectres de Marx* and the writings and interviews, lectures and seminars that either followed in its wake or that had prepared and accompanied the latter book's essential argument all along. How so? The answer, if I am not mistaken, lies in the way in which Derrida (quite literally)

21 Lawrence H. Tribe, *The Invisible Constitution* (Oxford and New York: Oxford University Press, 2008); Jeremy Waldron, *Thoughtfulness and the Rule of Law* (Cambridge and London: Harvard University Press, 2023); Scott Hershovitz, *Law is a Moral Practice* (Cambridge and London: Harvard University Press, 2023); Adrian Vermeule, *Common Good Constitutionalism* (London: Polity, 2022).

sounds out Hegel on Absolute Knowing and this nowhere more abundantly than in *Glas*.[22]

***

In the *Phenomenology of Spirit*, Hegel introduces the "*realm of ethical life* [*Reich der Sittlichkeit*]" as "nothing but the absolute spiritual *unity* of the essence of individuals in their self-sufficient *actuality* [Wirklichkeit]." In it, thought and practice meet in their objective and not merely subjective

22 Jacques Derrida, *Glas* (Paris: Galilée, 1974); *Clang*, trans. by Geoffrey Bennington and David Wills (Minneapolis and London: University of Minnesota Press, 2021). *Glas*, I must confess, has not actually been the text that originally mattered most to me since I first started reading Derrida. In fact, while researching my dissertation topic, I was blown away by Derrida's essay, entitled '*Violence et métaphysique*,' first published in two installments in *Revue de Métaphysique et de Morale*, in 1964, and subsequently republished as a chapter in *L'écriture et la différence* (*Writing and Difference*) in 1967. What he offered there was a rigorous as well as faithful rebuttal of virtually all of Emmanuel Levinas' central philosophical claims, theses and arguments, notably in the writings leading up to *Totalité et infini* (*Totality and Infinity*) and some fundamental articles preparing this author's later *magnum opus* and taking it further, such as "La trace de l'autre" ("The Trace of the Other").

When I asked a distinguished Hegel scholar and Levinas specialist, Adriaan Peperzak, what he thought of Derrida's rebuttal (which, it should be recalled, Levinas deeply appreciated and, in fact, admired so much that it occasioned a radical turn in his thinking, leading to his second major work, *Autrement qu'être ou au-delà de l'essence* [*Otherwise Then Being or Beyond Essence*]), Peperzak dryly said something to the following extent: "Derrida just plays all the good Hegelian arguments back to him, there's nothing new there, it misses the point Levinas is precisely trying to make." Confusing as this was, given Levinas' own favorable assessment of Derrida's text – one that he definitely did not have when reading the second iteration of the latter's engagement with his work, namely "*En ce moment même dans cet ouvrage me voici* [At This Very Moment in This Work Here I am]" published in *Psyché*, but, then again, might have had if he would have had the time of life to process what would become Derrida's homage in *Adieu à Emmanuel Levinas* – the fact that '*Violence et métaphysique*' did not intend to be radically critical at all. To complicate matters more, Derrida noted, in retrospect, that there was *absolutely nothing* in Levinas' work he had wanted to disagree with.

Was Derrida disingenuous, ironic or, perhaps, merely evasive, in stating as much? I now more fully understand that and why that was not the case. Thinking with Levinas against Levinas, like thinking with Hegel against Hegel, as both these authors, lest we forget, did themselves constantly when they discussed their sources – moreover, thinking of Athens and Jerusalem, tradition and modernity, even religion (here: of ethics and eschatology) and philosophy in terms of *translation*, thereby meaning *iteration*, that is, a repetition that does *not* withhold change, such that exact repetition, indeed, might well effect that very change – this, nothing else, was the deconstructive "logic" Derrida had espoused. And, we can certainly say that it is a translating practice, not to mention rigorous method, he largely inherited from Hegel and Husserl, indeed, from Marx no less than from Levinas himself. The first essay by Derrida I read, then, fully confirmed just that and the book that (occasioned by its most recent translation or retranslation) I read last, namely *Glas* or *Clang*, does so likewise. As he would later say about Blanchot and Heidegger, Derrida is here at once infinitely closely to *and* furthest removed from Hegel. There is no contradiction in saying so or, rather, it is in the very principle and practice of this very contradiction that "truth" in thinking is eventually found.

progress in the consciousness of their freedom. Indeed, Hegel notes of this hard-fought actuality:

> It is in itself a universal [*allgemeines*] self-consciousness, which, to itself, is actual as another consciousness in such a way that this other consciousness has complete self-sufficiency, or is a thing for it, and it is just therein conscious of the *unity* with the other self-consciousness, and it is in this unity with this objective essence [*gegenständlichen Wesen*] that it is first self-consciousness.[23]

Abstractly put, Hegel continues, this "ethical substance [*sittliche Substanz*]" is "the law insofar as it is thought [*das gedachte Gesetz*]," while concretely and immediately, historically or systematically, *de facto* and *de iure*, it is also "tradition" or "custom [*Sitte*]."[24] The meaning and force of law consist, as Hans-Georg Gadamer will come to say in terms of his "universal hermeneutics," not merely that of its "practical wisdom," but of its "effective history [*Wirkungsgeschichte*]." And the latter accrues in truth and significance, indeed, authority, over time.

This unity between thought and practice is further associated with the "life of a people [*Leben eines Volkes*]" or, a little later, with "the *power* of the whole people [*die* Macht *des ganzen Volkes*]."[25] This, all by itself, may give us reason for pause, at least as long as that perilous concept (i.e., "people") has not been fully determined and is understood, not as a *genus*, that is, some natural kind of its own kind, but *generically* rather than ethnologically, nationally or ideologically. Could this be done, with the help of Hegel's concepts and speculative argument, allowing us now, say, to differentiate and oppose an emancipatory or liberal *populism* (the Latin *populus* connoting people, next to nation and state), encapsulating the progress in our consciousness of freedom (and not just in thought alone), from its regressive and downright reactionary distortion and caricature, if not mirror image (as seen in the return and upsurge of alt-right, nationalist, supremacist, even fascist and Neo-Nazi populism of our days)?

Hegel, we know, started out as a Rousseauean educator of the people, fostering *Bildung* or cultural formation by means of *Volksreligion* (popular religion), first and foremost. Like the later motif of the spirits of peoples and of the world, of *Volksgeist* and *Weltgeist*, the motif of *Volksreligion* absolves

23 Georg Wilhelm Friedrich Hegel, *Phänomenologie des Geistes*, Theorie-Werkausgabe, vol. 3, Werke in 20 Bänden, ed. by Eva Moldenhauer and Karl Markus Michel (Frankfurt am Main: Suhrkamp, 1973), 264; *The Phenomenology of Spirit*, trans. and ed. by Terry Pinkard (Cambridge and New York: Cambridge University Press, 2018), 204, trans. modified.

24 Ibid.

25 Ibid., 264, 265/205.

itself from nativist and geographical particularities in Hegel's perspective, even as it falls certainly short of the genuinely universalist, let alone revolutionary as well as radically egalitarian idea of freedom that a heterodox reception history has associated with the apocryphal title '*Communismus der Geister* [Communism of Spirits],' often attributed to his contemporary and friend Friedrich Hölderlin. Yet even this motif of "spiritual communism," as I will call it, including the *denaturalization* of the concept of the people it clearly implies and further calls for, is not without some interpretive difficulties of its own. As Derrida notes in *Glas*:

> The people that has *Aufhebung* in its throat denies itself as a particular people, chokes and de-peoples itself but this is the better to extend its imperium and infinitely deploy its scope . . . There remains, then, the general question: how can the idiom of a familial generation be thought, i.e., denied by erecting itself into speculative-type universality? It supposedly starts with love.[26]

Since love is neither familial nor merely inter-generational per se, but extends itself – generically and in a strangely generative fashion – well beyond the spatial and temporal limitations we know, such that true love must be eternal, that is, virtually absolute and, in that precise sense, inspirational and aspirational, its concept and practice are consequently *spiritual* through and through, to be shared among all.

***

Of *Sittlichkeit* Derrida says, parenthetically: "One day, elsewhere, I'll say why I love this German word."[27] Did he ever do so and, if so, where and how, exactly? I do not have a final answer to these questions aside from the hypothesis that Hegel's use of the term *Sittlichkeit* conjured or summoned, for Derrida, if not an ethical "life" or "community" per se (as these were historical and overdetermined terms he would always approach with the greatest reticence, as he did with other concepts such as "subject," "decision" and "freedom"), then at least, in more formal or structural and generic fashion, something like "democracy," indeed, a "new international" – still, if not, therefore, necessarily forever – "to come." Strangely generative as these latter notions truly are, we cannot and ought not exclude the however *unlikely* possibility that the quasi-messianic and hauntingly spiritual communist realm they conjure (a Kantian "kingdom of ends," if ever there was one) *actually arrives* in the present, indeed, in our present; nor should we disregard the

26 Derrida, *Clang*, 17.
27 Ibid.

co-extensive possibility that the bottom may once, if not necessarily once and for all, fall out from underneath us. "Democracy dies in darkness,"[28] when no one lights a candle, much less carries a flaming torch, for it any longer. Would Derrida have judged that this moment has come now?

As Derrida rightly noted in *Avances*, the future indeed may very well be that there is none anymore. Consequently, there would not merely be a regressive turning back to – or relapse into – what was presumed to be a bygone past, nor the no less fatal experience of being stuck in an unproductive present, but, on the contrary, no *visible*, much less *determinable*, path for us to march slowly forward. And yet, given the indeterminacy, immediacy and urgency with which each historical moment calls out to us invisibly, the standing possibility of there *being*, quite literally, *no future* (in French, *avenir*) would not, all by itself, disqualify the generic "to come [*à venir*]." Paradoxically, aporetically, on the steep and winding, tortuous, and come to think of it, finally inconclusive path toward *Sittlichkeit* and everything it stands for, the all-redemption of all created and fallen things – the *apokatastasis ton panton*, as Origen of Alexandria believed, the *restitutio in integrum*, as Benjamin added – is neither excluded nor indeed inevitable. Yet as regards this undeniably theological leitmotif, we have only the in principle endless series of "nonsynonymous substitutions," its "iterability," to further go on, as we cannot avoid wagering that "necessities" will eventually give way to "chance," just as apparent contingencies may well have to become necessities – and that means: categorical, universal and absolutely imperative injunctions – for us, here and now.

To make this out, requires in principle an ongoing set of singular "negotiations" (to cite yet another important dialectical term in Derrida's vocabulary) within the *general structure* of an "infinite" *différance*, itself nonetheless considered "finite," and this each step along the way. After all, if "to think is to say no [*penser, c'est dire non*]," then the negations of our thoughts and acts must be *always* and *everywhere* "determinate," as thought, and whatever follows from or upon it, does not consist in pure abstractions alone or primarily. As not only Hegel but, well before him, Spinoza had made abundantly clear, *omnis determinatio negatio est*. But what then, if anything, might yet lie beyond this inherent negativity of all things *existing*, phenomenally or otherwise experientially given to us in one way or another? In other words, in what would the *apokatastasis* and *restitutio* consist when all is said and done? Nothing is less clear, or so it would seem.

28 'Democracy dies in darkness,' the slogan first used by Bob Woodward in 2007, is the official motto of *The Washington Post*, now owned by Jeff Bezos, which, like the *Los Angeles Times*, the property of yet another billionaire, decided not to endorse a presidential candidate in 2024, in a radical break with its long-standing tradition advocating democracy openly, in the light of day.

Derrida helpfully offers that "what" eludes whatever "is" – all powers that be – might call for an altogether different register that speaks of that which (neither here nor there in actuality) no longer even can be said "to be." Ontology itself and as such, in its very "essence" (and not merely addressing the sublunar realm of ontic existence, that is, of historicity and empiricity), finds itself put into question accordingly. What is thus called for and calls out "is," if one can still say so, an "originary affirmation," of sorts. By this Derrida means a quasi-mystical quasi-postulate that regards neither a thesis nor a hypothesis (i.e., theoretical proposition) per se, but a gesture or gesturing, first and foremost; in other words, a non-phenomenal and non-phenomenologizable "showing," as Wittgenstein's *Tractatus Logico-Philosophicus* suggests, one that neither historical positivity nor its dialectical or determinate negation, nor, for that matter, any formal logical operator of negation itself – let alone its psychoanalytic counterpart, namely that of denial (*Verneinung* or, as Derrida says, "*dénégation*") – can ever pretend to fully capture, much less silence or disempower, mediate or mitigate.

As Derrida notes with reference to Hegel's *Grundlinien der Philosophie des Rechts* (*Elements of the Philosophy of Right*): "*Sittlichkeit* sublates *Moralität* as it separates itself from it."[29] Kant, to whom the concept of "morality" refers here, cannot so much as think the abstract possibility, much less the material necessity, of *Sittlichkeit*, the social life of morals that Hegel's philosophical work both announces and concretizes.[30] This may seem a harsh and unfair judgment on Derrida's, even more so than on Hegel's, part.[31] This said, if one keeps Derrida's later direct and indirect discussions of Kantian moral law, most notably in *Apories* (*Aporias*) but also in "Force of Law" and *Specters of Marx* firmly in mind, then one can discern in *Glas* the first prefiguration of an *infinitizing* concept and far more emphatic, if elusive, *idea* of "justice" as always already and, perhaps, forever "to come."

The very *Aufhebung* of morality into ethical life (here of Hegelian *Sittlichkeit*, elsewhere of Levinasian responsibility, that is, of eschatology and justice, or later indeed of Benjaminian messianism and divine violence) entails, Derrida explains, "the whole procession of the negative."[32] Derrida's subsequent meditations on Kant drive home the same point. They further interrogate the generality and formality of the law, but also question the

29 Derrida, *Clang*, 12.

30 Ibid., 13.

31 In the first chapter of my *Religion and Violence*, I offer a reading of Kant's *Religion innerhalb der Grenzen der blossen Vernunft* (*Religion Within the Limits of Reason Alone*) and *Der Streit der Fakultäten* (*Conflict of the Faculties*), which would seem to cover many of the points Derrida, in *Glas* and elsewhere, seems to wish to gain from probing Hegel's concept of *Sittlichkeit*.

32 Derrida, *Clang*, 16.

largely ignored implications hidden in the analytical distinction between acts undertaken "in conformity" and those committed "out of respect" of the moral law, thus truly obeying a paradoxical "cause through freedom," which knows neither time nor place and gives itself in what Adorno, in critical conversation with both Kant and Hegel, will call a "spiritual" rather than intellectual or sensuous "experience": a *geistige Erfahrung*, which is "metaphysical" and "moral" at once.

While Derrida thus seems to largely reiterate the Hegelian critique of Kantian morality, insisting that the latter, in its purity and formal separation from all ethical life, remains *merely* counter-factual and, in this sense, "virtual" – and, thereby, "immoral" at that – his own position remains somewhat of *a post-Hegelian Kantian*, come to think of it. True, as he notes, for Kant:

> The two sides face each other, without being able to come together or complete each other, like the two halves or the two abstract walls of one and the same spiritual body. They must negate their unilaterality in the concept.[33]

But this same concept, since it comes at the heavy price of objective, speculative or absolute idealism, is never provided by Derrida himself, in turn, or presented without contradiction (paradox or, rather, aporia), that is.

But was it indeed Hegel's claim to have provided the universal concept as an ultimate stopgap? Does Absolute Knowledge or Knowing function as the definite solution for all chasms and dualisms opening up between what are, each time, exactly two seemingly irreconcilable poles rather than pillars integral to the "experience of consciousness" (e.g., essence and appearance, finite and infinite, inner or in itself and outer or for itself, self and other, identity and difference)? As Spirit progresses – almost "pilgrimage"-like – from individual sense-certainty, via general understanding and reason to ever greater speculative heights, expanding onwards into even further, deeper dimensions as well as wider horizons, that is, from objective to absolute Spirit, by way of the outer and inner representation of art and religion, respectively, culminating in their philosophical summa and summit, which is Absolute Knowledge (or Knowing), does its spiritual experience come to a halt? Or, alternatively, is some "virtuality," if not potentiality but a more formal inexhaustibility, a no less structural element of the speculative Absolute as Hegel defines it? Perhaps.

Freely adopting a Levinasian neologism, we soon realize that the Absolute in its very realization and actualization is marked by an *infinition*, of sorts. Yet where *infinitization* is the name of the game (i.e., the play, the "*Spiel*," at hand,

33 Ibid., 17.

as Hegel confirms), Levinasian *infinition* must likewise *necessarily* work, that is, "produce" and phenomenalize itself. Indeed, it must do so logically and not merely deontologically speaking. And yet, when all is said and done, not every saying – a "saying without said [*Dire sans Dit*]," the "patience" of a "passion" more fundamental than either "passivity" or "activity" – is thereby also silenced, much less sublated, Levinas claims. Moreover, we need not await the Hegelian "judgment of History," to learn its verdict, which can be rendered solely by an *absolute*, more and other than categorical, *imperative*.

This said, *Sittlichkeit*, in which the "Idea of freedom becomes actually present" and is, hence, "not merely in the heads of subjective individuals,"[34] metaphysically and practically, must remain just as elusive – that is, as absolute – as it was, first, in Kant and then in Levinas. For while "ethical life" conjures "freedom as living, present and concrete Good in the present (*vorhandenen*) world, which implies actual elaboration (*Wirklichkeit*), action, operation (*Handeln*), . . . the concrete substance of mores (*Sittlichkeit*)," none of these can have the last word, much less the first. For while these motifs and moments alone exceed and overcome mere "*Meinen* (according to Hegel's play on words between the subjective vacillation of the opining I and what is 'mine')," thus constraining "subjective caprice and vague intention (*Belieben*)" and, instead, finding "consistency in laws, enduring organizations (*Einrichtungen*), *institutions*,"[35] the latter do not found, maintain or exhaust the meaningfulness (Levinas writes "*significance*") of all signification, let alone its true, ethical *force*.

A novel positivity – a positing to the point of "exposure," Levinas quips – thereby inserts itself surreptitiously into the "divine economy [*la Comédie divine*]" in which Providentialism and Prometheanism change places more often than we can count. In fact, an at once novel and age-old *negativity* thus announces and inscribes itself with *at least* equal force, outweighing its speculative *dialectical* impact, and of far greater pragmatic consequence than even Hegel could fathom.

***

An unforgettable lesson, elements of which surfaced time and again in Derrida's seminars at NYU, concerns his engagement with Hegel's conception or, I will now suggest, *absolution* of Absolute Knowledge (or, as more recent English translations of the 1807 *Phänomenologie des Geistes* [*Phenomenology of Spirit*] render "*das absolute Wissen*," "Absolute Knowing"). Derrida's *Glas* – recently retranslated as *Clang* by Geoffrey Bennington and David Wills – opens, just as it no less tellingly ends, in mid-sentence. The

34 Ibid., 18.
35 Ibid.

voluminous book, whose pages and columns, with interspersed glosses, resemble a page from the Talmud, is thus without a determinable, absolute beginning. It surges forth *ex nihilo*, as it were, while it also lacks a proper end, shunning a Hegelian result, a syllogistic conclusion, but also a riddle's resolution, as it breaks off in and with a half-thought, it seems.

Prima facie, neither the reference to theologoumena such as the *creatio ex nihilo* and revelation, nor the incarnation and eucharist, the *apokalypsis* or *eschaton*, the *parousia* or *pleroma,* form *Glas*'s first or last explicit, much less primary, theme and concern. The book is an anti-book, an anti-Bible or, at least, anti-Gospel in so many words, a Scripture with, as said, neither beginning nor end, neither alpha nor omega. Taking off in midflight and disappearing, no less abruptly, across the horizon, *Glas* nonetheless conjures a whole semantic and hermeneutic universe, a quasi-semiotic *sériature* and infinite set, one whose polysemy or, as Derrida will come to say, "*dissémination*" ("dissemination") *goes on* to *survive* the very opening and concluding phrases among its own words ("having counted without" and "the debris of"). And yet, while the work contains neither a rabbinical Midrash nor a medieval *summa*, neither an ecclesial catechism nor idealist system, in any strict sense, it scrupulously guards an immemorial archive, an involuntary memory as well as a deliberate recollection and reconstruction of each single one of its detailed allusions, thus *doing justice* to all of its enabling, indeed, constitutive motifs and moments, moods and modalities. This, if nothing else, is what *deep pragmatism* – again, Derrida, himself in *Limited Inc*, speaks of "pragrammatology" – stands for, as it taps into the furthest removed recesses, the deepest and widest resources and repositories, endowing given *occasions* with the momentum they need to be noticed and take the effect, here and now or eventually, over longer stretches of time, with a material and institutional, even legal, impact that they may merit and call for.

In the process, a host of (quite literally) loaded notions, among them accounts of historical revelations or announced apocalypses, prove to phenomenologically manifest themselves *virtually anywhere* and also *in full.* Each step along the way of the stations and stages of the Cross and of profane theatricality, *Glas* passes through and by them, salvaging not only their putative original or accrued meaning – dialectically and hermeneutically, semantically or semiotically – but also their performative and, as Hamacher quipped, "perverformative," force. In a lecture presented in 1968 in Jean Hyppolite's seminar and entitled '*Le Puits et la pyramide*,' published in *Marges de la philosophie* (*Margins of Philosophy*) Derrida presents this insight as an "introduction to the semiology of Hegel," as a kind of "apprenticeship of signs" (as Gilles Deleuze said of Marcel Proust's *Recherche*). In so doing, on each textual, here Scriptural and literary, occasion that it probes, as it reads Hegel and Jean Genet alongside, with, and against each other, *Glas*' philosophical and theological, literary and psychoanalytic concepts, and modulated tropes aim at nothing less (and nothing more) than to *absolve the Absolute.*

For all intents and purposes, such an at once interpretative, polysemic and, indeed, disseminative project equals *traditio.* As Adorno proposed in the opening pages of his 1966 *Negative Dialektik* (*Negative Dialectics*), this age-old concept might well be rendered by the very name and spiritual experience or practice of "*Kabbalah.*" For any intellectual apparatus and its more contemplative as well as practical analogues, indeed, each motif and moment, mood and modality that their texts and histories have on offer requires a distinct, unique – and on each occasion "*relevant*" – act of "translation." It is only in the movement of this seemingly interminable process and progress of making texts and the things they treat "*relevant*" that hidden or forgotten origins and ultimate referents (or what goes by these names and the presumed realities they conjure) find their "*expression*" and can be "*iterated*" (to echo these eminently Spinozist and Cartesian terms, respectively).[36]

Critiquing or deconstructing Hegel – and, in his footsteps, Marx – then, would be to write their work also further, while remaining "haunted," if not therefore transfixed, by their respective "ontologies." And this implies taking their respective metaphysical and economic theses *absolutely*, precisely by *absolving* them from their residual historicism and naturalism, idealism and materialism, semanticism and structural formalism. This does not mean to pick and choose motifs and arguments as one sees fit, but to play the melody of these authors' writings as it were back to them *in toto* while modulating, if not changing, their tone, discerning and respecting what Cavell come to call their philosophical "pitch." In so doing, as Cavell's muse, the later Ludwig Wittgenstein suspected in his *Philosophische Untersuchungen* (*Philosophical Investigations*), philosophy begins by "leaving everything as

36 See my 'Spinoza, Levinas, and the Theologico-Political Meaning of Scripture', in Hent de Vries and Lawrence E. Sullivan, eds., *Political Theologies: Public Religions in the Post-Secular World* (New York: Fordham University Press, 2006), 232–248; and, with respect to Derrida's reading of Descartes, '"*Et Iterum de Deo*": Jacques Derrida and the Tradition of Divine Names', in Edward Baring and Peter E. Gordon, eds., *The Trace of God: Derrida and Religion* (New York: Fordham University Press, 2015), 13–38. The very nature or, let's say, structure and method of *iterability* – inspired by Descartes' *et iter de Deo*, which, one will recall, introduces his second proof for the existence of God in the *Meditationes de prima philosophia* – entails a "repetition plus change," an at least nonformal tautology or non-synonymous substitution of the self-same (in Descartes: of the *causa sui*) that prefigures and models all further engagements of Derrida's interpretative as well as political endeavors. This pivotal motif in Derrida's writing plays the same role as Adorno's wild suggestion that all philosophy, not least in modernity, fundamentally revolves around – and continues to mimic conceptually as well as practically – the ontological proof for the existence of God.

it is," even as it changes the rule of the game altogether. By the same token Derrida has written,

> the problem of the introduction to Hegel's philosophy is *the whole* of Hegel's philosophy: *already* posed everywhere, in particular in his prefaces and forewords, introductions and preliminary concepts. So one would find oneself, already, drawn into the circle of Hegelian beginning and set skating or sliding endlessly in it.[37]

This, then, is the way Absolute Knowledge or Knowing, as Hegel presents it, seems to sound off on all it could possibly lay its sight and hand on. As Derrida will seek to demonstrate throughout the two columns that make the text of *Glas*, this sounding off is not so much the dialectics' sonorous murmur or white noise (as in the "white mythology" Derrida suspected in Western metaphysics in his 1971 essay with the same title), but the latter's very *Klang*, its *glas* or *clang*, its death knell, of sorts: "the knell of *Sa*, the knell as *Sa*," epitomizing the meaning and force of "*Savoir absolu*," to begin with, which reverberates and resonates through all things, said and done, in past, present and Hegel's "future" as well.[38]

This said, while we are seemingly inevitably and irrevocably under the spell of this *clang's* echo and *basso continuo*, call it its driving beat, we can nonetheless, *Glas* reveals, not avoid attempting to exit and free ourselves. It is as if *exile* and *diaspora* are integral parts of the journey to selfhood, the very Odyssey of the soul, as much as they must trace and brace themselves both *within* or just *beyond* the realm of reason, in its totality, so to speak. "Escape" or "*évasion*," then, as Levinas knew early on, "is" a *standing* – that is, necessary and logical as much as virtual – "possibility," even if only as the very "possibility" of the opening up of all further, past, present and future possibilities, including those that seem completely closed off at first glance. As such, exile, diaspora, and, *a fortiori* escape are rarely realized, much less actualized, as much as Hegel, from early on, invites and inspires us to "think abstractly" and "act concretely." He does so in registers for which phenomenology and dialectics, logic and – speculatively – politics, even political theology, offer a method, a path, a ladder, whose services are principally and ultimately subservient to us *freely* learning *to see and set things aright*, as we must.

To aspire to nothing less (i.e., to pursue totality, the whole, spiritually re-experiencing its original "before" and eventual "beyond" of what is

37 Derrida, *Clang*, 10.

38 Cf. Catherine Malabou, *L'Avenir de Hegel. Plasticité, temporalité, dialectique* (Paris: Librairie Vrin, 1996); *The Future of Hegel: Plasticity, Temporality, and Dialectic*, trans. by Lisabeth During, with a Preface by Jacques Derrida (London and New York: Routledge, 2004).

historically and empirically, its "*en-deça*" and "*au-delà*," as Levinas, in *Totality and Infinity* and elsewhere so often intimates), is to enter the realm of *Sittlichkeit* of which Hegel's *Elements of the Philosophy of Right* sketches the formal scaffolding. It is to fulfill – and this means in essence, to theologically incarnate and economically materialize – its deepest and highest purposes, its *parousia*, *pleroma* and then some. Hegel, Derrida suggests, reading with and against him, aimed and, perhaps, accomplished nothing else. To illustrate this overall point, here is *Glas*'s opening line:

> what remains today, for us, here, now, of a Hegel?
> For us, here, now: that's what will not, henceforth, have been thinkable without him.
> For us, here, now: these words are quotations, already, always, we will have learned that from him.[39]

It should be noted, at the outset, that what thus "always" and "already" remains of Hegel – even and, perhaps, especially *in* and *beyond* every subsequent disavowal of his objective or speculative idealism and system of philosophy that we may yet feel entitled to, "today . . . here, now" – sheds light on *infinitely more* than the sheer possibility or presumed necessity of Absolute Knowledge or Knowing in its true (positive) or false (negative) totality. But this is not all there is to it: "what remains today, for us, here, now, of a Hegel?" is a question that – next to its tentative, unqualified answer, namely, virtually *everything* – is *emblematic* in that it can, in truth, be extended to (principally, practically) *all* of "tradition" or, as we said, following Adorno, all of its *Kabbalah*.

As much as *traditio/Kabbalah* stands in need of being "negated," in Hegelian, dialectical parlance and is, in this sense, and not just in part, suspended, but set aside, conserved, and elevated or salvaged "as such" and "*in toto*," in this irrepressible (and, Hegel thinks, irrevocable progress) process, its truth is revealed, that is, *made apparent*. In other words, its "truth moment" or "truth content," to use the Adornian idiom, is "sublated" and thereby *made relevant*. The negation, which is the very way "mediation [*Vermittlung*]" and the "labor of the concept [*Arbeit des Begriffs*]" operate together and on each other, is thus no longer merely "abstract" but "concrete" and "determinate." Indeed, the "determinate negation [*bestimmte Negation*]" is the organizing principle of both speculative and negative dialectics, as Adorno insists throughout his philosophical oeuvre, explaining why and how our difficulty ("*Skoteinos*") in reading Hegel gives way to deeper understanding once we realize that this fundamental and methodic premise can neither be set aside nor overcome. Indeed, as a logical operation, it is the *predicament of all our predications*, discursive and other, and, hence, determines and affects

39 Derrida, *Clang*, 7.

all things individually and collectively. And yet, in so doing, the operation of negation in question is not one of annihilation *tout court*. As it happens, it schlepps along an at least minimal semantic content and thereby gives the negated entity, concept or context, an indirect pragmatic effect as it projects its meaning and force further and further. The dialectical, negative limitation delimits, therefore, opening new horizons of interpretation by creating ever-expanding spaces to judge and act accordingly. Therein, paradoxically, lies its "positivity."

As *Glas* aptly summarizes things, in three languages at once: "*Traditio* is *Aufhebung* [or: The *traditio* is the *Aufhebung*, *La* tradition *est l'*Aufhebung]."[40] And since, as we have determined, the very concept and act of thinking, at least, for Hegel, Marx and Adorno, is that of negation, such that not only sublation but all tradition, all *Kabbalah*, consists in its own ongoing negation, as it were, not even the presumably well-known "negation of [the] negation" in which philosophical thinking and experience cannot but result, can claim the last word. Its negation is virtually a "positive" and the latter – logically, experientially – must thus be open to negation, in turn.

It follows that all thinking is negation or, put slightly differently, that "to think is to say no [*penser, c'est dire non*]." Derrida borrows this telling phrase from the French thinker Alain in the early 1960–1961 lecture course whose very title it carries. Yet Spinoza's *omnis determinatio negatio est*, as said, had captured this insight before and therefore underscores a broader point.[41] As Derrida notes,

> the way in which Hegel takes the labor of the negative seriously lets us depart from a tradition for which negation was *at the deepest level* the impossible and the unthinkable, or, in any case, that which, as such, had no hold on being.[42]

But how, if this is the case, does this departure affect Hegel's own understanding of the – at once phenomenological and logical, encyclopedic and legal, aesthetic and theological – *summing up*, whose *summation* in "the Absolute" Derrida portrays and acts out, indeed, mocks and mimics, in *Glas/Clang*? And, more importantly, perhaps, what role do "Absolute Knowledge" or "Knowing" continue to play in Derrida's own subsequent writings and teachings as what I am tempted to call *undeconstructables*, of sorts?

40 Ibid., 15.

41 Cf. Yitzhak Y. Melamed, '"*Omnis determinatio negatio est*": Determination, Negation, and Self-Negation', in Spinoza, Kant, and Hegel, in Eckart Förster and Yitzhak Y. Melamed, eds., *Spinoza and German Idealism* (Cambridge: Cambridge University Press, 2012), 175–196.

42 Jacques Derrida, *Penser, c'est dire non*, édition établie par Brieuc Gérard (Paris: Éditions du Seuil, 2022), 56.

In an altogether different sense, perhaps, in which, elsewhere in Derrida's oeuvre, only "justice" and "*chora*" qualify to be called "undeconstructable" (surprising, indeed, less than compelling as that may seem on Derrida's own terms), "Absolute Knowledge" or "Knowing" know *no outside*. The reason may well be that the persistent mention and use of the "absolute," including that of "Absolute Knowledge" or "Knowing," allows Derrida to effectively "crossover," if not therefore "cross out," ancient and modern distinctions between the finite and infinite (or, indeed, Infinite), and do so *in light and virtue* of an "inexistence," whose distinctive notion has unmistakable Levinasian contours, if not origins, and should not be ignored. Indeed, Derrida's extensive rendition of Absolute Knowledge or Knowing, I would suggest, is nothing short of a phenomenology of the "inexistent."[43]

43 For a more extensive elaboration of this claim, see my 'On Inexistence, Divine and Other', in Dika and Shuster, eds., *Religion in Reason*. A consequence of this analysis is that the distinction between the absolute and the relative, *relevant* to a historical or empirical situation, as it is revealed or manifested – and, we found, incarnated, phenomenalized and materialized or economized – at a *given* self-sufficient and saturated moment in time and space, is no longer fundamental or final. What has metaphysically been called an *occasion* in so-called *occasionalism*, is an offered occurrence and event, *not of this world*, hence, "inexistent," neither finite nor infinite, unless it "is" both. Heidegger in his 1930/31 seminar on Hegel suggests as much: "*Ist dieses Verstehen und Sprechen des Seins, die Sprache, göttlich in dem Sinne, dass sie absolut ist? Ist das Verstehen des Seins, so können wir auch sagen*, absolvent, *und ist das Absolvente das Absolute, oder ist die Absolvenz die verhüllte Transzendenz, die Endlichkeit? Unsere Auseinandersetzung ist auf diesen Kreuzweg von Endlichkeit und Unendlichkeit gestellt, ein Kreuzweg, nicht ein Gegeneinanderhalten von zwei Standpunkten.* [[T]he question arises as to whether this understanding and speaking of being, or language, is divine in the sense of being absolute. We can also put it this way: Is the understanding of being *absolvent*, and is the absolvent absolute? Or, is what Hegel represents in the *Phenomenology of Spirit* as absolvence merely transcendence in disguise, i.e., finitude? Our confrontation with Hegel arrives at this crossing which is located between finitude and infinity, a crossroads, which is not the same as the opposition of two points of view." (Martin Heidegger, *Hegels Phänomenologie des Geistes*, Gesamtausgabe Bd. 32 [Frankfurt am Main: Vittorio Klostermann, 1997], 92/*Hegel's Phenomenology of Spirit*, trans. by Parvis Emad and Kenneth Maly [Bloomington: Indiana University Press, 1988], 65, trans. modified). If the dialectical opposition between finite and infinite is, well, overcome, then this means also that the fullness (*pleroma*) of the putative infinite can and, perhaps, also must appear in the finite, just as it, perhaps, one fine or terrible day also may or must be instantly (and, again, on occasion) brought back to virtually *nil*.

This, then, is how I am tempted to understand Derrida's often-cited claim that "*la différance infinie est finie*," which is all too often misinterpreted in rigid *finitist* terms. Perhaps these words, first put in writing in *La Voix et le phénomène* (*Speech and Phenomena*), mean something altogether different. Just as, in Spinoza, the *natura naturans* is (the) infinite par excellence (more than any singular or even sum total of attributes and modes), since it does not let itself be reduced to the corporeally and extended or notional and intelligible manifestation in which it is nonetheless *expressed* by the substance's (i.e., Nature's or God's) other aspect or *natura naturata*, so likewise the infinity of "generalized difference," while it 'is' also nothing without, beyond or aside from its endless process of spatialization and temporalization, does not limit itself to any of these latter's particular instantiations or iterations (without which it

***

On Hegel's reading, in *Phenomenology of Spirit* and elsewhere, the answer to the Kantian question "What is Enlightenment?" reveals the latter as a definite, hence, finite, if not therefore finished, phase. Enlightenment, he observes, while it exhibits reflexivity, itself an emerging speculative quality, lacks a proper understanding of what knowledge is, seeing it as the relationship with an externality ("an *other*"), thus missing out on the in-difference in difference, if one can say so:

> the still unconscious activity of the pure concept which, to be sure, comes back round to itself as object but which takes this object for an *other* and which is also not aware of the nature of the concept, namely, that it is the non-differentiated, which absolutely separates itself [*dass nämlich das Nichtunterschiedene es ist, dass sich absolut trennt*].[44]

On a certain early – as of yet undeveloped, hence, limited or restricted – conception of "the absolute," the latter's idea knows neither previous nor current history. Thus, in the *Differenzschrift*, Hegel writes:

> If it is the case that the absolute, like its appearance, reason, is eternally one and the same (and it is the case), then every reason which has directed itself toward itself and has come to know itself has produced a true philosophy and completed the task which, like its solution, is the same in all times.[45]

Yet, on account of Hegel's own later – fully developed, indeed, radically unlimited and unrestricted, in George Bataille's idiom, "general" – conception, the absolute of speculative reason, it turns out, knows or, should we say, acknowledges no further History either. It no longer needs history to shore up its credentials, to prove or phenomenalize its arguments. Its mediation is immediate, once more and all over again. Or, alternatively, *mediation* only now reveals itself to have been fundamentally *immediate* all along. It flatly ignores

---

nonetheless cannot appear or make itself felt, that is, *touched*). Nor does *différance*'s range so much as equal the sum-total of all finite appearances and their expression. And yet, *différance*, in its very essence and operation, 'is' the appearances' – as Derrida says, "*quasi-*" or "*simili*-transcendental" – condition of possibility, their immanent or intrinsic, if abysmal and virtual, "ground," as it were, and *nothing besides* and *above*, *before* or *beyond* them. This is why infinite *différance* is finite and, quite literally, *inexistent* anywhere else.

44 Hegel, *Phenomenology of Spirit*, 329, trans. modified/*Phänomenologie des Geistes*, 419.

45 Cited after Eckart Förster, *Die 25 Jahre der Philosophie. Eine systematische Rekonstruktion* (Frankfurt am Main: Vittorio Klostermann, 2011), 285; *The Twenty-Five Years of Philosophy: A Systematic Reconstruction*, trans. by Brady Bowman (Cambridge and London: Harvard University Press, 2012), 286.

and avoids, negates and denies any prior, contemporary or ulterior story or history that would significantly (i.e., meaningfully or forcefully) add to its concept. For Eckart Förster, this latter view only further confirms Hegel's final and, perhaps, initial metaphysical and world literary proximity to a Spinoza and Goethe, respectively, in its undeniable echo of the Spinozist third kind of knowledge, the "intellectual love of God [*amor Dei intellectualis*]" or *scientia intuitiva*, on the one hand, and the Goethean *Urphänomen*, on the other.

With this robust absolute idealist or speculative dialectical concept of the concept and its mediation or "labor" in mind, it may seem astounding that Derrida, in *Glas* and elsewhere, would – still or yet again – have a use for it (whether philosophically or strategically, pragmatically, even politically, the difference matters little).

Why and how is it, then, that Derrida can so much as even consider "the Absolute" as being *productive* of all thought (including his own)?[46] Moreover, why and how is it that "the Absolute," as it is defined here – and, lest we forget, virtually *indistinguishable* from and *interchangeable* with "the Infinite," as modern philosophy, at least since Descartes and Kant, followed by Levinas, had conceived it – *produces*, that is, *knows*, *experiences* and *expresses* itself in his thought and writing, in *Glas* and well beyond? As Derrida once mused with reference to the Jewish Talmud, which he said he "did not know," namely that, perhaps, the latter knew itself in him, the motif of "the Infinite," similarly, seems present and used too ubiquitously to merit its mention or even citation. Levinas said as much of the presence of Franz Rosenzweig in his own *Totality and Infinity*, and Derrida, for his part, did roughly the same when asked about the quasi-total absence in his writings, if not thinking, of Samuel Beckett.[47]

Lastly, how does *absolving* "the Absolute," not to mention its conceptual abstraction and immanent realization, go *hand in hand* with its essential

46 I use the term "production" and its semantic register deliberately here. As Levinas says in *Totality and Infinity* (and Derrida well knows and affirms), the "Infinite" *produces* itself, even insofar as it creates, sustains and redeems the world and all (or most) that inhabits it. Indeed, Levinas clarifies: the Infinite does not exist first, in order to only then reveal itself (subsequently, that is, as an aftereffect resulting from a more supreme cause, of sorts). In that sense, all there "is" of it, is always already "there," eschatologically, even messianically and apocalyptically, so to speak; it does not withhold itself, for example by holding itself in reserve until the final Hegelian "judgment of History," surreptitiously anticipated by its "ruse of Reason [*List der Vernunft*]," have had their say or paved its way. Revelation is *apokalypsis*, phenomenologists like Jean-Luc Marion and Jean Vioulac have recently reminded us. It "is" or "happens" *instantaneously* and *in full*, as any genuinely "saturated phenomenon" does and, insofar as it is a "counter-experience," certainly must do, as it cannot be grasped by approximation or even asymptotically, let alone from this or that (spatiotemporal or perspectival) angle.

47 Cf. Asja Szafraniec, *Beckett, Derrida, and the Event of Literature* (Stanford: Stanford University Press, 2007).

appearance and at times fateful apparition and specter (the *Schein* and *Gespenst* that shadow the spirit, as Kant and Marx, respectively, knew)? This much seems clear, in Hegel as Derrida reads him, one movement and moment, mood or modality, gives in to the other, and, in so doing, cannot but *hand itself over*. But then, what would the reverse or inverse of such gesture – again, the negation of its negation – look like in the end? When and where this sublation just so happens *in fact*, we must also assume that this will always and, indeed, everywhere be possible *by right*. Even if not necessarily in this or that concrete form or format, what Derrida, in *De la grammatologie* (*Of Grammatology*), calls the "non-synonymous substitution" of one sign (name, thing or concept) by yet another, without beginning or end, first or last word, is the name of the game, its rule and law, so to speak.

* * *

An anecdote may help us out in preparing an answer to the many questions these observations still leave open. One of Hegel's major translators and commentators, Terry Pinkard, ends his massive *Hegel*: *A Biography* with the following, quite moving story:

> The German literary scholar Christoph Theodor Schwab visited Hölderlin shortly before his death on June 7, 1843. He asked him whether he had thought of Hegel. Hölderlin [having spent long years of isolation and madness, in the meantime, in his own words in "*traurige Dämmerung*" or "sad twilight"] answered that of course he had, muttered something incomprehensible, and then noted simply, "The Absolute."[48]

Endearing as this *fait divers* is, Pinkard's rendition of this anecdote is not fully exact, it seems. Schwab, who gave the funeral address after Hölderlin's passing and was the editor of *Friedrich Hölderlins Sämtliche Werke*, to whose second volume, published in 1846, he added a first biographical sketch, entitled "*Hölderlins Leben*" – incidentally one of the great "*Dichterbiographien*" that Benjamin highly praised and Paul Celan made direct use of – had, in fact, said something to the following extent:

> I asked him [Hölderlin] whether he had had exchanges with Hegel and this also he affirmed while adding some unintelligible words, among them 'the Absolute.' [*Ich fragte ihn, ob er mit Hegel umgegangen sei, auch dies*

48 Terry Pinkard, *Hegel: A Biography* (Cambridge and New York: Cambridge University Press, 2000), 664–665. The quoted is attributed to Günther Nicolin (ed.), *Hegel in Berichten seiner Zeitgenossen* (Hamburg: Felix Meiner Verlag, 1970), par. 39a, 35.

bejahte er und setzte einige unverständliche Worte hinzu, worunter 'das Absolute' vorkam.][49]

Whether Hölderlin expressed this reference to "the Absolute" *viva voce* or scribbled it on a small sheet of paper (as was his habit when he communicated with visitors during his later years), all this remains somewhat unclear and does not affect the overall gist of the indirect argument I am trying to make here. What is evident from this second and, we must assume, original version of the anecdote is that Hölderlin affirmed the "Absolute's" central importance *among* and *in addition to* some other – apparently equally or presumably even more "unintelligible" (i.e., inaudible or unreadable) – words. Needless to say, these may have been simply words that Schwab either did not capture or did not take the trouble to report.

What we can take away from Schwab's anecdote is this: *why* or *how* "the Absolute" inserts itself into language, into the spoken or scribbled word, in all of its linguistic signification and pragmatic force (or lack thereof, as this depends on context), is anything but obvious. *That* it apparently does is (and this so much that it is this word, name or concept that "comes to mind" [*vient à l'idée*, to use Levinas's helpful expression], even when, as is the case for Hölderlin here, nothing else with regard to Hegel – the person or his system of thought – evidently does). To pin down a precise answer to the question as to *why* or *how* "the Absolute" *comes to mind* – one way or another, one is tempted to say – seems to fundamentally miss the point. And this is the speculative point the "Absolute" is precisely making as it is cited and recited, *ad infinitum*. Suffice it to say that, in both recounted versions of the previous anecdote, "the Absolute" *stands out somehow*. But then again, it does so *without* its putative reference, meaning or force, being *either* directly posited and affirmed (i.e., spoken out loud or scribbled down in legible writing) *or*, for that matter, explicitly denied or indirectly ignored and disavowed.

Was Schwab suggesting that Hölderlin, in response to his question whether he (still) thought of Hegel, was indeed recalling, perhaps, invoking the main protagonist of Hegel's speculative logic, namely "the Absolute" and, thereby, *also* God or Spirit? Or was he merely testifying to a cherished memory and to the striking impression Hegel himself had made on him over the years? Was he merely babbling, citing or mentioning, but nowhere intentionally and actively *using* the words "the Absolute" as those that spoke

49 Nicolin, *Hegel in Berichten seiner Zeitgenossen*, par. 39a, 35. For Schwab's biographical sketch, see *Friedrich Hölderlins Sämtliche Werke, Zweiter Band: Nachlass und Biographie* (Stuttgart and Tübingen: J.G. Cotta Verlag, 1846), 263–333, https://archive.org/details/bub_gb_JR9VAAAAcAAJ_2/page/n267/mode/2up. Christoph Theodor Schwab was also the contemporary in whose handwriting the brief apocryphal text, entitled "*Communismus der Geister*," at one point attributed to Hölderlin, would be transmitted.

to or for him in this very moment, standing out among all the possible *faits divers*, for no obvious reason whatsoever? There is no one – decidable – answer to this simplest of questions. Yet this uncertainty, nothing else, reveals and, at each turn, reiterates the very point that is being made here, the beating *heart of the matter*.

Another illustration may be helpful in this context. In Paul Celan's poem "*Tübingen, Jänner*," the final word "*Pallaksch*" was drawn by the poet from the aforementioned biographical sketch by the same Schwab in which the latter reported on Hölderlin's repeated use of yet another (or even more) singular word; indeed, this time, not much of a word or name, let alone concept, but a genuine neologism (with enough determinateness, however, not to be a murmur or inarticulate outcry, thus eventually becoming part of a – poetic – language or idiom). As Schwab explains:

> one could sometimes take it for 'Yes' and at another time to mean 'No.' Yet, typically, he [Hölderlin] hardly thought much of it, but used it when his patience of what remained of his power to think was exhausted and he did not want to make the effort to reflect whether what needed to be said was 'Yes' or 'No.'[50]

The earlier Hölderlin anecdote, apocryphal as it may further be, suggests to us the unique way in which he himself may well have thought or believed that the reference or invocation of "the Absolute" ought to be taken in relation to Hegel (perhaps even as Hegel).

How come, then, that "the Absolute," among the innumerable words, including the better and lesser known philosophemes and theologoumena, we utter, speak and write, mention and use, holds what seems *the greater promise of intelligibility and efficacy*? How come it does so even as the historical and, we should add, more than merely historical weight it carries, as Hölderlin gives us to think here, has, in all appearance, very little to do with the alternative of either affirming ("*Ja*") or negating ("*Nein*") its existence or nonexistence (hence, motivating the intellectual and pragmatic pursuit of some form of "inexistence," once more)? Indeed, both in fact and as a matter of principle – that is, metaphysically and logically, speculatively and dialectically speaking – the question of "the Absolute" is not one of either "being" or "not being" and, therefore, not so much an ontological or ontotheological problem to begin with or, indeed, *at all*. Put differently, where

50 "*man konnte es das einemal für Ja, das anderemal für Nein nehmen, aber er dachte sich gewöhnlich gar nichts dabei, sondern brauchte es, wenn seine Geduld oder die Reste seines Denkvermögens erschöpft waren und er sich die Mühe nicht nehmen wollte, nachzudenken, ob Ja oder Nein zu sagen wäre.*" (Christoph Theodor Schwab, *Hölderlins Leben* (Triptychon Literaturverlag, 2003), 72).

"the Absolute" is concerned, it would seem, neither pompous positing nor adamant denial carries the day, let alone has the last say.

Derrida knew as much and, throughout his oeuvre, insists on nothing else, thereby casting a radically novel philosophical light on age-old questions of religion and mysticism, theism and atheism, faith and knowledge, including messianism and materialism, that does not identify with any of these particular (and all too often particularist) positions or traditions per se. In fact, he takes them to be "haunting" our thoughts and acts, until they wear out. Rather than questioning them critically, I would say that Derrida takes them *in a certain spirit*.

What would it mean, then, if our "patience" with this word ("the Absolute," taken as a term and name, concept or referent) – in spite of the immense power and range of traditional, modern as well as contemporary philosophical and theological, legal and political, next to aesthetic, efforts at thinking, justifying or representing and expressing it – may very well *run out of steam* and *lose its semantic and imaginative purchase* one fine or terrible day? Would we know and be able to tell and gage its metaphysical rather than ontological ramifications, its presumed normative deficit, our lack of any further "spiritual experience [*geistige Erfahrung*]," if that came to pass? Could the spirit of the times indeed be that of a spiritless world, the proverbial "iron cage" Max Weber resented, fearing a new "polytheism of values," a new mythology of coming gods, might come to fill its horrific vacuum?

Whether this happens or not, has already happened or not, our individual and collective response in the matter would undoubtedly have to resound like yet another, doubly reiterated "*Pallaksch*, *Pallaksch*!" (as, indeed, it does in Celan's *Tübingen, Jänner*). This singular utterance, in its very structure of repetition, connotes, as we have seen, neither "Yes" nor "No," nor even "Yes or No." In other words, it expresses neither some p nor its non-p, thus violating the very principle of noncontradiction, of the *tertium non datur*. On the contrary, if one can still say so, where elementary Western logic is thus boldly defied, it conjures possibly *something different altogether*. And yet, by claiming or reclaiming as much (or as little, as we enter the terrain of "minimal things" and of "minimal semantics" and its "dual pragmatics" right here), we are neither deliberately nor unwittingly admitting a certain "defeat of thought."[51] In an at once metaphysically deep and resolutely pragmatic sense of the term, thinking "the Absolute" *all the way through its end* (*zu Ende*, in full Hegelian rigor) requires *a more thinking* "*thinking*" than we can presently envision, let alone articulate. And the latter only will *get off the*

51 Cf. Rodolphe Gasché, *Of Minimal Things: Studies on the Notion of Relation* (Stanford: Stanford University Press, 1999); Emma Borg, *Minimal Semantics* (Oxford: Clarendon Press, 2004), and Bruno Bosteels' forthcoming study, entitled *Philosophies of Defeat: The Jargon of Finitude*.

ground and *go onward* the very moment it rids the world of all too abstract and stale, petrified and reified, fetishized, that is, *falsely absolutized* oppositions; and this *almost* irrespective of the propositional and political positions, positionings or posturing involved (theoretical and political anti-fascism or, as Richard Rorty said, "anti-authoritarianism" being the sole exception that proves the rule in question).

On this reading, the very heart of Derrida's teaching and legacy would seem to lie in his tireless attempt at *absolving "the Absolute."* By this I mean his quasi-phenomenologically and quasi-hermeneutically *reducing* this notion's ancient no less than modern metaphysical and presentist premises, not least by deconstructing their meaning and force – decentering and disorienting the undeniable ways in which "the Absolute's" name, idea and concept have come to structure Western thought and societies and much else beside. It means to do so in a manner neither Husserl (in his ever-refined *epochés*) nor Heidegger (in his *Destruktion*, *Schritt zurück* and *Kehre*) fully envisioned.

***

The fact that Derrida's program of study and instruction perennially turns not only *away from* but also – and, it might have seemed, increasingly – *back to* the archives and virtual repositories of religion and mysticism, theology and testimony, apocalypticism and apophaticism has, on this view, little to do with his presumed early or late ethical preoccupation with Judaism and messianism. Describing oneself, not without self-irony, as "the last and the least of the Jews [*le dernier des juifs*]," as he would first do in "*Circonfession*" ("*Circumfession*"), reveals a different kind of relating or even belonging to a tradition that, like the language of "monolingualism," is "the only one one has" and yet "not one's own" per se or "owned up to," in the end. Still, if there was ever one single Levinasian insight into the nature of ethics and justice, even law, it is the following: *one has obligations to what one owes nothing to*. This said, there is nothing in such obligations that resembles or amounts to paying a belated tribute to what has come to be called, for various reasons, "secular faith," to say nothing of an "atheism" presumably more "radical" than "humanism" and committed to "this life" alone.[52] Quite the contrary.

For complicated reasons that I cannot hope to unpack here, Derrida's project was from the outset, throughout its mature development and until the very last one of *thinking* and *acting upon* a motif best described as one of "*inexistence*" or, as has been suggested, of "*inexistance.*" I borrow the latter term from Alain Badiou, who, in *Logiques des mondes* (*Logics of Worlds*), uses it to describe Derrida's undertaking, even though I am aware of the fact that the invocation and

52 This would be my friendly amendment and riposte to Martin Hägglund in *This Life: Secular Faith and Spiritual Freedom* (New York: Pantheon Books, 2019) and to his earlier *Radical Atheism: Derrida and the Time of Life* (Stanford: Stanford University Press, 2008).

use of "inexistence" takes multiple forms, offering alternative courses of both thought and action, not only in these two thinkers but also in other contemporaries, Jean-Luc Marion and Quentin Meillassoux among them, for whom "inexistence" is clearly an operative, generic and generative concept as well.[53] And, lest we forget, the later Levinas's insistence on what he terms the "otherwise than being [*autrement qu'être*]," in its own way, suggests nothing else.

For a phenomenology or speculative philosophy of "inexistence," to *see and set things aright* would – for obvious reasons, given the virtual nature and stringent "anti-naturalist" character of its very "object" and "objective" (if we can still say so) – require neither Kantian deductions nor formal procedures, and, least of all, a deliberative proceduralism in which "the force of the better argument," as Jürgen Habermas calls it, might or might not eventually prevail by means of a communicative praxis that has consensus written all over it as its very telos.

Instead, what is needed is a genuine *sense of and for the absolute*. And the latter, while it eludes the exclusively discursive grasp of concepts and categories – if not, thereby, the dis- and reorientation of its speculative idea – "traverses" as much as it "transcends" (Badiou writes) each and every being and thing, norm and value. That it does so methodically, in a determinate negative fashion, that is, in a theoretical practice of *askesis* that shuns even all too confident forms of silent allegiance to a purported "logical alien"[54] of whatever nature, makes this figure of thought all the more striking.

* * *

Derrida's project in *absolving* as well as *guarding* the absolute, that is, of negating and thereby determinately *affirming* it just as thoroughly – or, not unlike Hölderlin and Celan, doing something altogether different, beyond dialectical logic, still – is also and, perhaps, first and foremost, a form of "forgiveness" or "pardon." In this, Derrida unmistakenly harps on a motif already introduced in Hegel's *Phenomenology*, namely that of "the forgiveness [*die Verzeihung*]," which, Hegel says, is a "renunciation of itself."[55]

53 Alain Badiou, *Logiques des mondes. L'Être et l'Événement 2* (Paris: Éditions du Seuil, 2006); *Logics of Worlds: Being and Event II*, trans. by Alberto Toscano (New York: Continuum, 2009) and Quentin Meillassoux, *Après la finitude. Essai sur la nécessité de la contingence* (Paris: Éditions du Seuil, 2006); *After Finitude: An Essay on the Necessity of Contingency*, trans. by Ray Brassier (New York: Continuum, 2008) as well as Stéphane Vinolo, *Jean-Luc Marion, Apologie de l'inexistence*, Tome I: *La destinerrance des phénomènes*; Tome II: *Une phénoménologie discursive* (Paris: L'Harmattan, 2019).

54 Sofia Miguens (ed.), *The Logical Alien: Conant and His Critics* (Cambridge and London: Harvard University Press, 2020).

55 " – The forgiveness . . . is the renunciation of itself [*Verzichtleistung auf sich*], of its *non-actual* [*unwirkliches*] essence, an essence which it equates with this other consciousness which was *actual* [*wirkliches*] action, and it bestows recognition as good on what thought

Again, this task of absolving the absolute is undertaken nowhere more directly and exhaustively than throughout the pages of *Glas*, in a partial, if "systematic," reading of the whole of Hegel's oeuvre. Here, Derrida seeks to delineate what he comes to call "the infinite proposition of the hetero-tautological speculative dialectic," which encapsulates the very "truth" of an irrepressible and irresistible "phantasm" of philosophy. After myth and mythology, idolatry and all the idols of knowledge and the marketplace, including the fetishism and "theological niceties" of the commodity form Marx brought to light, "phantasm" is the ultimate frontier, then, the one we'll never cross. After all, Derrida writes: "What can there be aside of an absolute phantasm? What can one still add to it? Why and how could one desire to get out of it?"[56] It is this stunning triad or quartet of questions (so much for the phantasm of a "postmetaphysical thinking," à la Habermas and others) that guides the remainder of *Glas* as it zooms in on Hegelian idealism's quasi-circular logic, as illustrated by this longer passage:

> Everything that is, all [the] time [i.e., all time, at all times, HdV], is precomprehended, strictly, in the circle of *Sa* [i.e., *Savoir abolu*, Absolute Knowledge and Knowing], which always comes back to itself, presupposes its beginning and reaches it only at the end (*in sich zurückgehende Kreis, der seinen Anfang voraussetzt und ihn nur im Ende erreicht*).
>
> Try to *think* (but this word already holds us back in the circle) a remainder of *time* (but time already engages us in the circle), which would not be, which would not come under a present, a mode of being or presence that would consequently fall outside the circle of (the) *Sa*, would not fall outside of it as *its* negative, ready to get back on the tangent so as to remain bonded by the circle and let itself be drawn back by it. The remainder, moreover, would not fall out of it at all. All that falls indeed still comes under *Sa*.
>
> So it would be about a suspended remainder.
>
> Which would not be: neither presence, nor substance, nor essence. In general, we think that what remains is permanent, substantial, subsistent. Here the remainder would not remain in this sense.[57]

In other words, it would "be" the "inexistent" (although Derrida, admittedly, does not use that term in this context), at any rate, a non-factuality or

had determined acting to be, namely, evil; or, instead, it lets go of this difference between determinate thought and its determining judgment existing-for-itself, just as it lets go of its own, existing-for-itself, determining of action. –" (Hegel, *Phenomenology of Spirit*, 387–388/*Phänomenologie des Geistes*, 492).

56 Derrida, *Clang*, 252.

57 Ibid., 252–253.

virtuality, that reveals a deeper and wider sense or, for that matter, nonsense – more precisely, non-sense – without which no emergence or reemergence of new and old things, thought or acts, would ever happen, or could never end.

If the previous passage makes anything clear, it is that *Glas* is not an easy work. As an early commentator and Hegel scholar, Heinz Kimmerle, wisely observes, the massive work is an "anti-book":

> The unity of the book is broken up in that a plurality of texts are assembled, all of which are without beginning and end. The unity of the book is at the same time doubled. There are two books in one here – one column on and by Hegel and another on and by Genet. According to Derrida, if one can read a book within a book in this manner, 'the abyss . . . the bottomlessness of infinite redoubling,' opens up. 'The other is in the same.'[58]

Indeed, Hegel, his text and their counterpart – here: Jean Genet and his texts, not to mention all the marginal glosses interspersed through both columns of *Glas* – are *virtually* one and the same, forming a singular substantive body of work but seen under two seemingly altogether different aspects, each requiring a certain optics (and each calling for the other to be seen and acknowledged, one way or the other).

In *Glas*, mimicking the earlier reading of Levinas in "Violence and Metaphysics," we find the purported "other" right here, on the same page, "in the same." A simple consequence follows from this way of putting things. As there is nothing that Hegel's thought and system, as it is read here by Derrida, seems to exclude, moreover, as his philosophy, including his philosophy of religion, is just as fully *reflected* and *refracted* by Genet's literary and theatrical writing – again, as it is read by Derrida, in this particular context, *on* and *across* the other side of the empty space or abyss that separates two imposing, colossal "columns" – there is *prima facie* and *sensu stricto* absolutely nothing in which *Glas* contradicts or so much as "disagrees" with Hegel. What, then, would be the odds of such "generous repetition" achieving any significant and distinctive, that is, not merely noticeable but effective, pragmatic change in our understanding of our times, with its proclaimed *death knell* of philosophy, indeed, of *Bildung*, the humanities, respect for the law and much else besides?

***

Considering crossing the apparent abyss between the two columns of *Glas* or *Clang*, one wonders whether there is, indeed, a profound resonance, if not

58 Heinz Kimmerle, 'On Derrida's Interpretation of Hegel', in Stuart Barnett, ed., *Hegel After Derrida* (London and New York: Routledge, 1998), 227–238, 227; the quote is from Derrida, *Writing and Difference*, 296.

some analogy, correspondence or correlation between, for example, Hegel's motif of "the rose in the cross of the present," known from the introduction to the 1820 *Elements of the Philosophy of Right* and earlier, the 1807 essay '*Wer denkt abstrakt*? ['Who Thinks Abstractly']'), on the one hand, and Jean Genet's 1946 *Miracle de la rose* (*Miracle of the Rose*), on the other. There might be one or more, consisting, first and foremost, in a somewhat different or opposed view of and critical response to the presumably rational insight and accompanying (preceding or following) delight in our final or genuine reconciliation with what is considered our reality, the world as we find it. Or is such a comforting assumption precisely the kind of surface meaning and reading – aptly captured by the mantra "a rose is a rose, is a rose" – that *Glas* invites us to challenge in at least two different registers (and there may well be more)?

To answer these questions, it is important to ask ourselves, first, what does *glas* even mean? This much is clear, the word or term connotes a "clang" or, in German, a "*Klang*" but also, more specifically and ominously, a *Totenglocke*, which is the apt title of its published German translation.[59] Yet it is also clear that *Glas*' (or a glas') resounding announcement, not like the figure of the *shofar* in Celan's poem *Die Posaunenstelle* or "Trumpet-Part," as Derrida notes in one of his early, near-Talmudic glosses in the book, "is not yet a voice or a language . . . no longer mute, but not yet speaking."[60]

One is further tempted to find "structural correspondences among all the descriptions of the *Klang* in the *Aesthetics*, the *Phenomenology of Spirit*, the *Philosophy of Nature*, etc.,"[61] as Derrida himself indicates. But the question remains: what would it require to sound out this *glas*, and thereby, perhaps, succeed or risk silencing it once and for all? And, if this is not one's ambition (and how could it be, Derrida seems to tell each step of the way), how could we best *attune* ourselves to – indeed, *resonate* with – it? Could we harbor any hopes of turning ourselves into its true and effective *sounding board* and then also *trumpet* for it, one way or another? In any case, "*Klang*" stands opposed to "*Sprache*," and Derrida clearly equals it with "resonance,"[62] a

59 Jacques Derrida, *Totenglocke*, trans. by Hans-Dieter Gondek and Markus Sedlaczek (Paderborn: Fink Verlag, 2006).

60 Derrida, *Clang*, 9. On Derrida's reading of Celan, see my 'The Shibboleth Effect: On Reading Paul Celan', in Bettina Bergo and Raphael Zagury-Orly, eds., *Judeities* (New York: Fordham University Press, 2007), 175–213.

61 Derrida, *Clang*, 9.

62 Ibid., 14. Clearly, Derrida has in mind the, perhaps, impossible, yet all the more necessary, transition, not just of sounds to words, but, as it were, downstream, also of words to concepts, as is apparent in the following passage: "the family speaks and it does not speak; it is a family from the moment it speaks – passing from *Klang*, if you will, to *Sprache*, from resonance to language – but it destroys itself *qua* family as soon it speaks and abandons the *Klang*. Like natural language, like language in general, it stops being what it is as soon as it

concept that is at least as overdetermined as that of "relevance." What then is *Glas*' resonance, and what is its (ongoing or renewed) relevance, for us here and now?

***

Of course, what Derrida calls philosophy's inescapable "phantasm" here, Hegel, for his part and precisely insofar as he is invoking, expressing, evoking Absolute Knowledge in its ongoing Knowing, considers to be fully *rational*. Indeed, *de facto* and *de iure*, the Absolute is, on his view, the consequential development and explicit embodiment of *reason* in the most emphatic sense of the Kantian term "*Vernunft*," whose apparent terminological substitute, namely "*Geist*," comes to carry far more metaphysical and theological *weight* in Hegel's phenomenology, logic and philosophy of law than most of Western thought ever deemed itself capable or worthy of *conceiving speculatively*. Each of the Spirit's terms and rhetorical motifs, names and concepts, including what they come to stand or stand in for in Hegel's system, encyclopedia and lectures, are, moreover, taken as completely real, as wholly actualized already, such that the historical – and resolutely Christian – aspiration towards achieving its *pleroma* is seen and portrayed by him as having effectively come to fruition, *in his own day and age*.

This said, it is not immediately clear whether or to what extent, not to mention why and how, the "absolute phantasm" Derrida's *Glas* conjures in its pages – ultimately and resolutely – also *parts ways* with Hegel, with the Absolute's Spirit. With the benefit of hindsight, one could claim that Derrida, perhaps, follows a line or schema of argumentation here, which already anticipates his later answer to the question *Whither Marxism?* In the book based on his intervention at a conference devoted to this conundrum as well as several accompanying clarifications, Derrida would suggest that one could, should and, perhaps, even must take one's leave of *virtually* all Marxian theses that make up its historical, anthropological and economical premises and conclusions, including the dialectical and materialist ontology that may have originally grounded them (up to what point remaining an unresolved matter in scholarly debate up to this day). And yet, Derrida continues in that later post-1989 context, one could not be but "haunted" by the "specter" of Marx and Marxism, that is, by the

posits itself as such, it denies itself as nature in becoming what it is naturally, just like nature itself for that matter. . . . The family is essentially spiritual. Language too. . . By positing itself as a system of signs, existing in exteriority, language rises to the concept (internal ideal signification) and from then on denies itself as a system of natural signs. The thing (the referent) is sublated (*aufgehoben*) in the sign: raised up, spiritualized, magnified, embalmed, interiorized, idealized, named, since the name accomplishes the sign" (*Clang*, 14, trans. modified).

unrequited, if not broken, promise of socialism and communism, whose "New International" one would need to constantly invent and reinvent.

To the extent that Derrida's notion of "phantasm" not merely *mimics* and *redoubles* what is, from Kant to Hegel, postulated as a "fact of reason" – and a "total social fact" by Marcel Mauss, at that – the understanding of this notion is itself, in turn, *comprised* in and, hence, also *compromised* by the concept and practice of "Spirit." The "phantasm," in its very concept and, indeed, appearance cannot escape reason at will. Deconstruction, then, affirms "phantasm" and "spirit" alike, in one breath, as it were. It acquiesces in a, for all purposes, quasi-perennial process of interpretation and transformation that is as much observed in historical, political and even psychic reality as it is methodically espoused and, in so doing, *turned up a notch*. Adorno spoke of a logic of "exaggeration"; Derrida sees in it a *surenchère*, an outbidding, of sorts.

With this in mind, *Glas's* idiom and pursuit of "absolute phantasm" certainly also change the scene and tone (faithful to Hölderlin's *Wechsel der Töne*), while invoking, as mentioned, a *spectrality* that can no longer be expected to *wither away*, like the so-called "Diamat" states (to cite Adorno's disparaging characterization of Eastern European "real existing socialism") would end up doing in fact. By contrast, in its formal preparation and revolutionary initiation of modern *Sittlichkeit*, which is the very name and concept of the substance and eventual overcoming of civil or bourgeois society, Hegel's and Marx's texts, on Derrida's and notably *Glas*' view, bequeathed a certain *Spirit of Trust*, strange as that expression (and, as we will see below, title) may further sound *at present* to rather disillusioned, if not nihilistic, contemporary ears.

***

"Deconstruction," if we insist on keeping that somewhat technical term, given its recent history and obvious merits, might be redefined as *equally Hegelian and Marxian* in outlook and overall strategy. Counterintuitive as this may sound, it resembles, to a point of indistinction, dialectics *zu Ende gedacht* (i.e., thought through and executed consistently). As a methodic injunction, in its redefinition of Kantian "critique" as much as, in its praxis, in espousing both Hegelian contemplation and Marxian struggle, deconstruction further also *provisionally* and *strategically* joins Frankfurt School Critical Theory's efforts and institutional endeavors.[63] It does so by offering and fostering a novel form of so-called "immanent criticism." This redoubled "critique" steers clear not only from the formalism of Kantian epistemology, its ethics and aesthetics, but also from the all too self-assured, self-indulgent forms of

63 See my "Jacques Derrida and the Theodor W. Adorno Prize of the City of Frankfurt," in *Modern Language Notes*, Vol. 131, No. 5, December, 2016, 1276-1294.

moralist posturing, of so-called "beautiful souls," whether portrayed as Romantics (in Hegel's mature view), as utopian socialists (as a seasoned Marx saw them) or, indeed, as left-wing infantile, wannabe communists (as V.I. Lenin put it more brutally).

It is deconstruction's *infinite nearness to* as well as *infinite distance from* objective and absolute idealist dialectics alike, in its relentless engagement with the former's speculative logic as well as presumed phenomenological and historically materialist inversions (in Marx and, more importantly for Derrida, at one point certainly, in Tran Duc Thao and Louis Althusser), that once again deserves our attention. And not only on the occasion of the twentieth anniversary of Derrida's passing, which invites us to revisit his teaching and writing, his library and archive, far more deeply and broadly than we usually have occasion to. There is an equally poignant reason to be found in the fact that Hegel's metaphysics and logics, next to his phenomenology and practical philosophy, have become a source of renewed interest, not least in recent studies published under the heading of so-called *analytical* German Idealism and also in revised forms of Hegelian Marxism (both of which, by the way, take an almost opposed approach compared to that of so-called analytical Marxism). These two emerging schools of thought (if one can call them that) not only seem to largely *corroborate* but also significantly *expand* on some of Derrida's guiding intuitions in his readings of Hegel and Marx and, hence, help us to elaborate on his lasting insights into the nature of "the Absolute" and its ongoing "relevance" to questions and matters of "theory and praxis."

Among these recent studies, Robert Brandom's 2019 *A Spirit of Trust: A Reading of Hegel's Phenomenology*, a title I alluded to previously, stands out for several reasons.[64] Its massive tome forms a lone column of formidable reinterpretation that awaits another, separated, no doubt, by an "empty space," and that, in that sense, stands "apart." Yet it lends an attentive ear, an "echo chamber," to use the idiom *Glas* adopts, to Derrida's musings about a *Klang* (*Clang*) he both sounds out and incessantly modulates, as if mindful of Hölderlin, whose *Dichtung* and, it seems, apocryphal "spiritual communism [*Communismus der Geister*]" Derrida tracks more obliquely here.

For Brandom in his *magnum opus*, as for Derrida in *Glas*, the concept of *Sittlichkeit*, next to that of forgiveness (and, Brandom adds, "magnanimity"), are among the key takeaways from the reading of Hegel, of the *Phenomenology of Spirit*, first and foremost. Moreover, in *A Spirit of Trust*, what Brandom calls "semantic holism" and what I have come to call "deep pragmatism" go hand in hand to provide a radically novel account of

64 Robert B. Brandom, *A Spirit of Trust: A Reading of Hegel's Phenomenology* (Cambridge and London: The Belknap Press of Harvard University Press, 2019). Cf. Gilles Bouché, *Reading Brandom: On 'A Spirit of Trust'* (New York: Routledge, 2020).

normativity and institutionalism that salvages fundamental intuitions of German Idealism, albeit in a new systematic key. Brandom's analytical reading is at once rigorous and, when compared to some recent Hegelian-*cum*-Marxist interpretations pursuing what seem to be very similar theoretical and practical objectives, also highly selective in the motifs it "makes explicit."

Yet, sadly, Brandom has apparently little patience for Derrida, mentioning the latter only just once and in this single instance characterizing him only somewhat stereotypically as an exponent of "Ferdinand de Saussure's conceptually pre-Kantian and pre-Fregean terminology." Derrida, Brandom goes on to conclude all too hastily, offers "a picture of a world consisting only of signifiers, with the only things available to be signified being further signifiers," at which point, he concludes, "things have gone badly wrong."[65] Brandom thus merely follows the interpretation his teacher Richard Rorty had already proposed in *Consequences of Pragmatism*, where he characterized Derrida's philosophy as "a kind of writing." Rorty would later add that Derrida's, in origin Husserlian, penchant for systematicity and quasi-transcendentality – as opposed to just enjoying idiosyncracy, celebrating "irony" and "contingency" – meant that he was merely pouring "Nietzschean wine" into "Kantian vases" (thus leaving the formal structure or schema of "metaphysics" – according to *Grammatology*, "our language" – firmly in place).

One need not accept these gross simplifications, to observe a surprising parallel between Brandom's "semantic holism" in a pragmatic key in *A Spirit of Trust*, on the one hand, and Derrida's account of Hegel, in *Glas*, on the other. After all, the generalized "semiology," which the early Derrida reads into Hegel, is, on closer scrutiny, not all that far removed from the "semantic holism" Brandom here calls his own. By the same token, Derrida's later introduction and understanding of "pragrammatology," notably in *Limited Inc*, likewise resonates with the motif of the "deeply pragmatic" that Brandom, for his part, attributes to each of these mutually constitutive and, it would seem (also in his eyes), opposite terms (i.e., "deep" and "pragmatic"). Yet a further parallel might even be found in the figure of the inexhaustible "archive" (to cite Derrida's term, in *Mal d'archive* [*Archive Fever*]), which takes up a comparable place in Brandom's earlier work, entitled *Making It Explicit*.[66] What to make of these parallels?

***

As Brandom reminds us in his discussion of the final pages of the "Spirit" chapter of the *Phenomenology of Spirit*, asking for and offering *forgiveness*

65 Brandom, *A Spirit of Trust*, 52.

66 For a discussion, which I will not summarize here, see my 'Introduction: Why Still "Religion"?', in Hent de Vries, ed., *Religion – Beyond A Concept* (New York: Fordham University Press, 2008), 1–98.

in response to "confession" (yet another parallel with one of Derrida's important motifs) is, in fact,

> the *final* form of recognition Hegel envisages. On the practical side it is to be the overcoming of modern alienation, reachieving *Sittlichkeit* in a higher, self-conscious form. On the cognitive side, it is the social and institutional framework for bringing to bear the metaconceptual categories of *Vernunft*, and so for achieving the final, adequate form of the understanding of the relation between the normative and the natural that Hegel calls 'Absolute Knowing.'[67]

Further expanding on his own understanding of the concept and its practice, which is likewise considered "spiritual" and expressive of an essential "truth," Brandom sees in *Sittlichkeit* the very condition and horizon without which no modern polity could emerge, much less respect and maintain the rule of law, which must be applicable to – and, where its judgment and ruling is just, also enforced on – all. Tied to confession, forgiveness thus plays for Brandom a role that is not unlike that of "originary affirmation" (Derrida), the "hermeneutical right" (Hans-Georg Gadamer) or, in a more analytical philosophical register, the very preponderance of assumptions of "truth" over "falsity" and the "skepticism" that the latter may inspire (Donald Davidson). In Brandom's reconstruction:

> Forgiveness [*Verzeihung*] is a recognitive attitude that practically acknowledges the complementary contributions of particularity and universality to individuality – both the way the application of the universal raises the particular to the level of the individual and the way application to particulars actualizes the universal in an individual. It is a practical, community-instituting form of self-consciousness that is structured by metaconceptual categories of *Vernunft*, rather than *Verstand*. It is *sittlich*, rather than alienated, in understanding the complex interdependence of norms (universals, on the side of content; necessity, on the side of force) and attitudes and the process by which together they institute and articulate normative statuses (commitments). It is, in short, what ushers in the form of community Hegel calls 'Absolute Spirit,' and the form of self-consciousness he calls 'Absolute Knowing.'" Understanding this is what the whole *Phenomenology* has been aiming at: "that one far-off event, toward which the whole creation moves."[68]

Brandom ties this fundamentally "backward-looking" notion of "forgiveness," itself a "speech act" and discursive gesture, of sorts, to that of

67 Brandom, *A Spirit of Trust*, 598–599.
68 Ibid., 598. The latter quote is from Alfred Lord Tennyson's poem 'In Memoriam.'

the more "forward-looking" notion of so-called "trust" (Hegel's term is *Vertrauen*). It would seem that the latter's implicit ground and mode of operation is not discursive in essence, from beginning to end, but instead what Brandom, modifying Hegel, calls a "recognitive attitude." Importantly, this disposition relies on a spirit and, we might add, spiritual practice of "magnanimity" (yet another form of "originary affirmation" and its "yes, yes," in the Derridian lexicon), nothing less, nothing more. Neither demonstrable nor explicable in conceptual and discursive terms, its mode and mood, in its very moment and potential momentum, is far more ethereal (if also, strangely, far more forceful, indeed, effective). One wonders with Brandom's earlier work in mind whether it can so much be "made explicit" to the fullest extent (or, come to think of it, even at all). And yet, it is "complementary" to the discursive act of "forgiveness," as Brandom goes on to note:

> Prospective trust that one will be forgiven for what one confesses is the recognitive attitude complementary to forgiveness. Together these reciprocal practical attitudes produce a community with a symmetrical, *edelmütig* [generous, noble, HdV] recognitive structure. The choice of the term 'trust' is motivated by Hegel's use of it [*Vertrauen/vertrauen*] to describe what was progressive about Faith [*Glauben*, HdV], in spite of the cognitive errors for which it stands condemned by Enlightenment: the reciprocal recognitive structure of the religious community.[69]

What this means is not hard to fathom. One-third into the text of the *Phenomenology of Spirit*, Hegel claims that we have already "before us" the elementary "Notion of Spirit." Yet to acquire this notion is only the first next step on the ladder that is the process and progress of consciousness realizing its subjective as well as objective, social and political freedom, including its legal underpinnings and guarantees. The elementary form of "notion of Spirit," like the "recognitive structure of the religious community," thus merely prefigures and anticipates what is a far more substantial and full Spirit-to-come, as it were, its *pleroma*, as we found. As Brandom comments:

> What still lies ahead for consciousness is the experience of what Spirit is – this absolute substance which is the unity of the different independent self-consciousnesses, which, in their opposition, enjoy perfect freedom and independence: 'I' that is 'We' and 'We' that is 'I.'[70]

69 Ibid., 621.
70 Ibid., 622.

In the very transition from the "Spirit" to the "Religion" chapter in the *Phenomenology of Spirit*, Hegel had spoken of the two "I's" – the inwardness of consciousness as it is or has turned in itself and the real or actual self, oriented outward – mediating and emphatically or finally reconciling singularity and universality concretely (rather than mere particularity and generality all too abstractly). The two I's, distinct as seemingly opposed poles as they are and must remain, conceptually and systematically, if not thereby also speculatively speaking, *revert to each other*, thus relinquishing their alienating separateness. In so doing, they open up a perspective in which nothing short of a divine presence becomes apparent, as if the early eighteenth-century mantra and pamphlets entitled *vox populi, vox Dei* were given new meaning, thereby obtaining a renewed political as well as historical-cultural and institutional force:

> The word of reconciliation is the *existing* spirit which immediately intuits in its opposite the pure knowing of itself as the *universal* essence, intuits it in the pure knowing of itself as *singular individuality* existing absolutely inwardly [*der absolut in sich seienden Einzelheit*] – a reciprocal recognition which is *absolute* spirit.
>
> Absolut spirit comes into existence only at the point where its pure knowing of itself is the opposition and flux [*Wechsel*] of itself with itself. . . . The reconciling *yes* (*Ja*), in which both I's let go of their opposed *existence*, is the existence of the *I* extended to two-ness, which therein remains the same as itself and which has the certainty of itself in its complete self-relinquishing and its opposite – It is the God that appears [*der erscheinende Gott*] in the midst of those who know themselves as pure knowing.[71]

In his 1830 Berlin address on the occasion of the three hundredth anniversary of the so-called *Augsburg Confession* (1530), drafted by Melanchton and inspired by Martin Luther, Hegel duly noted that, before the Confession, the "'Christian world was divided in two classes,' one that had all the rights and privileges (the ecclesiasticals [but Hegel will hardly have limited his reference to the oppressive class of the priests and prelates in Roman Catholicism]) and the other that was 'reduced to servitude [*Knechtschaft*].'"[72] As Terry Pinkard continues:

> But since what was always implicit in Christianity was its declaration of itself as committed to the dignity of all, working out that implicit belief in Christianity came to require us to adopt the Protestant principle that

71 Hegel, *Phenomenology of Spirit*, 388 and 389/*Phänomenologie des Geistes*, 493 and 494.
72 Pinkard, *Hegel*, 629. The citation is from Hegel's 'Rede bei der dritten Säkularfeier der Übergabe der Augsburger Konfession', in Hegel, *Berliner Schriften 1818–1831*, 31.

> each individual is ineluctably in the position such that with regard to 'the relationship which he has to God and God to him, [he] himself produces it with God, and that God Himself for his part completes [*vollendet*] Himself in the human spirit.'[73]

And what is true of the individual I of each Christian here holds true even more so of the collective, communal, popular "We" Hegel invokes and relies on to bring the "science of the experience of consciousness," to recall his early title for the project of the *Phenomenology*, to fruition and its completion, that is, again, its *pleroma*.

***

What exactly, in this light, does Derrida make of Hegel's *infinitism*, that is, of his metaphysical, onto-theological as well as deeply and broadly "logical" conception of Absolute Knowledge or Knowing, with all the fullness, the *parousia* and, as said, the *pleroma* it also entails? Do deconstructive and speculative "logic" fundamentally differ in their respective conceptions of the Absolute or, indeed, God? And this, notwithstanding their similar path of deploying a consequent – that is, virtually negative as well as strangely "originary" and "affirmative" – thinking that takes its avowed phenomenological and dialectical method in different directions, *in a different spirit*, as it were? In the words of the recent translators of the reedition of *Glas/Clang*, David Wills and Geoffrey Bennington, we may surmise that, like its two imposing columns, Derrida's and Hegel's own works are not only "[a]part – you immediately see the empty space – but contiguous or adjacent enough to produce an echo chamber."[74]

What Hegel pursues, Derrida's reading makes amply clear in these pages, is an emphatic and comprehensive idea that resembles neither that of the "Tragic," "Romantic," "Literary" or even "Fragile Absolute" (to mention just these few mischaracterizations that have figured prominently in recent and not-so-recent studies of German Idealism). If anything, Hegel's Absolute (as in Absolute Knowledge or Knowing, including the Absolute Religion leading *up to* – and leaning *into* – it) is a *metaphysical* and *political* as well as *logical* notion. It is even a governing concept in his philosophy of law, the legal aspect of governing and the very idea of justice. As the dot on the proverbial "i" of all past and present things existing, indeed, as the necessary horizon of all possible events and institutions that the future may yet allow for, the Absolute is thus more than the sum total of all that has happened or may still arrive. Logically, its infinity is *transfinite*, its idea is that of a

73 Pinkard, *Hegel*, 629. The citation is from Hegel's *Berliner Schriften 1818–1831*, 33.
74 'Translator's Preface', ix.

"beyond" of and "otherwise than" all being. Its infinity, we said, "is" (if we can still say so) "inexistent."

Is Brandom's analytical effort at pairing Hegel's "semantic holism" with deep "pragmatism," while shunning the presumed extremes of "pansemanticism" (i.e., of concepts and discursivity going all the way through, down and up), on one end, and of "panpsychism,"[75] on the other, not too far off, then? After all, what "is" the Absolute, if it can not only be said to "exist" or "inexist," but must, first of all, be seen and *phenomenalized* as "coming into existence"; in other words, if this Absolute, on Hegel's own terms, must be said to "become" and is "actualized," if not *all at once*, then at least without reserve. Transfinite and inexistent, its *once and for all*, its *parousia* and *pleroma*, reveals itself not merely *in* but also *after* all that can be said and done.

To seriously raise, let alone answer, these questions, one would have to consult and discuss several relevant other commentators in the matter. I am thinking not only of Catherine Malabou's 1996 *L'Avenir de Hegel. Plasticité, temporalité, dialectique* (*The Future of Hegel: Plasticity, Temporality, and Dialectic*), prefaced by Derrida, but also of Hamacher's massive 1978 preface to Hegel's early writings (1796–1800), notably *Der Geist des Christentums*, and entitled "pleroma – *zu Genesis und Struktur einer dialektischen Hermeneutik bei Hegel* (translated, without its added corpus of Hegelian text fragments, as *Pleroma – Reading in Hegel* and recently reissued in German (as in the English translation, without Hegel's fragments).[76] Other publications, not least an early essay by Gayatri Chakravorty Spivak and an edited volume entitled *Hegel After Derrida*, come to mind.[77]

To give just one example, taken from this still growing dossier, Malabou's open question, in *The Future of Hegel*, perhaps best captures the issues at stake: "Does Absolute Knowledge mark the *end*, in the twofold sense, of all events and any possible event? Must it be interpreted as the reduction of all temporality and the advent of the *parousia* of spirit?"[78] The possible answer to this pertinent summary of Hegel's predicament, as the latter seems to close off the course run

75 Brandom, *A Spirit of Trust*, 241.

76 Catherine Malabou, *L'Avenir de Hegel. Plasticité, temporalité, dialectique* (Paris: Librairie Vrin, 1999); *The Future of Hegel: Plasticity, Temporality, and Dialectic*, Preface by Jacques Derrida, trans. by Lisabeth During (London and New York: Routledge, 2005); Werner Hamacher, 'pleroma – *zu Genesis und Struktur einer dialektischen Hermeneutik bei Hegel*', in G.W.F. Hegel, ed., *Der Geist des Christentums*. Schriften 1796–1800, introduced by Werner Hamacher (Frankfurt am Main, Berlin, and Vienna: Ullstein Verlag, 1978) and republished and edited by Shina Sara Ottenburger and Peter Trawny (Frankfurt am Main, Klostermann, 2021); *Pleroma – Reading in Hegel*, trans. by Nicholas Walker and Simon Jarvis (Stanford: Stanford University Press, 1998). See in the context of law and justice also Werner Hamacher, *Sprachgerechtigkeit* (Frankfurt am Main: S. Fischer Verlag, 2018).

77 Stuart Barnett, ed., *Hegel After Derrida* (London and New York: Routledge, 1998).

78 Malabou, *The Future of Hegel*, 127.

by the dialectic all too prematurely, must be *either* a resolute "No, not at all!" *or*, on the contrary, a qualified, more cautious "Yes, perhaps, it might well be." Do Derrida and, with him, Malabou choose or hesitate between these two alternatives, assuming that is what they are, two poles of a dilemma that must be resolved?

This much seems clear: for Derrida, the future, when all is said and done, may turn out to be 1) that, *one day, there is actually none* (for all or some) such that (for all or some) there will be nothing (more) to come and hope for, or 2) that *there is one and will be one for all – with all one could wish for – at long last*, perhaps *for the long haul* (excluding dystopian scenarios and outcomes or so-called massive extinction events). But, even in the improbable eventuality that either 1) nothing will happen or 2) all will be fine for the foreseeable future, we cannot exclude that the *standing possibility* of even the apparent *end of all things* – and be it that of the very *parousia* and *pleroma* – might, at some point, in turn, be *retracted*, hence *negated* in its very negation again. Such a reversal could well take place in full and in either direction. It could take the form of a rebooting and resetting of the dismal end and ends of history, allowing us to wake up from its nightmare, shedding "old forms and thoughts"; or, it could be a dreaded catastrophic one-off event that brings everything to an abrupt, everything but messianic, standstill.

The future of the very concept and experience of the future (the *arrive-t-il?* of which Jean-François Lyotard makes so much in his *Le différend* [*The Differend*]) thus "continues" to be virtually exposed to *either* revelation and revolution *or* their counter-manifestation and counter-revolution, at any moment, on each occasion. And this even when and where the Kojèvian motif of "the end of history" has come to pass *already*. After all, what's over and done with *cannot* and *must not* have the last word (logically, legally, etc.). Such is the essential nature of every "to come," whether something (worthwhile or terrible, with much in between) is coming or not.

***

As one recent commentator on Hegel's life and work, namely Klaus Vieweg, aptly notes:

> In principle, freedom should orient human communities; this is Hegel's only theory about the future. He promises no paradise on earth, nor does he claim to have any mystical visions about the future. . . . The end of history requires people to continually determine freedom in new ways and constitute it in new forms.[79]

79 Klaus Vieweg, *Hegel: The Philosopher of Freedom*, trans. by Sophia Kottman (Stanford: Stanford University Press, 2023), 350.

All this is a way of saying, as Malabou does, that "freedom never becomes habituated to itself."[80] Both Derrida and Brandom would surely agree on this point.

Yet from the perspective I have outlined here, such an account, elegant, plausible and even necessary as it is, also risks underselling the Hegelian motif of our progress in the consciousness and realization of freedom somewhat. It tends to underestimate to what extent or in what way theologoumena rather than mythemes or literary tropes ("allegories," as Brandom calls them) entice and enable Hegel and, in his footsteps, Derrida to *reach farther out* and – paradoxically or, rather, aporetically – *even well beyond the thinkable*. And to do so, no one has shown us more compellingly than Derrida, who inaugurates and exemplifies a philosophical type of inquiry that *absolves* Absolute Knowledge and Knowing from whatever traditional mythological and theological as well as modern metaphysical preconceptions that refuse to enter the deeper and wider recesses, reservoirs, repositories and, indeed, "labor" of the concept, in Hegelian and Marxian parlance.

This, all by itself, instills yet a different sense of – and relation to – "tradition" as such and in toto. Again, *Glas* leaves no doubt: "*Traditio* is *Aufhebung*."[81] This sublation, insofar as it is neither abstract nor completely off but, instead, provides a "relevant translation," remains traditional or, at the very least, an integral part of that very same tradition ("the circle") and does so by definition, of necessity. This perhaps then, is what Absolute Knowledge or Knowing can only aim or pretend to "be." For even the most revolutionary, novel and innovative thought or act fulfills a promise of old and, in so doing, absolves its past (at the presumed or postulated end of which stands *pleroma*).

A reference to "religion" may make that clearer. For if Hegel "takes God for a subject, both in the sense of a 'subject of the exposition' and of 'the constitution of God as a subject'"; moreover, if it is "in God and as God that we see manifested the 'becoming subject' of substance,"[82] then we may rightfully ask what conceptual lines of differentiation and demarcation can still be maintained between, say, the *Phenomenology*'s introduction and its later discussion of "revealed religion" in the last segment of its "Religion" chapter and the one addressing "Absolute Knowledge or Knowing" toward its end. The two are not separate, that much is obvious, as all "essence" must surely "appear." But to say that the latter (i.e., Absolute Knowledge or Knowing) merely or fully sublates – that is, sets aside, guards and elevates – the former (i.e., religion) is also to *short-circuit* the system, squaring its "circle," if one can say so. For the very concept and practice of *Aufhebung* are modeled after an operation

80 Malabou, *The Future of Hegel*, 81.
81 Derrida, *Clang*, 15.
82 Malabou, *The Future of Hegel*, 82.

whose transition and figuration are *theological* as much as they are *logical* and *ontological.* At a minimum, Hegel is somewhat "hermetic" in this respect precisely. Yet, if Absolute Knowledge or Knowing negates and sets aside, maintains and elevates Revealed Religion, thus salvaging it *quasi-theologically*, then which of the two, speculative philosophy or revealed theology, has the last word?[83]

One is reminded of Derrida's opening reference to Hegel's riposte in the 1802 article '*Glauben und Wissen*' ('Faith and Knowledge'), echoed in Derrida's '*Foi et savoir*' ('Faith and Knowledge'), arguably one of the latter's most revealing texts ever devoted to the archive of religious historical moments and motifs, including their modern momentum and mediatic modalities. Here, likewise, Derrida falls back on an insight that may well have been Hegel's own, especially if we are to follow Pirmin Stekeler's apt summary judgment that

> for a sufficiently patient and competent reader . . . [Hegel] makes sufficiently clear that the word 'God' is yet to be understood in its proper [*rechten*] sense and cannot simply be read as a name of *a presumed referent* [or object] *that is already known* [*eines schon als bekannt unterstellten Gegenstandes*].[84]

On Stekeler's account of Hegel's view, "God" should not be equated with "Absolute Spirit" as their very sense and reference (their *Sinn und Bedeutung*, as in Frege's discussion of "*Gleichheit*") are surely *not exactly the same.* But then, do they need to be in order to mediate, if not sublate, each other as the respective traditional and modern as well as "relevant," translations of "Who" or "What" has, strictly speaking, in full logical rigor, neither name nor concept, sense nor reference? As Stekeler goes on to claim:

> It seems *prima facie* as if the expression 'absolute Spirit' [stands] simply for what is hardly more than a merely verbally secularized god. In

83 Of course, for Revealed Religion, as Hegel puts it in his *Vorlesungen über die Philosophie der Religion*, in the section on 'Absolute Religion,' the manifestation in question comes "from without [*von Aussen*]": "The absolute religion is the *revelatory* (*offenbare*) religion, the religion that has itself as its content and fulfillment (*Erfüllung*). But it is also called the *revealed* (*geoffenbarte*) religion – which means, on the one hand, that it is revealed by God, that God has given himself for human beings to know what he is; and, on the other hand, that it is revealed *positive* religion in the sense that it has come from without (*von Aussen*), has been given to them." G. W. F. Hegel, *Lectures on the Philosophy of Religion*, ed. by P. C. Hodgson, trans. by R. F. Brown and J. M. Stewart, with the assistance of H. S. Harris (Berkeley: University of California Press, 1984–1987), Vol. 3, 394.

84 Pirmin Stekeler, *Hegels Phänomenologie des Geistes. Ein dialogischer Kommentar. Bd. 1: Gewissheit und Vernunft* (Hamburg: Felix Meiner Verlag, 2014), 36. My translation, italics added.

> reality, however, Hegel distinguishes the objective Spirit as the inner subject matter [*Gegenstand*] of the *humanities* [*Geisteswissenschaften*], in other words, that which is thematized under History or Law, the State or Art, from a common We [*gemeinsamen Wir*]. This We is the absolute Spirit. It is the spirit that *We are*. This spirit forms a sort of background framework [*Hintergrundrahmen*], especially when we actively execute something and are, thereby, always already cooperative in one way or other. The absolute Spirit exists as the *generic-collective subject* of human forms of praxis.[85]

In sum, it is nothing but the "global" collectivity, spanning the European sciences from their ancient beginnings and promise to their modern (or, on Brandom's account, even "postmodern") fulfillment. And, again, this latter, as it takes the penultimate or final form of *parousia* and *pleroma*, is itself, qua *Aufhebung*, nothing but a part of something larger and strangely inclusive in turn. A further summation as much as summing up of "tradition," it is, *n'en déplaise* its Christian origins, stages and ends, a part and parcel also of *Kabbalah*. For this reason, Adorno (the ultimate consequent dialectician and negative metaphysician, if ever there was one) does not hesitate to invoke as his critical foil, virtual repository and final horizon.

***

Often used as an adjective or adverb, the term "absolute," derived from the Latin *absolutus*, the past participle of the verb *absolvere*, connotes the "loosening," "detaching" and "completing" of what can thus not be considered "dependent" on anything or anyone. Not grounded in some further, preceding or governing principle and, hence, self-positing and -moving, expressing and obeying only the nonformal tautology of the Biblical "I am I" (to the extent that it is, for Hegel as it will be for Fichte, a subject, indeed), the absolute is, in a sense, "self-contained" and "perfect."[86]

We know that "the absolute" or *absolutum* is first used as a noun by Nicholas of Cusa in his 1440 *De docta ignorantia* (*On Learned Ignorance*), where the term designates God, the *coincidentia oppositorum*. Elsewhere, God is also characterized by Cusanus as the *non aliud*, that is, as the one and only *not-* or *none other*, knowing neither determination nor, consequently, negation, as, per Spinoza's dictum, *omnis determinatio negatio est*: God has no "determinate negation [*bestimmte Negation*]" that we could give *voice* to; in Hegel's idiom, its meaning is not even "abstract."

85 Ibid., 56–57.
86 Michael Inwood, *A Hegel Dictionary* (Oxford and Cambridge: Blackwell Publishers, 1992), 27.

We also recall that *das Absolute*, in the wake of Kant and German Idealism, references the "unconditioned" and "ultimate reality" of all things and objects as well as of living and conscious beings.[87] By all counts, these seemingly concurring notions entail a plenitude, a fullness or, again, a *pleroma* of signification and force – one that is omnipresent and omnipotent – and that epitomizes the divine, at least in its theological, philosophical and then also onto-theological, that is, metaphysical understanding and definition. Further, to think of "the Absolute" as the "absolvent," then, derived from the Latin verb *absolvere*, translates itself into the modern philosophical vocabulary, with the connotation of releasing someone or something of blame, by acquittal or pardon. We are told that this meaning and usage find its first occurrence in English in Thomas Hobbes' 1651 *Leviathan*, which speaks of its aim to "absolve the divine laws" (here: from their presumed justification of political revolution).

Derrida, likewise, establishes a link between "the absolute" and "absolving" and makes explicit reference to "pardon," which in the English translation of his *Qu'est-ce qu'une traduction 'relevante'?* published in *Critical Inquiry*, is rendered as "mercy." The latter term appears to be borrowed from Shakespeare's *The Merchant of Venice* – "Mercy seasons justice" – a text Derrida comments upon here. As Derrida recalls, in Hegel's *Phenomenology of Spirit*,

> the movement toward philosophy and absolute knowledge as the truth of the Christian religion passes through pardon [*pardon*]. Pardon is a *relève*, it is in its essence an *Aufhebung*. It is translation as well. In the horizon of expiation, redemption, reconciliation, and redemption.[88]

All this takes place, in Hegel's text, Derrida reminds us further, at the end of the chapter on *Die offenbare Religion*, immediately before the chapter on *Das absolute Wissen*, which is where "absolute religion" transitions into absolute knowledge or knowing, itself the very "truth of religion."[89] This truth, one might add, is hardly *justified* through "faith alone [*sola fide*]," as if the gesture alone would allow us to tap into a stand-alone archive or already available resource and repository. Rather, it is through the concept's labor, through negation and mediation and, ultimately, through a potentially infinite series of translations that it – religion's "truth content" and "truth moment" (to use Adorno's philosophical terminology) – comes off the ground, into existence. Non-synonymous substitutions all, these translations, even

87 Ibid.

88 Jacques Derrida, *Qu'est-ce qu'une traduction 'relevante'?* (Paris: Éditions de l'Herne, 2005), 66; 'What Is a "Relevant" Translation?', trans. by Lawrence Venuti (Winter 2001) 27 *Critical Inquiry* 174–200, 197 (trans. modified).

89 Ibid., 77 n.11/197 n. 9.

where "relevant," a form of *Aufhebung*, do not add up to a script of signs *per se* or *exclusively*, as much as Derrida, early on, speaks of the need for "an introduction to Hegel's semiology," as we have seen. And since Derrida nowhere confuses semiology or even "generalized writing" with the reign of signs all the way up and down – lest we forget, in the phrase "there is nothing outside the text," text connotes "context," even "History" – Brandom, for all his impatience in reading Derrida's text, is largely in agreement with him when he differentiates between Hegel's "semantic holism" and "pansemanticism."

* * *

If phenomenological and dialectical "results" are at all pertinent where Derrida's absolution of Hegel is under discussion, then we must conclude that *neither theism nor atheism* are viable options and, hence, *irrelevant* to the questions that *Glas* revisits and reconsiders. Derrida absolves Hegel from Absolute Knowledge and Knowing insofar as the latter is revealed to be not fully integral to or eventually integrated in the latter's phenomenological, logical and metaphysical project. By the same token, Derrida and Hegel, as he reads him, absolve Absolute Knowledge or Knowing *in* and *for itself*.

What this means is that the latter is seen as justifiably put to the task of *infinite* justification, one that stops short at neither the name and concept of the Biblical God nor the ancient, medieval and modern metaphysical doctrine of the *ens realissimum*. If anything, Absolute Knowledge or Knowing, including even knowing "the Absolute" as "infinite" or "transfinite," is thus portrayed as a provisional designation, as a predication that is not without its own predicament. There is, in sum, nothing acquired by means of merely linear, asymptotic progression that we can or should *count* on here.

Quite to the contrary, "the Absolute" and its experiential, if not necessarily epistemic, mode of making itself "known" is *apocalyptic* through and through. It requires no eschatological horizon, but also no divine withholding or reservation, whose futurity (as in the Romantic idea of a "coming God") should make us pause and interest us the most. Like a thief in the night coming unannounced, its *parousia* and *pleroma* may, for all we will ever know, be right in front of us, *mirabile dictu* even ready to hand. To vary a motif that Derrida dwells on in his Jerusalem lecture devoted to the apophatics of mysticism and negative theology, "the Absolute" resembles a "secret" that need and cannot be kept, that sees and sets all things aright, thus affirming the traditional and proverbial "all in all," *all at once*.

In his Foreword to the English translation by A.V. Miller of Hegel's *Phenomenology of Spirit*, J.N. Findlay makes a reference to "the compassion which enables the man of conscience to forgive the sin-soiled man of action."[90] But given Hegel's invectives, in that work, against the "unhappy consciousness" and, somewhat later, the "beautiful soul," one should, perhaps, rather conclude that the two contrasting, indeed, opposing, normative attitudes of "the man of conscience" and "the man of action" in fact and by right *absolve each other*. Far from conditioning, explaining and determining or orienting each other unilaterally or even mutually, these virtual or polar opposites *relate without relating exactly*. Rather than "conscience" physically or metaphysically "causing," not to mention morally justifying, "action" (or the other way around), each pole of their constellation *implicates* and *engages* the other in all the schematizations of either thought or conduct. Indeed, they do so in ways and with possible outcomes (rather than speculative "results") that we have not yet begun to fathom, much less account for. Whatever criteriological terms "thought" and "agency" espouse and operate by, taken in isolation, they illuminate and accomplish very little.

But there is more. For "compassionate" conscience and "sin-soiled" action cannot but *let go*, and this not only of each other but of themselves just as well. Hence, their sole *modus vivendi* – extending itself, in Hannah Arendt's terminology, in and between the *life of the mind*, on the one hand, and the *vita activa*, on the other – is that of "conscious" or "thought" absolving "action" or "agency" and vice versa, as they revert to each other, flip or shade into each other and absolve themselves in this process in equal measure. Yet another *forgiveness*, including that of the thinking and acting forgetting and negating *themselves*, is quietly at work here.

Of course, such forgiveness – here: in absolving the absolute in both its historical, presentist articulations, including its age-old pseudo-Dionysian invocations of a *hyper-ousion* (a *plus d'être,* i.e., no more and more of being, Derrida says), and its novel, Levinasian expression of the *à Dieu*, the *être pour au-delà de ma mort* – does not escape the paradox and aporia of obtaining "pardon," more generally. The justification of receiving pardon, next to the act of pardoning, in turn, Derrida demonstrates rigorously, is as impossible as it is necessary, such that its wager cannot be but risked; in refusing or "avoiding" to do so, one risks a peril that is even greater.[91]

90 J. N. Findlay, 'Foreword', in G. W. F. Hegel, ed., *Phenomenology of Spirit*, trans. by A.V. Miller with and Analysis of the Text and Foreword by J.N. Findlay (Oxford and New York: Oxford University Press, 1977), v–xxx, viii.

91 The condition of possibility of the best and the worst are the same, namely an uncertainty that lacks clear or distinct criteria as to how to proceed any further; the best and the worst, while co-existing and co-extensive up to a point, do not have the same magnitude and also do not carry the same weight, come to think of it: a logic of "inverse proportions," to cite Peter Brown, may well be at work here with the smaller having the greater effect or, indeed, overall impact.

The "Absolute," then, cannot be forgiven, yet it must be; any, as Derrida might say, "non-synonymous substitution" for its presumed "transcendental signified," intended or not, stands still in its shadow and continues to share most, indeed, virtually all, of its metaphysical premises and contours, implications and consequences: as we found, "*La métaphysique c'est notre langue.*" To *deny* as much is either to think all too abstractly or all too concretely (i.e., all too ontologically or downright ontically). To *affirm* it, on the contrary, is to simply reaffirm the true and consistent nature of the dialectical logic, whose genuine negation is nowhere merely formal nor total. Far from being strictly tautological (offering more of the same), it is, as Hegel says, "determinate" (as in *bestimmte Negation*). More precisely, to negate – or, what comes down to the same, to mediate and sublate – this metaphysical tradition under modern or (as Brandom says) "postmodern" conditions is to think and experience these latter not only as *co-determined* and, indeed, *overdetermined* by what precedes and continues to haunt and surround them; it is also to think of modernity or presumed postmodernity, in all that it may have brought new to the table (as, in one sense or another, both caused and further causative) as *positively* and, even further, *absolutely* "free." And to fathom that latter intense Hegelian and Marxian "freedom" is to gage an at once exhilarating and daunting metaphysical or speculative "truth": when all is said and done, in fact, at any given instant, on any occurring occasion, the "System" and each and every one of its constitutive elements, parts and wholes, *can* and *must* take yet another turn, for better or worse. In itself first, against itself next, its circle keeps spinning, beyond our control.

***

As one commentator notes, it is clear to Hegel that "not everything is dependent on something else."[92] In Derrida, I would suggest, this restricted form of absolutism or infinitism is even further *generalized* and *formalized* to the insight that nothing is *necessarily* or *absolutely* dependent on anything, much less on anyone. Hence, much-debated conditions of possibility (of experience, truth or justice, transcendental and others) are just as much *in*-conditions (to use this neologism) of impossibility or even more so. Not only are conditions of possibility "conditioned," on their turn, by what they condition, in fact, the whole language of conditioning, with its accompanying logic of presuppositions, that is, of categorically or hermeneutically enabling horizons, falls short of gauging the deeper and wider meaning and force or effect of whatever it is it seeks to explain or explicate.

Paradoxically, as a consequence (but this language of cause and effect, one realizes, has now become somewhat problematic as well), the *principle*

92 Findlay, 'Foreword', viii.

of sufficient reason no longer obtains and necessity and chance, from here on, go hand in hand. As Meillassoux suggestively argues in *Après la finitude. Essai sur la nécessité de la contingence* (*After Finitude: An Essay on the Necessity of Contingency*), only contingency can be *speculatively* said to "be" ever necessary.[93] If I am not mistaken, Derrida's well-known musings about *la Chance* and *la Nécessité* (or *Ananké*) imply nothing else. If this is at all accurate, then one can call their shared perspective fundamentally an occasionalism with or without God (with or without "the Absolute") and philosophically, metaphysically, ethically and pragmatically, *the difference matters little*. The *counterfactual* claim is that neither origins nor ulterior aims can ever logically or deontologically, that is, criteriologically ever fully *determine* or *decide*, much less *predict*, how things will turn out, let alone justify them on purely procedural or criteriological grounds. Neither Providentialism nor Prometheanism, each of them based on unfounded theoretical and practical, more specifically, theological or teleological premises – "groundless grounds," as they remain – can ever claim or hope to guide us all of the way or even so much as get us started in earnest.

***

This said, the Hegelian-Hölderlinian – and, we may now add, Derridian – "Absolute," unlike some of its German Idealist, notably Schellingian, iterations, according to the Preface of the *Phenomenology of Spirit*, is not an unguided projectile and does not naively sink into *irrelevance* in the proverbial "night in which all cows are black." In its relentless and resolute negativity, the speculative and deconstructive "Absolute" proceeds, evolves and revolutionizes itself, *with* and *through* a "determination," whose minimal semantic distinctiveness and no less semiotic differentiation, prevents its "negation" and "negotiations" from becoming or remaining all too abstract. This is why its "consciousness [*Bewusstsein*]" need not be "unhappy" nor can its "soul [*Seele*]" ever consider itself to be "beautiful."

Its "determinate negations" mediate and mitigate the "truth moments" and "truth contents" that history accumulates or, more often, *piles up in catastrophe*. Even as it progresses and moves from the sense-certainty of consciousness, via self-consciousness, to reason, spirit and religion, reaching "Absolute Knowledge" and "Knowing" by way of the "world spirit [*Weltgeist*]," as Hegel sees it, *the* Spirit includes and effaces in itself each and every one of these, its, articulations. These latter eventually pass through nature and life, not just cognition, and are and remain embedded in an "experience

93 Quentin Meillassoux, *Après la finitude. Essai sur la nécessité de la contingence* (Paris: Éditions du Seuil, 2006); *After Finitude: An Essay on the Necessity of Contingency*, trans. by Ray Brassier (New York: Continuum, 2008).

of consciousness [*Erfahrung des Bewusstseins*]," whose complementing subjective and objective spirits are qua determinations as many negations, mediations and mitigations. As such and *in toto*, this process, and, in Hegel's view, progress, seems to experience and know no end that it could not, in turn, overcome or, indeed, turn against.

But that does not mean that its *pleroma* is thereby lacking (i.e., missing, hiding or withholding itself). If anything, the implied or intended totality of Hegel's system, which Derrida intimates and mimicks or parodies, is *virtual* and, in that sense, precisely, the *inexistent* par excellence. As Derrida seems to argue, one can forgive it for that, as it thereby keeps its age-old promise and eventual future relevance firmly and, indeed, fully intact. As was the case in his assessment of Levinas' oeuvre, in 'Violence and Metaphysics,' there is, on the whole, *absolutely nothing* one would need to disagree or part ways with in rereading Hegel.

* * *

Derrida's deconstruction, seen as a learned form of immanent rather than external critique (if one insists on keeping this term), affirms a simple, if far-reaching, insight: if we are always already "in" – since "metaphysics," our language, delineates the very limits of our psychic, social and cosmic-physical world – then the probability of our getting "out" is obviously infinitely slim, perhaps, *inexistent*. And the occasions to follow up on and follow through must likewise "be" equally rare, indeed, *invisible* or *inapparent*.

This, and nothing else, is what I have called the predicament of all predication (discursive or other). It would almost seem, as in the song "Hotel California," that in our individual and collective existence, while we may "check out" at all times, we can truly "never leave." Unless, of course, being "in" and "out" do not exclude each other mutually or necessarily. Assuming the latter insight places philosophy's traditional and modern absolutism, with its predilection for cognized finite and infinite totalities, into a bind, it also reveals such totalities, whatever their nature, to be surpassable – absolvable – in the end (whether in retrospect or from the get-go, again, the difference matters little as absolute *Idealism* finds itself "deconstructed" one way or the other). Against this foil, Derrida speaks of

> the possibility of a justice, indeed, of a law [*loi*] that not only exceeds or contradicts 'law' (*droit*) but also, perhaps, has no relation to law, or maintains such a strange relation to it that it may just as well demand [or require, urge and call for, *exiger*] this law [as system of rights] (*droit*) as it excludes it.[94]

94 Derrida, 'Force of Law: The "Mystical Foundation of Authority"', 924/925, trans. modified.

Yet such an "excessive" and "strange" concept of law – even as it absolves itself from any natural and positive, particular or universal existing law, while calling for another, including what is possibly a very different concept and practice of law, say, in the guise, of a quasi-messianic or otherwise utopian *idea* – would, as we found, nonetheless *stand and fall* with its applicability and justification. True, this might seem *impossible* – or at a minimum paradoxical, perhaps, aporetic – from where we find ourselves, "at this very moment." But law, emphatically, is neither written in stone nor a matter of "the spirit," when taken in isolation.

"Derrida's law," then, must be conceived as *the law of all laws*. In fact, it does not equal "justice" per se. It merely stipulates that when and where justice is erroneously – that is, unjustly – doomed to judge, rule and regulate *without force* and, hence, is neither applied nor enforced, its very content and form come to resemble the worst (*le pire*). Justice's very meaning and efficacy, seriousness and sincerity are instantly and cumulatively over time *destroyed* whenever and wherever law – and, as the nonspeculative "result" of its process, thereby also justice – is neither *thought* nor *followed through*, nor so much as *followed up on*. In its reasonable, considerate, even merciful and forgiving force, the rule of law – and, *a fortiori*, the reign of justice, call it the "kingdom of God" or of "ends," as Kant did, *Sittlichkeit*, following Hegel and Brandom, the "communism of spirits," attributed to Hölderlin, or the classless society, to echo Marx – requires, offers and promises *little less* than the Hegelian-Marxian "Absolutes." And for this, the latter, regardless of their respective – no doubt, deconstructible – totalities (which, all by themselves, on their own terms and by their internal logic, do not connote "totalitarianism," but are precisely its enemies), can and must be absolved, even forgiven.

Acknowledgment

I would like to thank Peter Goodrich, Anselm Haverkamp and Avital Ronell for taking the initiative of organizing the April 2024 event 'Derrida's Law,' honoring Jacques Derrida's legacy in matters of jurisprudence and justice, and for their kindness of soliciting and, now, for this volume, including my thoughts on the matter. In the following, notably in the second half of this chapter, I will also draw on my remarks presented, first, at the commemorative conference 'Re-Reading Derrida: A Library to Come,' organized by Marie-Aude Baronian and Joost de Bloois at the Amsterdam School for Cultural Analysis (ASCA), University of Amsterdam, in October 2025, and, second, at the workshop 'Derrida at NYU' at La Maison Française, NYU, in November 2024, organized by Avital Ronell and Zakir Paul.

6

DERRIDA'S WAKE

Radical Patience Between Justice and Forgiveness

Anselm Haverkamp

I. Looking Back

After the death of Jacques Derrida in 2004, several observations that had been in the air for a while took on a more definite form of curiosity towards his work's impact, importance and effect, whose force seemed to be both definite in crucial respects (and in these respects already a historical, even classical part of the canon) and at the same time limitless, undefinable, beyond limitation (and in this respect unforeseen, of a nearly sublime nature). The lifework of a great philosopher, one might say, confronts us with this double legacy, but there are not so many great philosophers in one's time, and thus one is rarely confronted in a lifetime with the double edge of this type of a legacy – and certainly not often enough to be prepared for such a moment of evaluation: a moment like a shock, in which time makes itself felt in the routine of history. It may be a mark of Derrida's singular importance that it is difficult if not impossible to decide what is important and what is memorable: what will be included of Derrida in the canon of philosophy as a historical achievement, and what is to be taken from his work as a desire to learn and to be further developed, contested and worked through, as unfinished labors towards a new politics of learning. For this meta-academic aspect of his legacy beyond the mere stuff left behind, Derrida has bequeathed us a lot of instruments, supplements and paleonyms like the old names of friendship and the love of learning.

In 1995, under the heading of *Deconstruction Is/In America*, Derrida had promised a "new sense of the political" emerging from the deconstruction,

DOI: 10.4324/9781003589419-8

in 1989, of the "Force of Law".[1] Is there more left of this event than the fading afterthought of a bygone era? In order to keep the following observations within the rememorative frame of the present occasion, I shall restrict myself to the surrounding debate of 1989 and refrain from further references to the mountain of literature of the years to follow.[2] The effect of having read most of it, discussed almost all of it, will be obvious. In retrospect, the seminal nature of the event clarifies. There is a reason at this moment for a reassessment of the recognition scene after Derrida. What can a Derridean legacy of philosophizing amount to in a moment like this one? We may have come to our own individual conclusions and lines of argument about this. We have argued, discussed, revised, rethought, but now we have more to do: to conceive of a history for deconstruction. A most urgent case is the "Force of Law," whereby the mutually determining force of "law and force" unravels an uncanny twist of older theological sources ("Mystical Foundation" is the ancient allusion in Derrida's subtitle). For Derrida, Benjamin's "Critique of Violence" served as the pre-text for an encounter with the law vis-à-vis the "de-" in de-construction and, as a consequence, with the law's stubborn insistence on having "a formal existence" (as Stanley Fish had it a little later, in 1991).[3] We know by now better, in the emerging historicality of deconstruction, the terms of discourse connected with Derrida's arrival, success and survival in the academy. They revealed in his writings "their *nomos*," as

1 The series of Derrida-events at the Cardozo School of Law and New York University started with "The Force of Law" in 1989, followed by the sequence of yearly seminars with Jacques Derrida (Fall term) and Stanley Cavell (Spring term) in NYU's *Poetics and Theory Program.* These conferences included 'Deconstruction and the Possibility of Justice' (1990) 11:5–6 *Cardozo Law Review*; 'On the Necessity of Violence for any Possibility of Justice' (1991) 13:4 *Cardozo Law Review*; 'Derrida/America: The Present State of America's Europe' (2005) 27:2 *Cardozo Law Review*, as well as in 1993 (between the first two and anticipating the last) a *Poetics Institute* conference of the NYU English and French Depts., *Deconstruction Is/In America: A New Sense of the Political*, ed. by Anselm Haverkamp (New York, NY: New York University Press, 1995). A German selection of the 1989 and 1990 volumes appeared under the title *Gewalt und Gerechtigkeit: Derrida – Benjamin*, ed. by Anselm Haverkamp (Frankfurt am Main: Suhrkamp Verlag, 1994), supplemented by the volume 'Walter Benjamin after the 20th Century: The Future of a Past' (2005) 26:3 *Cardozo Law Review*. The topic was continued in the 2012 Derrida-Conference, organized by Francesca Raimondi and Thomas Khurana in Frankfurt am Main, 'The Present of Deconstruction' (2014) 36 *Oxford Literary Review* 1.

2 Neither do I repeat the many well-known places in Derrida's work which I use beside "The Force of Law," but I make a limited use of *The Politics of Friendship* as perspectival help. As often, I have to thank Erica Weitzman as well as, besides Peter Goodrich, Christoph Menke who was unfortunately unable to participate in this volume.

3 Stanley Fish, 'The Law Wishes to Have a Formal Existence', included In *There's No Such Thing As Free Speech* (New York: Oxford University Press, 1994), 141.

Peter Goodrich has elegantly put it with a Greek name that relates not only to the sphere of the law, but to education and politics in general: spheres marked by the *caesura* of a "suspension of judgement" (for example), an ethics of indirection (in the exemplary sense mentioned), and thus of the unprecedented aporia of a waiting that is not an a-waiting, no utopian or messianic expectation, but a question of radical patience. Derrida's "new sense of the political," which comes under the old name of friendship – *amicitiae causa* – displaces the contractual terms of amicitial, unconditional (even if there were no friends) friendship.

In retrospect then, two points are to be drawn from the "Force of Law" (there were more, but these two are fundamental), both of which had already been highlighted by Benjamin and were connected in the twist of force and law: "something rotten in the law" and the importance of "life". The meaning of, and resistance to the death penalty, American obsession, was one of the projects to follow alongside the *Politics of Friendship*. Like Benjamin before him and Agamben after him, Derrida questioned the empty priority of the life-word: there is more than just life in a life, but the question is how the law is to deal with it, while at the same time being bound to deal with it through force. "Violence and the Word," Robert Cover's title of 1986, confronted the violence of legal acts; he spoke of the violence of the law as a "shadow" that runs from Dante's *Monarchia* to Shakespeare's *Hamlet*, whose "something rotten in the state" is cited in Benjamin's "Critique of Violence". It is tempting to meditate the curve ball thrown in Derrida's Cardozo intervention of 1989, if he had chosen Cover's 1986 text instead. Instead of Benjamin's "rotten state," Cover ended even more pointedly with "the shadow of the violence of law, *itself*."[4] It is the "itself" of the law, the law's 'self' in Cover's words, that points to the "de-" in deconstruction. The law has to forgive itself, to abandon its very self, in what it does not – cannot? really not? – forgive the subjects subjected to its very own, inherent violence. A violence that does not just change or terminate the lives subjected to it, but infiltrates their form of life *as if* it were, like Benjamin's "divine violence," the return of an unaccountable mythical violence in whose name the law feels forced to self-fulfill its formal, institutional existence. Cover's learned footnote on the institution of law as that which "chang[es] the contingent to the necessary" (ib. 1611.25) equals (practically cites) Aristotle's definition of tragedy.[5]

4 Robert M. Cover, 'Violence and the Word' (1985) 95 *Yale Law Journal* 1629. Compare my and Cornelia Vismann's contribution to the 1995 conference of the Amsterdam School of Cultural Analysis (ASCA), 'Habeas Corpus: The Law's Desire to Have the Body', in Hent de Vries and Samuel Weber, eds., *Violence, Identity, Self-Determination* (Stanford, CA: Stanford University Press, 1997).

5 Richard Sorabji, *Necessity Cause and Blame: Perspectives on Aristotle's Theory* (Chicago, IL: University of Chicago Press, 1988), Appendix 'Tragic Error', 296 f. The coincidence of

This tragic view of things was not Derrida's; it was the Greek conditioning he tried to overcome and leave behind.[6] Like democracy, justice – as a condition of politics, even if purified in friendship – "remains to come." Where does this hope leave us with respect to the formal nature of the law vis-à-vis the institutional force that comes to bear upon one's individual life – on the lives of the many not (yet) exactly friends in the shadow of the violent acting out of the law itself? How is the precarious shadow of the law's "formal existence" further perverted through the threat of 'security' (the paranoia of every potential friend being a potential threat) to be met by the force of a law, which is predominantly concerned with the maintenance of its own forceful self? Is this legal self's 'phallocentric' conditioning responsible, and to be held responsive, for the friendly fire of the police-enforced self-fashioning of the 'rule of law'? In other words (again going back to the Derridean 80s), if a pragmatism like "Justice as Fairness" (Rawls in 1985)[7] is not up to the law's task and proves – against all American "affinity" (Michel Rosenfeld's hope 2005)[8] – incapable of providing the adequate fairness towards the so-called 'other' on the grounds of this fairness's unabashed phallo-logocentric identity, what might be a fairer rule, a rule that deserves the interminable patience needed?

II. Meditating the "To Come" – An Interlude

Let me add a parable that Derrida may have appreciated: Mozart's *La clemenza di Tito*, an opera, which recalls in the wake of the French Revolution a lost hope called 'Enlightenment'. By a curious coincidence, the Julliard School offered a splendid performance of this memorable piece a couple of days after the conference on Derrida's Law as a supplement. Mozart's deconstructive transposition, in 1791, of Metastasio/Caldara's 1734 *opera seria* into

---

tragedy and legal violence is a common theme since Plato's *Nomoi*, most recently discussed by André Laks, *Plato's Second Republic: An Essay on the Laws* (Princeton, NJ: Princeton University Press, 2022), 107 ff. Laks does not explicitly mention Derrida's *Politics of Friendship*, which he has most certainly taken into account, but illuminates the platonic background of Derrida's book, esp. in his introductory remarks, page 5, on "friendship *(philia)*" and "*nomos*" as "meta-legislative" terms with Plato's characteristic of the normative intention of the law as "the finest and truest tragedy."

6 How this may connect with, or follow from (or illustrate, in a certain sense) the Derridean deconstruction of the logocentric 'presentism' (notably in the young Derrida's essay "Mythologie blanche" of 1972) remains as yet, half a century later, an unanswered question.

7 I refer here to the first version of John Rawls, 'Justice as Fairness: Political Not Metaphysical', (1985) 14 *Philosophy and Public Affairs* 223–251, passim. Compare in the following Stanley Cavell's Carus Lecture of 1988, *Conditions Handsome and Unhandsome* (Chicago, IL: Chicago University Press, 1990), Preface, xxxviii.

8 Michel Rosenfeld, 'Derrida's Ethical Turn and America: Looking Back from the Crossroads of Global Terrorism and the Enlightenment', (2005) 27 *Cardozo Law Review* 815–845, 819.

the *buffa*-like scenario of a happy comedy (in its first appearance, no doubt, innocently conservative) unmasks clemency, the ideological centerpiece of pre-revolutionary sovereignty, as a defense mechanism, the last resort of the enlightened ruler's inability "ein Mensch zu sein."[9] Like the Schmittian decisionism of the sovereign, the structural precondition and remaining implication of the entitlement that is mercy falls flat in *La clemenza di Tito:* no politics of friendship may ever escape the predicament of justice, even in the case of a well-meaning tyrant's insight that mercy towards a friend's treason does not solve the legal crux. Mozart neither offers nor implies a critique of this outdated ideological issue (on the contrary, his opera seems perfectly in tune). But in the same moving move, which decomposes what it exposes as sovereign prerogative, his art, seemingly in tune, also lays the political remedy, the phallocentric republic of friendship, to rest. Not that "there may be no friends, my friends" (as the saying goes of old, and Derrida explains in dialectical detail), and not that these non-friends may be even traitors, but that their shared inability, their in-capacity to recognize any of the so-called 'others' (except for these others', maybe, at best, phallocentric enmity, as Carl Schmitt's politico-theological cynicism has it), is the comedy called 'human'. The crucial equality, the legal form of a democracy not just to come but to survive in the process of its possible coming, is one of brothers, not others, whereas the egalitarian intention ("alle Menschen werden Brüder," the common Freudian slip) remains the law's crux in whose shadow the life-threatening "misery" of the law's violence lingers.[10] Its "urgency" arises, Cover had to admit, through "the law itself." The possible, occasional intervention of the Hegelian monarch remains a faint consolation.[11]

III. Friendship, the Benefit of a Doubt

At the end of his meticulous reconsideration of the philosophical tradition's lament that there may be, in the end, no friends for certain, Derrida's *Politics of Friendship* turning to history, to a new type of history as radical as the patience it affords, is radical in the face of the urgency to be faced. Deconstruction happens in art, in Mozart's music, but not as or in a critique. It

9 See Ivan Nagel, *Autonomie und Gnade*, 3rd ed. (München: Hanser Verlag, 1985), 13. *Autonomy and Mercy: Reflections on Mozart's Operas* (Cambridge, MA: Harvard University Press, 1991).

10 Christoph Menke, *Reflections of Equality* (Stanford, CA: Stanford University Press, 2006), 191. The translator highlights the pragmatic "urgency" instead of the existential "misery" (Cover): "die Not, die zu wenden ist" in the German original, *Spiegelungen der Gleichheit* (Frankfurt am Main: Suhrkamp Verlag, 2004), 317.

11 See Jean-Luc Nancy, 'The Jurisdiction of the Hegelian Monarch', trans. by Mary Ann and Peter Caws (1982) 49 *Current French Philosophy*.

takes place in the shadow of the law, rather than in an ideological setting that deserves to be critiqued nevertheless (and to little avail, as far as politics is concerned, while progress remains an uncertain hope). The deconstruction to be faced in the conundrum of friendship is what causes history to happen; it happens in the spectral form of (a) 'history'. Art is this happening's unreliable witness and, at times, narrator (Homi Bhabha's "right to narrate" entertains this hope). Adorno, Hegel uppermost on his mind, spoke less hopefully of a 'negative dialectics' (almost like the poet John Keats, who intuitively spoke of poetry's 'negative capability'). Negativity is both, the trademark of a critique that seems necessary, and the impediment of the form, in which the critique may be effective.

In American criticism, the "de-" *of* or *in* deconstruction was at first (and not least in Paul de Man's adaptation) taken in the sense of Keats's 'negative capability' (the heritage of Romanticism), but on a second glance it featured, announced and enabled a productive outcome, in which a post-romantic or, probably and more precisely, a postmodern art turns the crossed-out ideological leftovers of salvational expectations, the potential of a promised future, into an interminable work on the mystical foundations' unaccounted-for violent imput. Mythical violence is remembered as foundational and mystified as divine positioning by the creative force of a god, preferably the God of the Jewish and Christian Bibles. The revelation of their pre-established nature comes along and about as the normative address of an immanently manifest *trans*-cendence, which subjects the subjects of its revelatory impact to the law's primordial violence in view of a higher justice incorporated and implied by the law's formal administration. Is this anything but a flawed consolation, which defers compensation as promise? The question is old; among "preexisting conditions" (as Samuel Weber's recent title reminds us), it remains a permanent companion to the rule of law that does not just manifest, but "demonstrate" – the *demonstrativum* is essential here – "the violence to which living beings are susceptible as mortals."[12] And, even worse, upon which these mortals' subject-condition qua 'authoritarian personalities' relies (investigated by Adorno & al. in New York 1950).

Derrida's turn, in *The Politics of Friendship,* to an alternative history, which is all the more evident in deconstruction's historical fate after Derrida, includes a long list of political sites, but also a number of methodological questions to be faced in the so-called Humanities and their linguistic framing or, more to the point here (as Paul de Man and, following him on the occasion, Sam Weber argued), the "hidden articulations and fragmentations" in

12 Samuel Weber, *Preexisting Conditions: Recounting the Plague* (New York, NY: Zone Books, 2022), 40.

these academic fields.[13] For deconstruction, art was, from Derrida's beginnings, the central phenomenon to be dealt with. Deconstruction was an art- and literature-related project from the start. As a consequence, the rhetorical origin of both, the arts as well as the law, was to be reconsidered not as the hermeneutical surface crux of any understanding, but as the structural logic of a positioning and presentation, which de- and re-constructs its normative ups and downs in a de- and re-structuring *like* (the analogy may be of dubious value) the autoimmune conditioning of a 'movement' that is no 'process' (since a 'process' is what it is precisely not).[14]

The more or less ostensive self-referentiality of this moving of horizons of understanding depends on a pre- or, rather, post-romantic understanding of 'theory' and leaves the means of a 'critical' reflection behind as a hermeneutically too involved, ideologically entangled procedure and is historically too superficial to approach the underlying 'infrastructure' (Rodolphe Gasché's update of the Derridean linguistic groundwork).[15] The underlying 'infra' of the structure is relevant, insofar as law's rhetoric, like literature's, was from the start a linguistic affair that depended – even in the case of the 'good old law' and its 'common law' continuation – on the translatability into a written form, a writ, which (in Goodrich's apt shorthand) is "all that there is for law to be law". What is important for a de-constructive (and not just more or less fictitiously re-constructive) application is not the awkward intuition of bygone intentions of past law-makers and their linguistic ability to write the law (an act of conceptual 'know-how'), but the analysis of a given problem-situation, to which the law's written condition once may have responded and to which it gave a more or less durable answer. The linguistic infrastructure – not the time-bound intentions of those subjected to it in a more or less self-conscious fashion – is the legal challenge to be met. And thus no free-floating play of the signifiers is the answer, neither in the application of laws, nor in

13 Cited from Paul de Man, *Allegories of Reading* (New Haven, CT: Yale University Press, 1979), 249.

14 Let me add here a footnote on an inner-Derridean divide not without consequence in the afterlife of "The Force of Law," the divide between deconstruction as a radicalized hermeneutics (1) vs deconstruction as a post-structuralist methodology of 'infrastructures' (2). To the first I cannot pay as much attention as it deserves; it would have to include Werner Hamacher's proposal of the 'afformative' (13 CLR 1991) as a pre-performative degree zero of the law's force, an intuition, which takes the Benjaminian idea of a 'pure language' as a model and postulates a state of law *before* the writ as the "all there is" (of Goodrich's laconic formula). As a sublime first act, which is echoed by Benjamin's 'pure language', the 'afformative' would connect an intuited 'actuosity' (Fichte's 'first insight' according to Dieter Henrich) with a practice of law that would metaphorically coincide with the Mosaic model of Longinus's essay on the 'Sublime'.

15 Rodolphe Gasché, *The Tain of the Mirror* (Cambridge, MA: Harvard University Press, 1986), 150.

the reading of literary texts – with the rare exception, perhaps, of texts, in which an avant-garde wish for an unlimited indeterminacy, would co-thematize and in this sense implicitly 'deconstruct', the phantasmatic delusion of an unlimited freedom of expression. What defies such a lofty approach is the unrecognized and unforeseeable latent burden under the lay of the ordinary lexicon's diachronically transmitted semantics.

IV. Forgiveness, a Categorical Imperative

Paradoxically, the law's quest for 'justice' proceeds in a decisive (but rarely explicitly stated) break from the legal 'ordinary' in Cavell's sense. It fulfills the expectations of the ordinary as little as any breaking of the law would merely deviate from a generalizable common norm. Justice *does* justice in singular acts, acts of individually adapted transgressions of the generalized 'other's' legal subsumption. Whereas the singularity of each judgement may be (or may become) a common feature, the law's breaking away from the norm, which it represents, remains in and of "itself" an incommensurable act. This non-commensurability is no reason for pardon or grace; it is the acknowledgment of the 'other' in order to be just in the sense of adequate. The judge does not "invent the rule; rather, he should *follow* it *as if* he were inventing it."[16] The judge's inventive part is to "assume, approve, confirm (a rule's) value," is Derrida's Solomonic formula. There is no need, therefore, to apply exeptional grace, as long as the other's otherness is taken care of, or, more difficult to ensure, as long as it *can* be taken care of (Cover cites an impressive instance, when this was *not* the case). Procedural critique is not superfluous; it may be effectively put into practice through changes in a law or in the form of amendments. But the deconstructive insistence on the preconditioning of a case does more. It does more in that it pays attention to the case's individual, situationally specified, never entirely commensurable, but historically graspable format. The difficult mortgage of the legal tradition addressed by Derrida may be explained or thematized in a 'critique'. But that is not enough, since its *latent content* needs to be transferred into a productive reading and must be adapted in legal practice. The reconstructive necessity must be met, sure, but further developed on the basis of that which has been de-constructed and, that means, not on the basis of the content's pre-decided dogmatized form.

General forgiveness may be desirable, may be even economically more effective than the violent insistence on a revenge-oriented politics of punishment – I leave this question open, in spite of the fact that this is a vital consideration.

16 Thomas Khurana's shrewd formula departs from the following Derrida-quote in 'Derrida and the Philosophy of Deconstruction', in Sacha Golob and Karen Ng, eds., *Cambridge Companion to Continental Philosophy* (Cambridge, UK: Cambridge University Press, 2025).

The question with and after Derrida is whether forgiveness can be more than part of a certain 'messianicity', of a messiah never to arrive, while, on the other hand, the democracy "to come" is cultivated by the well-meaning as an expectation that appears more "real" (which it is evidently not, but asks for unlimited patience). The vestiges of, say, the practice of lynching, a form of common law of the worst type, betray the relentless desire for an untamed revenge, which should have been (once upon a time already) overcome by the rule of law, but which has in fact still not been left behind and cannot be appeased by a critique without its deconstructive other's cunning of reason. Mozart's art – *Cosi fan tutte* is the scandalous example, a masterpiece of such cunning – is just this, and is 'just' in this.

The law's intermediary position between institutionalized (instead of 'wild') justice on the one hand, and forgiveness on the other is as little utopian as 'the other' is other; it is approachable. It is, in other words, consistent with Kant's 'categorical imperative'. A merely formally guided piecemeal strategy like the Freudian 'working through' may reward a certain critique of procedure, but the critique's aim cannot be a mere making good – Rawls' 'justice as fairness' is too elusive. Fairness needs to include the other and not exclude even the enemy. Instead of an unquestionable, ideal justice, unreachable as it is, the possibility of a deconstructive "giving *in to* the name of the other," as Sam Weber has put it already in 1989,[17] needs to remain in play, as long as the unforeseeable returns of a mythical violence are in play, not least in the Benjaminian guise of a 'divine violence'. The quasi-categorical imperative of a forgiving in the name of the other – since what is the 'other' but a name for the other's right? – is to *dis*-place the guilt-management of mythically induced, mystically recalled origins, which do nothing but serve as an administrative cover for "setting it right" (Hamlet, again). The violence is in the setting (Cover's insight).

The question remains (or is to be rephrased): How far does the urge 'to set it right' in the face of the law's crucially dis-jointed settings go beyond the old maxim *in dubio pro reo?* Is the deconstructive insistence on a justice beyond the juridically justified violence more than a consoling ornament of philosophical naivety? How would the quasi-transcendental idea of forgiveness work as an alternative to the guilt-ridden social bond on the phallocentric road to a democracy to come? Forgiveness may come at the cost of some possibly unavenged crimes, but also with the loss of revenge as the worst of consolations. Does the triviality of such post-Derridean ruminations add more than a touch of sentimentality to the age-old uncertainty

17 As a reminder I cite Samuel Weber's contribution at the time, in 1989, starting from Paul de Man's analysis of the "hidden articulations" (as quoted previously), 'In the Name of the Law', (1990) 11 *Cardozo Law Review* 1538 (emphasis added).

of the uses of the word 'justice'?[18] And even if this question may remain undecided, how does this diminish or modify the impact of Derrida's legacy to any relevant degree?

V. Tail Piece

As far as the mystically intuited ground and the demand for a transcendental reasoning is concerned, the definitive loss of the God-term may even enable (and not just necessitate) some helpful evidence. In the deconstructive working-through of the shadows of an unreadable history, which is dominated by violence and remains susceptible to the narrative distortions of quasi-mythical errors, a phenomenology of 'the just' may arise: a recognition of *if, when and how* justice did in fact happen or may have happened. Since this it did and still does: happen now and then. For Pascal, a founding father of deconstruction for Louis Marin, Paul de Man and Jacques Derrida alike, the key was 'grace'. We may want to conceive of Derrida's alternative take on a history that would *not* be one of violence, but a history of the impasses of friendship. The categorical, quasi-transcendental point to be made by a deconstructive conception of history (like, say, in Kant's essay on *Eternal Peace*, Derrida's example) would not be to forgive in general and not to forgive or to ask for a forgiving at any cost or beyond tolerable understanding, but to replace the anthropologically mistaken phallo-centric guilt complex in the administration of justice with the democratic acceptance of more than what the self fears and needs in its self's defense. An acceptance, for which a mere understanding cannot be the sole precondition (although a self-critical hermeneutics of understanding might very well, let's hope, take its departure from there).

The most recent reinvention of the enemy, as Giorgio Agamben reminded us just in time (*Quodlibet*, 31 maggio 2024), offers a pertinent point, whose spell equals the shadow of the law's violence without any foreshadowing of justice. On the contrary, it justifies itself as a self-defense against the threat of what is felt and ominously named a universal 'nihilism'. In this self-defense, legal violence joins the recurring apocalyptic overtones in many

18 Phil Mitsis reminds me at this point of Derrida's much discussed piece "On Forgiveness" which responds, however, to an entirely different debate, whose theo-metaphorical underpinnings Derrida is careful to avoid: "of the forgiveness, in truth, of God, etc. I must leave these immense questions open," *On Cosmopolitanism and Forgiveness* (London: Routledge, 2001), 38. Consequently, he cannot find any juridical value in this "most often abused" of words, forgiveness – in Kantian terms at best an "hypothetical imperative," he concedes (ib. 39). But, Derrida adds: in that forgiveness is "excessive, hyperbolic, mad," namely, "heterogenous to the order of politics" (and thus different from a concept like 'revolution'), this heterogeneity qualifies forgiveness against the grain of its theo-metaphorical genealogy as the categorical imperative of a justice *above* or, maybe, even *independent of* the law: "be it as a dream for thought, this madness is perhaps not so mad . . ." he concludes (ib. 60, last words).

post-Derridean discourses, although (again) this may be not much more than the continued denial of the deconstructive undercurrent of history: an uncannily "inaccessible" point in the comeback of Schmitt's 'absolute hostility' whose violent return "can only be denied" was Derrida's brief, laconic, almost hopeless, response at the end of *The Politics of Friendship*.[19] No 'radical atheism' seems the appropriate answer to such 'theo-metaphorical' projects (Blumenberg's refutation of Schmitt),[20] self-centered as they remain, religiously bound to the spectre and name of the father. The revengeful god-conceptions' guilt-threat, whose truthful image is the shadow of violence, *must* be dissolved (a 'categorical imperative' if ever there was one), however useful the guilt and the blame may still seem for the legal practice of the ordinary – not to speak of the sociological aspects, the "games people play" in the many not yet really democratic, in fact still most authoritarian phallocentric regimes.

19 Here I come back to my brief remarks in one of the follow-up conferences, 'The Enemy Has No Future: Figure of the Political' (2005) 26 *Cardozo Law Review* 2553 ff.

20 See my juxtaposition Blumenberg v. Nancy in 'La sécularisation comme métaphore: Hans Blumenberg interprète de la modernité' (2003) 87 *Transversalités* 15 ff.

PART II
Force

7

THE DIVINE TANTRUM

On Law and Anger

Avital Ronell

It was a Fulbright year, and then some. After more than a year of high-strung research in Berlin, I had to junk the whole thing. A few months after providing my thesis director with the fifth version of the requisite prospectus, I was officially notified. Despite wall-to-wall rewrites and hairsplitting edits, my thesis proposal was rejected out of hand. The news took some temporal warp to reach me, since email and other texting devices apart from snail had yet to be invented. Having misinterpreted the silence around the newly revised fate of my project, I thought I had made it through this time. That kind of wait could go either way. "Sure, go ahead," was the mistaken introject of another's unspoken judgment. Nonetheless, his decision was final: Walter Benjamin, neither a literary critic nor a pure philosopher, was not an appropriate object for a Ph.D. dissertation at a German department of distinction – in this way I repeated the trajectory of Walter Benjamin on a point of institutional violence, having my thesis snuffed out, denied authorization before it could take hold. The nascent career, a lesson in ritual submissiveness, was put in jeopardy. On all matters of theo-administrative viability, it was inadvisable to question the authority of an advisor.

Still, to me, the advisor, however eminent and immovable, represented no more (nor less) than a tollbooth along the N.J. Turnpike or a spot check on Kleist's fateful throughway, even a fixture appointed by God – not much more than some minor deterrent to block the way forward that I thought I could clear. If, however, you came from the wrong class or chose your theoretical direction imprudently, you were pretty much done for. One could not speed through or magically bypass the checkpoint by means of a make-believe permit that you fabulated out of silence. Nor could one reasonably expect a sudden wave of the assenting hand, inviting the fledgling scholar to pass through

DOI: 10.4324/9781003589419-10

a sublimated structure of contest (Benjamin asks that we observe the difference between test and contest). As a graduate student, I was gearing up for subtle greatness, strengthening my calling as a *passageway*: I wanted to be the head of the Anglo-American welcoming committee, a conduit to his ascension, before Benjamin became a brand. He was not a sure bet like Rilke or one of the big guns of German thought, like Goethe-Gott-Kot and Goethe's own excremental homophones for his name going up and down the scale of unbeatable grandeur, or Marx, Nietzsche, and Husserl, with the addition, but maybe less so, of Freud and Heine. Around that time, mostly due to Stanley Cavell, Wittgenstein, the Viennese philosopher, scored high, but he confused everyone in terms of placement with his Anglo-Austrian stripes.

In those days we were not pursuing "careers" but mythically fated to reveal something more exalted, differently violent, following precise hazing protocols. You were supposed to make a discovery, or produce signs of positing stunts – or destroy, with parricidal finesse, a predecessor. Job-wise, we were met with seriously precarious outcomes, not unsimilar to the compromised status of today's crop, if at some level of ideological insistence less formally hunted down. Sometimes one was doomed to wait it out in sheer stagnancy, and I myself saw intermittent stretches when I idled for years before being miraculated into a job. Granted, the slow drip of careerism has its own dosage of kill pill suicide. Every day, one wants to call the whole thing off, slip out of the tightening noose of bureaucratic entanglement, relieve the sting of recurring jabs. At least, let us close down the reception desk for rejection notices. But what's one to do in a chronically deprecating culture where face-saving options dwindle by the minute for the mortifyingly earnest scholar, a type targeted for extinction?

Berlin was different for Walter Benjamin, but lethal, as it had been for my family, with its steady cultural upgrades and racialized exclusions. Of course, Benjamin and I were riding different Autobahns, locked into different systems of thought and historicity, for which, in some of the cases he handled, I was a haunted inheritor. On the whole, and by necessity, we took and previewed different forms of punishment. There are a number of slight differences between us, to be sure. In terms, for instance, of the allegorical snippet showcasing the drama of disqualified theses, my project was aborted before it could properly get on its way; his thesis was finished when it received the rejection slip, having been read and reviled by assistant Horkheimer.[1] Still, I tell myself that we're both storytellers, inescapably bound by immemorial hounding, abysmal trajectories that made us thick as thieves and weirdly

1 Walter Benjamin, *The Correspondence of Walter Benjamin, 1910–1940*, ed. and annotated by Gershom Scholem and Theodor W. Adorno, trans. by Manfred R. Jacobson and Evelyn M. Jacobson (Chicago: University of Chicago Press, 1994), 275–276.

stuck on literature, craving, at each turn, a substantial dose of poeticity. I do not mind such hyperbole in the making of plausible kinship. Benjamin was my pain threshold, intellectually bound, if as a regulatory ideal, and grown in adjacent neighborhoods of expulsive fury. We often share the task of the translator, getting it wrong (in my case) yet re-originating a text, scanning its minefield, sometimes blowing up in the process (in my case). Despite so much pressure of disruption and difference, we're family – not always a good thing, and transferentially hazardous. Aggrieved, I would still like to advocate for Benjamin's infinitely lost pass. I'll leave it at that, understanding that I am walking out empty-handed, like allegory in the book of *Trauerspiel*.[2] It's part of the muted *Schreiben-Schrei* (*cri/écrit*, screeching screed) of an unbearable history that keeps returning. By "lost pass" I also refer us to a missing passport to America, which should have been secured by a university outlet or a Californian landing pad, but was issued "too late" as the biographies remark.[3] The visa requested from Cuba was not processed, which is another story. Nor was the coveted contract from Schocken Books in New York, negotiated to the tune of a losing battle by Scholem. Benjamin was devastated by the rejection. On this terrain, Kafka had beaten him out.

*****

Since *mood* and other affective pre-givens are notoriously difficult to convey with exactitude in writing, let me just say that I am still mad. The dismissive violence of the rejection Benjamin suffered, if only as a metonymy of an irreparable historical slight – and I in his shadow, under safety of his name and generational difference – remains a hotspot in my overly sensitive psychic setup, an overwrought reception center. ("You're too sensitive!" say the perps). I can't help it. It's my job. I wanted to be his sentinel, but he keeps rolling into troubled zones. The suicide of Walter Benjamin, sucked into his work as inerasable marker, continues to notch a lacerating jointure, hermeneutically pulsed. How does one read the historical wrongdoing that bore down on him? The brunt of force that we identify in Benjamin's predicament cannot be simply detached from the approaches we take – or avoid – when reading him in reverse-forward,

2 Walter Benjamin, *The Origins of German Tragic Drama*, trans. by John Osborne (London: Verso, 1977).

3 See Hannah Arendt, 'Introduction', in Hannah Arendt, ed., Harry Zohn, trans., *Illuminations*, by Walter Benjamin (New York: Schocken Books, 2007), 1–58; Momme Brodersen, *Walter Benjamin: A Biography*, trans. by Malcolm R. Green and Ingrida Ligers, ed. by Martina Derviş (London and New York: Verso Books, 1996); Howard Eiland and Michael W. Jennings, *Walter Benjamin: A Critical Life* (Cambridge, MA: Belknap Press of Harvard University Press, 2014); Esther Leslie, *Walter Benjamin* (London: Reaktion Books, 2007); Bernd Witte, *Walter Benjamin: An Intellectual Biography*, trans. by James Rolleston (Detroit: Wayne State University Press, 1991); and Gershom Scholem, *Walter Benjamin: The Story of a Friendship*, trans. by Harry Zohn (New York: New York Review Books, 2003).

convoking one of his angels. The brutal *Erlebnis* of shock that he discerned in Baudelaire plagues his own oeuvre, a battered sign that looms over his life and work.[4] He was forced to waive the sphere of protected life, exposed to the unjust closedown. I cannot unsee Benjamin panting across the Pyrenees, barely managing the overloaded crush of manuscript pages in his custody, a suitcase pushed along, despite fearful counterwinds, and the experience of *Atemwende*, breath-turning: a catastrophic respiratory crisis as he treks uphill.[5]

On the run yet impeded, he is assailed, we could venture, by an historical police force. Benjamin, arguably, has a different relation to the police than Socrates or Rousseau, or even Derrida, who was picked up in Prague in 1981, taken into custody, released only when French President Mitterrand intervened by means of ministers who had been students of the cuffed philosopher. From Benjamin's perspective, the police force discharges its duties as a phantom body: the police give chase everywhere; they have a way of swarming you invisibly when they are not making you eat the pavement. When Derrida repeats an aspect of Benjamin on violence, he underscores this point: the police are *everywhere*, even where they are not. For our purposes here, Benjamin's step treks with Freud's thesis on trauma, which psychoanalysis measures as *Schritt*, proceeding step by step in *Beyond the Pleasure Principle*.[6] Let us take measure of the step (*Schritt*), shaping the scene in terms of hermeneutic *Fürsorge*, a caring-for. Both in hindsight and as a condition for moving forward, *Fürsorge* watches over the confrontation Benjamin set up with the existentials of justice meted, suppressed, rerouted, or painfully deferred. Signaling from Benjamin's legacy, this staggered transmittal, at once unique and still partitioning among emerging generations of readers, continues to press for heuristic attention.

4 Walter Benjamin, 'On Some Motifs in Baudelaire', in Hannah Arendt, ed., Harry Zohn, trans., *Illuminations* (New York: Schocken Books, 2007), 155–200.

5 He was a relative of Heinrich Heine, also on the run, or rather on the panting end walk. I have quite a bit more to say in this trailer or teaser and a number of scenes of traumatic disruption to disclose, but I will cut myself down to size, staying with only a small cluster of blends with which to conclude what was meant to open. Honestly, I can no longer tell if the melancholia that sets the tone for my being-in-the-world is somehow original with me and my so-called experiences or a knockoff of his oeuvre, a splinter of hysterical identification and adoption policy, a sequel to his impaired legacy. I wanted merely to turn to the melancholic that I borrow or rather take in a violent sweep of surrogation from Benjamin – a stance or *Stimmung* or disposition, or even *Gestell* that grafts originarily, prosthetically adapting, making it my own by injecting myself with Benjamin's melancholia. In so doing I remember what my teacher Derrida said about this state of affairs, turning melancholia in turn into an injunction: he said, if I am remembering correctly, that melancholia is a way of remembering, refusing to forget ("le mélancolique est celui qui refuse d'oublier"), resisting the intoxication of appeasements of forgetting, the closing of woundedness over time, holding vigilance and incessantly reviewing that which cannot pass: "Il faut de la mélancolie."

6 Sigmund Freud, *Beyond the Pleasure Principle: And Other Writings*, trans. by John Reddick (London: Penguin Books, 2003).

Benjamin did not take his poison lying down. His brand of hemlock was mixed differently than the concoction that felled Socrates, but their state-dispensed potions bound them to all the walking dead of philosophy, including Rousseau and Spinoza. Socrates' fall became an ongoing trauma of murder-suicide, according to Arendt, tailing all philosophers who cannot shake the state's chilling hostility.[7] Benjamin's fate, constellated differently but registered with the same takedown techniques of state, now frames and joins the future-forward image of the police coming down on those persecuted prey who cry out, "I can't breathe." When the Franco-Spanish border closed that day, the timing, also according to Arendt, was catastrophic.[8] Benjamin availed himself of the relief-stash obtained in his last stopover in Marseilles – reportedly enough morphine to have killed a horse.[9]

*****

In my corner, it's become a syndromic habit to pursue an inquiry into material defeat and to scan the inscribed vulnerabilities of a body's struggle with irreversible decline. I am thinking in terms of latency in Freud's terminal illness, textual markers such as Irma's throat that forecast his cancerous outbreak, describing where psychoanalysis begins and ends, or the inner conviction that had me taking the suicide run from Werther to Emma Bovary, back through Benjamin, when fielding the calls of singular others in modernity, all of whom deserve to be named, even lamented, if the *lament* were still a viable form of grievance and part of the desperate wrangle with legal animus.[10] "Animus," of course, has become a contested term in legal pursuit, undermining in some cases serious juridical engagement in the United States, a tropological provocateur that was already at issue in some of Plato's stage directions for rational adjudication. Nonetheless, despite the inconclusive standing of detectable strains of animus in my plaint, it seems to me that one cannot help but file a complaint at this time, historically cast and stirred by unresolved anger, on behalf of Benjamin and the companion species of undead plaintiffs forced out by a politics of annihilation. Despite its spectral contours, this petition to no one and nowhere – Celan's searching *unWo* – forms a renewed appeal to justice unserved. For his part, Benjamin seized upon the fine print of our heritage, not only in terms of his enigmatic

7 Hannah Arendt, 'Philosophy and Politics', (1990) 57:1 *Social Research* 73–103.

8 Arendt, 'Introduction', 18.

9 Howard Eiland and Michael W. Jennings, *Walter Benjamin: A Critical Life* (Cambridge, MA: Belknap Press of Harvard University Press, 2014), 675.

10 Sigmund Freud, *The Interpretation of Dreams*, ed. and trans. by James Strachey (New York: Basic Books, 2010), 131–132. These concerns are further investigated in Avital Ronell, *Complaint: Grievance among Friends* (Champaign, IL: University of Illinois Press, 2018); and Avital Ronell, *Crack Wars: Literature, Addiction, Mania* (Lincoln: University of Nebraska Press, 1992).

essay, "The Destructive Character," but also by umpiring the empty-handed walkout of the *Trauerspiel*, calling down a metaphysics stripped bare of transcendence, offering the doomed player . . . *nothing*, precisely.[11] Still, he stood his ground, however ungrounded, on problematic survival techniques, switching up *überleben* with *fortleben*, eventually captured and reset by Derrida's *survivance*.[12]

My arbitration here, at once miniscule and over the top, is without hope, yet fired up and righteous – an admittedly ambivalent relation to rights. I stand in *Fürsorge*, taking up a position of advocacy for the wrongdoing dealt out to my Walter, my inmost *geWalter*, seeking incalculable retribution, stalking imaginary courtrooms for audience, presenting his case to angry gods and, in the grand scheme of things, beseeching indifferent mortals. In *Fürsorge*, I'm a füry, a wrathful fairy, if that is imaginable, on the threshold of what is legally viable, one holding a steady gaze while short on authority, powerless except to the worlds of children.

Entering our sphere by a lingering infantile threshold, fairies rule over their own danger zones and established field of fear factors – just ask the Grimm brothers and other weaponizers of narratives fed to concocted subspecies and minors. Hungry for the persuasive supplement or oriented toward a go-to cognitive leap, legal advocates and philosophers find themselves reaching for the poetic word in moments of stalled confidence. At such fragile junctures the philosophical holdout, in any case, may take recourse to poetry and make-believe, drumming up fictions to which even Kant was beholden in stern determination (I am thinking of the "as-if" that shapes the categorical imperative as well as his sober-enthusiastic remarks on the French Revolution).[13] But can any poetics serve the cause of those whose argument is unappeasable, stoking the sensibility of a plaintiff who is boiling mad, running on overtime and past the statute of limitations, tacitly assumed? It is not always clear whether one can plead a class-action suit on behalf of the furious, or how to situate such a brief when animus-based petition is (or was), in some legal precincts, unconstitutional or, at the very least, on the edge of dismissal. A posture to be wary of, such instigating piques invite further investigation.

11 Walter Benjamin, 'The Destructive Character', in Howard Eiland, Michael W. Jennings, and Gary Smith, eds., *Selected Writings*, vol. 2, pt. 2: 1931–1934 (Cambridge, MA: Harvard University Press, 2005), 541–542; and Benjamin, *Origins of German Tragic Drama*.

12 Jacques Derrida, *The Beast and the Sovereign, Volume II*, ed. by Michel Lisse, Marie-Louise Mallet, and Ginette Michaud, trans. by Geoffrey Bennington (Chicago: University of Chicago Press, 2011).

13 Immanuel Kant, *Critique of Practical Reason*, trans. by Mary Gregor (Cambridge: Cambridge University Press, 1997); and Immanuel Kant, *The Conflict of the Faculties*, trans. by Mary J. Gregor and Robert Anchor (Lincoln: University of Nebraska Press, 1992). For further discussion, see Jean-François Lyotard, *The Differend: Phrases in Dispute*, trans. by Georges Van Den Abbeele (Minneapolis: University of Minnesota Press, 1988).

Duly agitated and cognitively thrown, one goes to the poets. Celan issues an injunction to *stay upset*; in some respects even Wordsworth, not to speak of Homer through Plath and the more modern raging poets, makes us wonder if chronic or flash rages can be transposed, brought to bear on legal procedure. Such a questioning stance requires, no doubt, an integration of a wholly other phrasal regimen within the order of legal disputes led by Lyotard in tandem with Celan and Derrida.[14] I shall return to the matter of the upset shortly, including Nietzsche's chronically upset stomach, politically pitched – a stomach ever turning, reversing dialectics, calling ahead to Camus' sense of revolt, the revulsion that deals precisely with what is revolting, turning, and churning.

Any living being, when standing defenseless before the law, and striking a stance of growing discouragement, whether in revolt or frozen in fear, can find themselves pinned by the "big A, *Autre*."[15] The defenseless come up against a crushing surge of power-alterity, linked in familiar German letters of modernity to themes crafted by Benjamin, Kafka, Musil, Jelinek, and their spectral cohorts, but also, more generally (as in the writings of Marcuse, Kojève, and Arendt), to the motif of parental authority, or whatever holds sway over our finite wriggles – including the law, a mentor, or the comeback Kaiser. Radical defenselessness (*Hilflosigkeit*), a starting point for psychoanalysis, has developed pushback techniques, of which a part may be sought in the *Agressionstrieb*, the start-up with which we are all equipped, primordially, as Melanie Klein argues.[16] Among other qualities, the aggressive drive, which Freud eventually replaced with the death drive, provides a means of defense, an instigation to fighting back. Yet, defeat, castration, and mortality unavoidably spell out the law of the land. This predicament of losing out to the *Autre* can bear good news, as all good losers know, but I'm not going there now. The capacity to summon protective maneuvers, however minimal, in the wake of defeat is outsourced at times to fictional frontiers, powerful allies in the realm of defeat.

While never reducible to a therapy or psychologistic lever, the poetic shield grapples with proposed representations or representatives of the authoritarian imposition, slipping out of a noose, but mostly rattled by a task. Benjamin's *Aufgabe* simultaneously means a task imposed and a surrender – *Aufgabe*, as in "give up," lose the shield. For Benjamin, instructed by the powerful flex of poetic utterance, the poet offers a figure of extreme exposure, delivering the word while courting danger and venturing bodily harm – a surrender

14 Lyotard, *Differend*.

15 Jacques Lacan, *The Ethics of Psychoanalysis (Seminar VII)*, trans. by Dennis Porter (New York: W. W. Norton & Company, 1997).

16 Melanie Klein, *Envy and Gratitude and Other Works, 1946–1963*, vol. 3 of *The Writings of Melanie Klein* (New York: Free Press, 2002).

to the experience, according to Hölderlin, of self-evisceration.[17] This is why Hölderlin's poem on poetic risk bears the title of "Dichtermut," which Benjamin comments with painstaking care: poetic *courage*. In this scan, Hölderlin and Benjamin have the poet in their sights, the *Dichter*, and not a *Dichtung*, poetry (or a body of literature, a dictation), which may survive the onslaught, leaving a trace. It may be useful to note that Benjamin keeps the focus on the poet, much in the way he considers the fate of the translator, as Derrida has pointed out in the work on translation.[18] As sacrificial – or at least *mortal* – carrier of a materially destructive yet inescapable assignment, the poet stays close to a presentiment of imminent doom. This exposure goes inward while it remains outside, involving our primal and externalized terrors, often projecting cultures of restrictive confinement when socially reconfigured. In his day, carceral encroachment, figuring embodied defeat, binds Benjamin specifically to Kafka, who leveraged his own nonaggression pact with history, continually renegotiating the ballistic quality of powerless deflation.

When facing patriarchal overload, Kafka and Benjamin each offered close-ups of the hits we've taken from effects of violence in law, bloodlust and its correlate in figures of justice. Weighing *Gerechtigkeit* and *sich (für etw. oder jmdn.) rächen*, homophones tying justice to vengeance, they often called for and received critical backup from Nietzsche, who rode vengeance back to its philological roots.[19] However, it was Freud who added the patriarchal pump from which violence issues as a borrowed feature of God's authority.[20] I bring this up now because the sudden burst of "God" in Benjamin's essay remains an enigma, most probably needing an assist from Kojève's understanding of authority in terms of a violent shakedown from "God," whether or not believably enthroned, whether or not legitimately sucked into the notion of Father, whether or not a complete collapse of the name, served up as a problem since the consternation over the fiction of paternity laid out by Plato.[21] Divine rage, though left unthematized, bursts on the scene inexplicably. In Lacan one has to choose or lose to the extent that we are faced from start to

17 Walter Benjamin, 'Two Poems by Friedrich Hölderlin', in Marcus Bullock and Michael W. Jennings, eds., *Selected Writings*, vol. 1: 1913–1926 (Cambridge, MA: Harvard University Press, 2004), 18–36.

18 Benjamin, 'The Task of the Translator'; and Jacques Derrida, 'Des Tours de Babel', in Joseph Graham, ed. and trans., *Difference in Translation* (Ithaca, NY: Cornell University Press, 1985), 165–207.

19 Friedrich Nietzsche, *On the Genealogy of Morals and Ecce Homo*, trans. by R. J. Hollingdale (New York: Vintage Books, 1989).

20 Sigmund Freud, *Totem and Taboo and Other Works (1913–1914)*, trans. by James Strachey, vol. 13 of *The Standard Edition of the Complete Psychological Works of Sigmund Freud* (London: Hogarth Press, 1975).

21 Alexandre Kojève, *The Notion of Authority: A Brief Presentation*, trans. by Hager Weslati (New York: Verso Books, 2014).

finish with "*le père ou pire,*" father or worse-than-father in a heated rumble of crushing consequence.[22]

*****

Muted yet pulsing, there is little in way of reprieve from a strangely inherited stock of anger, so let us finally get underway. One cannot simply control the flare-ups of choleric anguish by which one is punctually ambushed in a text such as Benjamin's on violence. Sometimes anger cannot be shaken loose, even when it goes into hiding, following the prompts of repression. Freud asserts that repression is actually good when it works, though it tends to fail us and concoct destructive jaunts. And so, the case of Benjamin becomes more a matter sublimated to grief – which still leaves an opening to grievance, legally and poetically pitched. The way anger is dropped on us by motives of critical unpreparedness raises questions about our own relation to law, modes of appeal, statutes of limitations. Aggrieved, I bring a question mark to the table of speculative anxiety. It comes down to a perennial matter of address attached to the legal implications of clocking out: Is it possible still to file a brief, to set down a complaint – or are we restricted by an implicit statute of limitations, the disruption of appeal? To whom or to what would one turn? Which placeholder, posited authority, or provisional respondent would one address? "*O einer, o keiner, o niemand, o du*" cries the plea put out by Celan, addressing the empty generality of no one and the singularity of You, all rolled up in none.[23] Without extending a temporary license to an offshoot of *Trauerspiel*, can we enter a plea before a larger, quasi-judicial authority, which, admittedly, involves on this point an element of *theatrics*? Whether or not supervised by reproducible technologies, there can be no ascertainable trial without representation, even where the unpresentable is at cause.

On the whole, Derrida reading Benjamin grants unique access to the call for justice and the aporias of appealing to the law, the staging of which implies an individual's plight pit against the mirage of universality – part of the voided but insistent generalizability of law.[24] Drawing on spectral appeal, my question seeks validity in some of the ways underscored by Benjamin and Derrida, but is also sponsored by Lyotard's phrasal regimens – asking, in other words, that we consider what remains strictly out of bounds,

22 Jacques Lacan, *The Seminar of Jacques Lacan, Book XIX: . . . Or Worse*, trans. by A. R. Price (Cambridge: Polity Press, 2022).

23 Paul Celan, 'O einer, o keiner, o niemand, o du', in Pierre Joris and Barbara Wiedemann, trans., *Memory Rose into Threshold Speech: The Collected Earlier Poetry of Paul Celan* (New York: Farrar, Straus and Giroux, 2020), 244.

24 Jacques Derrida, 'Force of Law: The "Mystical Foundation of Authority"', in Drucilla Cornell, Michel Rosenfeld, and David Gray Carlson, eds., *Deconstruction and the Possibility of Justice* (New York: Routledge, 1992), 3–67.

unlitigatable, juridically off the table in times that testify to upset's urgency, checking off moments when we are abandoned to uncodified idioms.[25] For his part, Lyotard refers us to those serious historical negotiations where an unscannable repertoire of evidentiary material is ruled out of order, necessarily exceeding juridical intervention by conventional means. Instances of an idiom's unrecognizability appear to foreclose the ability to judge according to code, covering material (as well as "immaterialities," a staple of Lyotard's lexicon) that cannot be legally primed or legitimately argued. In this regard, Benjamin and Derrida are, despite significant divergences, close allies when seeking out the a prioris of delegitimation and the language supply of legal standoffs.

*****

The Benjamin industry opened for operations only a few years after the rejection slip was nailed to my door. As far as sob stories go, the rebuff represented a mere episode in the roster of autobiographemes to which I am still grudgingly beholden. But, when the decision came down, twisting in Princetonian winds, I was a wreck and he was a complete unknown, unattended. He was certainly not on par with other visitors to our campus from Germanic precincts, such as Einstein, Panofsky, Gödel, Hermann Broch, Emily Noether, or Thomas Mann. I wanted to be the first on the block to field his call, discover the recondite stowaway, still unheard of even in Hannah Arendt's introduction to *Illuminations*, presenting to the English-speaking world the breakout phenom. Years later, in conversation with Levinas, I experienced another kind of triggering event when the philosopher bristled at the very mention of Benjamin, whom he dismissed as a mere *Schriftsteller*, a variant of popular writer that he had seen cluttering Parisian bookstores. He was incensed – his modulated, if mild downshift of anger – at my suggestion of plausible kinship on a shared topic. For I compared an aspect of Benjamin's work to one of his avowed obsessions. I had to backpedal to Heidegger, slowly regaining my composure. Levinas described the day he received his copy of *Being and Time* in the mail, his awe at the distinction immediately drawn between *vorhanden* ("present-at-hand") and *zuhanden* ("ready-to-hand") a breakaway moment in the history of thought.[26] He showed me by gentle hand gesture how he had cut open the pages with a knife. I was surprised by the swiftness with which Benjamin was disposed of in conversation, but later I could make some sense of the dismissal-knifing according to other protocols of reading that did not allow sufficient space for his commerce with Benjaminian revenants, Moscow, and playthings.

25 Lyotard, *Differend*.
26 Martin Heidegger, *Being and Time*, trans. by John Macquarrie and Edward Robinson (New York: Harper Perennial Modern Thought, 2008).

I bring to the table the wide-ranging abjection of Walter Benjamin (who, since those episodes, needs no introduction) in hopes of scoring a relatively minor point, one that was meaningful to me, and kept me going at the entry level of serious scholarly pursuit: Derrida's choice of texts and consistent protection of the names of the dismissed, the missed, the dissed – of those bound for extinction, muted arrival, or some form of death knell mockery, even archival chute – was important beyond measure. He was not the only one, but he weighed in strongly enough to make it count. When Derrida adopted Freud, for example, he took sizable hits from those dead and alive, from a host of undead authorities, still superegoically perched, locked, and loaded. One could feel Heidegger breathing down one's philosophical neck, scornful of the Freudian maneuver (and all psychologistic probes that *Dasein* would not abide). Even the next generation's refreshingly cool ones went anti-Oedipal, fed up with the tiresome habits of Mommy-Daddy-Pipi causalities, which nobody hosting significant symptoms was enjoying. At the time of "French Theory's" nascent upswing, Freud was greeted ambivalently, an easy target, especially for muscle-pumping, irony-avoidant foolosophers, to induct Erasmus to our cause, if anachronistically.[27]

The heckling bleachers did not deter Derrida, who also opened a sealed-off portal for poetry and literary aberration, bulking up his dossier with encrypted passwords of another zone of inquiry, including indications that locate art, lesbian cinema, paper machines, and photography. Derrida went so far as to read the blind in portraiture and scan provocative invisibilities, showing how to adjust philosophy to the silent exigencies of technology, medial bollards and other implementary techniques. Literature, for Derrida, was not simply literary, but pointed persistently to its outgrowth from law and other orders of impinging being. The juridical framework, essential and unavoidable, belongs in some ways to those relatively fragile contenders that Derrida took on, as if pushed by an inner dare and structural necessity. There is nothing of a "minor literature" in juridical pursuit, but Derrida sought the access code through Kafka – a champion of inaccessibility, referential turbulence, and the literary stall – as a startup to critical legal theory and its consequential support groups.[28] His encounter with Benjamin was of a different order and seemed to allow him to tighten his grip on the theoretical premises of jurisprudence.

27 Desiderius Erasmus, *The Praise of Folly*, trans. by Hoyt Hopewell Hudson (Princeton, NJ: Princeton University Press, 2015).

28 Gilles Deleuze and Félix Guattari, *Kafka: Toward a Minor Literature*, trans. by Dana Polan (Minneapolis: University of Minnesota Press, 2008); and Jacques Derrida, *Before the Law: The Complete Text of "Préjugés"*, trans. by Sandra van Reenen and Jacques de Ville (Minneapolis: University of Minnesota Press, 2018).

The comparison with Lyotard's reflections on acts of judgment, about which Derrida also wrote, holds only for a stretch before they part ways.[29] In shorthand, Lyotard delves into analytic philosophy where Derrida sets out to address the aporias of law and justice, strikes of violence, divine intervention, positing exploits, and the powering-down of authority. Leaving Wittgenstein to Lyotard, Derrida chose to ride with Benjamin on the edge of the law's legibility, scouring areas where things fall apart or are held together by a drop of hermeneutic superglue joining acts of precedent, mythological emergence, and historical analysis to the requirements of interpretive commitment.[30] From Derrida we glean that much of what we rely on discursively to make law stick, including the violence of "making sense" – the studied containment of incomprehensibility and inherited presumptions of legitimacy – hangs on the clash of undecidabilities, at best. By contrast, we must be wary when *decidability* is invoked, given its arbitrary and annihilating propensity, the logical presumption that allows judicial benches confidently to throw the book at you – *I simplify for effect.*

*****

We can now take a sidebar to address the "today" quality of our project, a corridor of thought that was not foreign to Derrida. When addressing relevant signals ascribable to legal messaging and discrete self-enforcement, Benjamin also made media technology part of the way we think about law, enabling us to consider how law, as an effect of media technology today, distorts and compels the contemporary scene of broken politics.

The obsession with law as a force that calls out for but cannot complete representation has shaped the history of medial output, if on a mostly thematic level. Media discloses its referent allegorically, we could say with Benjamin, while it keeps its phantoms covert and covered. Or, in another idiom, the technological medium always also shows up otherwise than being. Let me get a close-up as a sneak preview and review involving a speculative relation that *television* entertains with law, favoring stories that resolve themselves, compulsively offering closure on legal puzzles. The urge to resolve crime dramas, however traumatically truncated and simply narrated, covers for another drama that it avoids. We could file the untellable story that TV has covered under the category of an historical unsaid, that which defies its telling – shunning, yet replacing itself with uninterrupted storytelling.[31] A postwar phenomenology of urgent and impossible disclosure, television series and seriation abound in American programming, producing fresh batches that stem from *Dragnet* and *Perry Mason* to *Law and Order*, *Major Crimes*, *FBI*, etc. What binds a

29 Derrida, *Before the Law*.
30 Derrida, 'Force of Law'.
31 Avital Ronell, 'Trauma TV: Twelve Steps Beyond the Pleasure Principle', in *Finitude's Score: Essays for the End of the Millennium* (Lincoln: University of Nebraska Press, 1994), 305–327.

televisual metaphysics to law and the scripted pursuit of justice? The law has installed different engagement initiatives that play out by overflowing popular channels, as if to showcase its grip on thematizable aspects of legal dispute that erase yet leave a trace of what cannot be presented – the unthematizable pressure points that Derrida, following Benjamin on violence and technology, connects to the elusive withdrawal of justice. But withdrawal is not nothing ("Entzug ist Ereignis," Heidegger asserts: withdrawal is event).[32]

I will proceed by advancing the following hypothesis. The law saturates a televisual urge not only because it cannot be seen – theoretically, law does not manifest on the order of perception, hence the frenzied reliance on interpretation, explication, precedent, etc. – but because it compensates for the blindness it induces (as is the case in Kafka's man from the country). As a result, we have access only to a type of overrepresentation through varied representatives, bureaucratic substitutes, zealous administrators, identities arbitrated by means of flashing badges, insurance policies such as those Kafka, Esq., oversaw. In terms of medial appropriation, the law is non-presentable but generates representation and surrogate story, putting the legal ordeal of social organization on compulsive display. Derrida reminds us that Kafka read law as a force consistent with the refusal of genealogy: short-circuiting historicity and suspending believable origin, the law also stamps out authorship.[33] The attraction of the televisual technologies and platforms to the challenge of a thematic overabundance of law merits analysis to the extent, at least, that installed seats of power depend on media platforms, derived from a pathological dominance of television, for apportioning language games, moving forward and backward in the name of truth and knowing. The Trump regime has included in the roster of narrative tells the manic discernment of what counts as fake. Shifting the focus of what Lacoue-Labarthe saw as "national aestheticism" – the parades, rallies, films, concert series, the rebranding of cultural institutions, and the militaristic, fashion-backward uniforms sponsored by the Nazi fellowship – these regimes heavily rely on television to prompt political moves and stage their hyperbolic low-points.[34] End of Sidebar.

*****

The furlough accorded to the lie in *The Critique of Violence* complicates the testamentary itinerary without compromising its acuity.[35] Benjamin

32 Martin Heidegger, *Was heißt Denken?* (Tübingen: Max Niemeyer Verlag, 1954), 5; and Martin Heidegger, *What Is Called Thinking?*, trans. by J. Glenn Gray (New York: Harper & Row, 1968), 9.
33 Derrida, *Before the Law*, 43–44.
34 Philippe Lacoue-Labarthe, *Heidegger, Art, and Politics: The Fiction of the Political*, trans. by Chris Turner (Cambridge, MA: Basil Blackwell, 1990).
35 Benjamin, 'Critique of Violence', 244–245.

counts on the lie as a nonviolent offshoot of politesse in politics, capable of safeguarding diplomatic gains by downplaying violence. His recourse to fiction and literary device in the realm of legal dispute is never naïve, nor is it served up in bad faith. His *Kritik* indicates a number of aporetic routes that must be taken when delivering justice its due – acknowledging the problematic historicity and, by dint of necessity, the surfeit of fictions and nonhistorical idioms that accrue to any serious conception of Justice.

For these reasons, I want to adhere to Benjamin's playbook by dispensing another dosage of seriousness to the rollout of crucial stakes stacked in his legacy. This point has been a guiding thread in our discussion, yet has become hard to situate beyond a testimonial quiver that destabilizes the witness position. Always related, by etymology and a certain metaphysical logic, to *testicles* and a spermatic economy, testimony in English and German, indicates another relation to truth, a different ritual of swearing in since at least the Greek concept of *basanos* – where truth-testing ties to torture – and Roman law. I cannot divert at this time to the tradition bequeathed by Roman law, but defer to Hannah Arendt on the foundation she discovers in its articulation.[36] Here we can add only, if to keep the embers of anger stoked, that testimony historically required one to swear on one's testicles, which may give the appearance of excluding part of the contemporary demos when it comes to legitimate witnessing and oath-taking. The shuttle in the western tradition of *zeugen* (witnessing) launched between the phallus and testifying acts, the fragility of telling what happened, contours of different types of legal attestation and what constitutes an admissible record of events.

Allowing for the untouchable license of personal recollection, an ungeneralizable key to witnessing, we can ask what counts as a passable testimonial narrative. When, for instance, does testimony revert to *anecdotal* telling, too singular to anchor truth? Among the many sidebars, minoritarian traces, and off-ramps he continues to constellate, Benjamin taught us to respect the cognitive value of the anecdote, setting off a kind of rhetorical *forza del destino*, even when it comes to law, where, out of nowhere, fate rolls the dice. Whether fatefully thrown or retrieved from a highly subjective cache of souvenirs, the anecdote in Benjamin offers a tipping point in the constitution of knowledge and its often unavoidable reliance on non-knowledge. Derrida himself, that rogue, was not always averse to the anecdotal aside, however coded, when it came to unleashing a philosophically charged point on the order, say, of *Seinsgeschichte*. The destinal send-off secured by Heidegger is dispersed by the anecdotal envoi, which belongs to the stockpile of Derridean subjectiles and correlate programs for pushing off missives/missiles. The

36 Hannah Arendt, 'Foundation II: Novus Ordo Saeclorum', in *On Revolution* (New York: Penguin Books, 1990), 179–214.

anecdotal insert runs interference with authorized trajectories, redirecting cognitive assertion and recognizable pathways of thought. I revert to this subgenre in order to bear down on the implications of a motif underscoring that which evades transcendence or immanence in Benjamin, unable to take recourse to metaphysical staying power yet capable of disclosure – like a poetic flash without a stabilizing referent or legitimating authority to hold it steady. I cannot assure that all this theoretically motivated backstory justifies what is to come.

Following Benjamin's discursive values, let me draw down from yet another account in my anecdotal memory bank. An entry takes me to the time I was already an academic tween, maybe settling around the thematic timeline of my rejected Benjamin thesis. I can't remember for sure; actually, it may be a screen memory recap – this kind of narrating is not in sync with *Dichtung und Wahrheit*, when Bettina lent Goethe a steadying hand, or a memory stick prosthetically proffered, so that he could write his autobiography, filling in childhood memories that were barely retrievable by the adult mind. I have no Bettina dictating to me, fetching fresh supplies of anecdotes from my mother so that I can deliver a decent self-portrait hovering between *Poesy und Truth*.

What I can remember is that there was an experience of wrongdoing I didn't feel I could properly litigate, even in the soul-space of my heart (the heart becomes an important place and placeholder in Derrida's reading of Benjamin's *Kritik*).[37] I felt wronged; I unlocked a flash of anger. My father, after hearing me out, became anguished by my resolve to fix things. I was proposing a scheme of reparative justice, cast in young American insouciance. He sternly admonished me, "Please be careful. Don't become a Michael Kohlhaas." Even though he had been forced to flee Germany before finishing high school, my father carried a cultured inventory of ethical warnings. As a German-Jewish refugee, he didn't want trouble but was saddled with a troublemaker for a daughter. His own father, who didn't follow him out of Germany, despite his pleas, was removed to an extermination camp, sending only two postcards from Auschwitz, delivered by the Red Cross. I reveal these morose details, which exceed anecdote but don't amount to story, in order to scrape up clues from a shared sense of doom and a *Bildungs*-framework, a reading list cabled, I imagined, between Benjamin and my father. Both "fathers" were struck by an undertow of anxiety when seeking a measure of justice in the face of calamitous wrongdoing – a showdown with the event of unresolvable injury, when following Lyotard's analytic lead. Like Lyotard and Kleist, Benjamin reaches for that which flies beneath juridical radars, bringing interpretive gridlock to bear on gestures that cannot be adjudicated or legally registered. On par with Kleist, Lyotard specifically asks about outbursts and quasi-themes that the law cannot accommodate on the

37 Benjamin, 'Critique of Violence', 48–49.

order of a litigating language – part of his phrasal regime, including silence – inventorying, as we have begun to see, the kinds of utterance that no judiciary bench or branch can reasonably abide.[38] For Kleist, the *blush*, or moral flush of shame, delivers one such index of adjudicatory shortfall. A stain in Hawthorne, a reddening on the cheek in response to interrogation or judicial review, does not amount to a readable event in a legally framed dispute. I shall get to the short fuse that concerns Benjamin and Derrida (as well as Cicero, Lessing, Arendt) shortly.

Lyotard adds a number of non-prosecutable fluctuations of the nervous system and the speaking body that keep the phrasal regime down, irrecuperable in terms of maintaining legal meaning – and enforcement. Yet, the minor forces of law incite the nerves to speak. At one point, Benjamin and Kraus addressed the "rights of nerves" as a legitimate way to go about one's heuristic business.[39] And here I inch toward my point, but please, don't rush my approach to the problem of urethral sadism, which psychoanalysis understood only too well, becoming especially vivid under the instigation of Melanie Klein.[40] I return first to the ungovernable anecdote.

When my father urged me not to become a Michael Kohlhaas, it may have been too late. Kohlhaas had availed himself of every kind of legal recourse and feudal subterfuge, but was mocked and blocked when seeking juridical remedy for an injurious slam.[41] Having exhausted all procedural avenues and, by going so far as to pimp his wife in full expectation of obtaining a quid pro quo from the neighboring sadists – junkers intent on withholding an administrative pass to get on his way, allowing him to proceed – Michael Kohlhaas, despite relentless effort and surrogate envoy, dispossessed of power and property, could receive no hint of justice. This would be the time to remember that Kafka was a close reader of Kleist, a primal "K." in his intimate rolodex.

Kleist reflects on a number of legal theories on which something like *just affect* – affect-thresholds priming a "sense" of justice – depends. *Rechtsgefühl*, the sense of and feeling for justice, fortifies a notion of *equivalency* (*Gerechtigkeit*) as legitimate appeasement in matters of penalty appraisal.[42] For his part and partition, Kohlhaas wants what was stolen from him returned to him in the exact state it was forfeited. By means of a

38 Lyotard, *Differend*.

39 Walter Benjamin, 'Karl Kraus', in Michael W. Jennings, Howard Eiland, and Gary Smith, eds., *Selected Writings*, vol. 2, pt. 2: 1931–1934 (Cambridge, MA: Harvard University Press, 2005), 438.

40 Klein, *Envy and Gratitude*.

41 Heinrich von Kleist, *Michael Kohlhaas*, trans. by Michael Hofmann (New York: New Directions Publishing Corporation, 2020).

42 Heinrich von Kleist, 'Michael Kohlhaas', in Helmut Sembdner, ed., *Heinrich von Kleist: Sämtliche Werke und Briefe*, vol. 2 (Munich: Carl Hanser Verlag, 1961), 9.

number of ironic maneuvers, Michael K. finally wins his case, but only under the condition of facing the death penalty. Justice, in the end, is served, if only by execution – thus delivering finitude's in-your-face sentence, undecidably losing/winning the case and closing his monumental bout with the law. Well, I cannot leak completely into Kleist's story, and maybe, unlike Kohlhaas, whose overdetermined ironies bring him down, I was granted a temporary stay of execution, like so many of us whiling in non-ironical perplexity.

At a sensitive juncture of my deferred encounter with justice sought, the household patriarch shuddered with concern. Referring me to the Kleist story as a gold standard for ethical restraint, my father meant for me not to be overly cathected on the illusory goal of obtaining justice, going all-out German by exchanging life for principle, *überleben* for *fortleben*, heart for the sadistic prongs of reason. The still other K., Kant, makes reason and duty a bulwark of sadistic legalism, a position argued famously by Lacan, who, in his own way, took no prisoners.[43]

Michael Kohlhaas cued up a relation to the roots of jurisprudence that was fueled by rage, not far from a Puritan grasp of wrath, a death-driven tangle with urethral sadism – one of the three sadistic poses profiled by Melanie Klein, beginning with oral and anal forms of sadism, which we no doubt know only too well. I myself have been obsessed with the spread of anal-sadistic military strictures, the controls under which we barely live but continue to abide. Urethral sadism is part of the vernacular of rage that is connected to ambition and competitiveness, typically a reaction against shame. It involves the fantasy of drowning, poisoning, peeing on our adversaries. Thus, we tend to say how "pissed off" we are, or "pissed," which, in some pub cultures, is rerouted to mean drunk. Or, in the form of a quasi-curse, one can repel an offending other with the admonition, "Piss off!" While Hegel had something to say about *Piß* in the *Phenomenology*, Benjamin does not tend to go that low, not even in Marseilles, on a documented hashish romp.[44] But Benjamin does take a sidebar on anger, a sudden move that does not escape Derrida.[45] In the playoffs between divine and mythic justice, anger abruptly pops up, neither a concept nor lever, but an unaccounted burst of alien damnation that feeds violence and consumes itself as a flash that no more than stains, holding itself in a fizzle of nothingness, without determined aim or consequence.

The motif of anger in the unfolding of Benjamin's argument erupts close to the extreme deregulation induced by God's unannounced appearance in

43 Jacques Lacan, 'Kant with Sade', in Bruce Fink, trans., *Écrits: The First Complete Edition in English* (New York: W. W. Norton & Company, 2006), 645–668.

44 Georg Wilhelm Friedrich Hegel, *Phenomenology of Spirit*, trans. by A. V. Miller (Oxford: Clarendon Press, 1977), 210.

45 Derrida, 'Force of Law', 51.

the text.[46] The universality inscribed in the concept of justice (*Gerechtigkeit*) is shown by Derrida to stand in contradiction with God, the Decider who adjudicates the legitimacy "of means and the justice of ends *over and above reason and even above destinal violence.*"[47] Derrida remarks upon the intrusion of God in Benjamin's thinking on violence, the confusion brought down on human thinking, its relation to babbling nonsense (*Geschwätz*) that breaks with any notion of language as communicative, representative, or mediatory. This is where Derrida lands us:

> This sudden reference to God above reason and universality, beyond a sort of *Aufklärung* of law, is nothing other than a reference to the irreducible singularity of each situation. And the audacious thought, as necessary as it is perilous, of what I shall here call a sort of justice without *droit* [rights] . . . is just as valid for the uniqueness of the individual as for the people and the language, in short, for history.[48]

It gets better, and clearer, even if God's wrath should roll out a break with sense-making. To get a hold on the "nonmediate function of violence" ("*eine nicht mittelbare Funktion der Gewalt*"), Benjamin leads us to "the very place of decision."[49] Can it be merely by chance that he places God within inches of "the experience of anger to show that language is manifestation, epiphany, before it is mediation?"[50] Before letting go of anger, returning the responsibility of its always short-circuiting course to Benjamin ("Let us leave the responsibility for this concept to Benjamin"), Derrida will have promoted anger to a force that "in some way" shoots off as untamable immediacy: "the in some way disinterested, immediate and uncalculated manifestation of anger."[51] He ditches the problematic outburst of anger but soon relates it to the heart-space from which Benjamin's thought draws its passion. The beating of the heart, reminiscent by now of Jean-Luc Nancy's beats, is crucially bound to keeping time with unapproachable justice.[52]

Derrida finds the heart's beat to render "the exemplary instability of its status and its signature" that refers us to the core or heart of the matter with which Benjamin struggles to chart without abandoning the essential

46 Benjamin, 'Critique of Violence', 248.
47 Derrida, 'Force of Law', 51.
48 Ibid.
49 Ibid.
50 Ibid.
51 Ibid.
52 Jean-Luc Nancy, 'L'Intrus', trans. Susan Hanson (2002) 2:3 *CR: The New Centennial Review* 1–14.

ambiguity of his project.[53] I would want to enfold a second reading of "Dichtermut" here, the Hölderlin poem that keeps on flashing signals at moments of incalculability, and on which Benjamin carefully commented.[54] This was Benjamin's first major critical work, politically framed. In French, and in the interpretations of Lacoue-Labarthe, the poem's title is given as "Le courage du poète."[55] For Derrida's heart-core reading, the courage required of a genuine thinking of justice, its aporetic shortcomings and valiant overreach, reverts to the heartening brace meant to extend an abyssal embrace. Thus, Derrida obtains a permit to mesh *heart* and *courage* – here one can add colliding Hölderlinian tonalities – so that we take courage in disheartening times, in the heartless desolation of cruel encroachment that seizes the poetic sensibility. The assignment of responsibility shivers with the stress of overwhelmed knowledge and insufficient means of legal arbitration, even when served by God's thundering decree. Derrida states:

> I will have to content myself with stressing on the one hand the terrible ethico-political ambiguity of the text, on the other hand the exemplary instability of its status and its signature, what, finally, you will permit me to call this heart or courage (*ce coeur ou ce courage*) of a thinking that knows there is no *justesse*, no responsibility except in exposing oneself to all risks, beyond certitude and good conscience.[56]

As in Benjamin's reading of "Dichtermut," the poet stands exposed, fielding calls on the brink of suicidal resolve, putting the poet-body at risk. The poet, radically unshielded, surrenders any certitude of doing justice when delivering a word that issues from sacred nothingness. The risk assumed by clenching a divinely released flash of language – the poetic overreach required to do justice when bridging the divine and mortal breach in Hölderlin – looms over Benjamin's text.

For my part, allowing for a supplement of distortion and a smack of misprision (in graduate school, following the aborted mission on Benjamin, I was known as "Miss Prision"), I would like to underscore the *rage* in *courage*, catching the boomerang throwback to Benjamin following a narrow miss. Here I would offer to negotiate between "Dichter*wut*" and "Dichtermut," irreversibly entangled in the outrageous courage of poetic dare.

53 Derrida, 'Force of Law', 51.
54 Benjamin, 'Two Poems'.
55 Philippe Lacoue-Labarthe, *Heidegger: la politique du poème* (Paris: Galilée, 2002); and Philippe Lacoue-Labarthe, *Heidegger and the Politics of Poetry*, trans. by Jeff Fort (Chicago: University of Illinois Press, 2007).
56 Derrida, 'Force of Law', 51–52.

After mentioning anger in the analysis conducted by Benjamin, Derrida treats it more like a conceptual hot potato than anything else. Benjamin himself handles anger as an untreatable flare-up, blowing up the analytic scene only to let it fizzle. This is a Hölderlinian moment. The sky opens up, flashing on nothing that can be seized or semantically retrieved. It indicates epiphany without substance, which Derrida and Benjamin still place on the side of epiphanic blowup. Content to leave it be as part of the incalculable, Derrida quickly releases his grip on anger, like Benjamin, leaving the angry outburst for others to untangle, or pass on. Nonetheless, a philosophical history of such anger, justified or not, and however inappropriable by nature, must always risk an overstep in the context of law and justice.

From early on, among the Ancients, anger threatens to sideline our systems of justice to the extent that even Plato did not want stupid or raging partners to wrangle over the right side of philosophical dispute in *The Laws* and elsewhere. We are habituated to rule out anger within the limits of sober dispute in an effort to calm the edges of grievance. Given the complications of legal historicity, this sort of statement deserves more backing and evidentiary material, which, given the unavoidably stern sway of a scholarly imperative, one should not fail to supply. The perils of fast-tracking that I have not hesitated to provoke make one synthesize with a different view to the flexes of hypothesis and assertion, however.

There is another problem of anger identified by Arendt that discretely splits open Derrida's remarks on law and further unpacks Benjamin's library. Arendt broke out the political distinction between justified and unjustified anger, keeping one eye on Roman law and the other on Lessing, chief among German blockbusters of politically disruptive wrath.[57] She even made room for the kind of anger that makes one's contorting face *ugly* – hinting, as a good Kantian, at an aesthetic problem in the judgment of taste.[58] How does the law, when provoked, rip away at the beautiful form? Or is the relation between law and justice to be kept safely outside the sanctuarized space of the Third Critique? To the extent that Benjamin concerns himself with communicative and mediatory claims of language, the *communicability* of the experience of the beautiful form in *The Critique of Judgment* cannot be simply taken off the transcendental table.

Let me return to the problem at hand rather than continuing the habit of rummaging in the phrasing of quasi-transcendental judgment and the itinerary of transfer from Kant to Benjamin on this point, however compelling.

57 Hannah Arendt, 'On Violence', in *Crises of the Republic: Lying in Politics; Civil Disobedience; On Violence; Thoughts on Politics and Revolution* (New York: Harcourt Brace Jovanovich, 1972), 103–198; and Hannah Arendt, *Men in Dark Times* (New York: Harcourt, Brace & World, 1968).

58 Arendt, *Men in Dark Times*.

For the German lineage leading up to Arendt, Lessing's poetic anger, notoriously aimed at anyone who would listen or run, is of political consequence, prompting a thinking, in terms of desperate recourse, taken or rerouted through art history and small-state bureaucracies. Lessing was keenly tuned to frustrating and persecutory structures, packed with built-in torment. His specialty in drama (and personhood) involved muted indignity, vitriolic supremacy, coded attack, protest, and rage. He stayed focused, unrepentant, and refined. Arendt's reading of Lessing makes us ask, How many types of anger, under-theorized, feed the political agony of the day?[59] Does the outburst of anger wielded by Benjamin's reflection in the vicinities of mythic and divine justice carry a detonator that resists thematization or analysis? Or is this the core/*coeur* point of capture in a recalcitrant thinking of the *force* of law, which may or may not avail itself to presencing?

Now I must ("I must, I must," Lessing) restart the interpretive engine and test out some of Derrida's hypothetical checkpoints by telling a story of my unerasable *Berliner Kindheit*, a parental scroll down.[60] I started this section with my father's admonition because I remember well the wrath of God funneled into the domestic scene. As in Kafka's household, Mom would goad him on by inventorying a minor's crime spree, part of an accusatory discourse that was amended on a daily basis. As in Kafka and Benjamin, the *threat* of retribution was an even scarier splinter of homemade divine law, a real mom-and-pop little shop of horrors. I must turn to the maternal phallus to retrieve a piece of Benjamin. Mom had her own Berliner *Kindheit* and dubbed her particular brand of meanness as "Berliner Witz," the spite-tinged tease common to Berliners, not meant to cause serious harm, but if you couldn't take household Kombat, you were a weakling, unworthy of the slashes of Prussian malice. But enough of the metonymic anecdote, or what, as Derrida points out, Benjamin arrests under quotation marks, namely, my peculiar pursuit of "philosophy," idiomatically cast.[61] Why does Benjamin, at a crucial moment of his analysis, place philosophy in diacritical cuffs and under air quotes? We can ask Levinas, and my thesis advisor.

*****

I suppose that, among other acts of unconcealment, I am trying here to put forth a snarl of anger, barely suppressed, consisting in a child's relation to justice, of which one catches a psycho-sociological glimpse with the early wail, a first futile protest: "*It's not fair!*" The call for fair play, in terms of Schiller's *Spieltrieb* and ensuing speculative politics, reclaims an early rush to judgment, related to an infantile appeal to Justice, whose temporality begins

59 Ibid.

60 Walter Benjamin, *Berlin Childhood Around 1900*, trans. by Howard Eiland (Cambridge, MA: Harvard University Press, 2006).

61 Derrida, 'Force of Law', 54.

in a burst of *Jetztzeit* ("When do we want it? *Now*!").[62] Though infinitely deferred, the appeal to Justice demands immediacy and presence – turning us all back to childhood's righteous sting – and, simultaneously braked, into Kafka's man from the country, who spends his dwindling lifetime waiting for entry, stooped and stumped. We should not forget that the strained anger of the young-old man from the country wears down the guardian of the law, nearly exhausting him.[63]

*****

There is undoubtedly more to the breakout of anger in politics and law, as, for instance, when Benjamin allows for a brief flash of the divine tantrum to blast into the scene of destructive retribution, whether mythically or divinely cracking, law-giving or law-preserving. Anger, whether a divine bid for blowing off steam, strangely desperate and disarticulate – precisely aimed at the human and destructive scale as prelinguistic howl or scream – or intent on setting things right, arises in great part from a hermeneutics of frustration, emitting a cry of brokenness that also compromises the hermeneutic circle as it fails simply to retrieve meaning or round out the presumptions of sense-making, another form of violence. As broken address – or, when pushed dialectically, as a *purer* form of address – it still carries the burden of justice-seeking responsibility, disrupted and a priori soured, timed, and timeless.

*****

Anger, in terms of a classical rhetoric politically voided, out of place in jurisprudence and blocked out by the ground rules for genuine deliberation, is often doomed as device or method, revealing only the short fuse of action and arbitration. Still, it cannot be entirely ruled out of any invested forum for the adjudication of dispute. Arendt put it back in play, in an effort to take measure of the *justice* of claims, the plausible *justesse* of a rhetoric thrown on the debate floor by means of anger. As reactive and frustrated, anger, incited by and allied to grievance, is bound by a limit of language that has reached its boiling point in view of communicative qualities and representation. It is a force, rising for the most part in formless and sprawling turns, like Benjamin's police, ready to strike, patrolling the precincts of speech like a phantom attack squad, always there, says Derrida, even when it is not "there." A

62 Friedrich Schiller, *On the Aesthetic Education of Man: And, Letters to Prince Frederick Christian von Augustenburg*, trans. by Keith Tribe (London: Penguin Books, 2016); and Walter Benjamin, 'On the Concept of History', in Howard Eiland and Michael W. Jennings, eds., *Selected Writings*, vol. 4: 1938–1940 (Cambridge, MA: Belknap Press of Harvard University Press, 2006), 395.

63 Franz Kafka, 'Before the Law', in Willa and Edwin Muir, trans., *The Complete Stories* (New York: Schocken Books, 1988), 3–4.

stealth force, it tends to duck manifestation.[64] Impassioned yet pumped by juridical fixity of purpose, anger, when all is said and done, refers us in the end to law and justice: ineluctably, it implies a theory of rights, including the "rights of nerves" advocated by Benjamin and, in a different way, by Celan who profiled a posture of those thrown off, "the upset." Thus, Celan crafts a precise language of being-upset, *staying* upset, clenched, historically ticked off and, on the face of it, inconsolable and unmournably on message. Nietzsche had another recipe for staying boiling mad by "philosophically" entering the state of his chronically upset stomach to the rosters that describe his aroused ruminations.

*****

However pointless in terms of its modern pounce, anger scores a point in the history of reason. Framed in deficiency of aim and failing any identifiable measure of just return, anger lines up, since Lessing's reprisal of classically straitened rage (*Zorn*), on the side of reason. Alenka Zupančič supplied and parsed the utterance, apropos of Schiller, "I have reason to be angry."[65] To the extent that anger's home base has recourse to reason and law, it also presupposes speech. Even when flustered, anger demands language, wanting its day in court. We see the grab for law by the dispossessed and powerless as well as by the threatening gait of the booming Almighty. We see the disjunctive cry for Justice in German modernity from the first robber in Schiller, prompting the proto-terrorist in Kleist, and the population of post-punk destitutes, the *misérables* of global injustice. As for the "Angry Inch" of Hedwig, the trans philosopher and German scholar who was kicked out of the German university system, they could be shown to have some family resemblance to Benjamin's angry flash. Modelling a bit of an updated version of *Kultur*, Hedwig had been expelled from the university because of an East German-based *Trauerspiel* – their drama features a rejected thesis that analyzed the influence of aggressive German philosophy on the genesis of rock and roll.

*****

We could move forward with Benjamin's double take on anger in terms of law-positing and law-defounding destruction, an interpretive extension program, which, at this time, must be relinquished. I've probably made my point sufficiently clear, proposing *en gros* that one consider both the unreadabilty yet pivotal smackdown delivered by anger at home and in court, on the streets

64 Derrida, 'Force of Law', 51.
65 Alenka Zupančič, *The Chorus and the Real in Poetic Art*, lecture video (YouTube, 2011), https://www.youtube.com/watch?v=qp-otu2WqKU.

and in the classroom, muffled or in the shrill shape of *S_C_R_E_A_ M_E_D* indignation that Heidegger ascribes to Nietzsche.[66]

*****

In keeping with the syntax of overreach, one more point on this unsettled *topos*: psychoanalysis is at odds with itself over the status of anger. For some reason, Lacan asserts that psychoanalysis has shown little interest in anger.[67] I'm not sure why exactly he pitches the hypothesis and lets it stand. I'm not entirely convinced. This seems to be strategically necessary to Lacanian psychoanalysis, to deny anger a place or management office in the predecessors' corpora. Even without going to the effects of his own illness for Sigmund Freud, suppressed and rerouted, hysterically converted and somatically displaced, one wonders why the birthplace of psychoanalysis had no room for causalities driving the angry subject. I haven't yet cracked this case, but I am inclined to question Lacan's determination to downplay anger in the registers of the psychoanalytic vocabulary. Just ask Freud's Abrahamic lawgiver, Moses, about the angry outburst in relation to law, and let yourself review his holy tantrum – or ask Dora about the time she threw a pink slip at the great analyst when she gave him two weeks' notice.[68] I'd add the quarrels with Ferenczi and Jung here, if I didn't fear spectral retribution and a clap of thunder.

*****

On the whole, though, anger is not so easy to manage in terms of a genealogical probe. Plato gives it an ethical edge by raising the importance of getting angry *at yourself*, an honorable form of issuing a call to order, even if one can never fully be accountable to oneself or the polis – another cause for anger, never measuring up to what you should know or be.[69] Down the line, anger challenges the level of discovery associated with Nietzsche's ressentiment or his rundown of the Good as linked principally to goods, property, and greed, his transvaluations of values entailing the hoax of Christian softness.[70] Arendt pushes for another turn of the vise of valuation. For the Greeks and Lessing, she reminds us, anger was also viewed as a *pleasant* emotion that reveals and exposes the world.[71] Its transvaluation in Judeo-Christian thought deserves yet another round of interpretive re-

66 Heidegger, *What Is Called Thinking?*
67 Lacan, *Ethics of Psychoanalysis*, 103.
68 Sigmund Freud, *Dora: An Analysis of a Case of Hysteria* (New York: Touchstone, 1997); and Sigmund Freud, *Moses and Monotheism: Three Essays*, trans. by James Strachey, vol. 23 of *The Standard Edition of the Complete Psychological Works of Sigmund Freud* (London: Hogarth Press, 1975).
69 Plato, *The Republic*, trans. by Tom Griffith (Cambridge: Cambridge University Press, 2018).
70 Nietzsche, *Genealogy of Morals*.
71 Arendt, *Men in Dark Times*, 6.

flection, beginning with the Roman severance of the quasi-concept, which is marked by justified and unjustified anger-attitudes. On the Greek scale, before justification was at issue, anger was paired with *laughter* – an uncontrolled outburst that was to receive, in our times, its own attributes of endangering qualities from Benjamin's friend and chief archivist, Georges Bataille.

*****

If both Benjamin and Derrida light up only to abandon anger's blowout in the founding and breaking of law, maybe we can return in our designated reflections on the runaway philosopheme to Homer's valuation, where anger becomes a *duty* – a force that animates the warrior. The detestable anger of Achilles when he goes after Agamemnon shows up as a vital energy in *cholos*, cuing up the resources of anger as an action of noble capacity, hot and overflowing, raising the temperature of furious rejoinder in gods and mortals. Fueling a fight spirit, anger rises fast to move unstoppably, conducted as pre-Christian mission, a *duty*, and call. Young and combative at heart, it is shown to turn against the ruler's hubris, excessive and grotesque. Moreover, anger, in crucial sectors of Homer's world, names a *pleasure* linked to the mortal condition. Ha!

*****

Though the pleasure connection would yield yet another spiral down Benjamin's alley, a budding conspiracy with the death drive, aiming as it does beyond pleasure, I must leave the discussion of pleasure in law to another day, another vision of encompassing *jouissance* in the realm linking *Kritik* to violence. Let us just say in provisional conclusion, that anger recedes as quickly as it explodes – to no effect, or, rather to *pure* effect, without the reserve tropes of authority or any serious evidence of referential reliability besides the mettle that it calls up. In terms of pleasure and its likely transposition into *jouissance*, the explosion of anger implies a libidinally boosted force, fracturing law while heralding justice, blowing up the scene of indignities in a riot of surrender. When anger detonates in Benjamin's text on violence, it proves capable of cluster-bombing the holding cell of mere concepts or mediatory language. Angry outbursts overwhelm description or any system of responsibly assured motivation and consequence. In this way, the manifestation of anger mirrors and supports Derrida's displacement of form to *force*. Before discarding the ungovernable disruption that anger donates to the scene of writing, Derrida indicates that anger in Benjamin's text is "in some way disinterested, immediate, and uncalculated manifestation."[72]

72 Derrida, 'Force of Law', 51.

It belongs, moreover, to the alterations of "exemplary instability."[73] These terms underlie some of the deepest probes that deconstruction has undertaken, exemplified, for instance, in the restless interrogation of unconditional hospitality, forgiveness, amnesty – the purported other side of violence – and their recalcitrant requisites.[74]

*****

Wide-ranging and law-seeking – but also law-breaking, if you're not on Kant's watch list – unconditional hospitality demands the granting of asylum, no questions asked, the restoration of women's rights, immigrant sovereignty, and absolute forgiveness without recourse to amnesia (without the common supplement of a "forgive and forget"). For, in responsible (if obsessive) determination, deconstruction does not forget. The rogue surge of anger, at once indignant, raw, immediate, at once law-breaking and law-inaugurating, cannot be wrestled down to the spirit of stabilized or dialectizable signification, does not comply with a formal principle. Like force, the motif of anger, philosophically unhinged and largely unaccommodated, exceeds genre or categorial solidity, beating like a heart, fragile but ticking, ever about to shatter, looming over a broken horizon that has not known justice, except, possibly, for a short-lived session, maybe a heartbeat.

73 Ibid.

74 I cannot fail to acknowledge the importance of thinking close to the pulse of Derrida's work on Benjamin with Peter Goodrich and Anselm Haverkamp, learning also from each contributor to this volume. The outstanding acuity of my research assistant, Arielle Friend, helped bring this chapter to completion in a moment of stalled apprehension.

8

SACRIFICES

On a Footnote in 'Critique of Violence'[1]

Erica Weitzman

So Abram rose, and clave the wood, and went,
And took the fire with him, and a knife.
And as they sojourned both of them together,
Isaac the first-born spake and said, My Father,
Behold the preparations, fire and iron,
But where the lamb for this burnt-offering?
Then Abram bound the youth with belts and straps,
and builded parapets and trenches there,
And stretchèd forth the knife to slay his son.
When lo! an angel called him out of heaven,
Saying, Lay not thy hand upon the lad,
Neither do anything to him. Behold,
A ram, caught in a thicket by its horns;
Offer the Ram of Pride instead of him.
But the old man would not so, but slew his son,
And half the seed of Europe, one by one.

— Wilfred Owen, 'The Parable of the Old Man and the Young'

In the preface to the second half of 'Force of Law' as presented at the 1990 conference 'Nazism and the "Final Solution"' (and appended as a footnote to the published edition of the essay), Jacques Derrida states that one of the

1 I would like to thank Peter Fenves for his comments on an earlier version of this article, and Jeffrey Champlin for the conversations many years ago that eventually led to this chapter's realization.

DOI: 10.4324/9781003589419-11

reasons he has chosen to present on Walter Benjamin's 'Critique of Violence' for the occasion is his sense of it as a text "haunted in advance . . . by the theme of radical destruction." More precisely: "I believe this uneasy, enigmatic, terribly equivocal text is, as it were, haunted in advance (but can one say 'in advance' here?) by the theme of radical destruction, extermination, total annihilation" – and thus also haunted, in Derrida's words, "by haunting itself, by a quasi-logic of the phantom which . . . should be substituted for an ontological logic of presence, absence or representation", a logic which Derrida implicitly associates with the violent logic of the law as well as with its equally violent abrogation.[2] Leaving the methodological complexities of Derrida's statement aside for the moment: for Derrida, as is well known, Benjamin's positing of a "bloodless" violence of divine justice,[3] in contrast to what Benjamin styles as the bloodletting, "mythical" violence of the law, finds a kind of uncanny materialization in the murderous apparatus of the Nazi gas chambers, with their ghoulish promise, in the grotesque fantasies of their inventors, of eliminating entire human populations without leaving a trace. In his talk, Derrida admits that he is troubled by the possibility that beneath Benjamin's idiosyncratic revolutionism could lie a latent sympathy with such fantasies, a lurid attraction to both real and metaphorical violence in the service of an unknowable translegal future, a utopian horizon of anti- or non-law for the sake of which even what Derrida calls "the worst"[4] – genocide as political expedient – might be deemed to be justified.

Derrida's objection to Benjamin's notion of "divine violence" has of course been one of the most controversial and widely criticized aspects of Derrida's essay, possibly even of Derrida's work as a whole.[5] In what follows here, I

2 Jacques Derrida, 'Force of Law: The "Mystical Foundation of Authority"', in *Deconstruction and the Possibility of Justice*, Drucilla Cornell, Michel Rosenfeld, and David Gray Carlson eds., trans. Mary Quaintance (New York: Routledge, 1992), 3–67, here 63–64, note 6.

3 Walter Benjamin, 'Toward the Critique of Violence', in *Toward the Critique of Violence: A Critical Edition*, Peter Fenves and Julia Ng eds., trans. Julia Ng (Stanford: Stanford University Press, 2021), 39–61, here 58; 'Zur Kritik der Gewalt', in *Gesammelte Schriften*, II.1, Rolf Tiedemann and Hermann Sweppenhäuser eds. (Frankfurt am Main: Suhrkamp, 1977), 179–203, here 199.

4 Derrida, 'Force of Law', 63.

5 Werner Hamacher, while pointedly avoiding mention of 'Force of Law', implicitly rebuts Derrida's concerns in insisting that Benjamin's idea of "divine violence" has nothing to do with any crudely literal harms (be they of, or outside the law), but rather with the suspension of law per se; an "event which no longer posits and which represents nothing – nothing but the unrepresentable, in which the superiority of the moral order over any political order of statutory law announces itself." Werner Hamacher, 'Afformative, Strike', trans. by Dana Hollander (1991) 13 *Cardozo Law Review* 1133–1157, 1154, see also 1149–1150, note 34. For further criticisms of Derrida on these or similar grounds, see, e.g., Anselm Haverkamp, 'Kritik der Gewalt und die Möglichkeit von Gerechtigkeit: Benjamin in Deconstruction', in *Gewalt und Gerechtigkeit: Derrida – Benjamin*, Anselm Haverkamp ed. (Frankfurt am Main: Suhrkamp, 1994), 7–50, esp. 30–33; Bettine Menke, 'Benjamin vor dem Gesetz: Die *Kritik der Gewalt* in der

do not propose to take a position on the thorny question of the rightness or wrongness of Derrida's allegations against Benjamin, nor to judge the validity of the anachronistic connection he makes between Benjamin's notion of "bloodless violence" and the pseudo-hygienic extermination practices of the Nazi Holocaust. What I propose is something far more modest: to fill in a bit of missing context for Benjamin's essay – missed, perhaps, also by Derrida himself – and thus to reexamine some of the questions and tensions that haunt Derrida's own text, in the light of the debates, discourses, and events behind Benjamin's essay that this missing context reveals. For one, it is hardly necessary to summon up the Nazi Holocaust in order to evoke the idea of mass death in Benjamin's essay: the text appeared less than three years after the end of the First World War, in which up to 22 million people were killed,[6] and less than a year after the Spanish Flu pandemic, which cost the lives of at least 17 million more.[7] In other words, Derrida is right to ask – albeit only parenthetically and in passing – just how proleptic the theme of "annihilation" in the 'Critique of Violence' actually is: in 1921, at the time of Benjamin's writing, the wholesale destruction of human life is neither phantasmatic nor futural, but something in living memory and all too real.

For this reason, as Derrida himself notes, Benjamin's essay must be read not only against the background of the constitutional crises and internal legal debates of the Weimar Republic, as is often done, but also against the background of "a war and a pre-war that saw the European development and failure of pacifist discourse, antimilitarism, the critique of violence, including juridico-police violence."[8] It is to "critique of violence" – the opposition to killing of all kinds in the shadow of its excess – that the missing context previously alluded to belongs. I refer, namely, to the short and today all but forgotten manifesto 'Anti-Cain' (Anti-Kain) – written by the writer, activist, jurist, and publicist Kurt Hiller and published in his own journal *The Goal: Yearbooks for Intellectual Politics*

Lektüre Derridas', in *Gewalt und Gerechtigkeit*, Haverkamp ed., 217–275; Burkhard Lindner, 'Derrida. Benjamin. Holocaust. Zur Dekonstruktion der "Kritik der Gewalt"', in *Global Benjamin: Internationaler Walter-Benjamin-Kongress 1992*, vol. 3, Klaus Garber and Ludger Rehm eds. (Munich: Fink, 1999), 1691–1723, and Judith Butler, *Parting Ways: Jewishness and the Critique of Zionism* (New York: Columbia University Press, 2012), 76–77.

6 All sources emphasize that casualty counts in World War I (both combatant and civilian) are necessarily imprecise, but all also agree that whatever the exact number of deaths, it was in the many millions. See D. E. Showalter and J. G. Royde-Smith, 'World War I', *Encyclopedia Britannica*, 25 April 2025, www.britannica.com/event/World-War-I.

7 Here estimates vary even more widely, from as low as 17.5 million dead to as high as 100 million. See Max Roser, 'The Spanish Flu: The Global Impact of the Largest Influenza Pandemic in History', *Our World in Data*, 30 April 2025, https://ourworldindata.org/spanish-flu-largest-influenza-pandemic-in-history.

8 Derrida, 'Force of Law', 29.

(*Das Ziel: Jahrbücher für geistige Politik*) – which Benjamin, selectively quoting from in the concluding paragraphs of his own essay, both pours scorn on and, as will be shown in what follows, complicatedly co-opts. Hiller's text – billed as a "postscript" to the short essay 'The Disarmers' Final Battle' (*Endkampf der Waffengegner*), published in the same issue by the communist poet Rudolf Leonhard – is essentially an impassioned and acerbic appeal to renounce the use of murder as political tool, eponymously designated in the title of Hiller's essay by the biblical figure of Cain as the first homicide. Its main points are as simple as they are absolute: the Hobbesian anthropology of *homo homini lupus* must be rejected, leftists must not stoop to their opponents' tactics, all nations should agree to multilaterally and permanently disarm, and the preservation of human life as such should rank higher than any other principle or cause, as Hiller writes, in the sentence that will famously provoke Benjamin's ire: "We profess . . . that higher still than the happiness and justice of an existence – stands existence itself."[9]

Hiller's essay is unsystematic, reactive, and self-contradictory – but it is not abstract. Its immediate occasion, besides the aforementioned surge in antimilitarist sentiment after the disaster of the First World War, is the Spartacist uprising of January 1919, in which the police, together with right-wing paramilitaries, murdered more than a hundred activists – most infamously, Karl Liebknecht and Rosa Luxemburg – and which Hiller, for all his sympathy, here chides for resorting to the methods of its adversaries, methods that anyway badly backfired. While Hiller does not entirely equate leftist violence or Leninist class warfare with either police brutality or imperialist military conflict, he nevertheless condemns the former for adopting the latter's calculations:

> In his methods, the Bolshevik is just the inverse of the old Russian-Prussian militarist. . . . We demand that no one be permitted to take the life of one brother in order to bring freedom to another. . . . The notion that hundreds of thousands should be deprived of the fleeting miracle of existence so that millions can fare better is monstrous and hardly enforceable.[10]

Other targets of Hiller's polemic are just as concrete: strong-arm policing, Bismarckian saber-rattling, compulsory military service, mercenary reserve armies, and militarized national borders. Though Hiller also acknowledges

9 Kurt Hiller, 'Anti-Cain: A Postscript to Rudolf Leonhard's "Our Final Battle against Weapons"', in Benjamin, *Toward the Critique of Violence: A Critical Edition*, trans. Lisa Marie Anderson, 185–193, here 186; 'Anti-Kain. Ein Nachwort zu dem Vorhergehenden' (1919) 3:1 *Das Ziel. Jahrbücher für geistige Politik* 24–32, here 25.

10 Hiller, 'Anti-Cain', 186; 'Anti-Kain', 2425.

the economic violence of state capitalism and the power politics of the *Kaiserreich*,[11] he categorically dismisses the idea that the fact of such violence could justify taking recourse to the physical violence of the murder of others in opposition. This, for Hiller, is nothing but the faulty logic of the "intellectual terrorist": Hiller's term for a person who embraces killing as a means to a higher end, and thereby perpetuates the fallacy of retributive violence whose emergence is mythologized in Cain's fratricide.[12] Thus Hiller's demand, repeated as leitmotif throughout his essay: "Let us unequivocally decry Cain's methods as an abomination" (*Kains Mittel absolut verabscheuen*).[13] That the aims of the Bolsheviks and the Spartacists might be more noble than that of the militarized state makes no difference in terms of the rightness of their tactics:[14] not only does killing only lead to more killing, in Hiller's analysis, it also corrupts the person who kills, and debases the cause for which the killing is done in the first place.[15] Indeed, for Hiller, insofar as murder has been the *ultima ratio* of both statecraft and interpersonal conflict since, as it were, the dawn of time, to persist in violence as a political tactic, regardless of one's ideological position, is in the end to remain a reactionary; a truly radical politics, on the other hand, would be one that abjures physical violence in favor of "the struggle of the intellectual type against half-intellect and non-intellect and anti-intellect" (*den Kampf des geistigen Typus gegen Halbgeist und Ungeist und Widergeist*),[16] the struggle, as Hiller conceives it, of "nonviolence" versus "violence" per se.

It is surprising how little attention has been paid to Hiller's essay in the critical literature, particularly considering its placement as the last footnoted reference of the 'Critique of Violence', not to mention its status as the most immediate impetus for Benjamin's consequential meditations on the sixth commandment and the indefensibility of what he terms "mere" or "bare" life.[17]

11 See Hiller, 'Anti-Cain', 186; 'Anti-Kain', 24.

12 See Hiller, 'Anti-Cain', 186; 'Anti-Kain', 25.

13 Hiller, 'Anti-Cain', 185, 187, 190, translation modified; 'Anti-Kain', 24, 25, 30.

14 "The only difference [of the Bolshevik revolutionary Karl Radek] from [World War I general and right-wing politician Ernst] Ludendorff: the ethos of the final goal." Hiller, 'Anti-Cain', 186; 'Anti-Kain', 25.

15 Lewis D. Wurgaft stresses the specifically anti-pragmatic aspect of Hiller's argument: "In insisting on the pre-eminence of pacifism over socialism, Hiller was not simply distinguishing between the means and ends of revolutionary activity. Rather, the act of revolution was primarily a token of moral purity and testified to an awareness of the dangers of materialism in its social and political manifestations." Lewis D. Wurgaft, *The Activists: Kurt Hiller and the Politics of Action on the German Left 1914–1933* (Philadelphia: Transactions of the American Philosophical Society, 1977), 63.

16 Hiller, 'Anti-Cain', 187, translation modified; 'Anti-Kain', 25.

17 See Benjamin, 'Critique', 58–59; 'Kritik', 200–202. While Hiller still enjoys some recognition as an early advocate for gay rights, his intellectual production has otherwise gone largely ignored – a state of affairs evidenced, among other things, by the fact that 'Anti-Cain'

Benjamin's objection, as is well known, is that Hiller's elevation of "life" to the end goal of political activity not only implies an impoverished form of political thought, but also ultimately relies on a concept of life that, for Benjamin, is itself the primary object of "mythic" or legal-political violence – or rather, is precisely that which enables the establishment of "mythic" or legal-political violence in the first place. In this sense, according to Benjamin, Hiller's essay not only fails to recognize the inherent violence of the law itself, it also undermines the very nonviolence for which he advocates, upholding, despite Hiller's own intentions, the founding gesture of statist power and reducing the human being, for all Hiller's insistence on a "geistige" politics, to a condition of contentless, defenseless *Geistlosigkeit*.[18]

Benjamin had a complicated relationship with Hiller, who seems by all accounts to have been a difficult and combative character.[19] Hiller did publish an early essay of Benjamin's in the first issue of *Das Ziel*, but Benjamin was apparently disappointed in the issue as a whole – while Hiller was disappointed with Benjamin's contribution – and they never worked together or corresponded again,[20] though Benjamin did see fit to review Hiller's 1932 essay collection *Der Sprung ins Helle* for the *Frankfurter Zeitung*, where Benjamin's declared sympathy with some of Hiller's political aims does not prevent him from excoriating most of his arguments and philosophical methods.[21] This history notwithstanding, 'Toward the Critique of Violence' is in fact far more indebted to Hiller's 1919 polemic than Benjamin lets on. Not just

---

was first translated into English only in 2021, as part of the recent critical edition of 'Toward the Critique of Violence'.

18 The discourse that emerges out of Benjamin's objection is far too vast to take into account here, but its locus classicus is Giorgio Agamben, *Homo Sacer: Sovereign Power and Bare Life*, trans. by Daniel Heller-Roazen (Stanford: Stanford University Press, 1998), esp. 63–67 and 83. For a discussion of this problematic in the context of post-World War I medical technology, see Erica Weitzman, 'Human Fragments: Plastic Surgery and Bare Life in Joseph Roth's Feuilletons' (Winter 2013) 46:4 *Journal of Austrian Studies* 87–109, esp. 96–98.

19 See Wurgaft, *The Activists*, esp. 55–57. On Hiller's sectarian battles within his own pacifist movement, see Daniel Münzner, *Kurt Hiller. Der Intellektuelle als Außenseiter* (Göttingen: Wallstein, 2015), esp. 133–138.

20 See Lisa Marie Anderson, 'Translator's Preface', in Benjamin, *Toward the Critique of Violence: A Critical Edition*, 179–184, especially 181.

21 Walter Benjamin, 'Der Irrtum des Aktivismus. Zu Kurt Hillers Essaybuch "Der Sprung ins Helle"', in *Gesammelte Schriften*, vol. 3: *Kritiken und Rezensionen*, Hella Tiedemann-Bartels, ed. (Frankfurt am Main: Suhrkamp, 1991), 350–352. Benjamin reproduces part of his review in his 1934 talk, 'The Author as Producer': see Walter Benjamin, 'The Author as Producer: Address at the Institute for the Study of Fascism, Paris, April 27, 1934', in *Selected Writings*, vol. 2: 1927 (Cambridge: Harvard University Press, 1999), 768-772, esp. 722-73; 'Der Autor als Produzent: Ansprache im Institut zum Studium des Faschismus in Paris am 27 April 1934', in *Gesammelte Schriften*, vol. 2.1: *Aufsätze, Essays, Vorträge*, Rolf Tiedemann and Hermann Schweppenhäuser eds. (Frankfurt am Main: Suhrkamp, 1991), 683–701, esp. 689-90.

the central theme of political violence, but also – albeit in oblique or altered form – the framing question of means and ends,[22] the appeal to "myth" (in Hiller's case, as a mere synonym for conventional us-against-them thinking; in Benjamin's case, as the cyclical violence of temporal power itself),[23] the issue of universal military conscription,[24] and the case of the 1919 Greifswald Clinic doctors' strike, which Benjamin, for once in agreement with Hiller, calls "repellent," "depraved," and "a conspicuous case of violent default"[25] are all arguably prompted by elements of Hiller's own treatise.

The obvious point here is still one worth emphasizing: Benjamin's critique – or rather, his thinking "toward" a critique – is in no small part a response to Hiller's reflexive and *un*critical pacifism, which among other things exhorts his readers to "let us finally be satisfied with faith in the force of law [*Glauben an die Gewalt des Rechts*]" under the governance of "the League of Nations or the World Commune",[26] in the unstated and patently contradictory assumption that "violence" is something external to the law, that the law, as the purported antithesis of violence, could simply legislate the latter out of existence. In 'Force of Law', Derrida follows Benjamin in highlighting the aporetic nature of such a solution: for not only do wars and labor strikes, those seeming violations of the legal order, in fact operate perfectly well within it,[27] but also, more fundamentally, the very lawfulness of the law itself is dependent on acts of violence or force for its interpretation and execution – including, not

22 See Hiller, 'Anti-Cain', 185–186; 'Anti-Kain', 24–25; Benjamin, 'Critique', 39–41; 'Kritik', 179–181.

23 On Hiller's use of "myth" see 'Anti-Cain', 185; 'Anti-Kain', 24: "Myth creates an earthly state of being, the eternal validity of which we dispute, we who believe in becoming, we who devote our energy to the realization of a world we have seen in the mind, a not-yet-world." Benjamin, of course, makes a distinction between Greek "myth" and the Hebrew Bible in a way that Hiller, conspicuously, does not.

24 Hiller, 'Anti-Cain', 191–192; 'Anti-Kain', 31–32.

25 Benjamin, 'Critique', 53, translation modified; 'Kritik', 195. Compare Hiller, 'Anti-Cain', 188–189; 'Anti-Kain', 27–28. The strike consisted in the refusal on the part of the clinic's doctors to admit or treat patients after the raising of a communist flag above the clinic by the Greifswald Workers' and Soldiers' Council. Whereas Hiller cites the strike as an example of an act of real violence on the part of the establishment against a purportedly violent but in fact innocuous gesture on behalf of the oppressed, Benjamin treats it as an example of Sorel's "political" strike as opposed to the "proletarian general strike" – a difference perhaps above all of framing rather than of interpretation.

26 Hiller, 'Anti-Cain', 191, translation modified; 'Anti-Kain', 31. Anderson's translation of "Weltkommune" as "world community" fails to convey the institutional and legal overtones of Hiller's phrase.

27 "War is another example of this contradiction internal to law (*Recht* or *droit*). There is a *droit de la guerre*. . . . Apparently subjects of this *droit* declare war in order to sanction a violence whose object seems natural. . . . But this warlike violence . . . is always deployed within the sphere of law. It is an anomaly *within* the legal system with which it seems to break." Derrida, 'Force of Law', 39.

least, the power to determine what counts as "lawfulness" and "unlawfulness" in the first place. In this sense, as Derrida's argument suggests, Hiller's militant pacifism would be less straightforward than he supposes: insofar as violence is necessary for the survival of the juridico-political state, the blanket rejection of violence entails a rejection of the legal-juridical order itself – a criticism that Hiller's almost touching trust in the efficacy of international peacekeeping bodies fails utterly to realize.[28] Hiller forgets that the police and the League of Nations, too, must have their own methods of enforcement (or fade into irrelevance for lack thereof) – forgets, indeed, that the very "faith in the force [*Gewalt*] of law" on which he counts to protect people's lives is the same faith to which both the Wilhelmine and the Weimar governments appealed to justify the violent taking of them.

As Derrida writes, paraphrasing Benjamin:

> As long as they do not give themselves the theoretical or philosophical means to think this co-implication of violence and law, the usual critiques remain naïve and ineffectual. . . . Law (*droit*) in its very violence claims to recognize and defend . . . humanity as end, in the person of each individual. And so a purely moral critique of violence is as unjustified as it is impotent.[29]

And yet though Benjamin declares Hiller's defense of "existence itself" to be "false, even ignoble,"[30] he also grants it a certain truth, on the condition that it were to refer, not to "mere life," but to something like humanness as such: "False and lowly is the proposition that existence [*Dasein*] is higher than just existence," Benjamin writes,

> if existence is to mean nothing other than mere life [*bloßes Leben*] – and this is the meaning of existence in the reflection above. But the proposition contains a powerful truth if existence (or better, life) . . . means the unshakeable aggregate condition of "the human being" [*den unverrückbaren Aggregatzustand von "Mensch*]."[31]

"[Hiller's] proposition", Benjamin continues, "owes its plausibility to this ambiguity."[32] Despite such assertions, however, it is in fact not at all clear that Hiller's valorization of "existence itself" means the reduction of existence to "mere life", in Benjamin's definition "the (unconditioned: mere)

28 On Hiller's concession that weapons may still be produced for police (and hunting) purposes, see 'Anti-Cain', 192; 'Anti-Kain', 32.
29 Derrida, 'Force of Law', 41.
30 Benjamin, 'Critique', 59; 'Kritik', 201.
31 Benjamin, 'Critique', 59, translation modified; 'Kritik', 201.
32 Benjamin, 'Critique', 59; 'Kritik', 201.

not-yet-ness of the just human being";[33] the plausibility of Benjamin's own proposition rests on the ambiguity of his terminological interventions.

Here, however, we should take a detour into Hiller's early legal thought to clarify the logic of his later political stances. In a 1908 treatise bearing the title *The Right Over Oneself: A Study in Penal Law* (*Das Recht über sich selbst: Eine strafrechtsphilosophische Studie*), Hiller, anticipating his argument in 'Anti-Cain', declares "life" to be "the most important of all legal assets" (*das bedeutsamste aller Rechtsgüter*).[34] Hiller begins his study with a methodological argument for "the necessity of a critical-normative jurisprudence," based on "the hypostatization of a fundamental demand [*Grundforderung*]"[35] specifically, the basic legal postulate of *individual freedom*. As Hiller goes on to specify: "[I mean freedom] not in the current psychological sense ('free will'), but understood politically: personal freedom, the free configuration [*freiwillkürliche Ausgestaltung*] of one's own life."[36] It is from this fundamental demand – which, Hiller stipulates, "cannot be inferred from that which is historically given,"[37] i.e., which is not a legal precedent but a metaphysical premise – that Hiller moves to the actual theme of his treatise: "Where, and with what justification, does the German Criminal Code prohibit the individual from being able to freely dispose of himself" (*wo und mit welchem Recht verbietet das deutsche Strafgesetzbuch dem Individuum, über sich selbst zu verfügen*).[38]

The primary aim of Hiller's study, in other words, is to advocate for the decriminalization of certain forms of private behavior presently illegal under German law, in particular: dueling, abortion, self-mutilation, incest amongst consenting adults, and – of especial importance for Hiller's argument – homosexuality and suicide.[39] In the third chapter of his book, Hiller runs through a cursory legal history of suicide, arguing that suicide was in fact first deemed a sin only by the early Church Fathers – "in a very arbitrary interpretation" of the sixth[40] commandment[41] – and from there, declared a crime in canon and, eventually, civil

33 Benjamin, 'Critique', 59, translation slightly modified; 'Kritik', 201.

34 Kurt Hiller, *Das Recht über sich selbst. Eine strafrechtsphilosophische Studie* (Heideberg: Winter, 1908), 10. All translations from this and other texts where no translator is credited are my own.

35 Hiller, *Das Recht*, 3.

36 Ibid.

37 Ibid.

38 Ibid., 91.

39 Somewhat less convincingly, Hiller also defends bestiality on these grounds, declaring that, since an animal has the legal status of an object, it can be counted a "tool" for private use. See Ibid., 89–91. It should be noted that until 1935, bestiality was criminalized in Germany under the same statute as that which criminalized homosexuality.

40 Hiller writes "fifth," in accordance with Lutheran numeration. See *Das Recht*, 11.

41 Corresponding to the "fundamentally socialist nature of Christianity" (*sozialistischen Grundcharakter des Christentums*). Hiller, *Das Recht*, 11.

law. Therefore, as Hiller asserts, the current criminalization of suicide in the German penal code is not only arbitrary, but also historically contingent; in contrast, a legal based code on the normative precondition of personal freedom would require that one's life should be seen as a possession to do with as one will: a gift, as it were, that one is free to keep or relinquish.[42] Similarly, Hiller's chapter on homosexuality argues not only that the current legal and cultural animus toward homosexuality has no rational basis but also that, even *if* one were, for example, to consider homosexuality to be a practice detrimental to the individual – which Hiller, himself gay, anyway vehemently disputes –as a matter of private behavior, the law should have no standing to penalize it. The German state's criminalization of homosexuality (under the infamous Paragraph 175) thus not only constitutes an unwarranted and indeed anomalous intrusion into the private sphere,[43] but also amounts to a violation of the very principle of self-determination upon which the law should rest: as Hiller writes (quoting the sexologist Benedikt Friedländer), a "codified crime against personal freedom,"[44] the pure paradox of a legal infringement of the basis of the law as such.

As legal theory, none of this is particularly groundbreaking – even if its implications for the conservative culture of Wilhelmine Germany were radical enough.[45] Hiller's professed allegiance to a Nietzschean politics of will notwithstanding,[46] his argument in *The Right over Oneself* for individual liberty as the normative basis of jurisprudential theory is clearly derived from the liberal tradition's grounding of right in bourgeois notions of ownership, expressed succinctly in John Locke's famous declaration, "every Man has a Property in his own Person."[47] Here is one more genealogy to offer to

42 "This legal right is not only exposed to external threats, but also those who possess it have the ability to relinquish it" (*Dieses Rechtsgut ist nicht nur Gefährdungen von außen preisgegeben, sondern wer es besitzt, hat selber die Möglichkeit, sich seiner zu entäußern*). Hiller, *Das Recht*, 10.

43 Anomalous, that is, in view of the customary *non*intervention of the state in the marriage bed, as well as the non-penalization of other forms of frowned-upon sexual behavior such as extramarital affairs. See Hiller, *Das Recht*, 61–62.

44 Benedikt Friedländer, *Kritik der neueren Vorschläge zur Abänderung des §175*, quoted in Hiller, *Das Recht*, 89.

45 For a brief overview of the debates around homosexuality in Imperial Germany and an overview of Hiller's role in the Weimar-era homosexual liberation movement (including his disagreements with Magnus Hirschfeld), see Laurie Marhoefer, *Sex and the Weimar Republic: German Homosexual Emancipation and the Rise of the Nazis* (Toronto: University of Toronto Press, 2015), esp. 22–26 and 129–143. Hiller himself remained relatively unscathed during the Wilhelmine and Weimar eras, but upon the Nazi rise to power was arrested and imprisoned three times, after the last of which he managed to secure his release and go into (temporary) exile. See Marhoefer, *Sex and the Weimar Republic*, 200.

46 On Hiller's politics of "Activism" as a legacy of Nietzsche's philosophy of will, see Seth Taylor, *Left Wing Nietzscheans: The Politics of German Expressionism 1910–1920* (New York: De Gruyter, 1990), 60–88.

47 John Locke, *Two Treatises of Government*, ed. by Peter Laslett (Cambridge: Cambridge University Press, 1988), II §27, 287.

Benjamin's thought that "it would be worthwhile to track down the origin of the sanctity of life".[48] For Locke, the desire for the preservation of one's own existence is no less than "a Principle of Action [planted] by God himself,"[49] a principle that grants "Man" not only the duty to ensure his biological continuation, but also "the right . . . to make use of those things" – i.e. natural resources and nonhuman animals – "necessary or useful to his Being,"[50] the right, in other words, to exploit nature for the purposes of individual survival and propagation as the birthright of the human being qua handiwork of God.[51]

Hiller, needless to say, draws rather different conclusions from this principle than Locke (who explicitly excludes suicide from the sphere of permissible acts, not to even speak of things like abortion or homosexuality).[52] Nevertheless, his arguments in *The Right over Oneself* owe a clear debt to the Enlightenment conception of human life as God-conferred self-ownership: the "original Law of Nature",[53] in Locke's words, from which all other rights and privileges flow. In effect, what Hiller does is to radicalize Locke's idea of the God-givenness of life into a normative argument for absolute personal liberty, appealing to the supposed immutability of self-ownership for a progressive critique of Wilhelmine legal repression.[54] Furthermore, just as there is a direct line from Locke's notion of God-given self-ownership to Hiller's early advocacy for individual natural right, there is a direct line from Hiller's advocacy for individual natural right in general (and the rights of sexual minorities in particular) to the eventual militant pacifism of 'Anti-Cain'. As the Hiller scholar Lewis D. Wurgaft has shown, in the wake of the devastation of the First World War, Hiller's insistence on life as "the most noble of all legally protected interests" (*Das vornhemste aller rechtlich geschützten Güter*)[55] as the idea that one is free to lead one's life as one wishes comes to mean that under no circumstances should any individual or entity have the power to ask one to relinquish it.[56]

48 Benjamin, 'Critique', 59; 'Kritik', 202.
49 Locke, *Two Treatises of Government*, I §86, 205.
50 Ibid.
51 On Benjamin's analysis of Kant's "metaphysical" revision of Locke's idea of possession as one source for the 'Critique of Violence', see Peter Fenves, *The Messianic Reduction: Walter Benjamin and the Shape of Time* (Stanford: Stanford University Press, 2010), 187–226, esp. 190–202.
52 "But though this be a *State of Liberty*, yet it is *not a State of License*; though Man in that State have an uncontrollable Liberty, to dispose of his Person or Possessions, yet he has not Liberty to destroy himself. . . . Every one as he is *bound to preserve himself*, and to not quit his Station willfully." Locke, *Two Treatises of Government*, II §6, 271.
53 Locke, *Two Treatises of Government*, II §30, 289.
54 "Without this dogmatic generalization [that 'man is born free'] a normative criminal jurisprudence is impossible." Hiller, *Das Recht*, 3.
55 Hiller, *Das Recht*, 57.
56 See Wurgaft, *The Activists*, 61–62.

Whether or not one finds this argument convincing – Benjamin, for his part, would probably call it the "childish anarchism" of an unreflective civil libertarianism[57] – it is at least slightly more complicated than the simple-minded vitalism that Benjamin's comments on Hiller would seem to impute to him.[58] And yet, as Benjamin also intimates, such liberal jusnaturalism ultimately provides a weak basis for a politics of nonviolence: for not only does it rest on principles – such as individual ownership, generational inheritance, and the unrestricted anthropocentric exploitation of land and animals – in no way actually "natural," it also entails its own, possibly even more insidious forms of violence: including, not least, the violence of the absolute defense of private property and the fortress logic of personal identity itself.[59] At the same time, however, Benjamin's dismissal of Hiller's arguments (in 'Anti-Cain', but also, by extension, in *The Right over Oneself*) leaves unanswered Hiller's question of how individuals *may* claim rights, if the possession of themselves as autonomous living beings is no longer a sufficient or necessary criterion for doing so. Such an unanswered question also sheds new light on Derrida's controversial comments on the "theme of radical destruction" lurking within the 'Critique of Violence'. For Derrida's phrase refers not only or even primarily to the industrialized genocide of the Nazi Holocaust, the association for which Derrida has drawn such rebuke. It also refers (in a phrase I elided in my opening citation of the passage) to "the annihilation of the law and of right, if not of justice, and, among those rights, human rights, at least such as these are interpreted within a tradition of natural law of the Greek type or the *'Aufklärung'* type"[60] – that is, to the annihilation of the tradition that Benjamin, for his part, associates with the "groundless casuistry"[61] of means-ends logic, and to which Hiller, self-consciously turns in order to

57 Benjamin, 'Critique', 46; 'Kritik', 187. See also Derrida, 'Force of Law', 41.

58 It is worth noting that, despite the evident Biblical allusions of 'Anti-Cain', Hiller speaks of the "sublimity" (Erhabene) of the "idea of existence" (Idee . . . der Lebendige), and not, as Benjamin has it, of life's "sanctity" or "sacredness" (Heiligkeit). Hiller, 'Anti-Cain', 193; 'Anti-Kain', 32; Benjamin, 'Critique', 58, passim; 'Kritik', 201, passim. See also Hiller, *Das Recht*, 80, on the rejection of biopolitical justifications for prohibiting homosexuality, i.e., the argument that homosexuality is a crime against society insofar as the role of the individual is to provide new citizens for the state.

59 Significantly, Locke not only upholds the right to killing (in self-defense) as a natural right, but uses the selfsame figure that Hiller deploys as an anti-model in order to defend it: "And upon this is grounded the great Law of Nature, *Who so sheddeth Mans Blood, by Man shall his Blood be shed.* And *Cain* was so fully convinced, that everyone had a Right to destroy such a Criminal, that after the Murther of his Brother, he cried out, *Every one that findeth me, shall slay me*; so plain was it writ in the Hearts of all Mankind." Locke, *Two Treatises of Government*, II, §11, 274.

60 Derrida, 'Force of Law', 63, note 6. This phrase reappears, slightly altered and reframed, in the main body of Derrida's essay; see 'Force of Law', 61–62.

61 See Benjamin, 'Critique', 41; 'Kritik', 181.

advocate for personal autonomy and sexual freedoms against the repressive laws of the Imperial German state.

Derrida only mentions Hiller by name once in the body of his essay – once more than Benjamin does, anyway – where he appears to take Benjamin's representation of Hiller as a mere vitalist and *Lebensphilosoph* at face value.[62] Yet – and regardless of whether or not Derrida actually read Hiller's work – Hiller's pacifist call to arms echoes uncannily within Derrida's text, which insists doggedly, albeit not without qualifications, on the continued relevance and potential vindicability of "the classical emancipatory ideal" for contemporary legal thought.[63] In this sense, it is indeed telling that Derrida returns to the question of murder (as opposed to other meanings and forms of "*Gewalt*") in his conclusion to 'Force of Law', and especially to the millions of victims of the so-called Final Solution as one of its most extreme manifestations. Again, such remarks have been roundly criticized, both for missing the point of Benjamin's essay and for vulgarly reifying Benjamin's concepts into a concrete historical phenomenon. But even if the crude literality of Derrida's comments in this part of his essay represents a severe misrepresentation of Benjamin's thinking, this may perhaps be read less as an error than as a certain return of the repressed. For behind all Hiller's revolutionary posturing and philosophical naïveté also lies a real question, namely: How to *not* do violence to the other? More bluntly: How to *not* justify the persecution of individuals or the slaughter of millions through either reactionary fears of vulnerability to injustice or revolutionary promises of liberation therefrom, at least, in a form that merely perpetuates the violence of injustice itself? How to avoid the hermeneutic circle, observed by Derrida, by which the relative legitimacy of any act of violence depends on the degree of its future success, or rather, by which any successful act of violence produces its own legitimacy *as* its future?[64] How to prevent violence towards individuals without taking recourse to a law that depends on it? How to keep – in the words of one of Benjamin's discarded drafts for the 'Critique of Violence' – "human beings [secure] in the free community of their life"?[65]

It is no doubt in light of such questions that Derrida emphasizes, "the possibility of singularity"[66] in the thinking of justice, in contrast to the levelling logic of the bureaucratic or genocidal state: "because each individual murder and each collective murder is singular, thus infinite and

62 See Derrida, 'Force of Law', 53.
63 Ibid., 28.
64 See Ibid., 36–37.
65 Walter Benjamin, 'From "Life and Violence"', in Julia Ng, trans., *Toward the Critique of Violence: A Critical Edition*, 68.
66 Derrida, 'Force of Law', 60.

incommensurable"[67] – that is to say, because each individual or collective life is a question of justice prior to an idea of justice, including and especially those lives that are not to count as lives according to ideas of justice that are to justify themselves after the fact.[68] Such a "deconstructive affirmation"[69] of the singular, while it may well contain its own aporias and difficult genealogies, still eschews Hiller's liberal-absolutist valorization of "life" per se.[70] But it also refuses the temptation of the emphatically *non*-singular "aggregate condition of 'the human being'"[71] and the troublingly ambiguous "de-expiating force"[72] of divine violence that Benjamin opposes to it.[73] For while violence may sometimes be necessary, it is never bloodless: the drowned body of Rosa Luxemburg and the anonymized corpse of Karl Liebknecht are just two examples of the way in which violence seeks to cover its tracks, to present itself as the fight *against* violence, or as an act of God or a decree of fate – or, in another register, what a later Benjamin would call "the whore called 'Once upon a time' in the bordello of historicism"[74] – that might become, indeed, the founding moment of a new

67 Ibid., 62.

68 On the "deconstructionist approach to the boundaries that institute the human subject" as the first consequence of a thinking of justice, see Derrida, 'Force of Law', 19. Meanwhile, Derrida's comments directly before this on the question of animals as the subjects of rights can be read as an oblique response to Benjamin's annoyance that if "life" were to be considered sacred, there would be no possibility of distinguishing the claims of human beings from those of animals or plants. See Derrida, 'Force of Law', 18–19; Benjamin, 'Critique', 59; 'Kritik', 201–202.

69 Derrida, 'Force of Law', 63.

70 In a later essay from 1932 entitled 'The Fight against Murder' (*Kampf gegen den Mord*) Hiller revises his position from 'Anti-Cain' – while maintaining that this was always his position all along – to say that *obviously* pacifism requires armed struggle. While it is not certain that Hiller is responding to Benjamin, it is significant that he insists in the essay that the opposition to murder does not mean an opposition to violence *tout court*, that his argument was never directed against "violence" (*Gewalt*), but only against "violation" (*Vergewaltigung*). Similarly, Hiller's indignation in the essay at the idea that his pacifism would have anything to do with the defense of "naked life" (*nackte Leben*) is also worthy of note. See Kurt Hiller, 'Kampf gegen den Mord', in *Der Sprung ins Helle. Reden, Offne Briefe, Zwiegespräche, Essays, Thesen, Pamphlete Gegen Krieg, Klerus und Kapitalismus* (Leipzig: Lindner, 1932), 13–21, esp. 16 and 17.

71 Benjamin, 'Critique', 59, translation modified; 'Kritik', 201.

72 Benjamin, 'Critique', 60; 'Kritik', 203.

73 Samuel Weber makes the important point that, *pace* Agamben, the concept of "bare life" is in fact not sufficient to account for the extermination policies of the Nazis or other similar genocidal regimes, since such regimes aimed at eliminating not "life" as such but quite specific racialized or otherwise othered categories of existence considered a threat to "life" as a generality. See Samuel Weber, 'Bare Life and Life in General: The Question of "Concentration"', in *Singularity: Politics and Poetics* (Minneapolis: University of Minnesota Press, 2021), 57–76, esp. 62–67 and 74–75.

74 Walter Benjamin, 'On the Concept of History', in *Selected Writings*, vol. 4: 1938–1940 (Cambridge: Harvard University Press, 2003), 389–400, here 396, translation slightly

order, of a new regime, of a new state. . . .[75] If 'Toward the Critique of Violence' is a text haunted by the specter of "the annihilation of the law and of right" (even if that law and that right are ultimately, in Benjamin's eyes, neither lawful nor righteous), then 'Force of Law' is a text haunted by the specter of what could possibly be offered as an alternative to such juridical "annihilation," in the face of all those whose own annihilation or oppression the idea of an extra-, supra-, or post-legal order, or indeed the existing legal order itself, has been, or is, used to justify.[76] In this moment in which, yet again, nothing seems more fragile than the rights (and lives) of some, Derrida's call to ask who is sacrificed in the name of the law, including the law to come, bears rereading.

---

modified. Relevant in this context is Hegel's declaration in the introduction to his *Philosophy of History*: "But even regarding History as the slaughter-bench at which the happiness of peoples, the wisdom of states, and the virtue of individuals have been victimized – the question inevitably arises – to what principle, to what final aim these enormous sacrifices have been offered." Hegel goes on to assert that this slaughter-bench is "*the very field* which we, for our part, regard as exhibiting only the means for realizing what we assert to be the essential destiny – the absolute aim, or – which comes to the same thing – the true result of the World's History." G. W. F. Hegel, *The Philosophy of History*, trans. by J. Sibree (New York: Prometheus Books, 1991), 21.

75 As Julia Ng notes in her afterword to her translation of 'Toward the Critique of Violence,' Benjamin himself ultimately came to recognize the risks of his analysis, in the face of the "kind of violence that disguises itself as pure means," i.e., an authoritarianism that presents itself as an abrogation of violence, rather than its intensification. Julia Ng, 'Afterword: Toward Another Critique of Violence', in Benjamin, *Toward the Critique of Violence: A Critical Edition*, 113–160, here 114.

76 Judith Butler reads Benjamin's analysis of the commandment "Thou shalt not kill" as an exhortation to nonviolent resistance against state violence: more specifically, against the violence of a state (Butler is thinking of contemporary Israel) that orders the mass killing of others in the name of self-defense: "The commandment 'Thou shalt not kill' imposes a strong obligation to distinguish actual moments of legitimate self-defense from its cynical use in the service of an infinitely self-legitimating aggression. If all killing is proactively and retroactively named self-defense, then self-defense no longer operates as a credible justification for killing. Any and all killing is justified and approved on the part of the one who names all the violence waged as self-defense." Butler, *Parting Ways*, 97–98. Butler argues this point through Benjamin's notion of "divine violence" against the privileging of "mere life"; however, Butler's call to conscientious objection and the refusal of retributive killing places their argument far more in line with Hiller's "Anti-Cain" than Butler realizes, even if Butler would reject Hiller's emphasis on individual sovereignty as the basis of both rights and non-killing. On nonviolence as "a physical assertion of the claims of life," see also Judith Butler, *The Force of Nonviolence: An Ethico-Political Bind* (London and New York: Verso, 2020), here 24.

9

DE-EXPIATION AND THE BLOODLESS STRIKE

Mangalika de Silva

States of Desistance

What can Walter Benjamin, antifascist philosopher who committed suicide on the French-Spanish border rather than face incarceration and death in a concentration camp, instruct us about death fasts as acts akin to political suicide he never explicitly theorized? To piece together a Benjaminian theory of hunger striking requires an inferential deconstruction of his theory of the general strike (*proletarischer Generalstreik*) as the collective suspension of corporeal engagement and complicity wherein bodies are withdrawn from the continuum of subjugating capitalist production. In 'Toward the Critique of Violence,' Benjamin's primary focus is a search for a force that would be a pure means without instrumental teleology; it is the vantage from which he interrogates the general strike in its various forms through a critique of law-conserving/law-imposing violence.[1] Jacques Derrida's 'Force of Law,' a wide-ranging interlocution of Benjamin's text, engages the labor strike's consignment to passive non-action as symptomatic of the failure of the state to preserve its exclusive right to law-conserving/law-imposing force.[2] I introduce a third dimension into this dialogical interplay between Derrida and Benjamin by staging a confrontation between their respective approaches to striking, law, punition and violence, through a political philosophy of the death fast. In

1 Walter Benjamin, 'Toward the Critique of Violence', in Peter Fenves and Julia Ng, eds., *Toward the Critique of Violence* (Stanford: Stanford University Press, 2021).

2 Jacques Derrida, 'Force of Law: On the Mystical Foundations of Authority', Mary Quaintance, trans. (1990) 11 *Cardozo Law Review* 919–1045.

DOI: 10.4324/9781003589419-12

restaging Benjamin's and Derrida's analyses of violence from the perspective of the political death fast, I extend the dialogic to the following conundrums: the vexed question of monopoly violence; a comparative analysis of auto-hetero-deconstruction as differential contamination; and the norm of bloodless de-expiation that Benjamin connects to divine violence, and Derrida to the abolition of the death penalty.

In 'Toward the Critique of Violence', Benjamin contends that the state identifies the agents of the strike (in its reformist/extortionist mode) to be lawful bearers of passive action in the form of withheld productivity through corporeal abstention. Somatic deactivation is the contingent basis of law's recognition of a right to strike as nonviolent [*Unterlassung*]. In this text, Benjamin does not explicitly anchor this treatment of striking in a theory of corporeal praxis. For Benjamin, however, the general strike is a delimited form of violence when it is mobilized as an act of extortion in order to secure benefits through concessions and ameliorations. The extortionist general strike then aligns its contingent suspension to the reified instrumentalism of capitalist economic logic, and law with its reliance upon computations that justify the use of force. The extortionist labor desistance against the violence of capitalism proceeds via the calculative logic at the root of capitalist violence. The *general strike* that constitutes itself as an act of computational extortion requiring a response from existing institutional power is contrasted to the *revolutionary strike*. The irruptive advent of the revolutionary strike entails the removal of corporeal action from the eventless continuity of hegemonic capitalist calculation rather than seeking concessions from it. The extortionist strike implicitly recognizes the legitimacy of law whereas the revolutionary strike seeks to abolish law whose teleological trajectories have arisen from the violence of the state. The revolutionary strike will not be greeted with concessions but is invariably violently opposed by state power. These dichotomies of the mass labor strike stand in positive and negative relation to law. No positive law sanctions hunger striking even when it is conducted in an extortionist mode. In death fasts particularly, but not only in carceral settings, the strike proceeds to withhold a body that the state claims as its property and biopolitical right. The hunger strike disrupts the property relations between the state and its subjects at the level of the body. This active desistance proffers a potentially law-founding act of force.

In 'Force of Law', Derrida notes that for Benjamin even the limited form of extortionist strike is a withdrawal which constitutes an act of "estrangement". Does this distancing mark an alienation from capitalism and the law, or an estrangement from violence as embodied action insofar as the strike requires the withholding of bodies in a zone of passive action with which Benjamin is methodologically uncomfortable as he associates all striking with particular modes of proactive agency? Derrida discerns something uncanny in this legitimated form of the strike as a threshold or limit formation of the law.

> In carrying the right to strike to its limit, the concept or watchword of general strike . . . manifests its essence. The state can hardly stand this passage to the limit. It deems it abusive and claims . . . there was a misunderstanding, a misinterpretation of the original intention, and that (*das Streakiest* "so" *nicht gemeint*), the right to strike was not "so intended." It can then condemn the general strike as illegal and, if the strike persists, there can be a revolutionary situation. Such a situation is . . . the only one that allows us to conceive the homogeneity of law or right and violence, violence as the exercise of *droit* and *droit* as the exercise of violence. Violence is not exterior to the order of *droit*. It threatens it from within.[3]

The extortionist strike that supposedly recognizes the lawfulness of the state is not reciprocally recognized as indisputably lawful by the state. This is particularly the case for the biopolitical state perennially concerned with the productive and disciplinary ordering of bodies. The legalized general strike does not affect the substance of law from outside as an aleatory accident. Rather, the strike threatens the law from within as it projects the possibility of its auto-mutation into a law-founding force that displaces extant legalities. Derrida argues that every claim to right by non-state actors is perceived by law-conserving executive power as a potential act of subversion threatening the 'homogeneity' of law, rights and legalized violence. For homogeneity, which implies the ipseity of the state, I would substitute the term monopoly; the state considers the extortionist general strike as participating in, and therefore estranging, its monopoly of a right to force as an exclusive *right to rights*. It is within this tense terrain that the hunger strike, extortionist or not, can be located. Even if it culminates in negotiation and conciliation, the death fast is never considered originally or retroactively legal, not even when it climaxes in an agreement that recognizes previously unrecognized rights; concessions as such never extend to the right to hunger strike.

Though only briefly referenced by Derrida and not at all by Benjamin in their distinctive disassembling of violence, I suggest that the hunger strike/death fast retains the potential to be an "ungraspable revolutionary instant that belongs to no historical or temporal continuum but in which the foundation of a new law nevertheless plays."[4] Since the hunger strike is never legalized as a political medium, irrespective of any demands that accompany

3 Derrida, 'Force of Law', 989.
4 Derrida, 'Force of Law', 1001.

its initiation and culmination that may be accepted or rejected, it exercises a (Hegelian) right of distress:

> in the necessity of the instant the poor can call upon the right of distress as the last resort to rescue their minimal life-preserving well-being in the form of a crime. . . . The right of distress . . . is . . . a right to be exempted from worldly laws . . . the action of the right of distress only applies to actions of desire that imply the most intensive lack of a differentiation of needs.[5]

Hunger striking contains in microcosm the effigy, schema and spectrality of a law-founding violence. Perhaps only as hauntology, it may nevertheless accommodate a transgressive vibration of lawlessness, regardless of any teleological set of demands that the striker may or may not name.

Derrida identifies the legal general strike, even in its extortionist mode, as "sharing the monopoly" of right and violence.[6] Monopolies, however, do not share a right to exclusivity; the problematically legalized general strike still violates the foundational right of the monopolistic formation of the state that perseveres even in the slippage between law-conserving, law-founding and transgressing force. Derrida implies that it is a structural necessity for the state to declare the extortionist strike as illegal, and even to declare a state of exception that reaffirms the ipseity of monopolized law and force. The slippage of the general strike into revolutionary agitation and law-imposing force will be one of a series of 'auto-deconstructionist' events of binary implosion to be encountered in Derrida's reading of Benjamin, whether afflicting the coherence of law or inflicted by the incoherence of law.

For Derrida, any singular positioning, no matter how estranging, is iterable. Political iterability that can intertwine or polarize constituted and constitutive power (*potestas* and *potentia*) is the precondition of hauntological repetition in the strike, the projection in time and space of ghostly and shadowy forms of subversive, mimetic auto-estrangement Derrida identifies as afflicting the self-conserving foundational force of law. The general strike and the hunger strike belong to the category of such 'toxic' iterabilities from the perspective of law-conserving monopolistic violence. The extortionist strike still belongs

> to the structure of fundamental violence . . . it calls for the repetition of itself and founds what ought to be conserved, conservable, promised to heritage

5 Frank Ruda, *Hegel's Rabble: An Investigation into Hegel's Philosophy of Right* (London: Continuum, 2011), 17–18.

6 Derrida, 'Force of Law', 987.

> and tradition. . . . A foundation is a promise. Every position (*Setzung*) permits and promises (*permet et pro-met*), it positions . . . it inscribes the possibility of repetition at the heart of the originary . . . there is no more a pure foundation or pure position of law, and so a pure founding violence, than there is a purely conservative violence. Position is already iterability, a call for self-conserving repetition. Conservation in its turn refounds, so that it can conserve what it claims to found . . . there can be no rigorous opposition between positioning and conservation, only what I will call . . . a *différantielle* contamination between the two, with all the paradoxes that this may lead to.[7]

In contrast, however, to the concordance between positioning and promising, the death fast, regardless of its extortionist demands, portends only one modality and outcome in being a right of distress as the preclusion of any positioning, iterability, conservation and promising other than serial denegation; the striker expropriates from capital punishment a mortal process that lacks the temporal finitude correlated to a finite subject of rights wherein a promissory structure can be recognized or sustained. Given the inevitability of autonomic shutdown of bodily functions, the death fast taken to its limit becomes a *will not to will*. It rebels against regimes of infinite expiation afflicting the striker by enacting a *de-expiation* (*Entsühnung*) beyond any externally mandated temporal limit or court of accountability and judgment.

Excursus: Autophagy

The quasi-legal general strike potentially wounds a monopoly right to violence; it cannot be readily recognized as legitimate due to the possibilities it poses as constitutive power. Hunger strike is a double wounding, a self-wounding that wounds and scarifies the otherwise unscathable apparatus of monopoly right. Despite the striker's immersion in *physis*, this law-wounding self-wounding is an unnatural use of force, an estranging element that heightens its threat profile. It overwhelms the fetish of just means in positive law by way of *parapraxis* and hyper-performance of eschatology in vitro. The hunger strike is invariably concerned with projecting political natality (Arendt's inception) as thanatology. Law's revulsion at the hunger strike, an abyss to be obliterated by law with forced-feeding and medicalization, is apotropaic: The foreboding of an unfettered law-founding violence. The estrangement effect of the hunger strike derives from its intersection with a "violence that is not an accident arriving from outside law. That which threatens law already belongs to it, to the right to law (*droit*), to the origin of law (*droit*)."[8]

7 Derrida, 'Force of Law', 997.
8 Derrida, 'Force of Law', 989.

If the hunger strike/death fast can be said to be positioned, it is emplaced *as* a de-positioning of violence and law, since its only stance and station is to be performatively anti-foundational. It is no coincidence that it tends to seize time and place in juridically foundational carceral-type settings traversing prisons, solitary confinement, detention camps, military occupations, border checkpoints and apartheid enclosures. The hunger strike de-positions these edifices of empirical foundation without replacing them with another ground; the strike permits and promises an anti-*Setzung*. For it is not concerned with self-positioning as self-conservation, but as the force of a deliberately excavated *Ab-grund*, a rupture by means of radical refusal and abstention. The hunger strike unfolds a polysemic immediacy of lack that must be conserved – a conserving politics of lack embodied in the striker. Lack projects human desire into a beyond, an immateriality estranging the subject of lack and desire from the mediacy of *physis*.[9] The hunger strike drives the desire for emptiness as a foundational denegation of iterability.

Werner Hamacher *theorizes* the suspension of consumption as reactively reasserting the opposition of self to a Big Other. The subject of consumption becomes radically exposed to the unassimilable, the politically and ontologically indigestible through its failure to repel, negate and sublate an invasive, dominating and alienating alterity.[10] Hamacher conceives of nausea as the failure to sustain a subject-centered foundation. He reads nausea, disgorgement, extrusion, expectoration and ejection as antithetical to consumption, establishing the vocation of an anti-foundational anti-subject to which inventory can be added autophagy: i.e., the self-consumption that accompanies the aporetic hunger strike as oppositional and appositional. These actions of anti-consumption bear a citational relation to one another and to the de-subjectifying anti-foundationalism identified by Novalis: "could we not say that the means of nourishment themselves also eat the one who eats them?"[11] Reactivity to the involuntarily introjected Other resulting in corporeal revulsion informs both nausea and autophagy as self-estranging disembodiment: "in nausea, the organism is directed against itself, and indeed against itself as something in excess of itself, sustaining this once more in which it threatens to lose itself."[12] The gestural network linking autophagy, nausea, expectoration and disgust entails a consideration of digestion in itself, digestion for itself and digestion against itself, all of which become indigestible for the

9 Alexandre Kojève, *Introduction to the Reading of Hegel*, ed. by Allan Bloom, trans. by James H. Nichols, Jr (Ithaca: Cornell University Press, 1969).

10 Werner Hamacher, *Pleroma: Reading in Hegel*, trans. by Nicholas Walker and Simon Jarvis (Stanford: Stanford University Press, 1998), 231.

11 Novalis (Friedrich von Hardenburg), *Schriften*, ed. by Richard Samuel (Kohlhammer, 1968 1997: 72: III, 99).

12 Hamacher, *Pleroma*, 250.

political nutrition of the subject seeking an exit from political and disciplinary foundation and its commanding iterabilities across time and space. The mouth, through political nausea or autophagy, becomes the primary organ of repudiation – though in so doing, it may abstain from speech as well as consumption when the striker sews her lips shut.[13]

Survivance and *Walten*

Derrida locates an estranged element of the strike within law itself and to Benjamin's protocol of reading as the fixation and unfixing of meanings. He seeks homologues between the text of law and Benjamin's discourse:

> for there is something of the general strike, and . . . of the revolutionary situation in every reading that founds something new and that remains unreadable in regard to established canons and norms of reading, that is to say the present state of reading or of what figures the State, with a capital S, in the state of possible reading.[14]

This is particularly apt if we recognize that the apparatus of reading is not limited to alphanumeric graphemes and digits. For hunger striking is an interlocution of the state via a reading from out of the stricken and striking body that addresses the unreadability of entrenched 'canons and laws.' It is both a depoliticization of the corpus in its estrangement from the carceralizing interpellation of the subject and a para-politicization of the corpus in making it the bearer of multiplex historiographies and contingencies of suffering and disaffection that demands a right to the heretofore unrecognized right of de-expiation "congruent with the disjunction between law and justice" that abrogates and reverses *lex talionis* (retributive justice) and its commensurations of guilt and punition.[15]

Derrida is concerned with the force embedded in communicative action, particularly language, because nomos as force cannot exist outside of the language of calculation and command. However, it is precisely this hierarchization and monopolization of lawful language by law that compels the hunger striker to de-linguistify her condition through bodily enactment of de-expiation in the non-name of no extant *nomos*. The hunger striker as embodied interlocutor may enact a gestural grammar of *physis* that no law can comprehend, and which can only be rendered even more untranslatable

13 Martina Tazzioli, 'Embodying the Intolerable: Refugees' Hunger Strikes and Governing by Debasing Lives,' (April 2026) 125: 2 *South Atlantic Quarterly* (forthcoming).

14 Derrida, 'Force of Law', 995.

15 Peter Fenves, 'Intervention, Encroachment: Walter Benjamin on Violence and Expiation', (2019) 2:2 *Critical Times* 209–220, at 216.

when foreclosed by the biopolitical injunction against suicide as the theft of what properly belongs to law. The hunger striker is not of the *civitas*, as she has already made her exit from that zone, if she was ever there. Nor is the hunger striker concerned with 'just means' or 'just ends' as the striker's means already violate extant laws, and its ultimate ends (no matter how eloquently stated) are buried beneath occluded indeterminacies of decay and death. The hunger striker, as a frequently carceralized body, falls under the category of those who have violated an unnatural, therefore mythic boundary of the law and have been "moralized which is to say pietized" in being subjected to regimes of expiation (*Sühne*).[16] Yet the striker goes on: she must go on, she can't go on, she'll go on, for she is solely preoccupied with contesting the mythic monopolization of force that has driven her to the extremity of a self-destructive anti-*physis*. As Derrida suggests elsewhere:

> *physis* is the *Walten* of everything, which depends, as *Walten*, only on itself, which forms itself sovereignly, as power, receiving its form and its image, its figure of domination, from itself. *Walten* as *physis*, *physis* as *Walten* is everything; *physis* and *Walten* are synonyms of everything or everything that is . . . as originarily sovereign power.[17]

The concept of *Walten* speaks to forms of force anterior and posterior, yet underlying any finite political-institutional determination, and to a conceptualization of *physis* irreducible to objectified nature. Walten refers to *physis* that which prevails, as the pre-vailing and pre-veiling of what prevails. The hunger strike as *Walten* is a veiled constitutive power (*potentia*) that is submitted to political undecidability as a trajectory that accumulates denegations around a magnetizing *abgrund*: is it suicide, mental illness or a human right?[18] As a sovereign act, self-starvation begins in the self-discrepancy between the striker as agent and simultaneously as patient, and yet culminates in *ipsocratia*, the sameness of self as *physis* in *stasis*. Derrida, commenting on Heidegger's equation of *physis* as force, invokes the Heideggerian notion of the uncanny to decenter and deconstruct *Walten* that he posits as irreducible to teleocratic designs. *Walten* masters, determines and grips humanity particularly when humanity misrecognizes itself as monopolistic mastery through force and law. However, the mastery and mystery of the hunger striker lies the *Walten,* her *will not to will* life, an autocratic abdication from *Walten* through *Walten*. It is this very decision that discloses the striker

16 Fenves, 'Intervention, Encroachment: Walter Benjamin on Violence and Expiation', 217.

17 Jacques Derrida, *The Beast & the Sovereign II*, trans. by Geoffrey Bennington (Chicago: Chicago University Press, 2011), 72.

18 Adam Knowles, 'Toward a Critique of *Walten*: Heidegger, Derrida, and Henological Difference' (2013) 27:3 *Journal of Speculative Philosophy* 265-276.

as a possible medium of law-imposing violence, which no law has authorized, and in which no teleology of a specific finite legality can be divined.

From another angle, the hunger striker can be said to present to law conservation its own disavowed origin in the anteriority of law-imposing force, now returning in the encrypted hauntology of a threatening alien form of living death. That is why the hunger striker, positioned across law, criminality and non-law, is spectral: the striker becomes ghostly in her diminution and attrition through survivance as *Walten*.

> Survivance in a sense of survival that is neither life nor death pure and simple, a sense that is not thinkable on the basis of the opposition between life and death . . . a survival that is not more alive, nor indeed less alive, than life, or more or less dead than death, a sur-vivance that lends itself to neither comparative nor superlative, a survivance . . . [that] is without superiority, without height, altitude or highness, and . . . without supremacy or sovereignty . . . the survivance I am speaking of is a groundless ground.[19]

Law-conserving force possibly recognizes in hunger striking a spectral recursion of the survivance of law-founding force in certain vessels of estrangement as variants of its own foundational imposition of law. Derrida associates this spectrality with ruination and the hunger artist is ruination in motion: a scathing temporality traverses her body minute by minute and day by day with its scarification; at the same time, the striker harbors as inheritance the ruins of extant law and law-conserving force that she exposes as always already being a law-imposing violence without legitimate foundation and without the right to exact expiation. Spectrality as the hauntology of disavowed origins accompanies any gathering of forces that harbors a law-imposing violence-to-come before which extant law is spooked by its own ghostliness in the form of a corpus that exceeds its grasp – whether it be the slow violence of the political refusal of sustenance or the instantaneity of self-immolation that ignited the Arab Spring.

Ipsocracy, Monopoly and Law Imposition

The monopoly of violence relies on the tautology and circularity of law immunizing itself against its own founding violence as re-presented in alien simulacra. Monopolization can never be just, for it is a symbolic and logistical theft of *Walten* and its conversion into disavowal, technique and metaphysics as the originary criminal abrogation of law imposition. This is the purloining of what has no owner, of that which cannot be submitted to any mastery, is

19 Derrida, *The Beast & the Sovereign II*, 131.

no one's property and certainly not even that of the law that requires it for its functioning and self-purification:

> to every good, limited as it is in the temporal and spatial order, there accrues a possession-character [*Besitzcharakter*] as an expression of its transience. But the possession, caught as it is in the same finitude, is always unjust. Therefore, no order of possession, however it may be articulated, leads to justice.[20]

Possessive monopolization is at the dysfunctional core of law-conserving violence – conservation as guaranteeing exclusivity and hierarchy. Law-preserving violence is not opposed to criminality per se, but to another de-monopolizing alien law-posing violence that could potentially displace law-conserving right. For felonies recursively solidify the positioning of extant law and secure its self-conserving consecration. Yet the law as institutional norm apprehends two disturbing elements in the hunger strike: a phantom body and an alien imposition of undomesticated force that may potentially displace extant legalities.

The ghostly ruination intrinsic to law-conserving force is its slippage into extrajudicial violence in the praxis of policing. Benjamin and Derrida gravitate to the police who have become spectral through their differential contamination of law imposition and law conservation.

> Today the police are no longer content to enforce the law, and . . . to conserve it; they invent it, they publish ordinances, they intervene whenever the legal situation isn't clear to guarantee security. . . . The police are ignoble because in their authority the "separation of the violence that founds and the violence that conserves is suspended" . . . each time law is indeterminate enough to give them the chance. . . . Where there are police, which is to say everywhere and even here, we can no longer discern between two types of violence, conserving and founding, and that is the ignoble, ignominious, disgusting ambiguity. The possibility, which is also to say the ineluctable necessity of the modern police force ruins . . . deconstructs, the distinction between the two kinds of violence.[21]

The police are a "faceless figure" (*figure sans figure*); a phantom body as their mode of apparition is institutionalized in legal undecidability. Is the unquestioned legality of the police within the law a desperate attempt by law

20 Peter Fenves, *The Messianic Reduction: Walter Benjamin and the Shape of Time* (Stanford: Stanford University Press, 2010), 188.

21 Derrida, 'Force of Law', 1007.

conservation to grasp its ungraspable origin in a founding violence (without law) in order to sustain its monopoly against all comers? From the perspective of Black Lives Matter (BLM), the police are the contemporary legates of the law founding institution of American civil society as a racist slavocracy both evoked and modernized by contemporary extrajudicial executions of Blacks. Katherine McKittrick calls current and anticipated anti-Black violence 'plantation futurity' insofar as it fast-forwards prior trajectories of raced violence into the present and beyond as slavocratic aftermaths and portended possibilities.[22] The police are criminality interiorized, sterilized and monopolized, permitted to remain 'dirty,' 'bent' and homicidal as an immunizing antibody to be deployed against that which threatens law's monopoly like BLM and the abolitionist movement. This is why collective demands to defund the police and to abolish mass incarceration, the core edifices and facades of monopolistic right, threaten law to its core unlike the abolition of the death penalty that merely reaffirms the sovereign monopoly to pardon – to give or take life.

Derrida excavates a passage from Benjamin's *Trauerspiel* to capture the empowering undecidability of the ghostly police. However, this fragment may just as well apply to the hunger striker as *Walten*: "spirit is the capacity to exercise dictatorship" (*Geist ist das Vermögen, Diktatur auszuüben*).[23] This capacity requires a rigorous internal discipline just as much as it requires the most unscrupulous action (*skrupelloseste Aktion*).[24] The hunger striker, in becoming faceless and ungraspable, is akin, though not equivalent to, the schizoid police who at least remain recognizable in being institutionalized and sanctioned as belonging to the law. The striker is an untranslatable, viral and spectral presence, yet she has not fallen into disfiguration from a height of identifiability as have the police. The striker, even before this action, cultivates disfiguration as an abstention from legal normativity imposed by carceralizing edifices and powers. To 'criminalize' the striker is to re-positivize and re-juridify this alien figure of substance depletion by virtue of an anachronism that the striker evades via a withdrawal of *physis* through *physis* as her own power of *ipsocratia*.

Law mystifies and occludes the differential contamination between law-founding and law-conserving force within itself and beyond itself through monopolization, which is the teleology of both natural and positive law. Under positive law meant to adjudicate the legality of means, monopolization as means, as the law of laws, is never deposed. At best, there are adjudications concerning jurisdiction that debate legal boundaries but not the right

22 See Katherine McKittrick, 'Plantation Futures', (2013) 17:3 (42) *Small Axe* 1–15.
23 Derrida, 'Force of Law', 1013.
24 Derrida, 'Force of Law', 1013.

to monopolization as a *right to be rightless* in the affliction of force. To the contrary, the war on terror, among other conflicts, has exported and extended monopoly right in what is euphemistically named 'extrajudicial' violence – targeted assassinations and drone crowd killings as an ever-expanding colonial frontier of monopolized force.

It is not the imposition of material acts of violence that instantiates positions. Rather, it is the metaphysical imposition of monopolization, of exclusivity and rarefaction as an embedded characterology of founding force that simultaneously interiorizes and retroactively legalizes instituting violence by means of immunizing remotion as symbolic capital and a state good. Derrida reading Benjamin proposes the displacement of the act of foundation by the forgetfulness of conservation.

> The violence that founds or positions *droit* need not be immediately present in the contract [*nicht unmittelbar in ihm gegenwiirtig zu sein*: "it need not be directly present in it as lawmaking violence."] . . . without being immediately present, it is replaced [*vertreten*, "represented"] by the supplement of a substitute. And it is in this *différance*, in the movement that replaces . . . the immediate presence of violence . . . it is in this *différantielle* representativity that originary violence is consigned to oblivion. This amnesic loss of consciousness does not happen by accident. It is the very passage from presence to representation. Such a passage forms the trajectory of decline, of institutional "degeneracy", their *Verfall* ["decay"].[25]

The simulated de-presentation of law-imposing violence by law-conserving violence is an apotropaic exercise mediated by monopoly right. The latter exposes law-conserving force as merely a spectral trace structure – the non-originary origin of the origin – law-founding force. Law-conserving violence is converted (particularly through the medium of the police) into the presence of an absence that exposes the forgetting of origins as representational. Policing remembers to forget the difference between law-conserving force and law-imposing force as its foundational transgression. This depositioning of law conservation from within by a parasitic foundational force simultaneously deploys and banishes a simulacrum, a supplement that reiterates law's *ipsocratic* exclusivity and homogeneity in vitro. Monopolization is a transaction with analeptic simulacral violence held in political amber for future release. This theater of *remembering-to-forget* anomic foundation confirms that what is being brought forth to be obliviated proceeds by way of monopolization itself that institutes the conservational edifice. Iteration as the

25 Derrida, 'Force of Law', 1015.

rehearsal of monopolization is nostalgia for law's pseudo-subjugation and interiorization of an-archic violence as a force deferred at the punctum that is foundation through its simulated re-suppression. These acts of substitution, displacement, deferment, and simulation effectuate the domestication and sublation of the an-archic act of foundation. Hamacher argues how law conservation must turn against its own principle in repelling law-founding violence.[26] However, the metaphysics of monopolization confirms law conservation by virtue of its de-positioning of law-founding force within the legal edifice. As Derrida elucidates this iterativity,

> A "successful" revolution, the "successful foundation of a State" (in somewhat the same sense that one speaks of a "felicitous performative speech act") will produce après coup what it was destined in advance to produce, namely, proper interpretative models to read in return, to give sense, necessity and above all legitimacy to the violence that has produced, among others, the interpretative model in question, that is, the discourse of its self-legitimation.[27]

The police as a bi-frontal artifact of monopolization, and anomic law imposition, are not forgotten but rather conserved in all their indeterminacy. They evoke law's distant origins in acts of violent institution as in the American cult of the militia that embodied the revolutionary situation of law imposition in the first place. July 4th in the United States is both the celebration and deferral of law-founding violence in which fireworks simulate the weaponry that brought that entity – the nomothetic and autotelic nation – into existence, and that is relied upon to preserve it. The celebration and its fireworks are fictive allegories of historical *ipsocratia* as mythic and inculpating force deployed against the Other. Monopolization both instates and seals sovereign self-sameness; it further alludes to who and what can never aspire to *ipsocratic* purity – immigrants, and Muslims/Arabs, for instance, are inculpated as harboring alien law-founding potentiality within their very essence; hence the persistent occidental anguish concerning the imposition of Islamic law by elected Muslim politicians and various imputed underground conspiracies. The violence and terror of ICE deaths, abductions, disappearances and deportations are the reenactment of law-founding violence encrypted as law enforcement (i.e., conservation) that ritually reinstitutes American nativity through dramaturgical expulsions of denaturalized "aliens" who are illicitly embedded in the fabric of American *physis*. This is the inherent xenophobia

26 Werner Hamacher, 'Afformative, Strike', trans. by Dana Hollander (1991) 13 *Cardozo Law Rev* 1133–1157.
27 Derrida, 'Force of Law', 993.

of all monopolized force and why the spectacle of ICE abductions invariably overshadows any depiction of later degrading detentions – the warehoused body no longer serves for the staging of law instituting spectacle. Such law-founding nostalgia can reach hysterical heights (in more ways than one) when fearful rumor is spread about Latinx migrant caravans having secreted Muslim 'jihadists' or the accusation of legal migrants assaulting American dietary customs by seizing and consuming Oedipalized pets. Only through the dramatized use of an-archic force (of masked, nameless, warrantless paramilitaries) can monopoly power posit and name the differential (and potentially law-founding contamination) that threatens its purity from outside in being virally transmitted by ungraspable phantoms of de-positioning.

The instituting of monopoly – the forcing of force – can be differentiated from the force it stratifies and rarifies that allows it to pathologize other imputably estranging forms of law-imposing violence.

> But isn't tautology the phenomenal structure of a certain violence in the law that lays itself down by decreeing to be violent, this time in the sense of an outlaw, anyone who does not recognize it? Performative tautology or *a priori* synthesis, which structures any foundation of the law upon which one performatively produces the conventions that guarantee the validity of the performative, thanks to which one gives oneself the means to decide between legal and illegal violence.[28]

Law enforces itself by exacting violence against those who do not recognize it or attempt to emulate it in fact or fiction. The perpetuation of American whiteness in such fraught times requires the reassurance of 'pet-eating Black cannibals' as a dietary law-deposing violence. Such hyperbolic criminalization, beyond the 'ordinary decent criminal' (*inimicus*), is the other side of *ipsocratic* monopoly. Self-sameness is affirmed through meta-criminalized disjuncture.

The monopolization of violence begins with the identification of an Other as potentially law-imposing, which becomes the essence of this Other's legibility and illegality. One can break the law (ontic incidents of criminality) but the penalty will not be as severe as transgressing the ontological ban on embodying another alienating law-founding violence as an alien existential threat against the esoteric law-conserving force. Law-founding violence only creates the terrain, the vacant proscenium, upon which its act of institution can be replicated, theatricalized, revived, repeated, and forgotten, i.e., the deportation of those who threaten, dilute and parody white American indigeneity through geopolitical miscegenation.

28 Derrida, 'Force of Law', 987.

The violence used to secure monopoly right – material or discursive – is definitive, for if a founding violence is necessary to achieve monopoly right ex post facto, this confesses that any empirical exploit not undertaken under existing monopoly and law-conserving right is inherently anomic having been self-instituting beyond any law. As Derrida points out, there can be no permissible democratic debate on the desirability of democracy or its rejection within democracy as this transgresses democracy's monopolistic natural right *to be* and to institute the political by which all other regimes are judged and found wanting. It is this inviolability and transcendental stature of democratic right as a right to political monopoly that legitimate all violence undertaken in its name from regime change in Iraq, Venezuela and Iran to targeted assassination of American citizens judged to be "Islamic Jihad," or "domestic terrorists," to the criminalization of pro-Palestinian protestors as "antisemitic."

Auto-hetero-deconstruction

Derrida links the self-erasing textuality of law with the 'nomothetism' of Benjamin's text that he considers to be a force-filled, "auto-hetero-deconstruction." Across multiple interventions, Derrida assembles an archive of auto-hetero-deconstruction as a genealogy of differential contamination. The de-positioning of law conservation by the police reenacts the parricidal pharmacological mimesis, discussed earlier in 'Plato's Pharmacy' that structures the iteration and contamination between *phoné* (φωνή) as sovereign command and *graphê* (γραφή) by (in)fidelity, that resolves into the pharmacological blurring of the mnemic supplement as remedy (like the police) with lethal juridical toxicity.[29] This schematic subsequently reappears in the pharmacological-pathogenic conversion of the sovereign into the engulfing maw of the beast – the police are a legal ouroboros that both enact and consume legality by consuming its progenitor – the law in the name of the law. The sovereign can auto-deconstruct into the law-devouring state of emergency. Derrida identifies this auto-hetero-deconstruction of sovereignty with the differential contamination of politico-nomological miscegenation – "an onto-zoo-anthropo-theologico-political copulation."[30] The prolonged conjugation linguistically incarnates the anamorphic, self-substituting motion of sovereignty traversing terrains of the transcendental, and the corporeal immanence in the figure of the beast. In 'Force of Law', the miscegenation between sovereignty

29 Jacques Derrida, *Dissemination*, trans. by Barbara Johnson (Chicago: University of Chicago Press, 1981).

30 See his *The Beast & the Sovereign I*, trans. by Geoffrey Bennington (Chicago: University of Chicago Press, 2009), 18.

and monstrosity is the destructive copulation between law-conserving force and the law-transgressing beastly police.

Initially sanctified as foundational and sovereign, law-conserving violence reappears as an-archic law-imposing force; law functions like a *pharmakon* – a remedy that transubstantiates into a toxin. The legal *pharmakon* as the medium of differential contamination is associated with dis-ease, prescription, the medicinal, the body and a particular *physis* – *Walten* as the locus of dedifferentiation between law-founding and law-conserving force, which gestates open wounds, decay and degeneracy strewn across the body of law and its organs and subjects. "An effective critique must lay the blame on the body of *droit* itself, in its head and in its members, in the laws and the particular usages that law adopts under protection of its power [*Macht*]."[31] We are confronted with the police as rabble. The police-rabble are an organ or a member of the corporate body of law sundered from it in being inadequate to its concept. Hegel posits the rabble as an organ severed from a body-politic, and its *Sittlichkeit* (corporate ethicality); such amputation leads to a state of decomposition (*Verfaulen*) and decay (*Fäulnis*) that applies to the body of police.[32]

The mimetic impulse of law-conserving violence originates in its retrospective domesticating, legalization and encapsulation of anachronistic/anomic law-founding violence. This formulation follows the trajectory and pathos of Benjaminian mimesis as the compulsion and ability to become as Other – the recursion of identity through deforming alterity. Benjaminian mimesis as *Vermögen* – the mimetic faculty of physiognomic relation – is evident in the decay of law-conserving violence ultimately unfolding as the law-transgressing, law-imposing force of the police. The physiognomic dimension of mimesis as sensuous contact with Otherness is witnessed in the slippage of the abstract of law conservation into the material violence of police praxis that violates and cites the texts of law conservation at every opportunity. The inherent spectrality of the police originates in their mimetic yet parricidal expropriation of law-conserving force and its mutation into law-imposing/transgressing force. This auto-hetero-deconstruction of law conservation proceeds through the mimetic *physis* of police praxis as an echography, a recalling of, and to, an anterior anomic law-founding violence. What is undecidable here is the trajectory of mimetic power that can either proceed from law conservation's mimetic devolution into law-transgressing (extra-juridical force) as a recursion of its foundation or via the police's appropriative and parricidal mimetic parodying of law conservation.

31 Derrida, 'Force of Law', 1003.
32 G. W. F. Hegel, *Hegel's Phenomenology of Spirit*, trans. by A. V. Miller (Oxford: Oxford University Press, 1977).

The imprints and tracks of such wounding and decay of the corpus of law exposed to auto-hetero-deconstruction cannot be disassociated from a pharmacology of law and force. Does such transgressive imagery refract some hidden perhaps unwritten law of the normal and abnormal that on occasion Derrida seems to mourn or at least identify with a fall? A fall from what? Does this fall and decay originate in the inadequacy of the substance of law to its concept as embodied in the police? As much as Derrida seeks to navigate the difference between *physis* and *nomos*, *Walten* from positive law, the identification, infiltration, wounding, contamination and autoimmune disorders of law appear to refract the resurgence of *physis* at the heart of law and sovereignty. Derrida recognizes this when affirming, at the core of law's foundation, conservation and monopolization, the right to capital punishment as the right to take life and to shed blood, i.e., to destroy *physis*. Both Benjamin's and Derrida's texts are preoccupied with the decay and the degeneracy of a law that deconstructs itself through the vehicle of the police who align law with the spectral, that (for Derrida), is the locus of undecidability. At this juncture, with the spectral police hovering over law like an autonomic drone, it appears that the very principle of deconstruction in its diremption of violence is to incarcerate law in the *abgrund* of auto-contamination and undecidability with no exit – that is a tautology between text and *praxis* that must rebound on the text of deconstruction in its act of 'sentencing' the law. Merely identifying the slippages of law-conserving force into law-founding force through the disavowal of law's origins or the impunity enjoyed by police does not emancipate one from the aporetic. Such epistemic vertigo is neither here nor there as an inherent ontological undecidability. For if anomic undecidability is crucial to the evaluation of the impossible possibility of justice, then differential contamination must be conserved in Derridean legislation as its foundational right, if not monopoly, that upholds its ultimate assault on those very institutions dedicated to decidability.

One cannot help but notice the positioning of Derrida who speaks of contamination, decay, degeneracy, open wounds and, elsewhere, of autoimmune disorders; from where is he speaking? From what pharmacological site of normation and stability can he identify wounding, contamination and the suicidal degeneracy of autoimmunity as such while disavowing any possibility of deconstruction "becoming an available set of rule-governed procedures, methods, accessible approaches?"[33] What is the derivation and locus of this violence that in Derrida's interpretation lacerates Benjamin's text and the law? Decay, wounding and contamination cannot be disentangled from a set of rule-governed procedures and norms that name them

33 Derrida, 'Force of Law', 980.

as aberration or prescribe a deconstructionist therapy. Nor do such terms escape foundational calculation between the normal and the abnormal if the medical metaphor is taken to its limit. Perhaps at this juncture, what can mediate between Benjamin and Derrida (and his pharmacological lexicon) is a Canguilhemian philosophy of law as a theory of values, of normativity and the abnormal – a thematic not alien to law. This would be a paleopathology of law as the pathos of law is rooted in its remote aberrant foundations – a genetic coding of the law's metastatic mutation. "Health is a margin of tolerance for the inconstancies of the environment. . . . This is true enough of the human social environment where institutions are fundamentally precarious, conventions revocable, and fashions as fleeting as lightning".[34] This certainly applies to the law as a system of inconsistencies concerning the use of force disassembled by Benjamin and Derrida, and as experienced by the hunger striker exposed to law-transgressing violence in a variety of carceral environments that routinize inconsistency through arbitrary privations and force. However, in such inconsistent conditions, there are also "environments where there are leaks, holes, escapes and unexpected resistances" – architectures of undecidability and aperity that can lead to other forms of bodily alterity, which are promised by the eschatology of deconstruction as justice.

Medico-physiognomic dynamics appear in the ungraspable and spectralized body of the hunger striker who wills auto-hetero-deconstruction upon herself by willing the violence of starvation as a counterpoison upon herself to reenact, homeopathically, the residual toxicity extant as a parasite in her body, alien within and without her consent. The striker now repudiates law and policing through mimetic self-wounding, self-liquidation and self-depletion. For like the true and the untrue, law-founding/law-conserving violence, monopoly and the hunger striker are all "species of repetition."[35] The term 'species' should be taken literally here for the law enables the speciation of the police as beast, and the speciation of the hunger striker as the parricide of law-conserving violence. The autophagy of the hunger striker viscerally converts the law-conserving violence that subjugates the striker into an imposing lawless violence destroying its stature as a monopoly. The hunger striker resembles the *pharmakos*, the scapegoat – perhaps a self-sacrificing scapegoat – who scapegoats her own body that has been chased from the polity and subsists on the margins in heterotopic spaces of intensified law-transgressing policing. The strike rarely occurs at instituted centers. It unfolds at the margins in order to provoke a crisis of borders, walls

34 Canguilhem, *The Normal and the Pathological*, trans. by Carolyn R. Fawcett (Princeton: Princeton University Press, 1991), 197.
35 Derrida, *Dissemination*, 168.

and checkpoints through an emerging centration of that which has been excluded and confined.

> The city's body proper . . . reconstitutes its unity, closes around the security of its inner courts, gives back to itself the word that links it with itself within the confines of the agora, by violently excluding from its territory the representative of an external threat or aggression. That representative represents the otherness of the evil that comes to affect or infect the inside by unpredictably breaking into it.[36]

The hunger striker, like law-imposing violence, is positioned on the boundary between inside and outside, and ceaselessly traces and retraces border zones to deplete them through subversive mimesis. For hunger strikers resemble "all the exemplary figures of the violence of law (who) are singular metonymies, namely, figures without limit, unfettered possibilities of transposition and figures without figures."[37] This retracing is the strikers' recursion of the violence that shaped their embodiment from the outside that named itself as law-conserving. The hunger striker retraces law's violence from within the depths of her own body in ways that expose the pharmacological vibration, the unstable oscillation of its gestures between cure and toxin thereby concussing law's station as uncontestable foundation. In so doing, the pharmacological hunger striker reenacts differential contamination as her own auto-hetero-deconstruction that repositions law conservation as lawless imposition. The strike is an act of parricide directed at the law itself which has gestated and parented the striker as an institutional cipher – a number, a cell, a uniform, an inmate, a patient, a 'terrorist' and stateless. Such parricide is not an extreme act for the incarcerated *pharmakos* for it has been perennially divorced from origins in being transformed into an uprooted signifier for sundry labile frames of stigmatic reference and pathologization, for

> having strayed from the correct path, the right direction, the rule of rectitude, the norm . . . like someone who has lost his rights, an outlaw, a pervert, a bad seed, a vagrant . . . with no guarantor . . . uprooted, anonymous, unattached to any house or country, this almost insignificant signifier is at everyone's disposal.[38]

The hunger striker mirrors the auto-hetero-deconstruction of the law in her own body that decays and rots while assuming the role of court of conscience that

36 Ibid., 133.
37 Derrida, 'Force of Law', 1009.
38 Derrida, *Dissemination*, 143.

replicates a legal institution which is unconscious of the latent presence of anarchic violence in all that it says and does – a disavowal that rots law and decision from within. In the hunger strike, both the striker and the law become necrotic. Derrida associates decay with the falling away from an origin when it pertains to law; however, the striker's exile from origin occurs in the departure of the striker from her own body through that body that has become both the striker's natal and thanatological medium. The hunger striker in her 'degeneracy' transforms herself into the silhouette of a ruin; if the striker is ghostly, it is because what remains and abides is the flotsam and jetsam of auto-hetero-deconstruction.

> But this deconstruction is . . . the operation or rather the very experience that this text, it seems to me, first does itself, by itself, on itself. What does this mean? Is it possible? What remains . . . of such an event? Of its auto-hetero-deconstruction? Of its just and unjust incompletion? What is the ruin of such an event or the open wound of such a signature? And also, in what does its strength consist, strength precisely in the sense of *Gewalt*, that is, its violence, authority and legitimacy?[39]

De-expiation and the Hunger Strike

In 'Capitalism as Religion,' Benjamin identifies inculpation *or* guilt/indebtedness (*Schuld*) as

> the highest category of world history for guaranteeing the unidirectionality [*Einsinnigkeit*] of what occurs. . . . Cause and effect can never be decisive categories for the structure of world history because they cannot determine any totality. . . . It is a mistake of the rationalistic conception of history to view any historical totality (that is, a state of the world) as cause or effect. A state of the world is however always guilty with regard to some other later one.[40]

In 'The Meaning of Time in the Moral Universe,' Benjamin extends this argument of the temporal structure of inculpation and violent expiation as historical causality.

> What endows the law with this interest in the distant past and with power over it . . . is something very different indeed from the representation of the presence of morality in the past. . . . This is the tendency to retribution.

39 Derrida, 'Force of Law', 981.
40 Walter Benjamin, 'Capitalism as Religion', in M. Bullock and M. Jennings, eds., *Selected Writings Vol.1: 1913–1926* (Cambridge: Harvard University Press, 1996), 289.

> In modern law, retribution is confined to thirty years, a generation, even in the extreme case of murder – as if it were afraid to exceed the span of a human life. Yet we know from older forms of law that the power of retribution was able to extend its sway to succeeding, increasingly distant generations. Retribution is fundamentally indifferent to the passage of time, since it remains in force for centuries without dilution. . . . This idea . . . which mocks all delay as vain procrastination, fails to understand the immeasurable significance of the Last Judgment, of that constantly postponed day which flees so determinedly into the future after the commission of every misdeed. This significance is revealed not in the world of law, where retribution rules, but only in the moral universe, where forgiveness comes out to meet it. In order to struggle against retribution, forgiveness finds its powerful ally in time.[41]

Derrida discerns a similar archaic infinitude of expiation in the contemporary disjuncture between the atemporal formation of the death penalty in relation to the finitude of the condemned. In contradistinction to Benjamin, Derrida writes of de-expiation as embedded in the finitude of a delimited punishment contravened by the death penalty, which interdicts any possibility of de-expiation within its process and telos that knows no limit in negating all time-bound incalculable events. Derrida questions the logic of capital penalty in terms of its lack of correlation to the temporality of the condemned.

> For there to be punishment, this punishment must supervene upon the punishable subject, and it must be finite, or at least commensurate with life . . . a punishment worthy of the name must be commensurate not only with the crime but also with the capacity that a punishable and finite subject has of undergoing, of suffering, of living through the punishment. By eliminating the subject of the punishment, you eliminate the punishment and the right to punish . . . once it exceeds the limit, and precisely exceeds the finite life of the subject . . . the death penalty . . . becomes infinite and thereby loses . . . its punitive value.[42]

The death penalty, according to Derrida, contravenes itself by de-temporalizing expiation, rendering it paradoxically infinite through the infliction of death. The most violent and terrorizing instrument of the death penalty for

41 Walter Benjamin, 'The Meaning of Time in the Moral Universe', in M. Bullock and M. Jennings, eds., *Selected Writings Vol. 1: 1913–1926* (Cambridge: Harvard University Press, 1996), 286.

42 Jacques Derrida, *The Death Penalty II*, trans. by Elizabeth Rottenberg (Chicago: Chicago University Press, 2017), 33.

him is neither the syringe nor the electric chair but the clock that counts down to the termination of all temporality for those condemned to death. However, both Derrida and Benjamin coincide in associating unlimited expiation and inculpation with the hellish and suppressive dominance of calculation over that temporal aperity called history as the milieu of possibility.

Benjamin sought an exit from the dominance of retributive, inculpating time signatures over history and the incalculable event by rescripting capitalist modernity as the author of a political theology of law, guilt and debt with no possibility of de-expiation. In the 'Critique', he pitched mythic violence against divine violence in order to turn capitalism as political theology against itself:

> If mythic violence is law-positing, divine violence is law-annihilating; if the former establishes boundaries, the latter boundlessly annihilates them; if mythic violence inculpates [*verschuldend*] and expiates [*sühnend*] at the same time, divine violence de-expiates [*entsühnend*]; if the former threatens, the latter strikes; if the former is bloody, the latter is lethal in a bloodless manner. . . . *For the domination of law over the living ceases with mere life*. Mythic violence is blood violence over mere life for the sake of violence itself; divine violence is pure violence over all of life for the sake of the living.[43]
>
> (*emphasis mine*)

The 'unidirectionality' or 'one-senseness' (*Einsinnigkeit*) of world history is interrupted by a counter-directional and reversable time signature that Benjamin names divine violence, yet that reversibility is also embodied in, among other entities, the temporal detouring of hunger striking for the sake of the living. The death fast, like divine violence, "is lethal in a bloodless manner" that effaces all unnatural (therefore mythic) boundaries imposed upon the striker through the performance of de-expiation as self-determination through autophagy. These gestures bring the dominance of law over what Benjamin terms the threshold, i.e., "mere life" (*bloßes Leben*), to an end in an act of bloodless violence by which mere life extends itself beyond a law soaked by, and grounded in, the blood of retributive punition.

Benjamin's 'divine justice' anticipates the insurrectionary hunger strike arrayed against the compulsive bloodletting of a sovereign power as mythic violence. Bloodletting is the emblem of mere life colonized and moralized by inculpation and expiation. Law as mythic *lex talionis* – arbitrary relations of commensuration, adequation and retribution – trades in blood in its demand for calculable value equivalence in the form of corporeal and psychic

43 Benjamin, 'Toward the Critique of Violence', 57–58.

atonement, culpability, expiation and indebtedness. However, the lawful violence over-exerted against mere life confesses mere life's troubling excess and resistance to law – mere life as unassimilable surplus immanence. This surfeit of mere life to law opens the political logic of the hunger strike. The insurrectionary hunger strike is the rebellion of mere life against law that has historically and ontologically encapsulated mere life, threatening and decimating with bloodletting expiation and inculpation, and incarcerating mere life as inherently criminal in relation to law. This is the disciplinary thrust of biopower, which seeks to domesticate and consume mere life and submit it to rectitude and to render it commensurate with law. The asymmetrical war of the hunger striker is a forceful rupturing seeking the de-expiation of those for whom the strike is mobilized in the name of their mere life as such. The hunger strike's mediality is the putting into action and political play of the bio-semiotic forces of mere life against extant nomothetic incarcerations of the body. The extortionist labor strike seeks the striking body's incorporation into law as a biopolitical project; it is in search of an affirmational re-embodiment insofar as the law concedes the striker's juridical personality and corporeal admissibility. However, the insurrectionary hunger strike seeks law's abolition by disavowing expiation and *lex talionis* as legitimate and lawful calculations upon which the law feeds. The bloodlessness of the insurrectionary hunger strike speaks to the hauntological impact of the spectrally infused and radiating corporeal gestures, by which the starving body becomes its own ghost, paralleling its spectral doubles in the halls through which the law administrates flesh and blood subjects. Hunger striking scissions the body like the incorporeal motion of the Stoic's knife that bifurcates the striking body by sundering it from law and returning it to mere life through a de-expiating willfulness. In striving against the state and its bloodletting instruments of punition, this attrition of bodily integrity through self-imposed starvation/spectralization subversively parodies and thereby inflicts *kenosis* upon the formalized iconography of expiation associated with the mythic violence (*mytische Gewalt*), on which the authority of law resides.

For Derrida, the de-expiation of those consigned to the death penalty begins with staunching institutional positioning and promising in bloodletting, whether in the form of carceral legality or ecocidal, genocidal and ethnocidal mass liquidations deemed necessary to the production of a polity, that is culturally, economically and technologically dependent on, and addicted to, unquantifiable pools of blood as its political currency.

> Whether it comes to concepts or blood, we are . . . a long way from being done with the impermeable [*l'étanche*]. We are a long way, a very long way, from being done – will we ever be done? – staunching the flow [*d'étancher*]. What does staunching [*stancher*] mean? We were present at the scene of the hemorrhaging, if not the hemophilia, of the wound and

> the bleeding to be staunched, of the effusion of blood to be staunched (by draining, suturing, ligaturing, stricturing, closing the wound, binding), the hemoscenography, seemed to us to demand a certain privilege, a certain prerogative, even if water and tears could also be seen figuring among the liquidities to be staunched . . . we felt called upon by the death penalty to see red, to see the red of blood return or disappear.[44]

By foregrounding the finitude of the striker as her medium of dissensus, the striker alters moral relations between herself and surrounding institutional edifices. According to Fenves, Benjamin does not credit an alteration of moral relations as occurring between bodies. This alterity, however, is emplaced between the hunger striker and her auditors. Fenves observes a shift in Benjamin's thinking of expiation from acts of spectacular and omnipotent violence to the immanentization of forgiveness and redemption, which the hunger striker unfurls by means of their body.[45] The lack of bloodshed in the de-expiatory catharsis of divine violence is reliant upon the intervention of a transcendental agent upon an inculpated patient. However, the secularizing shift to immanent de-expiation presupposes the forgiveness of another, divine or not, and does not account for the radical immanence of the hunger striker who seeks no forgiveness from outside herself and unleashes a *Walten* of radical immanentization in the mode of motion of her body towards depletion and death. The immanentization of the hunger strike as a bloodless relation between agent and patient is encompassed in a continuum of citable gestures, extending beyond the striker's body limit, as an allegory of mere life's extension beyond the law as a surplus immanence. Benjamin speaks of an echography of embodied gestures, which combines speech and kinetic corporeality as the performative interruption of existing temporal orders potentially citable by others, and their gesticulations through retention as a mode of protention.[46] He is concerned with the iterability of the forwarded ekphrastic gesture across gesticulating bodies as the expressivity of mere life's potentiality to signify beyond any institutional inscription and enframement. The temporal structure of gestural citation entails self-altering repetition, by which ekphrasis takes as its object and impetus a prior ekphrastic gesture that is no longer apparent beyond its citation and substitution.

The gestural elongation in time and space of the hunger strike events stands in contrast to the organization of the death penalty, which, in modernity, has striven for de-spectacularization of the execution and its normalization through the occlusion and treatment power of medicalization – the *pharmakon* used

44 Derrida, *The Death Penalty II*, 214.
45 Fenves, 'Intervention and Encroachment: Violence and Expiation'.
46 Samuel Weber, *Benjamin's-Abilities* (Cambridge: Harvard University Press, 2010).

to accelerate and anaesthetize death for the prisoner. Medicalization is also strategically deployed to interrupt hunger strikes by deferring death through forced feeding often supervised by medical authorities. The use of the latter in Guantanamo prison against hunger striking prisoners who have never been tried or sentenced, discloses the gestural force of the hunger strike as the mobilization of de-expiation while reciprocally aligning the reactive medicalization of strikers with their renewed inculpation; being punished in Guantanamo for imputed terrorism and for hunger striking. Medical intervention used against imprisoned strikers is not meant to save them but to salvage the regime of inculpation and expiation. Opposition of hunger striking to the capital penalty is nowhere better expressed than by all the efforts taken to prevent the suicide of the condemned and to ensure the prisoner's good health before their execution, including feeding them; in all such cases of execution, the self-determination and the will of the prisoner must be interdicted and removed from the scene if proper punition is to occur, and law conservation to take place, to ensure the temporal permanence of the law over life and after death that Derrida critiques as undermining the project of punition. Derrida is correct; what is punition in the absence of the will of the punished?

If the retributive violence of law is "the ineluctable passage from quality to quantity, from the in-calculable or the non-calculable to the calculable," then the bloodless hunger strike is an exiting from the talionic quantification of life to dequantifiable and incalculable mere life, as self-qualifying aleatory life that can turn to a death as emblematically beyond calculation, at least by what is measured under law and medicine.[47] If blood is the emblem of retributive talionic punition and therefore integral to, and substrate for, the violence of juridical calculation, the hunger strike as bloodless violence is beyond calculative logic and reasoning, even its own political legitimation of its action. Given the addictive economies of bloodletting in the institutional and political ecologies under which the striker acts, hunger striking becomes the interiorization of blood as *le sang sans le sang*. The de-expiating hunger striker being emblematically bloodless does away with the quantifications of *lex talionis* that feed on blood materially and symbolically:

> this old and unintelligent talionic law, this law of blood for blood. What would happen if suddenly there were no more blood? Or if suddenly blood no longer counted for humanity? What happens when blood can no longer flow, so to speak, or have this phantasmatic virtue of expiatory sacrifice . . .? Why is it that, according to the manner in which it is done, the effusion of blood is here regarded either as a means of purification or as a crime? Why do all shed blood in one manner or the other?[48]

47 Derrida, *The Death Penalty II*, 140.
48 Ibid., 342.

10

THE SUICIDE OF THE CRITIQUE OF VIOLENCE

Chris Power

Jacques Derrida's keynote at the Cardozo Law School in October 1989 was split between speech and writing: he read the first part ('Of the Right to Justice/From Law to Justice') aloud and distributed the second ('First Name of Benjamin'). Six months later at a colloquium at UCLA on 'Nazism and the Final Solution' he inserted a prolegomenon composed of two numbered series of justifications before delivering the initially silenced conclusion. It begins with the admission that his reading of Benjamin's 'Toward the Critique of Violence' is "somewhat risky."[1] The prolegomenon concludes with an enigmatic anthropomorphism: "a kind of self-destruction, if not suicide of the text."[2] Of this suicide Derrida writes that it "lets no other legacy appear than the violence of its signature – as divine signature."[3] It is as if hedging introduced a greater problem that dooms his efforts in advance: a text that kills itself cannot be thought of as such without betrayal. It is as if marking his hesitation only consigned "First Name of Benjamin" to a more absolute silence.[4]

Derrida's hesitations betray his investment in what he calls, thinking of Benjamin, "a thinking that knows there is no *justesse*, no justice, no

1 Jacques Derrida, 'Force of Law: The "Mystical Foundation of Authority"', in Drucilla Cornell, Michel Rosenfeld, and David Gray Carlson, eds., *Deconstruction and the Possibility of Justice* (London: Routledge), 63.

2 Ibid., 66.

3 Ibid.

4 The editors of *Deconstruction and the Possibility of Justice* betray this self-betraying prolegomenon by resituating it at the margins of the text as the sixth footnote. Derrida, 'Force of Law', 63.

DOI: 10.4324/9781003589419-13

responsibility except in exposing oneself to all risks, beyond certitude and good conscience."[5] Calculating for the incalculable, Derrida tries to cautiously follow Benjamin into the singular aporia of textual suicide but he can neither bring it back to the life of speech nor belatedly justify it. It is as if the problem has infected him: the radical dream of deconstruction, Derrida writes, is "to introduce the equivalent of AIDS into the organs of transmission, into the hermeneutic *Gespräch*."[6]

Derrida takes great pains to rigorously expose Benjamin in all of his exposure to the line of fire: 'Toward the Critique of Violence' does not just risk right-wing revolutionary thought,[7] politicizing theology, and theologizing politics. It is not only, as Derrida writes, "too messianico-marxist or archeo-eschatological for me."[8] It not only risks politicizing blood ("Blood makes all the difference"),[9] reifying an opposition between the Greek and the Jewish,[10] and romanticizing crime and terrorism.[11] It does not merely bleed (as Friedrich Nietzsche and Georges Bataille write of their texts). It also somehow kills itself, either foreshadowing or rhyming with Benjamin's decision at the Franco-Spanish border in 1940 or coming from some incalculable future. All that it leaves for thought and history is Benjamin's name (Walter) as the name of the altogether other ("*waltende Gewalt*": pending violence).

The great enigma of this climax, which nothing survives other than its signature, is signaled by Derrida when he acknowledges that he cannot do it justice.

> Here begins the last sequence, the most enigmatic, the most fascinating and the most profound in this text. For lack of time but not only time, I cannot claim to do it justice. I will have to content myself with stressing on the one hand the terrible ethico-political ambiguity of the text, on the other hand the exemplary instability of its status and its signature, what, finally, you will permit me to call this heart or courage [*ce coeur ou ce courage*] or a thinking that knows there is no *justesse*, no justice, no responsibility except in exposing oneself to all risks, beyond certitude and good conscience.[12]

5 Derrida, 'Force of Law', 51–52.
6 Ibid., 37.
7 "The analogy with Schmittian or Heideggerian schemas does not need to be spelled out." Derrida, 'Force of Law', 46.
8 Derrida, 'Force of Law', 62.
9 Ibid., 52.
10 "If we trust the Benjaminian schema, is the deconstructive discourse on the undecidable more Jewish (or Judeo-Christian-Greek) or Greek?" Derrida, 'Force of Law', 56.
11 Derrida, 'Force of Law', 52.
12 Ibid., 51–52. I cite *Deconstruction and the Possibility of Justice* because the 2002 republication of the essay in *Acts of Religion* omits the following sentence: "For lack of time but

Violence has deposed the grounds of (its) reading, leaving traces neither of itself nor of its self-destruction. It can only be perceived in what Benjamin calls its incomparable effects. For Benjamin it has various names: divine violence, pending violence, sovereign violence, and deposing [*Entsetzung*] to which Werner Hamacher has added the term afformance.

Derrida deploys the term suicide to name an event that never occurs at the level of figuration, phenomenality, or legibility but that deposes itself and thus threatens the basis of socio-phenomenological positing. This suicide cannot be thought of as the means to an external end, just like a name does not refer to a person. It traces "a dismaying trajectory, one that is at the same time aporetic and productive of strange events in its very aporia."[13] It does not lead anywhere that could be cognized or experienced, but I will attempt to analyze some of the strange events that it produces or cannot resolve. Derrida describes this suicide variously as an explosion, an implosion, or an auto-hetero-deconstruction, but it never achieves a definitive form or takes place in a present tense or localizable passage. At the conclusion of his essay Benjamin notes that "not equally possible, and also less urgent for human beings is, however, the decision concerning when pure violence was realized in a particular case."[14] Divine violence could only manifest itself (self-)destructively, as it cannot be imagined either as such or otherwise.[15] It is irreducible to a given, immediate, phenomenological presence. That being said, it cannot be approached otherwise than through the metaphor of suicide: only this theatrical anthropomorphism exposes the radical pathos of what Derrida calls its "amour du droit" (love of law)[16] that goes to the extreme of ending itself.

Derrida's recognition of the radical violence that burns through Benjamin's text has since been repressed by both critics and apologists. David Lloyd's essay "Rage Against the Divine" articulates a secular critique. He shows that divine violence shares with mythical violence a foundational structure: divine violence, Lloyd argues, maintains the power of the priesthood, specifically the authority of Moses and Aaron that is contested by Korah and

---

not only time, I cannot claim to do it justice." See Jacques Derrida, 'Force of Law', in Gil Andijar, ed., *Acts of Religion* (New York: Routledge, 2002), 287.

13 Derrida, 'Force of Law', 66.

14 Walter Benjamin, 'Toward the Critique of Violence', in Peter Fenves and Julia Ng, eds., *Toward the Critique of Violence: A Critical Edition* (Stanford: Stanford University Press, 2021), 60.

15 Benjamin writes in the conclusion of 'Toward the Critique of Violence' that divine violence cannot be perceived as such. He elaborates in a fragment titled 'World and Time' included in the new critical edition of 'Toward the Critique of Violence': "genuine divine violence can manifest itself other than destructively only in the coming world (of fulfillment). Where, by contrast, divine violence enters into the earthly world, it breathes destruction." Benjamin, 'Toward the Critique', 83.

16 Derrida, 'Force of Law', 44.

his followers.[17] On the other hand, Judith Butler's "Walter Benjamin and the Critique of Violence" deploys Benjamin's thought to articulate a Jewish critique of Zionism and in doing so places Benjamin's thought in the context of what she calls at turns "a different Judaism"[18] and "another Judaism"[19] (one influenced by the *Kabbalah*). Lloyd's critique and Butler's defense of Benjamin's text both turn away from what Derrida called its suicide. Lloyd emphasizes that divine violence is not messianic, while Butler argues that Benjamin's thought troubles the foundations of a universal, secular humanism that could erase religious and cultural difference. Butler notes a Kafkan Judaism in the text:[20] like Benjamin writes of Kafka's gestures, the invocation of the divine explodes any framework (secular or religious) that would attempt to enclose it and make it legible and meaningful. In killing itself, the text also kills God and all foundations for religious and secular authority.

In different ways and towards different ends both Lloyd and Butler turn away from what Derrida asks us to permit him to call "this heart or courage [*ce coeur ou ce courage*] or a thinking that knows that there is no *justesse*, no justice, no responsibility except in exposing oneself to all risks, beyond certitude and good conscience."[21] Whereas Butler is working against an association of Judaism with vengeance, Lloyd rages against the divine violence that founded priestly authority.

Butler works against a Zionist monopolization of Judaism on the one hand, and the specter of resurgent antisemitism on the other; one intuits the spectral nature of the latter in Butler's references to "the vulgar representation of Judaism" and "the reduction of Judaism we confront in popular representation."[22] The Nietzsche of the *Genealogy of Morality* is perhaps one of its most canonical vulgarizers; the following passages will be quoted in full because they spell out some of the political dangers of divine violence and its differing interpretations.

> Nothing that has been done on earth against 'the noble', 'the mighty', 'the masters' and 'the rulers', is worth mentioning compared with what the Jews have done against them: the Jews, that priestly people, which in the last resort was able to gain satisfaction from its enemies and conquerors only through a radical revaluation of their values, that is, through an act

17 David Lloyd, 'Rage against the Divine: In memoriam Jacques Derrida' (April 2007) *South Atlantic Quarterly* 352.
18 Judith Butler, 'Walter Benjamin and the Critique of Violence', in *Parting Ways: Jewishness and the Critique of Zionism* (New York: Columbia University Press, 2012), 75.
19 Butler, 'Walter Benjamin and the Critique', 96.
20 Ibid., 94–96.
21 Derrida, 'Force of Law', 51–52.
22 Butler, 'Walter Benjamin and the Critique of Violence', 73.

> of the most deliberate revenge [*durch einen Akt der geistigsten Rache*]. Only this was fitting for a priestly people with the most entrenched priestly vengefulness.[23]

Nietzsche here returns to and revises the narrative of "master and slave morality" recounted only a year earlier in *Beyond Good and Evil*. In an act of priestly transvaluation, he acknowledges in the *Genealogy* that the weakness of the priestly type is the historical origin of anything interesting and dangerous:

> In any case, with some justification one could add that man first became an interesting animal on the foundation of this essentially dangerous form of human existence, the priest, and that the human soul became deep in the higher sense and turned evil for the first time – and of course, these are the two basic forms of man's superiority, hitherto, over other animals![24]

Insofar as he presents Jewishness as unified and monolithic, Nietzsche seems to agree with Korah and his followers who appeal against the authority of Moses and Aaron "to the supposed sanctity of 'the whole [Jewish] community'":[25] Nietzsche's description of the Jews as "a nation of priests" corroborates Korah's claim that "Every member of the community is holy and the Lord is amongst them all."[26] Despite this coarse, undifferentiated treatment of "the Jews," Nietzsche's distinction between the priestly and knightly modes of valuation can help illuminate what David Lloyd calls the showdown between Korah and Moses and thus the political valences of divine violence.[27] This showdown pits Moses' otherworldly "authority" against the earthly privileges of Korah and his followers and yields a univocal victory for priestly weakness against the totems of power and the ostensibly healthy and natural knightly mode of valuation that christens them as good without betraying any interest in external references, second opinions, or points of comparison. Lloyd reminds us of "Moses' and Aaron's Lot-like remonstrations to the Lord" that failed to prevent the earth from opening up and swallowing Korah.[28] As in Nietzsche, the priestly caste is not defined by authority, power, or violence but rather by weakness.[29] Divine violence

23 Friedrich Nietzsche, *On the Genealogy of Morality* (Cambridge: Cambridge University Press, 2007), 17.

24 Ibid., 16.

25 Peter Fenves, 'Introduction', in Peter Fenves and Julia Ng, eds., *Toward the Critique of Violence: A Critical Edition* (Stanford: Stanford University Press, 2021), 33.

26 *Book of Numbers* cited in Lloyd, 'Rage against the Divine', 351.

27 Lloyd, 'Rage against the Divine', 351.

28 Ibid.

29 "As we know, priests make the most evil enemies – but why? Because they are the most powerless." Nietzsche, *On the Genealogy of Morality*, 17.

strikes and destroys the privileged without leaving any traces, because they are "exponents of law."[30]

David Lloyd rages against the injustice of divine violence: he argues that it "not only shares with mythical violence a foundational structure" but that moreover it is "maintained through a highly elaborated code of law- and boundary-preserving measures whose application is attended with the threat of a merely suspended violence."[31] Instead of defending divine violence, I will try to understand what Derrida calls the suicide of the text in which it appears[32] by "showing" that neither divine violence nor the suicide of the critique of violence appears as itself. This suicide takes with it the foundations of secular and theological reasoning and preemptively silences its now storied reception history.

Instead of attempting to localize this suicide in a particular passage, I will argue that it occurs throughout the essay. The critique of violence is, in other

30 "Abstracting from the immense commentary on Numbers 16, which is in itself confusing enough, Benjamin identifies 'Korah's horde' with a single trait: as Levites – like Aaron and Moses, who remain conspicuously unnamed – they are 'privileged' [*Bevorrechtete*], which indicates that they are willy-nilly exponents of law in accordance with the recently articulated theorem '[A]ll law [*Recht*] was the privilege [*Vor-recht*] of kings or grandees'. Privilege equals law." Peter Fenves, 'Introduction', in *Toward the Critique of Violence: A Critical Edition*, 33.

31 Lloyd, 'Rage against the Divine', 353. Elsewhere Lloyd writes that it is "not only the fact of [the fate of Korah and his followers], the bloodless slaughter of some 15,000 Israelites" but moreover it is "the association of such punitive, end-directed violence with the unbounded, excessive wrath (*Zorn*) that it shares with the 'mythical violence' directed by Apollo and Artemis against Niobe" (Lloyd, 'Rage against the Divine', 355). He accuses Benjamin and Derrida of "passing over . . . the moment of rage in the passage from mythic to divine violence": "Only in the discounting of mortal rage in the face of an immortal, ineluctable violence can the profound injustice of divine violence and its inaugural force be overlooked" (Lloyd, 'Rage against the Divine', 366).

32 In the following passage, Derrida suggests that we leave the rage that animates and burns through the critique of violence to Benjamin. It indexes the deliberate slippage between affective and juridical registers that frustrates Benjamin's text.

> To explain this 'nonmediate function of violence,' Benjamin again takes the example of everyday language as if it were only an analogy. In fact, it seems to me, we have here the true mechanism, and the very place of decision. Is it by chance and unrelated to such a figure of God that he speaks then of the experience of *anger*, this example of a manifestation that passes as immediate, and alien to any correlation between means and end? Is it by chance that he takes the example of anger to show that, before any mediation, language is manifestation, epiphany, pure presentation? This explosion of violence, in anger, would not be a means toward an end; it would have no other aim than to show and to show itself. Let us leave the responsibility for this concept to Benjamin.
>
> *(Derrida, 'Force of Law', 51)*

Lloyd spurns this suggestion by raging against the divine: he positions himself as a "secular intellect" (Lloyd, 'Rage against the Divine', 347) surveying murderous or even genocidal feudal myths.

words, "haunted by *haunting* itself, by a quasi-logic of the phantom which, because it is the more forceful one, should be substituted for an ontological logic of presence, absence or representation."[33] This quasi-logic of the phantom raises many questions: the text might be dead on arrival or it might die again in each sentence; it might begin having already passed through its own end, or it could repeatedly kill itself. It does not, however, stand outside of history: if 'Toward the Critique of Violence' precedes Benjamin's death and the implementation of the final solution by twenty years, Derrida maintains nonetheless that it "would be reckless to say . . . that Benjamin knew nothing about it":

> One will always find ways to support the hypothesis according to which Benjamin, already in 1921, was thinking about nothing else than the possibility of this final solution that would be all the more challenging to the order of representation from having perhaps arisen, in his view, from radical evil, from the fall as fall of language in representation.[34]

Following Derrida, I wager that the text has internalized as a literary game the possibility that it be read as a suicide (note) published in a journal of social scientific and legal thought. 'Toward the Critique of Violence' posits the law of deposition and thus deposes itself. This suicide is not a *fait accompli* of a plotted climax. It is rather, as Hamacher writes, "exposed not only to its own inherent historic disintegration but must already previously, in its own effectuation, have been exposed to the absolute other of deposing of afformance."[35] I will show that it does so most clearly in the many em dashes that interrupt, lacerate, and suture the text, unleashing an intransigent critique of language that undermines formulation and re-presentation.

1. Death to the Concept

The suicide of the critique of violence is an (im)possible figure and disfiguration of justice: it can neither be imagined nor subsumed under a concept. It revolts against the possibility of conceptualization by establishing and then destroying the terms of its absolute singularity. Suicide is the price that the text pays for its intransigent pursuit of justice in the rotten language of the law: "[it] does not escape the law that it states. It is ruined and contaminated, it becomes a spectre of itself."[36]

33 Derrida, 'Force of Law', 63–64.
34 Ibid., 65.
35 Werner Hamacher, 'Afformative, Strike', (1991) 13 *Cardozo Law Review* 1139.
36 Benjamin, 'Toward the Critique of Violence', 43.

In paragraph nine of 'Toward the Critique of Violence', Walter Benjamin writes that death is crowned as fate at the origin and in the very structure of law. The power of law "resides in the fact that there is only one fate and that the status quo [*das Bestehende*], especially what threatens the status quo, belongs inviolably to its order."[37] Derrida's gloss on this point is infected by the Wittgensteinian dimension of the text that he elsewhere notes:[38] "If the origin of law is a violent position, the latter manifests itself in the purest fashion when violence is absolute, that is to say when it touches on the right to life and to death."[39] One could hazard the following paraphrase: There can only be one law, one fate, and one death. To deprive any state of the right to legally kill its citizens does not contest the authority of its monopoly on violence. For this reason, Benjamin dismisses the proponents of the death penalty's abolition as naive.

What Derrida calls the absolute uniqueness of fate calls for a violent scene to legitimate the authority of its positing.[40] This scene representatively extends the origins of law-positing violence onto the stage of the existent; in it, the violent origins of the fateful order of law show themselves (again) hovering undecidably between conservation of the given and foundation of the new. Benjamin writes that its meaning is to establish "new law," for, "in the exercise of power over life and death, law reinforces itself more than in any other form of law enforcement."[41] This event announces something rotten and ruinous ("etwas Morsches") in law.[42] Instead of turning away from the ruin of law, Benjamin writes that the faculty of understanding must approach the conditions whereby the law establishes its fateful nature through the death penalty "all the more decisively."[43]

The faculty of understanding is responsible for subsuming particular cases under concepts. Derrida and Hamacher both follow Benjamin's implicit observation that the application of given concepts violates the irreducible singularity of any case. As Derrida writes, "A decision that didn't go through the ordeal of the undecidable would not be a free decision, it would only be the programmable application or unfolding of a calculable process."[44] According to Hamacher, "Singularity is for Benjamin a determination of justice—indeed, its determination *par excellence*—and thus a determination of pure mediacy."[45] Such generalizable calculation might be lawful but never just, because justice

37 Derrida, 'Force of Law', 46.
38 Ibid., 14.
39 Ibid., 42.
40 Ibid., 41.
41 Benjamin, 'Toward the Critique of Violence', 47.
42 Walter Benjamin, 'Zur Kritik der Gewalt', in *Gesammelte Schriften II* (Frankfurt am Main: Suhrkamp 1991), 188.
43 Benjamin, 'Toward the Critique of Violence', 47.
44 Derrida, 'Force of Law', 24.
45 Hamacher, 'Afformative, Strike', 1144.

calls for the suspension of all legal conventions and ontic data in the attempt to approach that which is irreducible to precedent and conceptual generality. The performance of the subject (of justice) in front of and before the law

> cannot be just, in the sense of justice, except by founding itself on conventions and so on other anterior performatives, buried or not, it always maintains within itself some irruptive violence, it no longer responds to the demands of theoretical rationality.[46]

The performative subject of justice suspends itself between given conventions and the (im)possibility of the irruption of a new code. This suspension threatens the authority of what has already been determined as truth.[47] Law establishes itself "in the exercise of power over life and death": the subject (of justice) must be put to death, because he "would be before a law not yet determined, before the law as before a law not yet existing, a law yet to come, *encore devant et devant venir*."[48] The subject of justice is still temporally and spatially before a law that is still to come [*encore devant*] before [*devant venir*]: like the French spatial preposition *devant* shifts its position in those two French phrases, the subject of justice will never have a place, and the fateful order of law requires his death.

Paragraph nine of 'Toward the Critique of Violence' unveils the program for the text's self-terminating auto-deposition, its suicide. Benjamin's critique of violence deposes itself through fatal exposure to the contaminating ruin of the law. In the critique of violence, the faculty that applies concepts to intuitions to make experience cognizable and thus possible (as "experience") subjects itself to the death penalty, because it partakes in the (de)positing that threatens law from the inside. Instead of theorizing a position that would be comfortably outside of the corruption of the law (as Hamacher does in 'Afformative, Strike'), Derrida observes that Benjamin radicalizes law's internal threat to the (unthinkable) extreme: the auto-deposition of the subject of justice.

2. The Auto-deposition of Revolutionary Violence

'Toward the Critique of Violence' sutures together disparate elements and ruptures the semblance of continuity with em dashes that produce curious fragments within paragraphs. Each resultant fragment calls for singular attention as a literary gesture, but in the following I will only consider two of

46 Derrida, 'Force of Law', 27.
47 Benjamin, 'Toward the Critique of Violence', 36.
48 Derrida, 'Force of Law', 36.

them that tear through and undo the "theory" of revolutionary violence. Both demonstrate a process of unworking that breaks through the phenomenal reality of a functioning text and that which it posits, represents, and references.[49]

The first of these em dashes in the eleventh paragraph underscores the monopolization of violence secured by the legal sanctioning of workers' strikes: "Law grants this right [to strike] because it restrains violent actions it is afraid to confront. Previously, workers resorted straight away to sabotage and set fire to the factories. —".[50] Law concedes the right to strike because it fears violent measures such as sabotage or burning factories. To preserve itself and its end, law (*droit*) must recognize the right (*droit*) to strike, lest it be taken otherwise through more violent attacks on the means of production. The following sentence calls for a closer reading because of the way that it disrupts the conventions of writing. Since the English translation rewrites it by eliminating its ambiguities, it is helpful to have the German: "Griffen doch vordem die Arbeiter sogleich zur Sabotage und steckten die Fabriken an. –".[51] The verb comes first in the German sentence, which "makes sense" as an irruption (in the codified, written language of social scientific and legal theory) of the spoken: it "speaks," interrupting the conventions and authority of the law, as if it were a shout from the street penetrating the tranquility of a seminar and the machinations of theoretical rationality. In other words, this insertion passes the acoustic test (it "sounds right": one can imagine hearing it spoken), but it fails within the codified genre of legal theory: it can be read neither as a question (there is no question mark) nor as an imperative (it does not address the reader in the second person). Both verbs ("*greifen*" and "*anstecken*") are moreover conjugated either in the past indicative tense or in the present subjunctive, exacerbating the ambiguity of the sentence by bifurcating interrogation and imperative, theory and irony, and the real as opposed to the imagined past. The concluding em dash opens the temporal gap between the past and the present, suggesting the return of a revolutionary past that can only be rescued from the decidability of the past perfect tense through the time-travel machine of literary license.

49 The pure manifestation of revolutionary violence can neither be symbolically mediated nor posited as a phenomena; it manifests itself in "ellipses, pauses, interruptions, [and] displacements." (Hamacher, 'Afformative, Strike', 1139). Unlike Hamacher's seminal reading, however, I will neither be reproducing the myth of the general strike nor the myth of "revolutionary violence" as a theoretically functional ("living") semantic unit that could be extracted from Benjamin's text and applied to other contexts. Unlike Hamacher, I will focus instead on divine violence and the suicide that distinguishes it radically from any functional or living theory.

50 Benjamin, 'Toward the Critique of Violence', 51.

51 Benjamin, 'Zur Kritik der Gewalt', 193.

This sentence sabotages (the factory of) legal theory. If it were an imperative statement, it would interpolate its readers as the revolutionary workers of yesteryear ("Resort at once, workers, to sabotage and set fire to the factories"), thus abolishing the distinction between manual and theoretical labor, exposing legal theory to its contested grounds and its solidarity with rioting workers. But this call echoes through the text without grounding itself in or as writing. Is it not the case, although it suggests otherwise as an unmarked rhetorical question, that threatening the state by sabotaging the means and modes of production causes the state to "concede" the right to strike, and that therefore the right to strike is only the political representation of the originary revolutionary violence that founded the state?

The concession of the right to strike betrays the state's fear of and not its control over its subjects. This em dash afformatively manifests the originary revolutionary violence that parliamentary democracy weakens through representation; it cuts through the illusion of the state's mastery (as if it had the right to bestow the right to strike instead of being the effect of that revolutionary force that it belatedly tries to control and that thus ironically diminishes its own authority). It exposes the ungroundedness of political determinations that arrive after the fact to establish the state's monopoly on legitimate violence. The conceit of legal theory is that its real domains of contestation are the barricaded street and the factory set ablaze by intransigent refusals to compromise. This em dash politicizes Derrida's claim that constative utterances always depend on the prior existence of performances of law imposition.[52] Whatever ends up being determined as "the case" testifies to a consolidation of language; this first emerges through the distinction between speech and writing.

The second em dash in paragraph thirteen marks the auto-deconstruction of the revolutionary general strike. In this passage Benjamin follows Sorel's attempt to distinguish between, on the one hand, a political strike that posits certain ends that would end the strike if they were to be realized, and, on the other hand, a general proletarian strike that posits no end other than itself. After neatly distinguishing between these two political events (the former reformist and the latter revolutionary), Benjamin allows the following slip: "With thought-provoking arguments Sorel has explained the extent to which such a rigorous conception of the general strike is liable to diminish the deployment of actual violence in revolutions."[53] This general rhetorical excess should not be dismissed given the tightly woven juridical text that it interrupts. The em dash alerts the reader to the irony undermining the argument.

52 Derrida, 'Force of Law', 27.
53 Benjamin, 'Toward the Critique of Violence', 53.

Sorel's argument is "very ingenious" insofar as it makes the paradoxical claim that the proletarian general strike is in the interest of the state, because it suppresses what would otherwise be a more violent outburst. The proletarian general strike that sets for itself the singular task of the destruction of state power ("die einzige Aufgabe der Vernichtung der Staatsgewalt")[54] is pitched as being in the interest of the state, because it does not cause but rather diminishes the unfolding of "actual" violence in revolutions ("die Entfaltung eigentlicher Gewalt in den Revolutionen)."[55] The em dash can be read as opening and closing the gap between the ingenious and the absurd and the gap between theoretical and actual violence.

The (non-)extortionary nature of the general proletarian strike appears as a bargaining chip mediating the relationship between the state and its subjects. Only the em dash does justice to the (im)possibility of absolute rupture by positing nothing other than language's interruption: the general proletarian strike calls for an end to mediation and thus for language that ends itself. The refusal to be absorbed by the symbolic (structure of the state) refuses itself and ironically reappears as the last word of a fatal ultimatum. The em dash marks the auto-deconstruction of the theory of revolutionary violence through its symbolic subsumption; it does not survive this paradox.

Revolutionary violence breaks (through) its own language as a pure manifestation of mediation that transgresses its own terms. Whereas traditional Marxism is a means to the end of revolution, this suicidal operation can be glimpsed in these markings that either connect or separate theory and praxis. While *The Communist Manifesto* famously interpolates its readers directly in the informal second person plural (exhorting workers of the world to unite in its famous conclusion), 'Toward the Critique of Violence' mobilizes an imperative interrogation coming from and directed toward the past as a politics of pure means that serves neither the goal of revolution nor any predetermined end. Where traditional Marxist theory justifies itself by positioning thinking and writing as useful in pursuit of the end point of revolution, 'Toward the Critique of Violence' dematerializes "actual" revolutionary violence by turning it into theoretical leverage to blackmail the state into recognizing the revolution that will abolish it as its own interest. Whereas the Marxist conception of history concludes in the dictatorship of the proletariat and the subsequent gradual wearing away of the state, 'Toward the Critique of Violence' mobilizes an interminable and anti-teleological mode of theory that either refuses or destroys every end.

54 Benjamin, 'Zur Kritik der Gewalt', 194.
55 Benjamin, 'Zur Kritik der Gewalt', 195.

3. "The Final Sequence"

Derrida reads 'Toward the Critique of Violence' as a ghost story. He calls us repeatedly to return to that which in Benjamin's text survives its suicide:

> Let us return to the thing itself, to the ghost, for this text is a ghost story. We can no more avoid ghost and ruin than we can elude the question of the rhetorical status of this textual event. To what figures does it turn for its exposition, for its internal explosion or its implosion?[56]

In short, Benjamin's text turns to God for its explosion or implosion. God names the vest that Benjamin detonates within the strictures of the law. Before invoking a theological vocabulary to situate the critique above legal jurisdiction, he first lays bare the intellectual desperation that forces him to do so. He writes, as if randomly, of

> the strange and initially discouraging experience of the ultimate undecidability [Unentscheidbarkeit] of all legal problems (which in its hopelessness can perhaps be compared only with the impossibility of deciding conclusively on what is "correct" or "false" in evolving languages).[57]

This passage interrupts the argumentation to make explicit room for (juridical) pathos. Towards the end of his torturously undecidable text, Benjamin acknowledges the discouraging hopelessness that it (like all rotten, legal language) can engender. Before the climactic theological finale, Benjamin seems to turn in this passage to (the humanity of) his reader as if to reassure them that it gets better: undecidability is only discouraging *initially*. One must habituate oneself to the rot of the law and the war at the heart of any symbolic order.[58] This reassuring note cautions the reader against what he elsewhere calls left melancholia in a text written in 1930, seventeen years after the political suicides of his dear friends and comrades Christoph Friedrich Heinle and Friederike Seligson in 1914. This brief affective turn de-ontologizes language: to make sense of the undecidability of all legal problems, Benjamin can only entertain the possibility of an analogy with evolving languages ("*werdende*

56 Derrida, 'Force of Law', 44.

57 Benjamin, 'Toward the Critique of Violence', 54.

58 Derrida repeatedly embeds his text with the Greek root of the word polemic ("polemos"): "If there is something of strike and the right to strike in every interpretation, there is also war and *polemos*" (Derrida, 'Force of Law', 39).

Sprachen" in the German: languages that are not in the manner of being but rather become, evolve, and change) – "evolving languages" might exist, if only to help stabilize the unthinkable undecidability of all legal problems.[59]

At this moment God enters the scene as a *Deus ex machina* saving the possibility of decision and language's being: "Reason, after all, never decides on the justification of means and the justice of ends; rather, fateful violence decides on the former, while God decides on the latter."[60] The first appearance of this monotheistic God fills the void of the ultimate undecidability of any end and the impossibility of justice. Like fate he appears only after the fact to retrospectively determine the grounds of decision. His mythic function is to mark the limits of the mortal world beyond which thought is impossible. The distinction between mythic and divine violence is undermined before it is even introduced: the first manifestation of the existence of the monotheistic God of divine violence marks the boundary between the undecidable becoming of languages and the symbolic death of their being. The monotheistic God arrives on the scene as the dead myth of an end to justice, which is exactly as unthinkable as an end to language. His arrival guarantees only the absolute limits of language and thought.

An urgent spirit of decision characterizes the final confrontation between mythic and divine violence. Mythic violence, exemplified in Niobe's punishment for comparing herself to Leto, confirms the need to annihilate the legal violence that can always manifest the authority of the gods by establishing new laws after they have been violated, making subjects responsible for the punishments and guilt inflicted upon them. What previously was only a "vague intimation of [law's] problematic character" has become a certainty concerning the perniciousness of its historical function, the annihilation of which thus becomes a task.[61] It is at the moment [*gerade*] of the manifestation of the gods that a question returns again for the last time: "Precisely this task introduces once again and for the last time the question of a pure, immediate form of violence that might be capable of putting a halt to mythic violence."[62] ("Gerade diese Aufgabe legt in letzter Instanz noch einmal die Frage nach einer reiner unmittelbaren Gewalt vor, welche die mythischen Einhalt zu gebieten vermöchte.)"[63]

Particular attention should be paid to Benjamin's emphasis on the time and space of the text: far from an opening to a purer sphere, we now ("*gerade*") find that the task of destruction ultimately poses a question that has been posed before. Although it has been posed before, it has apparently

59 Benjamin, 'Toward the Critique of Violence', 55.
60 Ibid., 54.
61 Ibid., 57.
62 Ibid.
63 Benjamin, 'Zur Kritik der Gewalt', 199.

never been posed like this. It is a recurring question and Benjamin avers that this is its last or ultimate instance. The recurrence of this question recalls the difference between the titular definite article (*the* critique of violence) and the indefinite article in the first sentence of the text (*a* critique of violence). The pathos of Benjamin's text corresponds to the urgent temporality that calls for immediacy.

Instead of a narrative progression from mythic to divine violence, Benjamin binds the two indissociably in a mutually (de)constructing constellation. Whereas all other iterations of this call for the destruction of the law are grouped together as an eternal return of the same by Benjamin's claim that the mythic violence that separated the Greeks from their gods is identical with all forms of legal violence, a confrontation is about to take place that will destroy these and all determinations: "Just as God is opposed to myth in all spheres, so divine violence runs counter to mythic violence."[64] The translation of the verb "*entgegentreten*" as "oppose" in the new English translation neglects the figurative undecidability of this encounter. It could be a meeting, a facing, or a face-off; these two faces could stand in opposition or they could be two sides of the same coin. This sentence could be otherwise translated as: "Just as in all spheres God faces myth, so the mythic faces divine violence." These two encounters (*entgegentreten*) are only belatedly established as such by means of a double deferral: the initially absent implied verb (*entgegentreten*) that relates myth and God first appears in the second clause as a separable verb that only manifests itself at the very end of the sentence. In its first instance ("Wie in allen Bereichen dem Mythos Gott") there is no boundary between these two words, only an empty space.[65] Divine violence appears and disappears in this void. It appears as a ruin; it ruins itself in its ex-position.[66]

This tête-à-tête between law and justice is figured by shifters (pronouns that could refer to one or the other) in the original German: "Und zwar bezeichnet sie zu ihr der Gegensatz in allen Stücken."[67] The English transla-

64 Benjamin, 'Toward the Critique of Violence', 57.

65 Benjamin, 'Zur Kritik der Gewalt', 199.

66 In a diary entry from May 20, 1934, Werner Kraft cites a conversation he had with Benjamin in which the latter disavowed the "theory" of divine violence: "In substance, [Benjamin] argues today the following position: just law [*gerechtes Recht*] is what benefits the oppressed in class conflict. – Class conflict is the center of all philosophical questions, even the highest. — What he earlier called divine ('pending' [*waltende*]) violence was an empty spot, a limit concept, a regulative idea. Today, he knows it *is* class conflict." Alberto Toscano, 'Preface to Sorel, Reflections *On Violence*', in Peter Fenves and Julia Ng, eds., *Toward the Critique of Violence: A Critical Edition* (Stanford: Stanford University Press, 2021), 200. My reading is an attempt to highlight here the repetition of the suicide of the critique of violence: divine violence kills itself again, (dis)appears in and as this empty spot.

67 Benjamin, 'Zur Kritik der Gewalt', 199. Derrida reproduces in his French: "A tous points de vue, dit-il, elle en est le contraire" (Derrida, 'Force de Loi', 123) and it is maintained in

tion reconstitutes a distinction that has collapsed: "Indeed, divine violence designates in all respects an antithesis to mythic violence."[68] There are no clear designations separating mythic from divine violence in the original German text: from all points of view, it is its opposite. In this mutually (de)constructing constellation, these terms can only exist in relation to each other. Notice further how the definition of divine violence is given entirely as an if-then (*ist-so*) statement:

> If mythic violence is law-positing, divine violence is law-annihilating; if the former establishes boundaries, the latter boundlessly annihilates them; if mythic violence inculpates [*verschuldend*] and expiates [*sühnend*] at the same time, divine violence de-expiates [*entsühnend*]; if the former threatens, the latter strikes; if the former is bloody, the latter is lethal in a bloodless manner.[69]

This moment of the text is a breakdown or a breakthrough. If earlier Benjamin declared that, "All violence as a means is either law-positing or law-preserving," the symbolic regime grounding that claim collapses in on itself in this passage.[70] Divine violence "kills itself" by destroying the boundaries that construct it; it is deposed by the terms that posit it. As Derrida writes, "[Benjamin] would like either to found it or conserve it but in all purity he can do neither. . . . Before your eyes a demonstration ruins the distinctions it proposes."[71]

How can one read a text that ruins itself? "For lack of time but not only time, I cannot claim to do it justice."[72] Despite itself and the appearances to which it gives rise, this suicidal text wills no end other than its own. Instead of positing itself, it (almost miraculously) deposes itself. It subjects the concepts that would make it legible to death, because they violate the absolute uniqueness of the singularity that is not "its" own as it cannot be generalized as the property of a subject. The text takes itself out of the universal exchange of the symbolic and the "life" of language in a kind of sovereign silence. A much longer analysis would be needed to exhaust the suicide that occurs not once but rather throughout the text at a micrological level that has escaped its storied reception history, which has tended toward abstraction or the application of functional theories.

---

the English translation: "From all points of view, he says, it is its opposite" (Derrida, 'Force of Law', 52).

68 Benjamin, 'Toward the Critique of Violence', 57.

69 Ibid., 57.

70 Ibid., 48.

71 Derrida, 'Force of Law', 43.

72 Ibid., 51.

Only the disfiguring figure of suicide can begin to do justice to the text's self-canceling operation. This operation cannot be reduced to the opposition between literary irony and theoretical authority without reifying both concepts and the metaphysical opposition that separates them: if, as Shoshana Felman writes, irony consists precisely "in dragging authority as such into a scene which it cannot master, of which it is *not aware* and which, for that very reason, is the scene of its own self-destruction,"[73] the authority, power, and violence of 'Toward the Critique of Violence' consists precisely in dragging irony into a scene it cannot undermine, of which it is *not aware*, and which, for that very reason, is the scene of its own self-destruction. Irony cannot undermine the rotten legal languages that serve as the basis for authority, because they are deposed by their positing.[74]

73 Shoshana Felman, 'To Open the Question', (1977) 55/56 *Yale French Studies* 8.

74 Derrida underscores the double genitive in the phrase "threat of law": "it both comes from and threatens *droit*" (Derrida, 'Force of Law', 42).

11

WHAT DOES A WEAK LANGUAGE SAY ABOUT LAW? DERRIDA AND HAMACHER ON LAW'S LANGUAGE

Juntao Lin

*****

In unfolding the force of law as a form of *différance*, Derrida presents an intriguing paradox: the "force" of law, in a truly deconstructive way, reveals a scene in which force and weakness exchange places:

> For me, it is always a question of differential force, of difference as difference of force, of force as *différance (differance* is a force *différée-différante),* of the relation between force and form, between force and signification, performative force, of affirmation by signature, but also and especially of all the paradoxical situations in which the greatest force and the greatest weakness strangely enough exchange places. And that is the whole history.[1]

Derrida does not, however, fully elaborate on this exchange between force and weakness. We are instead left without the specific conditions under which this exchange occurs, told only that this paradox, one that troubles both law and justice, constitutes "the whole history." Why, then, is it not "force" itself, but rather *le caractère différentiel de la force*, marked by strange exchange and paradox, that defines history? If the word "force" is "indispensable," how does it make Derrida "uncomfortable,"[2] as he goes on to say? Is

1 Jacques Derrida, 'Force of Law: The "Mystical Foundation of Authority"', in Drucilla Cornell, Michel Rosenfeld, and David Gray Carlson, eds., *Deconstruction and the Possibility of Justice* (New York: Routledge, 1992), 7.
2 Ibid.

DOI: 10.4324/9781003589419-14

it because of the nature of force itself, or because of the very possibility that allows force to shift between forcefulness and weakness?

Central to this question is Derrida's claim in 'Force of Law' that "force" has become an increasingly suspect category. Attending to the idiom embedded in law's necessity – its "enforceability" (to enforce the law) – he reveals a logic where "there is no law without enforceability, and no applicability or enforceability of the law without force."[3] The "mystical foundation" of law, he claims, lies in its mode of legitimation: law authorizes itself through the force that sustains it, a self-preserving force grounded not in any substantive value of justice but in performative enactment. The foundation of law is nothing other than its own operation. In this sense, force is not merely an attribute of law but its very language: it produces the illusion of justice merely through self-assertion. And this, according to Derrida, is the only ascertainable mode of law's existence. As a result, justice, ostensibly law's end, takes on an uncanny cast; it seems forcibly bound to the operation of law through its own speaking, or through the act of being spoken. Outside of this speaking, justice is nowhere else to be found. The question of language (and idiom), as Derrida stresses, "will doubtless be at the heart" of his enquiry.

If law and justice stand in a simple relation of means and end, then law sustains itself by exercising the force of its enunciation, working as a means to the means. This, in turn, compels us to ask whether justice itself can be spoken, or articulated, at all. Another way to pose this question: Can justice be expected to speak for itself under any circumstance or condition? And if so, in what form? When Derrida takes note of Montaigne's statement, "notre droit même a, dit-on, des fictions légitimes sur lesquelles il fonde la vérité de sa justice" ("even our law, it is said, has legitimate fictions on which it founds the truth of its justice"),[4] he is, in fact, reflecting on how "legitimate fictions" function as a linguistic structure that is inherently paradoxical simply because, on the one hand, law is affirmative, demanding legislative, performative action, and sustained by force; on the other hand, it is unstable, fictional, non-substantial, or, in a sense, *weak*.

In the following discussion, I seek further to explore the idea of "weak language" under the auspices of Derrida's aporia of force. "Weak language" is not necessarily the direct opposite of what might be called "strong language." More specifically, the very "force" of law inherently contains the possibility of a "weak language," which plays a crucial role in determining its undecidability, in the incompleteness of deconstruction, and, more importantly, in the constitutive premise of violence itself. As Derrida puts it, in those moments of deep paradox and indecision, while the greatest force and

3 Ibid., 6.
4 Ibid., 12.

the greatest weakness undergo a strange exchange, the task is not to precisely measure the accumulation of force, identify specific conditions, or pinpoint the exact moment when such an exchange happens. Rather, it is to recognize this transformation itself as implicating an act of deconstruction and to acknowledge that justice can only be articulated through this very process of deconstruction. That is to say, for justice to exist, this exchange *must* take place. Later, we will also see that this exchange operates in a way similar to translation – translation still happens even where the semantic or lexical situation seems untranslatable, in terms where Derrida presents his classic aporetic formulation.

I introduce Werner Hamacher's theory of the afformative to help clarify how language, in a non-performative way, gives rise to the exchange that Derrida notices. In many ways, Hamacher and Derrida share a similar premise while he takes a reorientation. By introducing Walter Benjamin's concept of the "general strike" as a scene in which justice may arrive, Hamacher pushes the discussion further and clarifies that language becomes "pure" only through its inevitable failure, its reliance on impurity. In doing so, he disentangles language from the coercion of legal acts, ensuring its complete detachment from speech acts. Following this logic, we come to see that in the unsettling exchange between force and weakness described by Derrida, this exchange stages a moment of translation – a fleeting, fragile, unrealized possibility. It exposes a purity of language as force, a purity so absolute that it reaches an extreme, a "weakness weaker than weakness itself."

1/

Starting by reading Pascal, Derrida seeks to show that as a form of force, law is always engaged in interpreting itself, and in doing so, it attempts to name, as Pascal announces: "At the beginning of justice there was logos, speech, or language."[5] This statement declares the beginning of a time in which the legal framework establishes itself. Derrida calls this interpretative force "a performative force", which is the cause of the very emergence of justice and law. Since violence is the only way in which law manifests at its emergence, its enforcement is subject to performative self-justification. Law constantly demands the self-assertation of its legitimacy, securing nothing beyond its own existence. This process of interpretation cannot stop because the entire structure depends on this fragile premise. Hence, Derrida acknowledges the limit of the discourse of law is "in itself, in its performative power itself."[6] While Derrida's broader critique of the theory of performativity and speech acts will be set aside for

5 Ibid., 10.
6 Ibid., 13–14.

now, it is worth noting that performativity nonetheless governs legal language itself. Law, he argues, only *appears* legitimate because it is governed by performativity. Its force and its weakness are both sustained by this mysterious authority, yet law itself lacks any intrinsic legitimacy. Before any interpretative, and therefore performative addressing, "no justice and no earlier and previously founding law, no preexisting foundation, could, by definition, guarantee or contradict or invalidate."[7] If law cannot enforce its own force, it collapses. This paradox explains law's "mystique", that is its authority arises not from strength, but from the precariousness of its self-justifying performance.

Derrida brings this paradox into view through Montaigne's notion of "legitimate fiction." For Montaigne, "legitimate fiction" functions as a necessary supplement for establishing justice, just as "law" (*droit*) is a historical or positive artifice of fiction that supplements the deficiency in nature while the natural law is lacking.[8] According to Derrida, it is fair to say that fiction does not so much supplement legitimacy but *becomes* legitimacy. Justice, in this view, moreover, relies on fiction as its sole foundation of legitimacy. This statement brings us close to understanding the weakness of legal language (or language of law). Because it is performative, legal language can only endure itself by repeating that performance. When the limit of law coincides with nothing but its own operation, law reveals itself a divided structure. It seems strong insofar as it *must* compel its own performance and carries it out forcefully; it is also weak insofar as that compulsion is unavoidable and its authority depends on constantly renewing the force it asserts.

This paradoxical contention is why Derrida says the following: "[S]ince the origin of authority, the foundation or ground, the position of the law cannot by definition rest on anything but themselves, they are themselves a violence without ground."[9] Derrida thus demonstrates the positionality of a law that lacks an external referent or object. At the moment of its inception, law has recourse to no foundational basis, nor external justification, to secure its legitimacy. Instead, it can only affirm itself, projecting its own authority back onto itself, creating a self-referential loop that Derrida believes is both "mythical" and "weak". Such a loop, severed from something like external reality, traps law in a cycle where its authority depends on the very instability it seeks to suppress.

Still, Derrida does not posit a complete separation between law and justice. Instead, he identifies a fragile, non-instrumental relation whereby the two remain linked without being reduced to a means-end logic. This connection, however, is still predictably fraught with tension, for if "weakness" defines

7 Ibid., 13.
8 Ibid., 12.
9 Ibid., 14.

law's structure, how does justice emerge? If we reject the violence of injustice, we simultaneously reject the violence of justice as well. What remains is an un-transformable, stalled, and static weakness that carries a general ethical significance but obscures justice's attainability. Here, Derrida is not simply advocating for the removal of violence or weakness. Rather, he locates the possibility of justice within this instability, framing justice as an unavoidable *aporia*: an encounter with the "impossible." Thus justice, for Derrida, is not a fixed reality but an *experience*. It is fleeting, seemingly perceptible, yet absolutely incapable of being fully recorded, reproduced, or reducible to legal calculation. While law depends on its performativity, its calculability, and its stability within rational frameworks, justice – by contrast – is what Derrida, drawing on Levinas, describes as the infinity of otherness.[10] The description of justice as "undecidability" and the "impossibility" of experience aligns with Derrida's account of the ethical experience of aporia, as it is stated in this passage:

> for a decision to be just and responsible, it must, in its proper moment if there is one, be both regulated and without regulation: it must conserve the law and also destroy it or suspend it enough to have to reinvent it in each case, re-justify it, at least reinvent it in the reaffirmation and the new and free confirmation of its principle. Each case is other, each decision is different and requires an absolutely unique interpretation, which no existing, coded rule can or ought to guarantee absolutely.[11]

Justice cannot be enforced, yet, it demands enforcement. Language cannot fully articulate justice, yet, it must still speak of it. The position of justice is precisely the position of aporia. This comprises the radically different account of language that Derrida suggests. Derrida tries to say that if a language concerning justice truly exists, it does not relate to external values, including justice itself, in a means-to-an-end manner. In other words, justice is never simply something external; it is not a corresponding entity that stands outside the law. At the same time, it is also clear that justice is not something lodged inside the law, as if it were a hidden core or the ultimate secret to be defended. Then where is justice? For Derrida, the striking point is that justice can come into view only when we admit that neither law nor any speech of justice is unshakable – that is, only when we acknowledge law's deconstructiblity does the possibility of justice arise. Here Derrida not only deconstructs the law, reassuring us that "law is deconstructible is not bad news,"[12] in order to rethink its relationship with justice; he also goes further

10 Ibid., 22.
11 Ibid., 23.
12 Ibid., 14.

by treating justice as something without a fixed consequence, or more simply, without a recognizable end.

Since an end no longer exists externally, its limit is itself. The language of justice has no external ground to depend on. When Derrida argues that justice is the one thing that cannot be deconstructed, then, as a paradoxical outcome, what he really means is that justice can never say anything about itself. This is why he states, "(t)here is a silence walled up," because "silence is not exterior to language."[13] Silence is not the absence of language; it is built into it, thereby forming its very foundation. In this register, silence functions as a kind of *weak language*. It cannot speak about its own origin, yet it conditions the possibility of speaking justice at all. Derrida sees deconstruction as addressing precisely this "foundation without a foundation," which we might consider as a language of irreducible weakness that continuously negotiates both its right to exist and the legitimacy of its own undoing in and through silence. The moment that unsettles Derrida, the exchange between the greatest force and the greatest weakness, is a moment when silence strains to speak about justice.

It can be said that the exchange of force and weakness mirrors the logic of translation. In its apparent term, force seeks self-maintenance by expelling weakness, just like speech would exclude silence. However, as in the previous discussion, in addressing itself to the task of preserving its own authority, force cannot but be aware that weakness is not an external remainder but a condition of its possibility, much as speech cannot but be aware that silence is internal to language. When force attempts to purge weakness, it immediately breaks down. Due to its lack of enforceability, weakness cannot naturally constitute the law itself; rather, it resembles something the law is meant to protect. Weakness is distanced from those who enforce and judge the law, standing instead as the subject of enforcement and judgment; indeed, it is more of the object upon which force is exerted. However, the paradox lies precisely in the fact that the oppression of weakness exposes a fundamental flaw within force itself, thereby causing it to confront its own limits in the very act of enforcement. The presence of "weakness" triggers what Derrida remarks but does not fully elaborate as a mechanism of exchange. This exchange can be understood, if we view it literally, as an act of translation: something is exchanged and translated between force and weakness. From what he indicates, it is not simply a matter of justice being translated into injustice, or vice versa. Instead, what is being translated is force, which shifts into something that is no longer comprehensible as merely force itself. Rather than being the opposite of force, "weakness" represents a non-force, a condition that opens up legal language to a fundamental form of translation – a

13 Ibid.

dynamic structure rather than a fixed opposition. As this exchange and translation take place, the concepts of justice and injustice no longer hold their stability through mere opposition, while at the same time, they essentially allow justice to be *experienced* rather than codified.

This is where Werner Hamacher's account of the afformative provides a more decisive vocabulary to extend Derrida's thread of thought. Written around the same historical period, Hamacher's essay is not solely a supplement to Derrida's logic of law and justice, but runs alongside the mechanisms of exchange by troubling the linguistic aberration on the path toward a "homogeneous, empty history." Hamacher distinguishes "weak language" from what we might call the language of the weak, or a social position that lacks power. The term refers to a language that refuses its own manifestation – a language of "afformativity." Silence, accordingly, synchronizes in a "missed time" and points toward pure language and pure violence.

2/

Historically, both Derrida and Hamacher's reflections on the language of law emerge at a moment of transition. The renewed attention and unease that Benjamin's *Critique of Violence* provoked in the late 1980s – at the so-called end of the Cold War – was far from incidental. Benjamin's political-theological turn, represented by *Critique of Violence* (1921) and the fragment *Capitalism as Religion* (1921), gained renewed relevance since the 1980s amid global debates about the "end of history" qua homogenization of power. While this is not the place to delve into historical entanglements, it is still worth noticing how Derrida's critique of justice's "undecidability" resonated with the suspended political realities: sovereignty, democracy, and justice were in flux. It was a moment when the voice of the powerful was becoming homogenized, universalized, and unassailable. It was arguably within this climate of uncertainty that Derrida urged an ethical engagement with the aporia that troubles justice.

Werner Hamacher takes up the problem of justice's inexpressibility in his essay 'Afformative, Strike' (1990), a text that turns on Benjamin's figure of the "proletarian general strike".[14] For Benjamin, the proletarian general strike names a "pure means" that not just suspends but deposes law without grounding a new legal order. Hamacher later develops into the concept of the *afformative*, one that interrupts juridical force without instituting another act of legislation. In this sense, the afformative radicalizes the ever latent potential for

14 For a more detailed exploration of how *Critique of Violence* is connected to Benjamin's 1920s discussions on pure language, world history, guilt, and capitalism as religion, see the introduction to Peter Fenves and Julia Ng (eds.), *Toward the Critique of Violence: A Critical Edition* (Stanford, CA: Stanford University Press, 2021).

justice's "weak language". Read in this light, Hamacher's move also resonates with the Benjamin's famous notion of the "weak messianic power". Weakness does not name a deficiency to be overcome; it names the withdrawal of force as such, and the opening that this withdrawal makes possible. What appears as absence is therefore not passivity or impotence. It is what allows history to be transformed and what Benjamin calls "sacred time" to be restored.

By now, Derrida's critique of performativity has brought us to realize law's mythical foundation is nothing but its own performance. Legal authority must therefore be reiterated again and again through its own self-referential act, and this very need for reiteration makes the performativity of legal language unfortunately an empty form of its weakness as much as a source of force. Hamacher presses this problem further by raising a deepened critique of what makes any positing of authority possible. In his essay, he draws on the tradition of speech-act theory associated with J.L. Austin, but he also insists that the crucial question precedes Austin's taxonomy of performatives. It concerns the act by which something is instituted in the first place, self-maintained, yet structurally flawed, what he calls *positing* (*Setzung*). The term, originally from Immanuel Kant's definition of the act that posits existence, becomes a central concept here. According to Hamacher, Kant preestablishes an absolute subject of reason for Being, a subject that creates the self-authorization of a sort of autonomy. Hamacher writes:

> Existence [*Dasein*] is the absolute position of a thing. . . . The concept of position or positing [*Position oder Setzung*] is completely simple and is the same as the concept of Being. . . . If a thing is considered posited in and for itself, then Being [*Sein*] is as much as existence [*Dasein*].[15]

On this account, positing is supposed to refer only to itself (as it should not depend on anything external in order to be what it is) and should therefore be unconditioned.

Hamacher's objection is that this self-grounding positing cannot be made coherent. If positing must precede everything because it is the precondition for any act of positing, then it must already be *posited* before it can occur. An "original" positing would have to precede any act of positing, which means it would already differ from the *Being* it is meant simply to affirm.

Kant's framework cannot accommodate such a logic because, once one posits, positing becomes conditional – it must depend on something other

15 Immanuel Kant, *The One Possible Basis for a Demonstration of the Existence of God*, trans. by Gordon Treash (New York: Abaris, 1979), quoted in Werner Hamacher, *Premises: Essays on Philosophy and Literature from Kant to Celan*, trans. by Peter Fenves (Stanford, CA: Stanford University Press, 1999), 11–12.

than itself, something that exceeds it, in order to be. Otherwise, every act of positing would amount to the same positing, always belated rather than "absolute" in Kant's sense. Hence Hamacher's conclusion that "if a positing can be a positing only by allowing something other than itself – other than its thetic Being – then an original positing cannot be performed."[16]

We will return to the problem of whether a truly "unconditioned positing" exists. For now, it is enough to note that Hamacher reads Kant's position as making reason's universal and absolute *Setzung* of self-operativity the basis on which later accounts of linguistic performativity come to rest. Hamacher's critique of positing then extends to Benjamin's distinction of the two forms of violence in *Critique of Violence*. As Benjamin emphasizes in that text, *lawmaking violence* cannot, by itself, create legitimacy; legitimacy, in fact, originates from *law-preserving* violence.[17] Hamacher reformulates this in terms of positing. Since positing is never truly transcendental or unconditional, *lawmaking* (*Rechtsetzender*) violence cannot simply establish a "positive" order once and for all. Its "positivity" depends on being reiterated, and that reiteration takes the form of a performative maintenance that requires law-preserving violence to sustain it. Seen from this angle, law-preserving violence, as a form of "passive" violence, turns violence into a purely instrumental force, thereby stripping positing of its authoritative power. As one can recognize easily, "lawmaking violence" and "law-preserving violence" do not name two independent forces; they are two sides of the same structure, each defining and endorsing the other. The consequence is that the operation of "law-preserving violence" comes at the cost of depleting the very foundation of lawmaking violence, thereby exposing the groundlessness of violence itself. Hamacher identifies this process of self-exposure and the continuous, repetitive performance of language as "the dialectic of positing and decay" – or, more precisely, a dialectic of performance. He argues that the decay of positing, caused by the maintenance of legal violence, is equivalent to the decline of history itself.[18]

It is precisely this primordial positing of language that instrumentalizes violence, thereby turning (legal) language into a tool of enforced violence. Hamacher picks up on Benjamin's argument about "pure language" by emphasizing that language is not determined by external purposes but functions as a form of "pure mediacy". Following this logic, the possibility of breaking

16 Hamacher, *Premises*, 14.

17 By distinguishing between lawmaking violence and law-preserving violence, Benjamin famously calls law's authority into question. He argues that law-preserving violence operates like 'fate' (*Schicksal*) in its hold over human life, securing its authority precisely by repeatedly enacting and maintaining itself. See Fenves and Ng, *Toward the Critique of Violence*, 46–47.

18 Werner Hamacher, 'Afformative, Strike', trans. by Dana Hollander (1991) 13:4 *Cardozo Law Review* 1138.

free from this cycle of positing and performance is, to use Benjamin's own term, "deposing" (*Entsetzung*). Hamacher explains that deposing is not a predetermined or instrumentalized form of violence. Rather, it marks a break from the circulation of what is determined and posited by law. In this sense, "deposing could not be the means to an end, yet it would be nothing but means."[19]

Reconfiguring the formulation of Benjamin's account of pure language and pure violence, Hamacher argues that the "proletarian general strike", which is given a hopeful significance in *Critique of Violence*, serves as the very paradigm of this irreducible pure language – pure violence. As a pure means, it does not seek the fulfillment of any predetermined political goal. Rather, it aims to completely paralyze all visible and invisible forms of power. Pure violence possesses an absolute untranslatability, fundamentally opposing any form of representation and being non-performative. Based on that articulated premise, Hamacher introduces the idea of "afformative". The effort to clarify this concept is accomplished through a lengthy footnote in which Hamacher summarizes the "afformative" (and the language of the afformative) as follows: a) "Afformative" (afformation, afformance) is not the opposite of, external to, a subcategory of, or negation of the performative (performation, performance), but its indisputable precondition. "Afformatives" do not belong to the realm of acts or positions, but they influence acts indirectly, manifesting as interruptions, pauses, and ellipses; b) "afformative" is not *aformative*, but formless, incapable of being determined or presented by form. In that regard, it "deposes" not as the negation of positing, but as precondition for all positing. Deposing functions as an athetical, immediate mediation that transcends conventional laws or logic; c) the afformative stratum of language merely "lets" but never posits; however, this letting is neither external to nor opposed to positing but is instead dependent on it. It adheres to non-purity solely as a form of purity. "It cannot help becoming what it is not and will always have become what it never was."[20]

For Derrida, the performativity of law determines its sheer existence. Law must perform itself, yet at its core, there is a silence – an emptiness that ultimately cannot, by definition, serve as a foundation. This silence is weak enough to preserve the possibility of exchange between force and weakness within legal language. Hamacher makes the point even more explicit: silence inherent in language signals the potential interruption of the speech act. In contrast to the performativity of language, Hamacher identifies a form of language whose defining characteristic is pure mediacy,

19 Hamacher, 'Afformative, Strike', 1140.
20 Ibid., n. 12, 1140.

and which, as what Benjamin calls "pure language," has the capacity to interrupt language itself.[21] This distinction is crucial because, in Hamacher/Benjamin's theory of language, pure language and pure violence stand as equivalents. Both of these terms share a singular function, in Benjamin's language: impartability (*Mitteilbarkeit*).[22] Whether in language or in violence, it is not the content or purpose they contain, but rather this "possibility of imparting" as a pure means independent of any external condition that constitutes the possibility of resistance through pure language or pure violence.

Through his exploration of the connection between Benjamin's general strike and afformative language, Hamacher effectively seeks to juxtapose a series of cryptically interrelated concepts from Benjamin's writings across the 1920s and 1940s – namely, pure language, pure violence, and, ultimately, the elusive figure of the "weak Messiah." One can see that Hamacher is particularly attuned to the dialectical interdependence between weakness and force within the idea of the "weak Messiah":

> The deepest distortion of the possibility of messianic time, however, the distortion of the messianic ability itself, which Benjamin calls messianic "force", lies in its being exposed to the inability and thus the impossibility of perceiving itself, acting and fulfilling itself as the possibility, ability and power.[23]

Force and weakness are not in a simple opposition but exist in a dialectical, aporetic relationship. In an extreme situation, force is compelled to expose itself to inability, which in turn generates "the force of weakness." This force is without substance, without power, arising precisely from the absence of force itself. For that, Hamacher gives a very clear formulation of how this weak Messiah works:

> It is a "weak" force because it is the force of weakness, because it is force out of the missing of force. This weakness is not in contrast to force, but

21 Hamacher offers a precise distillation of Benjamin's notion of language as 'pure means': "[But] just as mediacy is the condition of possibility of instrumental language, the language of pure mediacy and pure impartability is also its interruption" because "pure impartability is in itself heterogeneous and discontinuous." Hamacher, 'Afformative, Strike', 1141.

22 The concept of *Mitteilbarkeit* originates from Walter Benjamin's essay 'On Language as Such and on the Language of Man' (*Über Sprache überhaupt und über die Sprache des Menschen*). In English, it is typically translated as either impartability or communicability. See Werner Hamacher's note 13 in 'Afformative, Strike' for his explanation, as well as Samuel Weber's extended discussion in *Benjamin's -Abilities* (Cambridge, MA: Harvard University Press, 2008), 38–52.

23 Werner Hamacher, '"Now": Walter Benjamin on Historical Time', in Heidrun Friese, ed., *The Moment: Time and Rupture in Modern Thought* (Liverpool: Liverpool University Press, 2001), 191.

> lies in its centre. For that force cannot be messianic that rescues only itself; messianic is only the force that rescues even its own failing. A messiah is only he who rescues even the impossibility of a Messiah. He can only come in such a way that he might also not come, and come as someone other than the Messiah.[24]

Therefore, one must take note that the operation of weakness does not function as a preconditioned positing – that is, it does not emerge from an already visible or fully formed position. Instead, it exists "as something that which it is not yet and never will have been." Rather than being a position itself, Hamacher defines it as a "promise of a position."[25]

3/

For Derrida, the tension between the endless approach toward pure violence and the impossibility of reaching it is itself justice. Undoubtedly, this is a question of language – one that extends from Benjamin to both Derrida and Hamacher. The boundary of language exists only with itself; language is not a means directed toward an external end, but rather, its ultimate nature lies in its very origin. In this regard, Derrida employs a different term from "undecidability" in his analysis of Benjamin: *Aussichtslosigkeit*, which encapsulates meanings of "insolubility," "hopelessness," and "despair." This suggests that the attempt to articulate justice through language inevitably leads to a dead end. However, a language that appears to have no exit and no hope also severs the possibility of being extinguished by external forces – particularly the force of what Derrida identifies as *Schicksalhafte Gewalt,* or "fate-imposed violence." In doing so, despair that emerges from within itself paradoxically generates a hope that surpasses fate and, in turn, transcends violence itself.

The issue of language's "failure" is even more clearly articulated in Hamacher's critique: language succeeds only in its failure. Through his examination of the afformative at its most radical level, Hamacher rescues language from the domain of representational function. For him, rather than asking what pure violence is, one should turn to the dimension of "what it has to be." Pure violence (alongside pure language) never succeeds, never appears, yet, it also never disappears as a promise. Afformative language is precisely such a thing – so pure that it is reduced to nothing but its own "has to be," and it is not even itself: "As the sheer possibility of language as such, the afformative cannot help but preserve itself in the diversity of performatives. It cannot help becoming what it is not and will always have become what it

24 Ibid.
25 Hamacher, *Premises*, 14.

never was."[26] Put another way, the weakness of language cannot but express itself through becoming something else, even risking becoming "force" in doing so. It is not the act of becoming other that is of primary significance. Rather, what is crucial is that, in order to avert its own disappearance, language must undergo a transformation into something other than itself. It must become other in order to be itself. Although the failure and collapse of language emerge precisely in its movement away from being itself, this movement marks not only the failure of language but also the failure of the world of performative force, the world outside of language. Only language can permit the emergence of a new world and a new time through its own failure. While afformative language, weak language, the language of despair, and the language of failure may be understood as distinct articulations of a singular aporetic structure of language, it is with this language that justice is promised – precisely because it is never positioned.

To conclude more explicitly: the very language that "must fail" is a language "weaker than weakness itself." Its failure is more probable than that of any other way, always appearing as the one that has "failed more." What it anticipates is not the realization of justice in an already determined way, but rather in an "undecidable" way: it creates a space that allows for exchange – or more concisely, for translation. Since it is so weak that it is not even itself, its force of weakness holds the potential to become anything else. It exists in its purest form precisely through all impure forms.

26 Hamacher, 'Afformative, Strike', 1140.

12

APRÈS LA LOI

Kafka, Benjamin, Derrida

Dominik Zechner

Every relation to the law, however evident it seems, is obscured by a different kind of law that constitutively prohibits all relation. To the extent that the law relies on language as the horizon of its presentation, a linguistic foundation precedes and enables all legal positings. This primordial linguistic condition, as inexhaustible as ever withdrawing, essentially *permits* legal structures but resists representation and direct reference. The law's pre-positional and prohibitive foundation is self-withholding and, paradoxically, the ground that makes possible all positive law and lawful relations. The present chapter thus considers what it means to put oneself in relation to the law. It correlates and constellates three authors whose works have profoundly influenced, through theoretical and literary means, the modern discourse on the law and its bearing on the possibility of justice: Franz Kafka, Walter Benjamin, and Jacques Derrida. Kafka's 1915 parable 'Before the Law' ('Vor dem Gesetz') and Benjamin's 1921 essay 'Toward the Critique of Violence' ('Zur Kritik der Gewalt') offer decisive touchstones for Derrida's legal thinking, though I will suggest that an equally important, yet rather implicit, intertext is the 1919 story 'In the Penal Colony' ('In der Strafkolonie'), which Kafka penned while taking a break from composing his second novel, *The Trial* ('Der Proceß'). I argue that "In the Penal Colony" presents the post-positional counterpart to the pre-positional conception of the law's unrepresentability offered in 'Before the Law' (and, by extension, in *The Trial*). This post-positional legality, in turn, becomes readable in the context of Benjamin's concepts of law-positing and revolutionary violence, which Derrida explores in his seminal discourse of 1989, 'Force of Law' ('Force de Loi'). There, Derrida develops three "aporias of justice," whose literary representation in the penal colony is at once astounding and ironic.

DOI: 10.4324/9781003589419-15

Prohibitions

Jurisdiction is the saying of the law – in German: *Rechtsprechung*. Demarcating the perimeter of a court's authority, the term "jurisdiction" indicates a realm wherein binding juridical pronouncements are made. Its purview, therefore, extends within the field of language. The inscription, preservation, interpretation, and expression of the law, as well as any enunciation of a verdict, are linguistic events whose very nature calls for an interrogation of the relationship between language and the possibility of justice. If the law can realize itself only to the degree that it is *said* and if judgment is a function of the field of language, then the study of the law finds its fundamental condition in the study of linguistic elements and structures.[1] Another name for the fundamental inquiry into the realization of the law would therefore be *philology*.

The legal scholar as philologist is interested in the ways in which language is open to and therefore *allows* expressions and inscriptions of the law. This original allowance is not itself subject to a given jurisdiction but offers a linguistic opening for the sheer "saying" of laws. It is the very law that allows laws to be expressed. Before anything can be prohibited or permitted, the law itself, its inscription and articulation, must already be permitted through the very possibility of language. Language *gives* the law in that it gives permission for the expression of the law, which is to say that language functions as the law of the law. Its permissive law is constitutively withheld so that the "saying" of particular laws is made possible. Language's primordial permission is the law of laws, and as such, it is withheld and thus prohibited.

When considering the title of Kafka's most famous parable, the problem of a constitutive prohibition is operative on the prepositional level: "Vor dem Gesetz." Similar to the English "before," the German preposition *vor* comprises a spatial as well as a temporal register: one either stands before the law, or else one waits for the law to make an appearance. That Kafka's text serves both registers is by now a commonplace among readers, though the parable's topographical arrangement that confronts a man from the country with a doorkeeper at the gate of the law is responsible for a conspicuous privileging of spatial interpretations. In the case of the text's French reception, this is particularly obvious, as translators, when forced to decide between the

1 One might object that language itself is in need of intra-linguistic regulation whose principles are stipulated by its given grammar, but that would miss the point. The existence of grammar serves less as evidence for language's dependency on the law than to demonstrate language's ability to carry and realize lawful structures. In other words, it is possible to think language apart from grammar, or, which amounts to the same thing, a language antecedent to grammar. Paul de Man located this language in the figural: 'Tropes, *unlike grammar*, pertain primordially to language', *The Resistance to Theory* (Minneapolis and London: University of Minnesota Press, 2002), 15; my emphasis.

spatial *devant* and the temporal *avant*, have favored the former, turning 'Devant la loi' into a text that topographically distributes various agents and elements, thus eliding the temporal dimension of the law's realization.

Prepositionality bears on the question of the law to the precise extent that laws are posited – in German: *gesetzt*. Laws mark calculated positions within a given discourse whose thetic anchoring is upset by prepositional dynamics. It follows that, on the one hand, laws are subject to the positing power of language, and, on the other, that this power itself rests on quasi-structures that are not themselves posited but pre-positional. Hence, the preposition occupies the impossible position before all positions and is thus indicative of a language that *allows* the positing of laws, but which is not itself under the jurisdiction of such positing – which is to say that the preposition bears testimony to an *apositional* language, one that occurs through the sheer vacancy of positions, theses, positings, laws.

"Prepositions thus indicate," as Kristina Mendicino explains,

> the articulation of political dispositions that precede and exceed all positive law and that may be traced not only through manifest political declarations, but also through poetic compositions whose purport is no less political for the fact that they fall outside the more restrictive range of institutional and legal documents.[2]

In that prepositions "precede and exceed all positive law," they essentially occupy a linguistic dimension *before the law*. In this sense, there is something superfluous about Kafka's title, as it tautologically spells out a truth inherent in the preposition it so prominently deploys: the *before* of *vor* already means as much as "before the law." As a preposition, the *vor* is itself un-posited (*ungesetzt*); at the very least, it's not-yet-posited. *Vor* is thus the ultimate, if not the truest, of prepositions because it articulates on the level of expression the very antecedence it structurally manifests. If law is that which is posited (*Ge-setz*), *Vor dem Gesetz* contracts to a kind of *Vor-Gesetz*, a law before the law, whose possibility is not owed to any kind of lawful positing but instead hinges upon the existence of an apositional language whose occurrence anticipates and permits lawmaking positings.

Prepositional language therefore implies "the pre-language of every language and thus the language of language"; this language, however, is "no meta-language in which the rules of speech could be registered only to be displaced, but a proto- and para-language that speaks with every language

2 Kristina Mendicino, 'Introduction: Of Rights, in Other Directions—Romantic Prepositions', (2018) 133:5 *Modern Language Notes* 1143–1152, 1147.

as a silent reservation against speaking, as the unspeaking denial of speech."[3] If *Vor dem Gesetz* evokes an antecedence to that which is discursively posited, it also eludes everything that can positively be stated, defined, specified, and avowed, thus indicating a pre-language or *Vor-Sprache*, whose expression remains inexpressible and whose inexpressibility accompanies all that is posited as silent reservation. Every linguistic position is thus haunted by the prepositionality that made it possible.

Mendicino emphasizes that the tension between prepositional speech and positive law is particularly tangible in poetic compositions, perhaps because the language of literature is perched on the very threshold between proto- and posited discourse. According to Julia Kristeva, it's the eternal function of poetry "to introduce through the symbolic that which works on, moves through, threatens it."[4] The name she offers for this threat is the semiotic *chora*, a nonspatial space where linguistic drives pulsate before condensing themselves into discrete linguistic elements that owe their identity to acts of positing. "The *chora*," Kristeva explains,

> is not yet a position that represents something for someone (i.e., it is not a sign); nor is it a *position* that represents someone for another position (i.e., it is not yet a signifier either); it is, however, generated in order to attain to this signifying position [*mais elle s'engendre en vue d'une telle position signifiante*].[5]

The French *en vue de* does not suggest the possessive teleology of "attainment" and is better translated as "in view of." Thus, if chora is "not yet" a position but "generated in view of" positionality, this means that its discursive location is pre-positional: its language would precisely be a semiotic pre-language not subject to symbolic positings, but which both allows for and accompanies every symbolic position. In short, chora's location is "before the law."

3 Werner Hamacher, 'Versäumnisse: Zwischen Theodor W. Adorno und Paul Celan', in *Keinmaleins: Texte zu Celan* (Frankfurt am Main: Klostermann, 2019), 57–91, 85; my translation ("die Vor-Sprache jeder Sprache und deshalb die Sprache der Sprache. Keine Metasprache, in der die Regeln des Sprechens nur verzeichnet werden könnten, um verschoben zu werden, sondern eine Proto- und Para-Sprache, die in allem Sprechen als stummer Vorbehalt gegen das Sprechen, in jeder Sprache als Sprach-Versagen mitspricht"). See Dominik Zechner, 'For Shame of Language', in Kristina Mendicino and Dominik Zechner, eds., *Thresholds, Encounters: Paul Celan and the Claim of Philology* (Albany: State University of New York Press, 2023), 231–256, esp. 238–245.

4 Julia Kristeva, *Revolution in Poetic Language*, trans. by Margaret Waller (New York: Columbia University Press, 2024), 80.

5 Kristeva, *Revolution in Poetic Language*, 24. See Julia Kristeva, *La révolution du langage poétique: L'avant-garde à la fin du XIXe siècle: Lautréamont et Mallarmé* (Paris: Éditions du Seuil, 1974), 24.

Kafka writes:

> Before the law stands a doorkeeper. A man from the country comes to the doorkeeper and asks for admittance to the law. But the doorkeeper says that he cannot grant him admittance now. The man reflects and then asks whether he will be allowed to enter later. "It is possible," says the doorkeeper, "but not now."[6]
>
> (Vor dem Gesetz steht ein Türhüter. Zu diesem Türhüter kommt ein Mann vom Lande und bittet um Eintritt in das Gesetz. Aber der Türhüter sagt, daß er ihm jetzt den Eintritt nicht gewähren könne. Der Mann überlegt und fragt dann, ob er also später werde eintreten dürfen. "Es ist möglich", sagt der Türhüter, "jetzt aber nicht.")[7]

The parable's opening demonstrates the double valence of the preposition *vor* as the spatial arrangement of the doorkeeper's place "before the law" soon shifts into a temporal delay: at the present moment, the visitor cannot be admitted. Much hinges on the prominent use of the temporal adverb – *jetzt* – that emphatically locates the visitor's demand in the present. As a matter of fact, the whole passage is written in the present tense, thus unfolding in the very *now* of his demand. Only the law cannot correspond to this demand and instead withdraws from its presentation in the present.

Kristeva confirms this dynamic when stating that the pre-positional chora "is *not yet a position* [*sans être encore une position*] that represents something for someone."[8] Its positive expression is *possible but not now*, which is the case precisely because *chora*, as the sheer space of generating presently present presentations, cannot itself become present in this present. Translating possibility into presence would mean actualizing it and thus stripping it of its potentia. Chora's being is therefore *sans être encore*, the without-yet-being of the pre-positional – which is to say pre-ontological, which is to say pre-onto-theseological – space of sheer emergence. This space allows for the generation of representations but cannot itself be represented. Its allowance is premised upon a fundamental prohibition.

Albeit with an eye to Melville rather than Kafka, Giorgio Agamben writes of "pure potentiality" as the ability "*neither to posit nor to negate*"; this

6 Franz Kafka, 'Before the Law', in Stanley Corngold, ed. and trans., *Kafka's Selected Stories* (New York and London: Norton, 2007), 68–69, 68.

7 Franz Kafka, 'Vor dem Gesetz', in Wolf Kittler, Hans-Gerd Koch, and Gerhard Neumann, eds., *Drucke zu Lebzeiten* (Frankfurt am Main: Fischer, 2002), 267–269, 267.

8 Kristeva, *Revolution in Poetic Language*, 24; my emphasis. See Kristeva, *La révolution du langage poétique*, 23f.

ability signifies "the Nothing from which all creation derives."[9] The choratic pre-positional space "before the law" is likewise one of pure potentiality because here, too, nothing is posited or negated. To posit something means to move from the *Vor-Gesetz* into the symbolic realm of organized, calculated, and networked positions – positions that can, in turn, be negated. A space of pure ability/potentiality would therefore have to precede these positional networks – as the very Nothing that permits their positing but that can itself never be the result of a thetic act. This pre-positional Nothing cannot be negated but is, in an entirely abstract sense, the structural origin of all negation. It also cannot be represented, yet as the sheer potentiality of everything that could become posited, it is the very principle of representability.

In his reading of Kafka's parable, Jacques Derrida is attuned to the retreat of representation. He understands the doorkeeper's reassurance that entry into the law "is possible" but "not now" as a necessary deferral, albeit not the deferral of an experience or a good, that is, of something that could become presently available. Instead, the doorkeeper's "not now" must be related to *any now* as any possible instant of presentation. "What is deferred forever till death," writes Derrida,

> is entry into the law itself, which is nothing other than that which dictates the delay. The law prohibits by interfering with and deferring the "ference" ["*férance*"], the reference, the rapport, the relation. What must not and cannot be approached is the origin of *différance*: it *must not* [*il ne faut pas*] be presented or represented and above all not penetrated. That is the law of the law [*la loi de la loi*], the process of a law whose subject we can never say, "There it is," it is here or there [*"la voilà" ici ou là*].[10]

The law of the law is therefore prohibitive, but its prohibition is not related to a determinable object, thing, act, thought, or transgression. It is a prohibition without positive content and thus the empty form of prohibition itself:

9 Giorgio Agamben, 'Bartleby, or On Contingency', in Daniel Heller-Roazen, ed. and trans., *Potentialities: Collected Essays in Philosophy* (Stanford: Stanford University Press, 1999), 243–271, 257, 253.

10 Jacques Derrida, 'Before the Law', in Derek Attridge, ed., Avital Ronell and Christine Roulston, trans., *Acts of Literature* (New York and London: Routledge, 1992), 181–220, 205. See Jacques Derrida, 'Préjugés: Devant la loi', *La faculté de juger*, Jacques Derrida et al. (eds) (Paris: Éditions de Minuit, 1985), 87–139, 122. The rhetorical tension between "forever" (*à jamais*) and "till death" (*jusqu'à la mort*) seems to suggest that the movement of deferral could find an endpoint, and thus a point of release and redemption, in death. Yet, if the moment of death coincides with the "never" of *jamais*, this indicates that the authority of death is itself subject to *différance*, infinitely deferring its realization. I discuss Kafka's suspension of death in greater detail in *Kafka und das Problem der Endlichkeit* (Vienna: Sonderzahl, 2024).

il ne faut pas. This "mustn't" does not apply to citizens, subordinates, or subjects of the law – but solely to the law itself, which *must not show itself* to all those it rules. That which prohibits prohibits itself as pure and self-prohibiting prohibition.

The law interrupts and defers, explains Derrida, "the reference, the rapport, the relation" to itself, which is to say that the law cannot be *referred to* as long as referential acts consist of indexing positively determinable phenomena. It is not possible to put oneself into relation to this law because this would assume that the law belongs to the order of empirically encounterable beings. This does not mean that the law is simply beyond relationality, however, but the relation it requires is of a different order. The Germanic lexicon touches on this order with the term *Verhältnis*. Rather than a simple relation between two positive entities, the relation of *Verhältnis* implies the register of *Verhaltenheit*, that is, restraint or holding-back.[11] This kind of relation is no longer reducible to the rapport between positive elements but occurs solely as the constitutive holding-back of positive relationality. What Derrida calls "the law of the law" therefore relates as that which withdraws from all predicable relations and every occupiable and thus relatable position. It is the primordial restraint of relationality and therefore the very *Verhältnis* that allows for the emergence of any positively determinable rapport.

The fact that the law cannot be represented or referenced does not mean that representation itself is void. Rather, the law of the law marks the eclipse of representability that serves as the condition of possibility for all that can be represented. Concluding that there simply *is no relation* would thus be to misunderstand Derrida, for the only relation that is constitutively withheld is the relation to the law of the law. This relation is *verhalten*, which is to say it is held back, guarded, or suppressed. Paradoxically, however, its prohibition is the very ground for the permission, the granting allowance, of everything relatable. The law of the law is therefore pre-positional inasmuch as it is pre-relational, for only posited elements can positively relate. *La loi de la loi* is not itself a posited law but names that which, in the law – in every law, in the discourse of the law, in lawfulness as such – remains radically unposited. It's the apositional element that grants positings, opening up the symbolic space of positive law. While this space can be described as one of prohibition, its interdictions are of a derived, secondary nature, for they owe their possibility to the primordial interdiction of the law of the law, which forbids only itself: "The law is prohibited."[12]

11 See Werner Hamacher, 'The Relation', trans. by Roland Végsö (2009) 8:3 *CR: The New Centennial Review* 29–69.

12 Derrida, 'Before the Law', 204. The idea that the object of the law's prohibition must remain unsayable is prominently developed in Lacan: "We must keep in mind that jouissance is prohibited [*interdite*] to whomever speaks, as such – or, put differently, it can only be said

Inscriptions

Kafka's 'Before the Law' belongs to the manuscript of the unfinished novel *The Trial*, which he began in the summer of 1914 and abandoned in January 1915. In October 1914, Kafka took a two-week vacation from work to focus on his writing, and while he made little progress on the novel, he managed to compose the story 'In the Penal Colony' during this period. The genealogical proximity between this story and the parable of the man from the country, which lies at the heart of *The Trial*, is rather astounding, not least because the two texts negotiate fundamentally different relations to the law. In an important sense, this difference is already evident in the respective titles of the two works, both of which make prominent use of prepositions. While the *vor* of 'Before the Law' indicates a space prior to the formulation of any positive law, the *in* of 'In the Penal Colony' renders the space of the law penetrable, occupiable, perhaps even inhabitable. In fact, the whole legal apparatus of the penal colony aims to inscribe the law not only as, in principle, presentable but as visible for all: "And now anyone can watch through the glass as the inscription takes shape on the body."[13] We are thus no longer confronted with the law as the pure form of prohibition. In the penal colony, it's both possible and desirable to point one's finger at the law, exclaiming, "*la voilà!*"

How does one read the relation between the obscure courts of *The Trial* and the penal colony's theater of justice? Did Kafka radically redefine his understanding of the law as he paused the recounting of Josef K.'s story in order to follow an unknown traveler to the tropics? It is more probable that the two texts negotiate two distinct kinds of law. Whereas 'Before the Law' is interested in the law of the law as the withdrawing principle of representability on which all representation rests, the colony's torture device is designed to make the law apparent. The violence done to the man from the country is therefore of a different order than the collective suffering of the colony's condemned men. It is a violence of withdrawal and withholding, the suspension

[*dite*] between the lines by whomever is a subject of the Law, since the Law is founded on that very prohibition." Jacques Lacan, 'The Subversion of the Subject and the Dialectic of Desire in the Freudian Unconscious', in Bruce Fink, trans., *Écrits: A Selection* (New York: Norton, 2002), 281–312, 306. The complication that Kafka adds to this logic is that the pre-positional pre-symbolic space (*Vor-Gesetz*) that allows for lawful interdictions is itself prohibited. There is an un-posited (*ungesetzt*) law that precedes all *Gesetze* and is itself not symbolizable in the form of a legitimate prohibition; this very impossibility to symbolize realizes itself as prohibitive. The law of the law is thus the prohibition of prohibition, and therefore the allowance of all that can be posited and interdicted. Only to the extent that prohibition prohibits itself do positings become permissible.

13 Franz Kafka, 'In the Penal Colony', in Stanley Corngold, ed. and trans., *Kafka's Selected Stories* (New York and London: Norton, 2007), 35–59, 42.

of positing power, and thus the forfeiture of insight. 'In the Penal Colony' responds with the open violence of law-positing.

The term "law-positing" belongs to the lexicon of Walter Benjamin, who, in 1921, wrote the seminal essay 'Toward the Critique of Violence.' Deriving from the Greek verb κρίνειν, to perform an act of critique is to separate, divide, and distinguish. It is in this literal sense that Benjamin approaches his task, developing a veritable typology of violence. Concretely, he isolates three styles of violence and names them "law-positing," "law-preserving," and "revolutionary."[14] In order to arrive at this disambiguation, Benjamin must first separate natural from positive law, focusing his analysis on the latter. Within the realm of positive law, one encounters sanctioned and unsanctioned forms of violence, that is, violent acts that are condoned and anticipated by the given legal order, in contrast to those that threaten this order. While sanctioned forms of violence pursue legal objectives, unsanctioned forms posit natural ends. Benjamin thus recognizes in the occurrence of an unsanctioned violence that abandons all legal teleology a power that threatens to topple the governing structures of legality.[15] He can conclude "that there inheres a law-positing [*rechtsetzender*] character in all violence used for natural ends."[16]

Thus, Benjamin arrives at the problem that sits at the core of his typology: sanctioned violence is a belated structural effect of unsanctioned violence. If law-positing violence is unsanctioned violence that occurs outside the precinct of legal ends, this means that any positive (i.e., *posited*) law in its sanctioned quality owes its very existence to a violent act that eludes the legal order. The law cannot account for its own foundation. Benjamin continues: "If the first function of violence is law-positing, then [the] second function of violence can be called law-preserving [*rechtserhaltende*]."[17] Law-preserving violence is the sanctioned maintenance of an institutional form

14 My discussion follows the translations proposed by Peter Fenves and Julia Ng in their recent republication of Benjamin's study. See Walter Benjamin, *Toward the Critique of Violence: A Critical Edition*, ed. by Peter Fenves and Julia Ng (Stanford: Stanford University Press, 2021). Especially the translation of "law-positing violence" for Benjamin's *rechtsetzende Gewalt* is much more accurate than Jephcott's rendition as "lawmaking violence," which had hitherto been considered the standard translation. See Walter Benjamin, 'Critique of Violence', in Marcus Bullock and Michael W. Jennings, eds, *Selected Writings*, vol. 1 (1913–1926) (London and Cambridge, MA: Harvard University Press, 1996), 236–252. What makes Jephcott's choice particularly misleading is that lawmaking qua legislation belongs to institutions that are themselves subject to law-positing violence. Thus, what colloquially is considered a lawmaker belongs to the structures of institutional law preservation.

15 Using the term "power" in conjunction with the concept of violence is sanctioned by the original terminology, as the German term *Gewalt* denotes both brute violence as well as institutionalized power.

16 Benjamin, *Toward the Critique of Violence*, 45.

17 Ibid.

founded by an unsanctioned positing blast. All pursuit of legal ends through law-preserving violence is therefore premised on an unforgeable act of unsanctioned violence.

The relationship between law-positing and law-preserving violence is both dialectical and representational. It is dialectical because law preservation works to curb, weaken, muffle, and stifle the illegitimate forces at work in law positing, thereby effectively working against its own ground of possibility. It is representational because every law-preserving structure symbolizes the law positing to which it owes its existence. Benjamin connects these aspects when stating that "all law-preserving violence, in its duration, indirectly, through its suppression of hostile counterforces [*Gegengewalten*], *weakens* law-positing violence, which is *represented* in it."[18] Every lawful institution is the representational image of the positing violence that founded it. This image weakens relative to the time that has passed since the founding event, until the institution becomes entirely obsolete: "If the consciousness of the latent presence of violence in a legal institution disappears, the institution falls into decay [*verfällt es*]."[19] Benjamin's legal theory thus unearths the dialectical predicament that the apparatus of legal institutionality is indebted to a positing power that it must, however, suppress in order to conserve itself. The project of law preservation implies a structural disconnect from the very violence it represents. This disconnect spells the inevitable ruin of all legal institutions, for preservation is but positing in decay.

'In the Penal Colony' was published in 1919, two years before Benjamin's essay first appeared in *Archiv für Sozialwissenschaft und Sozialpolitik*. At this point, Benjamin's engagement with Kafka had not yet commenced. His interest developed in the mid-20s, following Kafka's death, whose tenth anniversary Benjamin commemorated with a formative essay in 1934. While this essay makes no explicit mention of the typology of violence he had developed a dozen years prior, it is safe to assume that it was very much on Benjamin's mind, for the piece on Kafka verbatim repurposes an entire passage from 'Toward the Critique of Violence,' whose bearing on Kafka's works is thus spectrally inscribed.[20] Part of what I would like to suggest is that the story

18 Ibid., 60; my emphasis. See Walter Benjamin, 'Zur Kritik der Gewalt', in Rolf Tiedemann and Hermann Schweppenhäuser, eds., *Gesammelte Schriften*, vol. II.1: *Aufsätze, Essays, Vorträge* (Frankfurt am Main: Suhrkamp, 1991), 179–203, 202: "daß jede rechtserhaltende Gewalt in ihrer Dauer die rechtsetzende, welche in ihr repräsentiert ist, durch die Unterdrückung der feindlichen Gegengewalten indirekt selbst schwächt."

19 Benjamin, *Toward the Critique of Violence*, 49. See Benjamin, 'Zur Kritik der Gewalt', 191.

20 The passage concerns the concept of fate in Hermann Cohen. See Benjamin, 'Zur Kritik der Gewalt', 199. And compare Walter Benjamin, 'Franz Kafka: Zur zehnten Wiederkehr seines Todestages', in Rolf Tiedemann and Hermann Schweppenhäuser, eds., *Gesammelte Schriften*, vol. II.2: *Aufsätze, Essays, Vorträge* (Frankfurt am Main: Suhrkamp, 1991), 409–438, 412.

'In the Penal Colony' becomes readable as a literary mode of demonstrating a critique of violence in ways that are not too dissimilar from what Benjamin proposed in 1921.

"In the penal colony," Benjamin explains in his Kafka essay,

> those in power [*die Gewalthaber*] use an archaic apparatus which engraves letters with curlicues on the back of every guilty man, multiplying the stabs and piling up the ornaments to the point where the back of the guilty man becomes clairvoyant and is able to decipher the script from which he must derive the nature of his unknown guilt. It is the back on which this is incumbent.[21]

The torture device around which this justice system is centered inscribes the back of the condemned person with the very law that was supposedly transgressed. The entire topology of 'Before the Law' is flipped around a vertical axis, such that the subject no longer stands *before* the guarded gate, because the law is now *behind* him, stitching its signature into his back, removed from the field of vision, so that the whole body must transform into a hermeneutic instrument and learn to read through its wounds.[22] The condemned person literally has the law *im Rücken* as his back is broken by the very law he broke.

'In the Penal Colony' thus achieves what 'Before the Law' determines impossible: it spells out the law, elevating it to the level of symbolization through an ornamental script tattooed onto the prisoner's skin. Taking a break from gauging the law's desire for Josef K., Kafka moves from the level of eclipsed representability to that of presentation, which signals that the law he negotiates in 'In the Penal Colony' is not of the same order as the one that underpins *The Trial*. While 'Before the Law' stages the constitutive withholding of the law as the pure form of its self-prohibition, the colony's torture device renders the law a legible effect of law-positing inscriptions. The man from the country has no commandment inscribed on his back because the injunction *il ne faut pas* applies solely to the law itself, which exclusively prohibits its own presentation. Relative to 'Before the Law,' the penal colony's spectacle of torture moves from a pre-positional understanding of the law to a notion of the law as positional representation. The legal space of 'In the Penal Colony' thus unfolds as the law's permanent re-positing.

21 Walter Benjamin, 'Franz Kafka: On the Tenth Anniversary of His Death', in Michael W. Jennings, Howard Eiland, and Gary Smith, eds., Rodney Livingstone, et al., trans., *Selected Writings*, vol. 2.2 (1931–1934) (London and Cambridge, MA: Harvard University Press, 1996), 794–818, 811. See Benjamin, 'Franz Kafka: Zur zehnten Wiederkehr', 432.

22 See my discussion of this scene in *The Violence of Reading: Literature and Philosophy at the Threshold of Pain* (Cham: Palgrave Macmillan, 2024), 23–26.

Benjamin speaks of "those in power," *die Gewalthaber*, that is, the ones who *have violence* at their disposal. The phrasing fails to account for the political transformation the colony has been undergoing, because "those in power" no longer seem to be in favor of the infamous torture device. The latter had been invented by the colony's former commandant, whose reign, upon passing away, was replaced by a reformist leadership whose proponents increasingly consider the legal torture obsolete. In fact, the old regime lives on in the actions of a single person, the so-called officer, mentee of the former commandant and in charge of maintaining the archaic apparatus. If the first function of violence is to posit the law, then to carry out this function was the prerogative of the old commandant, the true *Gewalthaber* as the one who instituted the colony's system of legality and invented the justice-rendering apparatus. Upon his death, the colony falls into a state of disrepair and afterness in which his law-positing power threatens to become a decaying memory. While Benjamin understands law-preservation to be the degenerated representation of positing violence, Kafka's torture device seems precisely designed to elude this logic because every act of passing judgment appears as a violent iteration of the law positing to which the whole apparatus owes its existence. In other words, Kafka invented a machine that counteracts the decay of law preservation by turning every law-preserving act of passing judgment into the literalization of law-positing violence, stabbing the prisoner's body to death with the very letters of the law.[23]

Derrida's engagement with Kafka's parable 'Before the Law' dates to the year 1982, when it was first given as a lecture to the Royal Philosophical Society in London. When he revisits the problem of the law seven years later in the context of the conference 'Deconstruction and the Possibility of Justice,' held at the Cardozo Law School in New York, Kafka ceases to be his main reference, while Benjamin moves prominently to the fore. Indeed, Derrida mentions his work on Kafka only in passing, privileging a discussion of Montaigne and Pascal, before dedicating the entire second half of his contribution to a close reading of 'Toward the Critique of Violence.'[24] At the very heart of his deliberations, Derrida pronounces three so-called "aporias of justice." In what follows, I would like to suggest that these

23 Hence, there is a level on which the torture machine becomes readable as a device of law preservation: its operation is firmly on the side of the rule of the old commandant, whose authority it seeks to preserve as it is in the process of becoming displaced by the law-positing violence of a new regime. The story ends with a visit to the teahouse where the old commandant is buried. An inscription above his grave reads: "Have faith and wait!" Kafka, 'In the Penal Colony', 59. A law once deposed may still lie in repose, awaiting the day of its thetic re-realization.

24 See Jacques Derrida, 'Force of Law: The "Mystical Foundation of Authority"', trans. by Mary Quaintance (1990) 11:5–6 *Cardozo Law Review* 921–1045, 929, 993.

theoretical impasses correspond to 'In the Penal Colony' in a specific way, indexing Kafka's work as an implicit intertext of Derrida's 'Force of Law.'

The aporias Derrida names result from a necessary tension between justice and the law. Because there can be no law that could codify and render justice without instantly becoming unjust, any "just" decision implies an inevitable negation of the law. In the first aporia he cites, this negation takes the form of a suspension: "For a decision to be just and responsible, it must, in its proper moment if there is one, be both regulated and without regulation."[25] What regulates the just decision is its grounding in the law, but precisely this lawful basis must be suspended, the grounding unmoored, in order for the decision to arrive as just. Instead of simply following a given rule, a presiding judge must question the rule and its bearing on the case at hand, lest the act of passing judgment become a mere calculating process. The act of judgment confronts the rule with its own deregulation thus reclaiming the very freedom suppressed by the imperatives of administrative governance.

In the space of this freedom, every decision confronts its own undecidability, which is how Derrida frames his second aporia. "A decision," he explains, "that didn't go through the ordeal of the undecidable would not be a free decision, it would only be the programmable application of a calculable process."[26] The ordeal of the undecidable is located, paradoxically, both after and before the law: it leaves behind the law understood as a means of legal calculation in order to breach a space of pure freedom, which, in turn, is located before a law that every decision must respect and affirm. "There is," Derrida adds, "apparently no moment in which a decision can be called presently and fully just: either it has not yet been made according to a rule . . . or it has already followed a rule."[27] The undecidable thus marks the impossible juncture where the temporalities of *not yet* and *already*, where before and after, meet. The undecidable is before the law, which is to say, *après la loi*.

While the first two aporias of justice bear on the problems of freedom and temporality, the third and final one evokes the cognitive horizon of all decision-making. A just decision, Derrida observes, is driven by an extreme urgency dictating that it must not be postponed. At the same time, it is necessary for the decision to be properly informed, equipped with the knowledge that renders the intricacies of the case transparent and decidable. However, the decision simply "cannot furnish itself with infinite information and the

25 Ibid., 961. One way in which Kafka's penal colony is secretly inscribed in 'Force of Law' bears on the incision inherent in every decision: "Justice, as law, is never exercised without a decision that *cuts*." Ibid., 963. The colony's skin-slicing justice cuts and recuts, relentlessly – but in such a way that every incision causes a new wound of injustice.

26 Ibid.

27 Ibid.

unlimited knowledge of conditions, rules or hypothetical imperatives that could justify it," for such preparation would unduly delay the rendition of justice.[28] To make a just decision requires forfeiting the fantasy of comprehensive knowledge to embrace, instead, the sheer opacity of nescience. The possibility of justice therefore meets a three-pronged impasse – it reaches the same impasse in three guises as the just decision exposes itself to the suspension of legality, the ordeal of the undecidable, and the night of nescience. These aporias can only be encountered in the positional space of legality founded by law-positing violence.

Returning to Kafka, the reader of 'In the Penal Colony' observes a peculiar implementation of these aporias of justice. Indeed, Kafka's judgement machine is not only designed to forgo the distinction between law-positing and law-preserving violence by turning the law-preserving institutionality of justice into the violent reenactment of law positing – it is furthermore built to elude the very impasses of justice that Derrida works out with such enviable precision. The way this elision operates becomes evident in the officer's soliloquy, as he explains the legal foundation of the colony's justice system:

> The principle [*Grundsatz*] according to which I decide is: "Guilt is always beyond all doubt." Other courts cannot follow this principle, since they comprise various authorities and have even higher courts above them. This is not the case here, or at least it wasn't so under the former commandant.[29]

While *The Trial*'s netherworld still allows for a vertical tension that connects lower and higher courts, making it possible for a case to float up and down a perpendicular legal axis, the penal colony collapses this tension, tying all legal decision-making to the ground of but one *Grundsatz*.[30] This basic sentence is no law in itself; instead, it inscribes the law of the law, albeit not as the unposited *Vor-Gesetz*, pure retreat, and empty form of prohibition invoked in 'Before the Law.' The colony's principle does not prohibit; instead, it prescribes, thus designating the very relation between law and decision. This relation is no *Verhältnis* in the sense of a constitutive withholding, but a relation pure

28 Ibid., 967.

29 Kafka, 'In the Penal Colony', 40. See Franz Kafka, 'In der Strafkolonie', in Wolf Kittler, Hans-Gerd Koch, and Gerhard Neumann, eds., *Drucke zu Lebzeiten* (Frankfurt am Main: Fischer, 2002), 201–248, 212.

30 The court portraitist Titorelli explains this vertical movement when exploring the possibility of Josef K.'s "apparent acquittal." In this scenario, the painter submits, the case is "forwarded to the higher courts and then returned to the lower ones, and continues swinging up and down, with longer and shorter oscillations, with longer and shorter pauses." Franz Kafka, *The Trial*, trans. by Mike Mitchell (Oxford: Oxford University Press, 2009), 113.

and simple, the obvious link between rule and judgment. The principle dictates that all reported transgression amounts to a violation of the rule, which is why all decisions are the same: "Guilt is always beyond all doubt."

The penal colony's process of judgment is therefore not designed to suspend the rule; instead, it suspends the very demand for the rule's suspension. Put another way, Derrida's insistence that a just decision can only arrive once the governing rule is suspended is denied in defense of a principle that permits neither interruption nor delay. The very *Grundsatz* that grounds the law is never subject to destabilizing scrutiny, does not require reinterpretation or reinvention, and is thus never exposed to the possibility of its own negation. The decisions it informs are entirely calculable and programmable; in fact, they are a priori calculated and programmed – for if guilt is always beyond doubt, then the decision that is made is no decision at all but merely the belated pronouncement of a preordained reality. Even before the prisoner is fed to the colony's peculiar piece of machinery, the machine to which he is subject is one of total calculation, suppressing the very freedom required to keep alive the possibility of justice.

Derrida's first two aporias of justice are thus eliminated. Neither is the rule ever exposed to the necessity of its own deregulation, nor does the decision-making process meet the ghost of the undecidable. "Who will ever be able to assure us that a decision as such has taken place?" Derrida asks. The same question poses itself to the penal colony, albeit with the ironic bend that here it is not the undecidable that disturbs the certainty of judgment, but the very fact that all decisions are structurally preempted, for they have virtually already taken place. That guilt *is* always beyond all doubt means that it *has* always been beyond all doubt, which is to say that it *will* always be beyond all doubt. That this logic also affects Derrida's third aporia becomes clear when the officer discusses the circumstances surrounding the case at hand. The execution at the center of 'In the Penal Colony' involves a man rumored to have fallen asleep at his post. When reprimanded for the malfeasance by his captain, the man allegedly retorted: "Throw the whip away, or I'll eat you alive." The officer concludes his account to the traveler:

> Those are the facts of the matter [*Das ist der Sachverhalt*]. The captain came to me an hour ago; I took down his statement and immediately added the judgment. Then I had the man put in chains. That was all very simple. If I had first summoned the man and interrogated him, it would only have led to confusion. He would have lied; if I had succeeded in refuting these lies, he would have substituted new lies for them, and so forth. Now, however, I've got him and I will not let him go.[31]

31 Kafka, 'In the Penal Colony', 41. See Kafka, 'In der Strafkolonie', 213.

Based on the captain's sole account, constituting "the facts of the matter," judgment is passed with a strong sense of urgency. Is this not precisely the impasse Derrida envisions when insisting that every decision ought to expose itself to the night of non-knowledge, for rendering justice must not tarry? Kafka's officer, too, loses no time. So much so that a consultation of the alleged perpetrator is deemed unnecessary. No counter-narrative is added to the captain's account, simply because a man, once accused, is deemed guilty and therefore can only be considered a fraud: he would have lied and augmented his story with ever new lies.

We are not confronted with an aporia of justice in the deconstructive sense, but with the farcical pastiche of justice's aporias, not least because Kafka's officer never truly exposes himself to the threat of total nescience.[32] Instead, the captain's account is considered to contain the absolute knowledge whose wealth of information exhausts the case's complexity. All that could be added to this obvious *Sachverhalt* are falsehoods that would unnecessarily disturb its clarity. Precisely this clarity, however, clouds the relation between decision and justice – a cloud inscribed in the very notion of *Sachverhalt*, whose true matter or *Sache* remains subject to a withholding retention, another obfuscating *Verhältnis* operative underneath all obvious relations.

Annihilations

When Benjamin develops his typology of violence in 1921, there is one expression of violence that eludes the dialectic between law positing and law preservation. If the executive and administrative qualities of this dialectic underpin any effort of institution building, the third option confronts such efforts with their own impossibility, for its purpose lies in the sheer destruction of the law. Benjamin derives it from his engagement with Georges Sorel's *Reflections on Violence* and its theory of strike action, in particular from Sorel's crucial distinction between the "syndicalist" and the "political strike." Committed to "the strengthening of the State," the latter defines specific political goals whose achievement is accomplished through the preservation of state power.[33] Say, for instance, "the mass of producers would . . . change masters"; such a change would not affect the facticity of the state itself.[34] The syndicalist strike does not operate this way. Instead of preserving state power, it altogether denounces the doctrine of the state, engendering "the perspective of a total catastrophe" that "drags into the revolutionary track everything

32 In the penal colony, Derrida's aporias of justice do not constitute an impasse but allow, instead, for infinite permeability as depicted in the relentless cutting up of defenseless skin.

33 Georges Sorel, *Reflections on Violence*, ed. by Jeremy Jennings (Cambridge: Cambridge University Press, 1999), 162.

34 Ibid., 171.

it touches."[35] In short, while the political strike advances a reformist agenda that seeks to restructure the state, the syndicalist strike strives to make the state as such disappear. Therein lies its revolutionary claim.

Responding favorably to Sorel's strike dichotomy, Benjamin summarizes: "In contrast to the political general strike . . . the proletarian general strike sets itself the sole task of annihilating [*Vernichtung*] state power [*Staatsgewalt*]."[36] The revolutionary violence mobilized by the proletarian, i.e., syndicalist, strike is dedicated to the state's negation (*Nichtung*). It therefore eludes the representationalist paradigm that governs the correspondence between law-positing and law-preserving violence, and according to which all legal institutions manifest as the decaying image of the positing violence that afforded their founding. Revolutionary violence withdraws from all figuration, fantasy, and future vision – it does not counter the reality of the state with a program for its utopian improvement. Instead, it responds to the decay of all representational legality with the utter breakdown of representability. Another step in the direction *après la loi* has thus been taken: while the pure potentiality that Kafka's famous parable withholds from presentation is conceivable as the *pre*-positional law before the law, Benjamin's revolutionary violence announces a *post*-positional space within which all posited law is rendered impossible, which is to say *im-positable*.

The revolutionary aftermath no longer occupies the positional space of lawmaking. It returns all that was posited to its un-positedness, effecting the sheer evacuation of all positions, ultimately deposing all accomplished positings. Another name for this revolution would be *après la loi* – "after the law." Benjamin speaks of the "deposing [of] law together with all the forms of violence on which it depends, just as they depend on it, and finally, therefore, on de-posing state violence [*Entsetzung des Rechts samt den Gewalten, auf die es angewiesen ist wie sie auf jenes, zuletzt also der Staatsgewalt*]."[37] The post-positional reveals itself as the *depositional*, un-positing all that had been subject to positing violence. In an influential commentary on this passage, Werner Hamacher deems it "reasonable to term the 'de-posing' of acts of positing and their dialectic . . . as an absolute *imperformative* or *afformative* political event, as *depositive*, as political *a-thesis*."[38] This event of afformance, he specifies, can "never be represented in the form of a rule or a law" for it prevails as "the manifestation of a violence independent in principle from positing."[39] The *Entsetzung* achieved by revolutionary violence is therefore

35 Ibid., 124.

36 Benjamin, *Toward the Critique of Violence*, 52.

37 Ibid., 60. See Benjamin, 'Zur Kritik der Gewalt', 202.

38 Werner Hamacher, 'Afformative, Strike', trans. by Dana Hollander (1991) 13:4 *Cardozo Low Review* 1133–1157, 1138.

39 Ibid., 1139n12.

not the mere counterpart to *Setzung* in the sense of law positing. For all posited law belongs to the realm of representation within which the dialectic between positing and preservation oscillates in the form of decaying images. The violence of revolution does not add a negative to this set of images; the negation of its *Vernichtung* is not the logical opposite of positive legality. Instead, such *Vernichtung* must be thought of as the evacuation of all positings and thus as the effective deactivation of all performative and instituting effects.

The post-positional space *après la loi* is therefore essentially related to the irrepresentable potentiality *vor dem Gesetz*. Both neutralize the performance of positings and their representation in the form of rules or laws – once in the invisible guise of the as yet un-posited, then as the afformative occurrence of the depositive. From the standpoint of positional reasoning, the spaces before and after the law therefore appear to be the same, which is to say *they don't appear at all*. If Derrida detects in the shift from law-positing to law-preserving violence "the very passage from presence to representation," then revolutionary violence opens a passage of another kind: instead of manifesting a negative representation, it evokes the sheer eclipse of representability.[40] So it defies recognition. Indeed, it is quite impossible to state with any degree of confidence whether a depositive event has, provably, taken place. Benjamin unambiguously holds that only *Setzung* but not *Entsetzung* "can be recognized as such with certainty."[41] A depositive occurrence could only be ascertained if it were to assume a positive form, either as presence or representation; what we perceive and recognize are always positions, that is, results of positing acts. The deposing violence of annihilation therefore exceeds the horizon of phenomenal appearance.

Thus arises the question of how a literary work like 'In the Penal Colony' might grapple with the challenge of representing revolutionary

40 Derrida, 'Force of Law', 1015. In the same passage, Derrida understands the representation of "originary violence" as its consignation to "oblivion." This emphasis on forgetting bears on Hamacher's argument as well, especially to the extent to which it construes the afformative space *before* and *after* the law in terms of a certain *letting*, that is, the letting-happen of possible positings. He submits "that all positings depend on this letting," which implies that they "preserve [its] memory." Hamacher, 'Afformative, Strike', 1140n12. In other words, every presence preserves the memory of the unpresentable prohibition that originarily affords its presencing. If representation amounts to a form of oblivion, then what it forgets is not just the presence it supposedly represents, but the sheer un-representability *memorized* in and by this very presence.

41 Benjamin, *Toward the Critique of Violence*, 60. This discourse on un-representability returns us to Derrida's reading of 'Before the Law,' in which the law "appears as something that does not appear as such in the course of a history," for "it is the object of no possible experience." Derrida, 'Before the Law', 194, 212.

violence. Kafka's solution to this problem is allegorical. The story reaches its tipping point when the traveler, having been invited to witness a public execution and instructed about the procedures of the colony's legal system, is coerced into a favorable assessment of what he has seen. In this moment, the colony's system of decision-making, which manifests in the singular figure of a judge and allows for no appeal to higher courts, is itself subjected to another's judgment: "Don't hold back in your speech," the officer teases his guest, "raise a big ruckus with the truth, lean over the railing, roar, yes, roar your judgment, your unshakable opinion."[42] The confidence expressed in these words is soon betrayed, for the traveler's verdict comes as a shocking surprise: "I am opposed to this procedure."[43]

Passing judgment on the colony's system of adjudication, the traveler triggers a constitutional crisis. The public execution he was supposed to witness is at once called off, and the prisoner is freed. In his stead, the officer himself mounts the torture device, determined to receive the commandment "Be just!" on his back.[44] He straps himself down, and the machine begins to work. But almost immediately, it starts falling apart. Up top, a loose cogwheel appears, detaches, and falls to the ground, followed by countless others. In the meantime, the rest of the machine accelerates into overdrive, frantically stabbing the officer's body instead of writing on it. Made deeply uneasy by the murderous spectacle of disintegration, the dumbfounded traveler observes that

> the harrow where the body was impaled was already tilting to one side, as it usually did only in the twelfth hour. . . . And now the final stage also failed: the body did not become detached from the long needles; it poured out its blood but hung over the pit without dropping.[45]

In this last of executions, the concept of execution is itself executed, as the machine distills its law-positing effort – usually dilated across twelve hours – into the crystalline temporality of but a few moments. The officer's demise culminates in a figure of suspension, another form of strike, that allegorizes the grinding halt of all positing violence. His destruction coincides with the machine's self-undoing as the afformative deposing of its positing powers. While the apparatus was designed to counteract the decay of law preservation through the ever-renewed spectacle of law

42 Kafka, 'In the Penal Colony', 52.
43 Ibid., 53.
44 Ibid., 54.
45 Ibid., 57f.

positing in the form of the law's inscription and revelation through the prisoners' wounds, its last operation sends the frenzied law positing into such overdrive that the project of law positing itself meets the depositive limit of its annihilation. If 'Before the Law' imagines the law as pure pre-positional possibility, 'In the Penal Colony' moves through the terror of positionality in order to encounter its post-positional impossibility. Aghast, we witness the de-posing of the law. *Entsetzt vernehmen wir des Gesetzes Entsetzung.*[46]

46 I dedicate this essay to my Fall 2022 seminar "Justice & Violence," and am especially grateful to Emily Trujillo for her sharp eye and brilliant suggestions.

13

AFTERWORD

Derrida and Benjamin Repurposed

Avital Ronell

Decidedly, the task of the editor does not merit heuristic passion, though the job description of such a machinic interpolator, a quasi-writer whose allotment of transcendence remains minimal, involves policing every diacritical mark and paragraph shift of a text that becomes available to the reading public. On the downside of editorial assistance, everyone who writes for view – or purports to carry an argument – has experienced the horror of being cut down to size or manipulated into alien stipulations of sanctioned format and meaning. Responsible for different levels of textual administration, editors are on call even when they are in recess. Granting an address so that writing has a place of submission, they form a first horizon of reception, a gateway. Sometimes the editor is a sifter of language, a poetic shadow. In our case, the editor – while not cast as Hölderlin's poet or Benjamin's translator, but a neighbouring intrusion, on calm days a discerning umpire, on other days, a nursemaid – was compelled to stand before the perils of decision. What was our end goal besides marshalling effects of a somber anniversary – a trope closely reviewed by Heidegger and Derrida himself in terms of temporality and event? It had been twenty years since Derrida left us.

On one level, we wanted it all: to honour Derrida and Benjamin with a measure of *justesse*; to introduce to the public domain younger scholars, vibing off their intergenerational verve; to keep seasoned scholars in shape, urging renewed subscriptions to difficult thought without regressing or slacking off (sometimes an age-appropriate tendency, but not always, for there are those who get going only after a certain age, throwing off the brunt of institutional and conceptually branded shackles). In other words, our goal was to keep the heat on with newer forms of critical approach, to keep things reasonably agitated, queer and rigorous, spreading to domains of legal analysis

DOI: 10.4324/9781003589419-16

and poetic insight that Benjamin and Derrida took seriously when scoring a critical point. We needed to be clear without overreaching, steady and motored by restrictive determination. At decisive junctures we asked ourselves these questions: What is the wound to which Benjamin's continued poignancy testifies today? When does poetic utterance, as witness to what cannot be granted referential authority, become the mainstay of argument and demonstration, audacious and confident? How is *testimony* bound to poetry, dependent on fiction, straightened and delivered in a mode of disavowal? Whether explicitly stated or more unconsciously driven, these questions give us a framework for pursuing a speculative history, the "what-ifness" of persistent problems that Benjamin lobs into our courts. How, finally, does Derrida move through these checkpoints of Benjamin's thought?

But there is still more to this project than raising a renewed probe into the depths of the supra-juridical enigma posed by Benjamin and repurposed by Derrida in terms of law-flexing violence. In the course of gathering these papers, we recognized the perils of reconfiguring a titanic couple, Benjamin and Derrida, a cleaved figure that had known how to fall and crash, how to pick up, scatter, disappear and resurge. Their fates intersect, but also pull apart in ways that require us to read bifocally, sometimes strained, against any established grain. Admittedly, at least one lens was smudged at times, leading to anamorphic takes. Sometimes you have to squint to see, adapting a perceptive squeeze practiced by Lacanian analysis. We needed to see beyond the extravagant visibility they had attained: in some respects, not to be overlooked, both Benjamin and Derrida had become *too popular*, whether they showed up front and centre in a number of debates, or hung back, marginal and mired in footnote wars. On the other hand, despite auratic claims that can be made on their behalf, singly or in partnership, they were often taken out of the game by a default of perceived density. As a team or alone-standing, they are often deemed too difficult for our age of recovering readers, dominated by the wizards of technological abbreviation. (BTW, Heidegger had pointed out, in view of *The Question Concerning Technology*, that the use of abbreviation was a portentous techno-splice, grinding down language – hence, CIA, USA, FBI, NYU, etc.).[1]

The texts gathered here assume their fault lines while earnestly delivering yields, many aspects of which spring from unacknowledged areas of Derrida and Benjamin's reflections on violence and law. The critical translator-commentators have refrained from setting up strawmen or vulnerable precedents when carrying out their considerations for failure and renewal: They are rigorous and honoring, mindful of a generation of interpreters that took

1 Martin Heidegger, *Überlieferte Sprache und technische Sprache*, ed. by Hermann Heidegger (St. Gallen: Erker-Verlag, 1989), 24–25.

the first batch of calls. Some contributors wear the mantle of OGs, having stepped up at the first iteration of Derrida's encounter with Benjamin and troubled juridicity.[2] The returning exegetes may have supplied newer perspectives, having provoked a review that distributes pulses of resignification along the body of the two texts under study. The lineage itself invites the application of interpretive rigour, an institutional or disciplinarian hermeneutics often conducted by those who stray from the sanctioned parametres of their disciplines and refuse to stay in their lane in pursuit of critical demands placed on them.

The bulk of essays addresses tropes of disappointed legality, juridical gridlock, including the dumpster fire of acts of *justesse* within or removed from the legal systems under examination. Thus, the volume tends to follow a peculiarly contemporary undertow of Benjamin's text to which Derrida points or on which he *desists* (a term he used to describe Lacoue-Labarthe's philosophical stance, that of desistance).[3] They immerse themselves in demonstrations of a number of topoi: hatred and offshoots of hate speech, the prongs of general strike, the defeat of language, a bang up of grammar at crucial junctures of judicial articulation, citing recurrent withholding patterns of law, wayward grievance, the leakage of unthematizable effects of *force,* including insinuations of the "gift of death"[4] that looms over Benjamin's text – a work by some measure that can be grasped as one long suicide note, unbearable to read, yet appearing to issue an imperative to be read over and over again, in acknowledgement of its relation to the law's primal unreadability, a hypothesis pursued in Kafka's penal fiction.

When coaxing our colleagues to cast their thought on the fate and ongoing implications of the 'Force of Law', we had to concede a spark of ambiguity. Though driven by a relentless focus, the intentions leading the charge were undoubtedly overdetermined. Urged by Kafka's groundbreaking *Trial*, whose implications proved ever latent and coming for us, we understood how the relation to law can remain inscrutable and oppressive, ready to pounce, while it also promotes a theatre of care, miming protective stances of invasive enforcement. The police are everywhere, even where they are not. This phrasing, originating in Benjamin's thought, is repeated by Derrida when sighting the *phantom police* that binds policy to the polis, politics to a

2 Drucilla Cornell, Michel Rosenfeld, and David Gray Carlson (eds.), *Deconstruction and the Possibility of Justice* (New York: Routledge, 1992); and Werner Hamacher, *Premises: Essays on Philosophy and Literature from Kant to Celan*, trans. by Peter Fenves (Stanford, CA: Stanford University Press, 1996).

3 Jacques Derrida, 'Desistance', in Philippe Lacoue-Labarthe, ed., Christopher Fynsk, trans., *Typography: Mimesis, Philosophy, Politics* (Stanford, CA: Stanford University Press, 1989), 1–42.

4 Jacques Derrida, *The Gift of Death*, trans. by David Wills (Chicago: University of Chicago Press, 1995).

cut of politesse, a remnant of that practice which runs behind the veritably lost art of diplomacy.

Two points can be borne in mind, one stemming from Lyotard, an exacting reader of Kafka. According to Lyotard's grappling with "phrases in dispute," we have been served notice by Kafka: henceforth no one can prove their innocence. Some discursive measures simply cannot be fed into the legal machine. Then there is the matter of phrases that the law simply cannot register, such as nervous tics or hysterical blushing, even glum or sealed silence. Lyotard's reflections induce us to consider the premises of judgment and various indicators of adjudication governing the essential pressure points of performative claims. The plaintiff is always responsible for proving reality, Lyotard asserts with philosophical gravity and referential implosion.[5] The second consideration is that the Law, even when in your face and on your case, advocated or bearded and covered by outsourced representatives, is never present, as Derrida demonstrates with the anti-gravitational pull of phenomenological inquiry. Thus Kafka's man from the country in the mind- and back-bending parable, 'Before the Law,' wants to see the law, voicing a citizen's *demande,* an appeal replicated with another accent in Blanchot's 'La folie du jour,' also finely interpreted by Derrida, whose protagonist wants to *touch* the law as if it were a recoverable entity.[6] Though remote and largely unfigurable, the law taught by Kafka swarms the individual and seizes on the recesses of perversity, as psychoanalysis shows, stoking neuroses and mass cognitive decline, provoking a steely bout of overcompliance or practiced rebuff to legal offense – a remnant of adolescent negation.

An additional turn of the vice, part of a continued interrogation of premises, including that which accompanies super-egoical despotism, requires us to explore the unavoidable relation of law to masochism, the tie-in to precepts of domination and submission outlined by Deleuze's reading of Sacher-Masoch, a dignified professor of history who was appalled to have his name become the irremovable tag of masochistic depravity.[7] These topoi and themes are not far off from the inquiry led in tandem by Benjamin and Derrida, encompassing their understanding of violence, divine and mortal, precedent-making, juridically immersed in rules of conduct, legally binding and undermining, cratering a subject defined by different levels of sadistic and masochistic intrusion, beginning with Lacan's famous dictionary of punition that features the prohibitive "non/nom du Père" (the no/name of the Father). Many of these themes, as well as their unthematizable counterparts,

5 Jean-François Lyotard, *The Differend: Phrases in Dispute*, trans. by Georges Van Den Abbeele (Minneapolis: University of Minnesota Press, 1988).

6 Jacques Derrida, 'The Law of Genre', (Autumn 1980) 7:1 *Critical Inquiry* 55–81.

7 Gilles Deleuze, 'Coldness and Cruelty', in Jean McNeil, trans., *Masochism* (New York: Zone Books, 1991), 9–138.

are made relevant again in these essays, as irrepressible backstory of theoretical consequence in legal and philosophical studies.

The Genesis of Force

The quasi-concept of *force* was put in play to describe the work of Roger Laporte in 1975, when Derrida was interviewed by Radio France Culture. Subsequently, upon reentry in his work, force, which cannot claim a stable place in the philosophical lexicon, hovered between the semantics of *intimidation* and *fascination*, in the alternating sense of that which bespeaks *horror* and the capacity to set one in *thrall*. In some ways, force remains *hors jeu* in terms of classical philosophical rules of engagement and cannot measure up, for instance, to the abundantly commented repertoire of *violence* in critical and political thought. When reading Laporte, Derrida used force strategically. It was meant to indicate that which exceeds genre or categorial solidity, lacking for the most part referential authority. As literary inducement and poetic overreach, moreover, force seizes on rhetorical instabilities. It quickly upends classical rhetorical and material manoeuvres, even while making appeals to philosophy as it roams on the borders of *Wirkungsgeschichte*, a history of effectivity posed as marginal and problematic. Yet, modern philosophy remains wary. It does not easily recognize the heuristic merit or conceptual agility of something like force, which, by dint of ghostly shadowing practices, appears to sideline philosophical argument and the very possibility of demonstration. Force lines up with a history of neglect. Leibniz critiqued Descartes for ignoring force, and Derrida himself starts out in a formidable essay by underscoring the lapse of attention paid to force. In 'Force and Signification', which takes on literary criticism as practised by structuralism, Derrida positions force as the other of language, situating philosophy as the "twilight of forces."[8] He is scouring for the living force of meaning, something left in the dust by the structuralists' superseding concerns with *form* in literary criticism.[9] Down the road, Derrida appears at times to forego an analysis of force when turning to variations on mourning and their shivery residues – the trace, the destinies of *sur-vie* and other crypts borne by his oeuvre. Still, the question of force returns with a vengeance, one could say, to the extent that policing and policy amp up the stakes of politics and wide-ranging mechanisms of enforcement.

The paradox of binding force to law is further complicated by the different senses of force, juridical and philosophical, that are encountered in the

8 Jacques Derrida, 'Force and Signification', in Alan Bass, trans., *Writing and Difference* (Chicago: University of Chicago Press, 1978), 28.

9 Ibid., 5.

development of Derrida's work. By the time the use of "force" graduates to Derrida's essay on law and violent impingement in the work of Benjamin, philosophy, for its part, will have lost the force of authority, no longer divinely borrowed or sanctioned by legislative acts linked to the human order. Husserl commented on the lost vitality of philosophical reflection, which used to carry living meaning for our very existence, while Hannah Arendt and Alexandre Kojève zeroed in on the powering down of authority, seen by them as a calamity of irreversible proportions for securing political action in service of the idea of Justice.[10] Authority was needed, no matter how groundless, mystical or fatherless (Kojève says that authority derives from God-the-Father whether or not you cling to that trope hung around your historical neck).[11] Only the mysterious force of authority could be counted on to head off the pernicious threat of fascist overthrow, capable of crushing the riotous wresting plans of the various tyrannies. Authority could be redeployed, according to Arendt, Kojève and cohort, to change the course of an inescapability – a savagely uncontrolled historical onslaught they saw coming down the German pike.

Created as one of his dead serious coups of tactical inventiveness, Plato brought in authority where philosophy was stand-alone and powerless – he also invented hell to get leverage on the Good. Authority had the symbolic punch to stand against the perversion of state power, but was vulnerable to its fatal reach when they came for Socrates. From the moment Socrates was shut down, swarmed by invasive aggressiveness and murderous resolve, Arendt observes, we knew the state to be hostile to philosophers. The latter were outnumbered and needed to think of something quick. Philosophers had to come up with a ballistic shield, or at least a practicable countermeasure to the state's bloodthirsty readiness. Authority supplied such a lever.

But what was authority, asks Arendt in 'What is Authority?'[12] Does it hold the power of enforcement? Can authority secure for its purposes the overriding legitimacy of law? Force, for Derrida, is another matter, but makes similar destabilizing threats, taking recourse to a different rhetorical register. Like authority, it proceeds with little phenomenological backup. We cannot say with certainty what force is up to, nor how it will land in the precincts of political action and philosophical need, nor how it inflects the co-belonging

10 Edmund Husserl, *Cartesian Meditations: An Introduction to Phenomenology*, trans. by Dorion Cairns (Boston: Martinus Nijhoff, 1982); Alexandre Kojève, *The Notion of Authority: A Brief Presentation*, trans. by Hager Weslati (New York: Verso, 2014); and Hannah Arendt, 'What Is Authority?', in Jerome Kohn, ed., *Between Past and Future: Eight Exercises in Political Thought* (New York: Penguin, 2006), 91–141.

11 For more trouble with authority, see Avital Ronell, 'What Was Authority?', in *Loser Sons: Politics and Authority* (Urbana, Chicago and Springfield: University of Illinois Press, 2012), 19–34.

12 Arendt, 'What Is Authority?', 91–141.

of philosophy and politics, as Jean-Luc Nancy would say, citing their overlap. Historically tuned, even at the beck of universal positing – a persistent habit – philosophy itself has taken a downturn as politics dwindles into mere bouts of intrigue and vulgar power grabs. Despite the crisis in authority that philosophy's custodial claims consistently reassert, authority often relies on the supply line furnished by a certain concept of force when it concerns itself with the state and its citizens. Plato wanted to keep authority free of material coercion, an action plan that he could not credibly set up. In the first place, authority belongs to a rhetoric of *persuasion*, even a standing reserve in more Heideggerian terms. Inheriting these stances, Derrida, as we shall see, reverts to the usage of "performative force" when analyzing Benjamin's *Gewalt* in order to tap the elusive grasp of justice.[13] *Gewalt* is situated undecidably between force and violence, but also showcases Benjamin's signature: Walter "Gewalter" Benjamin.[14]

*****

The Task of Our Translators

The essays collected in this volume represent an effort to refresh reflections that have accrued to Derrida's reading of Benjamin. The editors were keenly aware of historical mutations that necessarily mark our engagement with these and other singular texts of consequence, the urgency of re-originating concerns that remained in latency, awaiting the disciplined pounce of translators, in Benjamin's logic. Benjamin puts the focus on the task of the *translator* which, following German strokes of ambiguity, involves both hermeneutic frustration and a gift, even if the delivery is missed or goes astray. The *Aufgabe* of the translator quietly displaces the imposing weight of translation, fixing on the finite and anxious commentator whose audacity impels a renewed approach, having accepted a call and calling that begin in the muted *lack* of a so-called original text that foresees its turn and turning. Primed to size the discovery of a text's innate perversibility, a new crop of commentators listens for the vulnerable tropological quiver and existential fault line, heeding the particular mode of the text's concealment, untapped historicity.

Absconding with a text while conferring value, the critical pouncer also provokes the bracing delight, a deep dive into abyssal recesses and remote calling systems – the long distance that troubles existentially alert technologists

13 Jacques Derrida, 'Force of Law: The "Mystical Foundation of Authority"', in Drucilla Cornell, Michel Rosenfeld, and David Gray Carlson, eds., *Deconstruction and the Possibility of Justice* (New York: Routledge, 1992), 7.

14 The *walten* in *Gewalt* plays a significant, if encrypted, role in Benjamin's interpretation of Goethe's *Elective Affinities,* where domestic justice goes to pieces.

from Benjamin to Heidegger, and beyond. Translators, as textual interlopers, take calls issued from afar or in perilous proximity, hitherto left unnoted. In the rhetoric of Benjamin's insight, translators come close to the description of essentially poetic beings who expose themselves to the brunt of finitude, capable of experiencing ongoing dejection and the failure to "do justice." They embrace a knowledge or facticity, understanding that their work never reaches the level of answerability that the text calls for. Yet, a so-called original text aims for the propulsion of justice as a kind of ego-ideal, calling for careful appropriation as it crosses over into the language of an alien territory. Such a call comes through, if it comes through, like an immigrant seeking asylum, seared in solitude and the sting of endangerment.

The Sequel: An Authorized Heist

In the main, we were bringing out a kind of *sequel* to previous articulations reflecting the complexity of violence and law ascribed both to Benjamin and Derrida, providing a thirdness that occurs between them or in the blind spots that their unique encounter designs. When one rides a double textual expansion – entailing the contaminations and types of relatedness that this particular force of stellar partnership invokes – the impetus to theorize the textual predicament is hard to resist and, in any case, worrisome if evaded. What does the power couple of Benjamin and Derrida create when they co-articulate a dare or a distinctly legal structuring of the philosophical question? Are we introduced into the theatre of two plaintiffs (or opposing counsel) meant to bring into view warring frames of historicity and thematic relevance? Or is something else at stake, as yet unfathomable while also too close to read?

As he sets his goal, Derrida assesses the magnitude of the encounter, the aporias of argument, the scope of intentionality and implications of a proper name. Preparing a Derridean sweep, he invites us to ask: Who is Benjamin to us? How does he operate as textual sentinel protecting a future as yet unsketched? How do we approach the unsaid embedded in Benjamin's reflection? Derrida takes into account how Benjamin often makes us do a double take as part of his performative repertory. There exist other qualities, perhaps less noted, that throw the modern reader for a loop, rendering one vulnerable as well to the *overexposure*, noted previously, on which much of the current relation to Benjamin pivots. After the period of relative anonymity he became the currency for cultural analysis, widely cast. He rebuked the values associated with "originality" at the level of material reshuffling, thematically urging incessant editing and splicing, allegorical resets. He practised the voiding of all sorts of aphoristic shots and stills that his work presents, ranging deep into *The Arcades Project*. On the whole, he was an original who placed his bets on the second infiltration of thought. That is to say, he liked us to start jamming on the *second* take, marking the sequel or what comes into view only under the rule of repetition and distortion. It may well be that we live in an age of sequels, in and on the second hand, which is why there is so much distress around the very thought of originality, a problem for the most part obsolesced by newer technologies to which both Benjamin and Derrida point. The *sequel*, whether historical or discursive, comes around, adds on, discontinues while it carries on – or, in a deconstructive idiom, it can be seen to *supplement* or press on the groove of iterability. Perhaps it even suggests a shift, in a minor key, in the concept and logic of inheritance, for the sequel also points us to a structure of descendance, of what comes purportedly after and before, though any such certitude will be submitted to a sorting machine that Derrida's reading has switched on. Given his stated proclivities, Benjamin pre-approves the reappropriation of his text, the thefts and shifts induced by his readers. With his keen sense of technological irony and sensitivity, his work asks how contemporary modes of repetition serve or at least inflect us today in our intersecting fields. Is sequelity not a way of starting from scratch, hitting reset, reverting back in order to have the illusion of moving forward, somehow advancing? Is the sequel the necessary place (if it is a *place*) where the original gets some relief, illumination or somehow benefits from critical start-up funds? Or is it a matter of a lame second try, a second marriage, maybe better than the first after all, but already on a downslide and in discontinuity with any fantasy of a forever and only. Commonly ascribable to cinematic *écriture*, the sequel is something Benjamin would have let in, even when it arrives as an announced letdown, a parasitical appendage, an annexation or retest of sorts. We are mostly all familiar with this logic of secondariness, an orginary grafting, and, if not, then at least you are living it, in the way Lacan kind of says somewhere that we *only* have second chances, and we exist from the start in the second-plus round. An overdetermined trope, it is in any case meant to indicate one of the signs of non-sovereignty with which Benjamin associates Goethe's work on affinity. Here we must face, perhaps too quickly, the abyss of human relations, the allotment of violence dealt among individuals and the laws overseen by science, including laws of chemical attraction. Goethe, through Benjamin – his sequel – asks by what means one can start over, and, if so, under what conditions?[15] How do scientific models of predictability emerge in the effort to reshuffle destinal cards in an era of reigning contingency?

If this volume represents a strategic resumption of Benjamin's work on law and violence, inflected by Derrida's skeptical passion for justice, this is because something programmed in the very structure of their encounter speaks to us today. The notion of strategic resumption advocates for the

15 See Walter Benjamin, *On Goethe*, ed. by Susan Bernstein, Peter Fenves, and Kevin McLaughlin (Stanford, CA: Stanford University Press, 2025), 91–161.

text's residue – that which was necessarily suppressed the first time around, including the share of non-knowledge with regard to its genesis and constitution. We can count on Benjamin's indications on this point, his determination to promote a quasi-concept, enveloping the value of the sequel and its correlate in citationality, which gains on acuity because it doesn't inflate into the pompous power punch of anything that would claim its own identity, having more or less given up the struggle with different levels, meanings and phantasms of highly invested categories on the order of autonomy, originality, singularity, uniqueness and so forth. What is bequeathed by Benjamin in view of the relinquishment that his text enacts is the abandonment of sovereignty. Given the overall premise of handing over your lack to the next generation, how must Derrida's intervention function here?

In view of these considerations, we have had to ask ourselves about the very status of 'The Force of Law,' continually wondering whether it counts as an extension of Benjamin, presents as commentary or fulfils the function of Afterword; or does Derrida's supplement rather overtake the "original" in the form of a belated surge released from the textual body, and, perhaps, in some measure, part of a corrective syntax, an inflection of *über-* or *fortleben* – two modalities of survival that Derrida reads out of Benjamin's corpus? How do petitioned sequels live or carry on, drag along, continue or reanimate a work in distress of itself? If a work still worked, in Derrida's idiom, and so could prop itself up as a totality, it would not tolerate a sequel; at best, it would have accomplished and fulfilled itself, sealing itself in, with only a flicker of a Warholian afterlife, animated by replay and seriality.

To the extent that Derrida's assist – the mechanisms of overtaking and reinscribing deployed by him – amounts to a sequel when approaching Benjamin, our anthology replicates in turn effects of a generative sequentiality. This is due largely to the way Benjamin's work explicitly indicates a necessary split in the work, a cleavage or doubling, a division and continuation, a form of splice and spin-off, opening questions of descendance, mutation, progression, repetition – even mimetic rivalry, played out with suspicious decoys of mirroring and internal zones of conflict. Otherwise articulated, Derrida responds to a distress call from within the work-and-life of Walter Benjamin with the understanding that he is responding to a lack in the work. The sequel says there was something missing that now asks to be re-originated. Such an "ask" is not limited to Benjamin, but is claimed by his work as legitimate for all texts, as something always in the first place called for by the parent text. None of this is inoffensive, without its own risk of violent aftermath. Propelled by attentive voracity, the sequel/offspring cannot always avoid making claims to supersede the original in a parricidal face down, initiating the destruction of the parent text as in Hegel's reading of the child whose arrival assumes the form of a death threat, marking a predatory ambush. The Derridean presumption would own that the mortal encroachment is law; "c'est la loi!" he'd say to us on occasions of violent disavowal, framing a hostile encounter in the standoff of finitude's grip: The death grip happens. Yet, the temptation of triumphalist supersession appears to loosen when Derrida receives Benjamin. By logical force, the impetus to sequentiality can have started up only by diminishing in value, renouncing the myth of an original start-off. Beyond their qualities of ensuring a dosage of repetition compulsion, sequels have gained in valency while keeping alive the losses that engage them.

Apart from the neurotic surplus, the value of the sequel serves to remind us that *everything* starts off by borrowing, citing, reclamation – the transfer of accounts as originary graft applies to economies as well as deconstruction. Still, one rarely identifies secondariness as if an accomplishment were to be touted, not even in consideration of the petri dish responsible for cloning and replication. What have we gained by means of Benjamin's grafts and Derrida's disrupted iterations? In their works, according to internal necessities, they both establish the difficulty of trusting a merely chronological lineup or first run. Let us scale down to consider the way relations configure and disband since Benjamin and Derrida have merged, beginning with the relation of two texts or two versions, or two theoretical entities orbiting a common, if un-plumbable, premise.

*****

How Many Texts?

The texts under study foreground a pairing of articulations in disrepair, in need of each other, or trying desperately to break off into autonomous spheres in an effort to void their bonds and contractual obligations to each other. Do we even know that we are dealing with the relation of texts to each other, that is, to a factor of *two* texts? One is tempted to say "two texts," but we cannot easily calculate or take measure of how many or how much is involved when we address such a level of exegetic complexity. As the encounter of Benjamin and Derrida reasserts, texts pass into one another with different prompts of motivation, technique and consequence. They practice a peculiar *Mitsein* that does not fail to mix formulae of accommodation with elements of repulsion and *allergy* – the inability to assimilate alterity, the base of "allergy." Texts are embedded according to a complicated algorithm of encounter and cannibalistic behaviour. They are on and with each other in a way that continually calls for decipherment. They devour. Wordsworth and Coleridge, among so many other lead poets and philosophers – and, by different measures of repetition compulsion, legal commentators and scientific-discursive investigators – have shown their hunger. As such, the sequel or supplement, the transfers that they hunt, are not new, despite their contemporary usage and edge, but a continuation of a long tradition in which texts go into and after each other, developing dependencies and, conversely, entire systems of disavowal, where they disclaim their origins or start-up points, minimizing their launch on the prompt of indebtedness, a problem addressed by Goethe, Freud, Heidegger according to a different scale and rhetoric of unpinnable beginnings.

A Narcotic Hypothesis

According to a register supplied by Benjamin and Derrida, the relation of texts tends to hold up a narcotic hypothesis that infiltrates outstanding pairings: texts draw on each other with steady voracity. To a certain degree, we could say, pushing the envelope, that since Benjamin's extended applications of citationality and alien incorporation, texts behave differently, craving others, standing in constant need of a supply line: Benjamin's ventures underscore the way texts are on each other, inject each other, shoot up, snort, interiorize, eat. They have a specific way of assimilating the foreign body, being equipped with receptors and – since Nietzsche – with a mechanism for rejecting what they down, releasing the alien other.

Derrida's 'Rhetoric of Drugs' essay leaves aside the catalogue of violent urges documented by Benjamin.[16] Nonetheless, the essay proceeds by picking up some steam along the lines of Walter B.'s drug-fueled discoveries, which anticipate aspects of the logic of supplementarity. Benjamin maintained a relation to rogue itineraries of directed surplus and repetition, loss and remnant, supplement and deficiency, pointing to a rich and melancholic mapping of his thought. He'd sometimes manage to take an off-ramp and experiment with zones of transfigured states and warped utterances, shaking down classical tropes of consciousness. In 'Hashish in Marseilles' – an experiential fugue that goes to France as a gateway space where foreign bodies multiply – Benjamin tries to give a sense of *what it is like* to get high, to hunger for a language jumble that seeks another sense and direction. We can put the focus on "like," emphasizing a rhetoric of approximation that generalizes this predicament of textual cleaving in troubled relatedness.[17] For, like Thomas de Quincey[18] before him, at the moment of describing his ownmost experience, in an effort to disclose a felt divergence to altered consciousness – understanding that so-called consciousness is ever-altering, but that's another

16 Jacques Derrida, 'The Rhetoric of Drugs', (1993) 5:1 *Differences* 1–25.

17 Walter Benjamin, 'Hashish in Marseille', in Howard Eiland, Michael W. Jennings, and Gary Smith, eds., *Selected Writings, Volume 2: 191–1934* (Cambridge, MA: Harvard University Press, 2005), 674–678.

18 Thomas De Quincey, *Confessions of an English Opium-Eater and Other Writings*, ed. by Robert Morrison (Oxford: Oxford University Press, 2013).

story – he takes a swerve *away* from a grounding self to quote Baudelaire. On his watch, de Quincey summoned Wordsworth when he tried to get inside his own head in order to secure the trope of interiority. This reliance on the experience of the other to describe one's own state in stubborn singularity is still part of the intertextual transfer, posing, furthermore, a problem in testimony. "Can you tell us what happened?" these narratives demand of the presumed subject. But, in order to get inside, they go out – if we manage momentarily to avoid all the problems of introjection and incorporation, encrypted objects and discarded parts where the lines between inside and outside blur.

Following Benjamin and Derrida as they conspire to read the law, we thus ask how we tend to regulate our speculative drive when locating our relation to a text, a problem plaguing every writer who has wrangled a unique experience that crosses a philosophical frontier or claims a psychic apparatus that plays hide-and-seek with evidentiary materials. In the legal theatre of yesteryear, with Baudelaire sitting on the bench as character witness for Flaubert (not the smartest strategy, as Mr. Flowers of Evil should not be called to vouch for Mr. "Emma Bovary, c'est moi"'s moral solidity), the contested object becomes identified by the court as a drug. Thus, at the end of the trial, the judge declares *Madame Bovary* to be juridically suited to the vague yet decisive definition of an illegal substance, as a poison, a drug – let us add here, as a *pharmakon* which, we know from Derrida, also stands trial as a scapegoat. A similar courtroom fate, with a different outcome, awaited James Joyce, when *Ulysses* was sprung in 1943 from the charge of obscenity. The judgment declared the unruly novel an emetic drug: a legally sound text can make us sick, the judge argued, as long as it did not arouse erotic sensations. As a proven emetic (the judge's friends had read the work and uniformly reported rising nausea), the censorship was lifted. And so, the censored novel was admitted into the United States.

Whether legally framed or rhetorically conceived, texts of modernity have been consistently assimilated to a rhetoric of drugs. By now they seem parked at Benjamin's reception desk and running out the Romantic clock. Ever since the admission policies of the addict Samuel Taylor Coleridge, a text tends to be seen in terms of a heightened state of urgency, particularly when nabbed as a foreign substance. Relegated to a level of unconscious assimilation, it effects a tremor in the readership jonesing for a poetic hit. Like Madame Bovary, whose depravity stems from an unmanaged craving for fiction, we are said to be shaken by the encounter with the foreign body-text that leaves one lacerated, whiplashed, blindsided, confused by its time-release invasion. Or, a bit off course yet part of the brunt of a foreign intrusion, the reader submits to a Kafkan thrall: the work hits one like an axe in a frozen sea. These rhetorical transfers, existential bleed-outs and legal determinations are inevitably violent. As with the emergent technologies that Benjamin interprets, drugs serve to filter and suspend poses of mastery to which critical thought aspires. What, finally, are the consequences of how texts shoot up only to be shot down – how they are policed – in terms of reading 'Force of Law'?

*****

The Problem

Following Derrida's lead, as we go to the encounter of Walter Benjamin today, we slalom between the poles and varieties of hot and cold media, travelling the zones of intricacy for which Benjamin is celebrated or watered down – even dumbed down and avoided. It seems as though Walter Benjamin, certainly under the protection of Derrida, should not be vulnerable to any act of dumbing down. However, his exposure has not always certified the difficult prestige of his oeuvre. In some measure, what has become known in past decades as the "Benjamin industry" takes the form of aggressive familiarity with his work, at times handing off a far too stabilized sense of its orientation, covering up pitfalls, blurs and types of leakage for which it is still responsible. Before sectors in the humanities and social sciences claimed a share of Benjamin, he was no more than a stowaway, hardly recognized or legitimated. Fairly late in the game, Hannah Arendt said that he was grievously overdue, a mere rumour. As pre-spectral emergence, his advent, slow in coming, proved visible only on a very high-tech detection system. These words lend themselves to a media technological translation of how she sought to present this rumoured speck that was significantly prevented from arriving, somehow resisted. Wherever he belongs in an updated *Geistesgeschichte* (intellectual history), he was long exposed to the *ver*-quartet of psychoanalysis: *Verneinung, Verwerfung, Verdrängung, Verschiebung*: the denial, disavowal, repression and displacement that continue to orient his positions in the vibrant worlds of thought and legal consequence. His problematic status contained the seeds of a great complicity; it may have enticed Derrida to propose a co-production. Not only did they share a date of birth, but the struggle over legitimacy bound them in telling ways.

*****

It is not entirely clear whether Derrida was on a rescue mission when choosing Benjamin. His m.o. included the focused hospitality extended to sacred strays, among whom we count the largely underestimated colleague-poet, Paul Celan. Taking into account the spare portion of hospitality offered to a neighbouring discourse, often shunned if not outright ignored, we must acknowledge that, prior to Derrida's intercession, psychoanalysis was consistently denied hospitality in strictly philosophical precincts. Doors were slammed. As witnessed by Arendt, Benjamin suffered a similar distancing. He certainly was not spared marginalization. One of the subthemes addressed in this volume involves the discrediting of Benjamin, given his inability to acquire the proper ID for philosophical and speculative thought. This happened in his time, not infrequently steered by his "friends" (this still happens – just a few years ago, it seems, Philippe Lacoue-Labarthe could not pass a programme through the University of Strasbourg in the philosophy *faculté* with Benjamin's name on the list). The spark of ongoing discrediting on the one hand, and the sheer prestige of the oeuvre on the other, is something that is not uncommon in our histories. The double fate of dismissal and the unquestionable weightiness of the name, "Benjamin," owns a piece of the turf of the critical and still-evolving reception of his breakthrough thought. The ambivalence shown to Benjamin may have been sufficient to draw Derrida in, mirroring his own strife with recurrent strains of misrecognition. Plus, though heavily read, they both remain constrained in some ways by their difficulty – a scholar's quiet dream and craving. The problem of obfuscation somehow links with Kant's anxiety around popularity. There is also the matter, covered in these chapters, of provoking the dread of the polis – an ancient anxiety of rousing the death threat shown toward the roving philosopher, street-wise, contaminating and enticing.

To the extent that we are responsible to these names and their inexhaustible currents, we are bound to calling out the snares, the false unconscious that accompanies their itineraries and legacy, without neglecting to point up the wonderful and probing works written and signed by many colleagues in contiguous fields. Writing on Benjamin is no easy task, under the best of circumstances. Writing on Benjamin writing, or writing on Derrida on Benjamin, staying on their medial trek and close to their relation to the agility of inscription requires great discipline and maybe even love. Though Derrida presents a different score sheet, there are not many haters in Benjamin studies. Still, it is not uncommon for academics to hate on the subjects they chose and occasionally to practise a politics of resentment, bullying and demeaning their topic. It is not uncommon, but it's not necessarily the rule. We bring this up only to consider, in perhaps an unphilosophical mood, the affect level of our responsiveness to Benjamin. We cannot be sure if he is *lovedlovedloved*, but there is a discernible mood of trust in Benjamin that remains close to philosophical interests, even when he veers off, as in the introduction to Goethe, into political overdrive after the trip to Moscow, and so forth. We should not want to lose sight of the theoretical stakes implicit in the philosophically stunted and sticky notion of affect: What are the terms of the lately unambivalent embrace that the name Walter Benjamin has encountered? Has Benjamin been *accepted*? On what terms? How does he fare in the standoff between his name and that of Adorno? And, finally, in view of the adoption papers filed and signed by Derrida?

To be sure, there are always spectral traces tied to the subterranean strains of a logic that emerges according to another metronome and series of determinations, especially when we are faced with a *double signature* that has shown the pumped vitality of a cult life. Abysses still need to be cleared in terms of the vexed trope of popularity in Kant, who shines a light on the problem of philosophy's popularity (even when class enrolments go down, flicker). One can link Kant's speculative struggle with his own popularity to something that has been happening to Benjamin and Derrida, though at a different pitch and level, according to a different notion of sequencing, remembering and erasing, return and relapse.

*****

A Final Note

Lacoue-Labarthe has said that the 20th century can be seen as having established three major categories that define thought and political action: struggle, task and mission. *Struggle* belongs to the Marxist intervention; *task* reverts to Benjamin; *mission* was assigned by Heidegger – Heidegger was on a mission, Benjamin signed up, interminably, for a task, and a material impetus motored the Marxian struggle.[19] The three tracks that Lacoue-Labarthe laid down for us in order to lend firm structure to the travel logs of twentieth-century thought by no means require us to practise a politics of the epistemic clean cut, or to seek areas of secured non-contamination.[20] There was surely struggle in scaling and backsliding on the *Aufgabe*, and there was a hint of mission, if messianically inflected, in every task that Benjamin set for himself as translator of world-historical stalls and allegorical disruption. According to his instruction, one is always leaving the stage empty-handed, coaxed by melancholia – so here, too, we could quietly raise the issue of affect (what Lyotard has said philosophical thought has failed to nail). The task before us may not rally the intensity of a libidinal surge that can be ascribed to struggle, and, slightly differently calibrated, the muscle tone of the task may not merge with a Heideggerian mission and factors of mobilization to which Ernst Jünger points us. "Struggle" and "mission" may not drop off as they push forward, reminiscent of the way "task" is meant to be upended, though the discrete burdens they may in the final analysis all share imply the same basic fatalities and end up in an unavoidable historical ditch. Nonetheless, the singularity of Benjamin's surrender, the way he located giving up at the heart of the task – marking the gift of surrender or the gift of death, the *Gabe* in *Aufgabe* according to Derrida's registry – indicates a kenotic stall, an essential unworkability at the core of doing, the giving of pause when we think we have vanquished violence or understood how to live under the force of law. These qualities, in Derrida's lexicon, give Benjamin an edge of ethicity that binds us as we confront the brunt of legal violence today.

19 Nidesh Lawtoo (ed.), *Conrad's Heart of Darkness and Contemporary Thought: Revisiting the Horror with Philippe Lacoue-Labarthe* (London: Bloomsbury, 2012), 266.

20 This triadic structure resurfaces in Lacoue-Labarthe's political theories. See the interpretations offered by Nidesh Lawtoo (ed.) in *Conrad's Heart of Darkness and Contemporary Thought.*

INDEX

For Product Safety Concerns and Information please contact our EU
representative GPSR@taylorandfrancis.com
Taylor & Francis Verlag GmbH, Kaufingerstraße 24, 80331 München, Germany

www.ingramcontent.com/pod-product-compliance
Ingram Content Group UK Ltd.
Pitfield, Milton Keynes, MK11 3LW, UK
UKHW020152200926
475702UK00016B/2671
* 9 7 8 1 0 3 2 9 6 4 2 9 4 *